INDOOR AND GREENHOUSE PLANTS

VOLUME 2

INDOOR AND GREENHOUSE PLANTS

ROGER PHILLIPS & MARTYN RIX

Assisted by Peter Barnes, James Compton and Alison Rix

Layout by Gill Stokoe
with the help of Jill Ryan & Debby Curry

RANDOM HOUSE
NEW YORK

Acknowledgements

Our particular thanks to Tony and Vera Orsbourne for the introduction and to Nicky Foy for the *Compositae*. In addition to those mentioned in Volume 1, the following helped with specific parts of Volume 2; John Wright for help with the fuchsias; Dr J. Heursel, the Research Station for Ornamental Plant Growing, Melle for help with the azaleas:

Most of the specimens photographed in the studio came from the following gardens and we would like to acknowledge the help we had from them and their staff.
The Crown Estate Commissioners at the Savill Gardens, Windsor Great Park; The Royal Botanic Gardens, Edinburgh; The Royal Botanic Gardens, Kew; The Royal Horticultural Society's Garden, Wisley; the University Botanic Garden, Cambridge; The Chelsea Physic Garden, London; Tresco Abbey Gardens, Isles of Scilly; Eccleston Square Garden, London; Sandling Park; Knightshayes Court; Trewithen; Trebah; The National Botanic Gardens, Kirstenbosch; Longwood Gardens, Pennsylvania; Huntington Gardens, San Merino, California; Santa Barbara Botanic Garden; the Harry P. Leu Gardens, Orlando; Oldbury Nurseries and Clay Lane Nursery for most of the fuchsias; Stanley Mossop for the achimenes; Blackmore & Langdon for tuberous begonias; Reads' Nursery; Green Farm Plants; Special Plants; Marston Exotics; Barter's Farm Nurseries; Holly Gate Cactus Nursery; Westfield Cacti; Fibrex Nurseries; Burnham Nurseries.

Among others who have helped in one way or another with Volume 2, we would like to thank: William Waterfield, Marilyn Inglis, Harry and Yvonne Hay, Derry Watkins, Peter and Wendy Dresman, François Goffinet, Graham Quinn, John Phillips, Brandy Cravens, Noel Kingsbury, Tania Compton, Alan and Carolyn Hardy, John Coke, Terrence Read, Charles Quest-Ritson, John d'Arcy, Susyn Andrews, Brian Shrire, John Bond, Hans Fliegner, Jim Gardiner, Mikinori Ogisu, Mike Nelhams, James Smart, John Marston, Leigh Walker, Pamela Egremont, Anthony and Anita Rix, Ted Rix, Julius Rix, Geoffrey and Katie Goatcher, Ray Waite, Peter Bradley, Rupert Bowlby, Jill Macphie, Anne Thatcher.

Published in Great Britain by Macmillan, an imprint of Macmillan Publishers Limited, London.

Library of Congress Cataloging-in-Publication Data is available

ISBN 0-375-75028-2

Random House website address: http://www.randomhouse.com/

Printed by Toppan Printing Co. (China)

98765432

First U.S. Edition

Contents

Heleconius charitonius, the Zebra

Danaus plexippus, the Monarch

Butterflies in the Conservatory

by Tony and Vera Orsbourne

Having filled the conservatory with exotic plants, it is possible to expand the illusion of the tropics and have free-flying exotic butterflies gliding around among the flowers. Even in a small greenhouse it is possible to keep and breed a number of species.

Certain butterflies are easier to keep than others under unnatural conditions. Probably the best are the Heliconius group from Central and South America. They are brightly coloured and have a lovely drifting, gentle flight pattern, ideally suited to an enclosed environment, whereas many other species tend to batter themselves in their efforts to reach the light source or tend to get caught up in vegetation. They are also long-lived, nine months is a normal lifespan for most species.

For Heliconids to breed, there must be a well-established passion flower in the greenhouse (*see Vol. 1, page 65*). The common *Passiflora caerulea* seems generally acceptable, but other more exotic species suit particular butterflies. Provided both males and females are present, they will pair and lay their eggs on the tendrils of the passion flower. Depending on the temperature, these hatch in 7–10 days, and the caterpillars or larvae feed on the tendrils and young leaves. As they develop, they shed their skins up to four times; they should not be disturbed while they are shedding. Finally they pupate and the

pupae hang from the passion flower. Depending on the temperature they take 10–14 days to emerge, then start the cycle again. Due to the longevity of the individual butterflies, there can be several generations at a time in residence in the greenhouse.

Another attractive and relatively undemanding butterfly is the Monarch, *Danaus plexippus*, a common butterfly in North America, but only an occasional vagrant to Europe. The larvae feed on *Asclepias* species (*see page 116*), and grow large, so a good stock is again necessary. When kept warm and humid, the caterpillars grow at a prodigious rate and will go from egg to chrysalis in two weeks. *Asclepias curassavica* doubles as both a good nectar plant and a food plant for Monarchs. The winter-flowering *Eupatorium* species are also useful for nectar and are an important food source for hibernating Monarchs in Mexico. The whole North American population of Monarchs flies south in the autumn to central Mexico, where millions of butterflies congregate on a few cloudy mountain tops, clustering together on pine and fir trees to keep warm during periods of freezing weather, and waking up in mild spells to drink water and feed on nectar-rich flowers. In spring the survivors mate and fly north again, producing four or five short-lived generations before the end of the following summer.

The Tree Nymph (*Idea leuconoe*), is another species that is worth keeping. It is an attractive species, delicate in flight, placid and long-lived. Because it is a challenge to breed, it is best to obtain pupae. The larvae feed on *Asclepiadaceae* and

Caligo the Owl

Heliconius erato, one of the easier species

Idea leuconoe, the Tree Nymph

Apocynaceae, especially species of *Tylophora*. The pupae are bred commercially in the Philippines and are obtainable. The Owl butterflies (*Caligos* spp.) are very impressive, having a wingspan of 12–15cm. They are mostly inactive by day and feed on overripe bananas. The caterpillars feed on *Musa* or *Canna* foliage, and will also eat *Strelitzia* (*see page 281*).

Before deciding which butterflies to keep, ensure that the plant collection includes a number of high nectar flowers. *Lantana camara* (*page 141*) is very popular with most butterflies, as is *Pentas lanceolata* (*page 198*). These are both easy to grow, provided that they are kept frost-free, and can flower almost continuously. A number of other familiar conservatory plants are also high in nectar including *Hoya*, *Stephanotis*, *Heliotropium* and *Verbena*. Some of the more tender *Buddleias* are worth growing. The autumn-flowering *Buddleia* 'Nicodemus' will give a wonderful display of cascading, highly scented flowers, set off by silver foliage. Other species of *Buddleia* can be grown to flower almost all the year round. Some other favoured species for nectar include *Lonicera*, *Clerodendron*, *Pelargonium*, *Leptospermum* and *Jasminum*. *Citrus* and *Choisya* are good for winter nectar as well as being food for certain swallowtails. Suitable flowers can be brought in from the garden if there is a shortage of flowers indoors.

When it comes to stocking with butterflies, there are a number of sources. If there is a butterfly house in the area, it would be worth getting to know the owners as they may be prepared to help. In England, World-wide Butterflies at Sherborne, Dorset DT9 4QN has a catalogue, and it is worth becoming a member of the Amateur Entomological Society, PO Box 8774, London SW7 5ZG. In the US, the equivalent is the Lepidopterists Society, editor Mark Minno, 600 NW 35th Terr., Gainsville, FLA 32607-2441.

Before starting, fit a bead curtain at each entrance of your conservatory to stop the butterflies escaping. Windows and ventilators will need to have frames fitted, covered with fine netting and a secondary net-covered door, if that is needed for increased ventilation in summer. The ideal temperature range for rearing butterflies is between 20–30°C.

Of course, having introduced exotic butterflies, under no circumstancies can pesticide sprays be used. The only way to treat an attack of whitefly or red spider mit, is to use the appropriate biological control. Other major pests are spiders, earwigs and woodlice. In commercial butterfly houses Chinese quail is used as a predator, but a more realistic control of spiders is to note cobwebs when misting with water and physically move their builders. It will be necessary in any event to mist spray regularly, as these butterflies need a fairly high degree of humidity. A pool or water feature is attractive and useful as an extra humidifier.

When buying eggs or pupae, ensure that they come from farm-reared stock and not from the wild, as many species are now endangered by over-collection. It should also be noted that it is illegal to release exotic or hand-reared butterflies into the wild, although the odd escape cannot be avoided. Those gardening in subtropical areas can plant the necter-rich flowers mentioned above to attract wild butterflies to the garden. Other flowers, especially evening-scented flowers, attract hawkmoths and the sight of these often huge moths can be exciting as they hover from flower to flower in the dusk. *Ipomoea*, *Impatiens* and Petunia are especially good at attracting moths.

Flowers for attracting nectar-feeding birds

In many parts of the world, nectar-feeding birds can be attracted to the garden by suitable flowers. In temperate and tropical America these will be hummingbirds, in Africa and Asia, sunbirds, and in Australia various nectar-eating birds and even marsupials. In Europe, tits soon learn to drink nectar from exotic bird-flowers, though there are few flowers which are primarily pollinated by birds.

A hummingbird visiting *Isomeris arborea* (*Capparidaceae*) in California

Typical hummingbird flowers from different plant families: the green and red colouring and tubular shape are common characteristics. *Phaedranassa carmioli* (left) in the *Amaryllidaceae* and *Fuchsia fulgens*

It is interesting that similar flower types attract different families of birds in different continents, and similar flower shapes have evolved in different families of plants. Bird-flowers are often tubular or have hanging bells, or bottlebrush-like flowers, and some, like *Puya alpestris*, even produce a flowerless perch for the bird to stand on while it sips from the flowers. In *Strelitzia* the perch is part of the flower and when pushed down, releases the pollen with a flick onto the breast of the bird. In other flowers like *Columnea* and some *Salvias*, the long curved stamens deposit their pollen on the bird's head or back.

Bird-flowers also have a characteristic range of colours and are often popular garden plants. Red and orange are the commonest colours, often combined with green or deep blue. Nectar is usually thick and copious, but may also be watery, as in *Canarina* (*see page 202*). Birds are attracted by sight, not scent, so most of these flowers have no smell. Flowers specially recommended to attract nectar-feeding birds include *Abutilon*, *Aloe*, *Anigozanthos*, *Banksia*, *Cestrum*, *Correa*, *Calliandra*, *Callistemon*, *Cyrtanthus*, *Epacris*, *Erica*, *Fuchsia*, *Kniphofia*, *Sutherlandia* and *Zauschneria*.

Hymenosporum flavum near Durban, Natal

Pittosporum crassifolium

Berzelia intermedia Schldl. (*Bruniaceae*)
A much-branched heath-like shrub with fluffy
flower heads, native of the SW Cape from the
Cedarberg to Uitenhage, growing in wet
places in fynbos, flowering in September–
January. Stems to 1.5m; leaves heath-like with
tiny flowers in heads 1–2cm across. The stems
below the flower heads become swollen and
reddish. Peaty soil. Min. –5°C.

Billardiera longiflora Labill. (*Pittosporaceae*)
A delicate climber with tubular flowers and
purple shiny berries, native of New South
Wales, Victoria and Tasmania, growing in
damp forests and along streams, flowering in
August–November. Stems to 4m. Leaves
linear to narrowly lanceolate, to 5cm long.
Flowers tubular, greenish-yellow, sometimes
suffused with purple, 2–3cm long. Fruits
oblong, 2cm long, conspicuous, usually
purple, sometimes white or pink. Needs moist
soil but good drainage. Min. –5°C.

Callicoma serratifolia Andr. (*Cunoniaceae*)
A dense spreading evergreen tree or large
shrub with creamy-white acacia-like flowers,
native of Queensland and New South Wales,
growing in damp places along streams,
flowering in September–January. Tree to 10m.
Leaves thick, dark green above with reddish
hairs beneath, toothed, to 12cm long and 4cm
wide. Flowers in fluffy heads 1–2cm across.
Tolerant of wet soil. Min. –5°C.

Hymenosporum flavum (Hook.) F. Muell.
(*Pittosporaceae*) Native Frangipani
An upright evergreen tree or large shrub with
yellow scented flowers, native of Queensland
and New South Wales, growing in rainforests
and temperate forest, flowering in September–
January. Tree to 20m. Leaves thin, dark green
and shiny above, to 15cm long and 6cm wide.
Flowers tubular, the lobes 4cm across,
opening creamy, ageing to yellow or orange, in
large bunches to 20cm across. One of the
loveliest small trees for subtropical areas,
requiring good soil and water in dry periods.
Min. –5°C when mature.

Liquidambar formosana Hance
(*Hamamelidaceae*)   A large deciduous tree
with round prickly fruit, native of the warmer
parts of Vietnam and China from Taiwan to
SW Sichuan, growing in moist forests at up to
2500m in the south, flowering in spring. Tree
to 40m; leaves 5-lobed when young, later
3-lobed, to 15cm long, colouring brown or red
in autumn. In dry areas it needs water in

Billardiera longiflora in Australia

Sollya heterophylla near Perth

Loropetalum chinense subsp. *rubrum*

Liquidambar formosana 'Afterglow' in California

summer. Min. –5°C. **'Afterglow'**, much planted in California, was selected for its purplish young leaves and red fall colour. Plants from W Hubei and NE Sichuan (var. *monticola* Rehder & Wilson) have proved to be hardier than the Taiwan form.

Loropetalum chinense (R. Br.) Oliver subsp. *rubrum* (*Hamamelidaceae*)
A red-flowered form of the white-flowered *L. chinense*, a native of Assam, S Japan and the warmer parts of China from Hong Kong to Yunnan, growing on rocky hills, often on limestone or in dry open woods, flowering in spring. A much-branched evergreen spreading shrub to 2m. Twigs stellate-pubescent; leaves ovate, to 4cm long. Petals 2cm long. An attractive small shrub for a pot and well-drained soil. Min. –5°C, but best in climates with warm summers.

Pittosporum crassifolium Banks & Sol. ex A. Cunn. (*Pittosporaceae*) Karo, Turpentine Tree   An evergreen with leathery leaves and scented red-brown flowers, native of New Zealand on North Island, growing on forest margins and by streams, flowering in September–December. Shrub or small tree to 9m; leaves 5–7cm long and 2–2.5cm wide, revolute, white-felted below. Flowers 12mm across, scented especially in evening. Seeds black. A good plant for shelter in mild coastal districts. Min. –5°C. The similar *P. ralphii* Kirk has longer, not revolute leaves.

Pittosporum undulatum Vent.
A spreading evergreen tree with scented flowers, native of Queensland to South Australia and Tasmania, growing in forests, flowering in September–December. Tree to 10m or taller in forests. Leaves smooth beneath, with wavy edges, to 15cm long and 4cm wide. Flowers about 1.5cm across. Easily grown and common in mild climates such as S California where it often seeds itself. Min. –5°C. *P. phyllyreoides* (*not shown*) is a pretty willow-like tree with weeping branches, creamy-yellow flowers and orange fruit; suitable for dry areas.

Sollya heterophylla Lindl. (*Pittosporaceae*)
A delicate climber or twiggy shrub with blue bell-like flowers and blue shiny berries, native of Western Australia, flowering in August–November. Stems to 2m. Leaves thin, narrowly elliptic, to 5cm long. Flowers 1–2cm long. Fruits cylindrical, 2cm long. Needs moist soil but good drainage. Min. –3°C.

Callicoma serratifolia in Madeira

Berzelia intermedia on Outeniqua Pass, Cape Province

Pittosporum undulatum in Los Angeles

Escallonia illinita var. *pulverulenta*

Escallonia bifida

Deutzia pilosa on Omei Shan, Sichuan

Carpenteria californica with *Phlomis*

Carpenteria californica Torr.
(*Hydrangeaceae*)   An upright evergreen shrub
with peeling bark and simple white flowers,
native of C California in the foothills of the
Sierra Nevada between the San Joaquin and
King rivers, growing on dry granite hills,
flowering in May–August. Stems to 2m; leaves
4–9cm long, narrowly oblong; petals 5–7,
2–3cm long. For well-drained soil in sun.
Min. –10°C. Suitable for dry gardens in light
shade when established; tolerates irrigation.
'Ladham's Variety' is an English clone.

Deutzia pilosa Rehder (*Hydrangeaceae*)
A small, probably evergreen shrub with white
starry flowers, native of SW China, especially
in subtropical forests at the foot of Omei
Shan, growing on wet cliffs and scrub at up to
1500m, flowering in May–June. Stems to
1.5m; young branches with spreading reddish
hairs; leaves sessile, subcordate, ovate,
acuminate. Flowers 3–9 in a cyme, long-
stalked, 1–1.5cm across. Min. –10°C for short
periods.

Dichroa febrifuga Lour. (*Hydrangeaceae*)
An upright shrub with masses of small blue or
pinkish flowers, native of the Himalayan
foothills from C Nepal to China and Vietnam,
growing in moist forest and scrub at up to
2400m, flowering in May–July in the wild,
later in gardens. Stems to 3m; leaves 10–20cm
long, lanceolate, toothed. Flowers, 5–6 thick
petals and blue stamens; dark blue berries. As
with *Hydrangea*, the best blue colour is formed
only on very acid soil. Min. –5°C.

Escallonia illinita Presl. var. *pulverulenta*
A large evergreen shrub smelling of pigs with
shiny green leaves and white flowers, native of
Chile, growing in thickets in mountains,
flowering in late summer. Stems to 3m; leaves
obovate or oval, 2–6cm long, sticky when
young. Flowers with lower part of petals
forming a tube 12mm long and 8mm across
the reflexed lobes. Min. –5°; often resprouting
if cut down by frost.

Escallonia bifida Link & Otto, syn.
E. montevidensis (Cham. & Schlect.) DC
A much-branched evergreen shrub or small
tree with masses of flat white flowers, native of
S Brazil and Uruguay, growing in thickets in
mountains, flowering in late summer. Stems to
3m in Europe, but taller in the wild. Leaves
narrowly oval to obovate, 3–7.5cm long,
slightly sticky. Flowers with no tube, about
18mm across. Min. –5°C or less against a
sheltered wall. One of the best shrubs for
attracting butterflies in early autumn.

Hydrangea serratifolia (Hook. & Arn.)
Phil. fil. (*Hydrangeaceae*)   An evergreen
climber with narrow leaves and white flowers,
native of Chile and nearby Argentina, at up
to 1800m, climbing on trees and cliffs,
flowering in summer. Climber to 5m or more.
Leaves 5–15cm long, usually not toothed in
spite of the name. Flowers enclosed in bud by
4 thin bracts, usually all fertile. For a moist
shady position or north wall, protected
from drying by the wind. Min. –10°C, perhaps
if sheltered.

Philadelphus 'Rose Syringa' on Tresco

Philadelphus argyrocalyx from NE Mexico near Saltillo, flowering in Devon

Philadelphus argyrocalyx Wooton
An upright shrub with masses of small sweetly
scented flowers, native of New Mexico in the
White and Sacramento mountains and of
eastern Mexico near Saltillo, growing on dry
limestone slopes, flowering in June–July.
Stems to 2.5m, arching when mature. Leaves
to 2cm long, elliptic to ovate, silky hairy on
both sides. Flowers about 2–3cm across (in
Mexico the petals are often blotched pink at
the base) with the outside of the sepals and
capsule silvery-hairy. An attractive shrub for a
dry sunny bank where the sweetly scented
flowers can be sniffed *en passant*. Min. –10°C.
Close to *P. microphyllus* Gray, but more silvery-
hairy and less twiggy in growth.

Philadelphus affinis Schlecht.
A large arching shrub with creamy-white
flowers, native of Mexico in the mountains of
Oaxaca at 2000m but cultivated elsewhere,
flowering in August–May (autumn, winter
and spring). Stems to 4m, often scrambling
into trees. Leaves to 7.5cm, with 5–8 teeth on
each edge. Flowers 2.5–3cm across, the petals
obovate and rounded. Min. –5°C.

Philadelphus mexicanus Schlecht. **'Rose
Syringa'**, syn. *P. coulteri* hort. (*Hydrangeaceae*)
A climbing or sprawling shrub with solitary
flowers stained pink at the base, native of
Mexico, flowering in summer. Stems to 10m
when supported; leaves ovate-lanceolate,
rounded at the base, acuminate, with about 3
small teeth on each side, about 6cm long but
shorter on flowering shoots. Flowers to 5cm
across, well scented, not always pinkish at the
base. This old cultivar survives climbing up
into trees in mild gardens in W Britain and N
America, and was the parent of many of the
large-flowered cultivars such as 'Sybille'.
Min. –5°C.

Ribes speciosum Pursh (*Grossulariaceae*)
Fuchsia-flowered Gooseberry   A spiny shrub
with masses of hanging crimson flowers,
native of California from Santa Clara Co.
south to N Baja California, growing on dry
coastal hills and shady canyons below 500m,
flowering in January–May. Stems to 2m; leaves
green in winter, 1–3.5cm long. Flowers about
1cm long with protruding stamens 2–3cm.
A valuable shrub for a dry sunny place, not
needing summer water. Min. –5°C or less
against a wall.

Philadelphus affinis

Ribes speciosum wild near Los Angeles

Hydrangea serratifolia at Trebah, Cornwall

Dichroa febrifuga in Coleton Fishacre, Devon

Grevillea rosmarinifolia Tresco form

Grevillea juniperina

Grevillea thelemanniana in England

Grevillea laurifolia

Grevillea juniperina

Grevillea banksiae

Grevillea aspleniifolia

Grevillea wilsonii

GREVILLEA

There are about 250 species of *Grevillea*, all native of Australia, named after Charles Greville (1749–1809), a founder of the Horticultural Society of London, now the Royal Horticultural Society. Most species need well-drained, slightly acid soil in a sunny position. Hybrids form easily and there are many named cultivars, especially in Australia. Propagate by cuttings in late summer.

Grevillea aspleniifolia Knight (*Proteaceae*)
A spreading or prostrate shrub with narrow flat leaves and one-sided spikes of flowers, native of New South Wales, growing in rocky or moist places in Eucalypt forest, flowering mostly in July–November. Stems to 5m; leaves 15–25cm long, entire or with teeth, giving the appearance of *Asplenium trichomanes*. Flower spikes 3–8cm long; flowers deep red, styles purplish-pink. Min. –5°C.

Grevillea banksiae R. Br. A prostrate shrub or small tree, native of Queensland from Port Curtis to N Moreton District, growing in sandy and rocky places near the coast, flowering mostly in summer. In the wild a tree to 9m; the cultivated form is a bush to 3m; and prostrate forms are found on coasts. Leaves 15–25cm long, pinnate, silky beneath. Flower spikes 8–18cm long, cylindrical; flowers red, pink or creamy white. The bush form is almost always in flower. Min. 3°C.

Grevillea juniperina R. Br. An upright to prostrate shrub, native of New South Wales, growing in moist places on acid soils, in scrub or open woodland, flowering all year, mostly in July–December. Shrub to 3m; leaves 0.5–3.5cm long, 1–6mm wide, lanceolate to linear, spiny. Flower spikes 2.5–3.5cm long, umbel-like; flowers red, pink, orange, yellow or creamy white. Commonly cultivated in Australia where many clones have been named. Min. –5°C. 'Sulphurea' is a good yellow clone found in Europe.

Grevillea laurifolia Sieber ex Sprengel
A prostrate shrub with broad flat leaves and red or maroon flowers in a one-sided spike, native of New South Wales, growing in dry rocky places in sclerophyll scrub or open woodland, flowering mostly in September–January. Shrub to 5m across; leaves 3–12cm long, 2–6cm wide, ovate to elliptic, leathery. Flower spikes 2–8cm long; perianth hairy outside. Popular as ground-cover. Min. –5°C.

Grevillea longistyla Hook. A spreading shrub with leaves divided into 5–7 linear lobes and red to orange flowers, native of Queensland, growing on sandstone ridges and in open forest, flowering in July–December. Elliott & Jones record that the plant grown in Australia under this name is probably a hybrid with the very similar *G. johnsonii* McGillivray, a native of New South Wales (this hybrid is the plant shown here). It forms a wide shrub to 5m, with narrow leaf lobes to 15cm long, a pinkish perianth and red styles. Quick-growing and easy. Min. –5°C.

Grevillea robusta Cunn. ex R. Br. A tall tree with ferny leaves and one-sided spikes of golden-yellow flowers, native of SE Queensland and NE New South Wales, growing in subtropical or dry rainforest, flowering in September–November (spring). A tree to 40m, leaves 10–34cm long, pinnate, with the 11–31 pinnae, deeply lobed, silky beneath. Flower spikes 12–15cm long, in groups, horizontal; flowers yellow-orange, rarely reddish. Easy and fast growing; commonly planted in mild climates as a street tree. In the past much grown for shade. Young plants are pot-grown for foliage. Min. –5°C.

Grevillea rosmarinifolia R. Br.
An upright or spreading shrub, native of New South Wales and Victoria, growing in poor sandy soils in open forests, often by streams, flowering all year, mostly in May–November. Shrub to 3m tall and 5m wide; leaves 0.8–3.8cm long, 1–7mm wide, linear to narrowly oblong, with a sharp point, silky beneath and usually revolute. Flower spikes 4–6cm across, umbel-like, hanging; flowers red. Drought-tolerant. Min. –10°C. Several similar clones are grown in England (clone shown here originated on Tresco)

Grevillea 'Superb' A hybrid which forms a small bushy shrub with large heads of pinkish flowers all year. Stems to 2m; leaves 15–24cm long, bipinnate, fern-like. Flower heads in groups, 15–18cm long, mainly one-sided, opening pinkish-yellow, becoming deep pink. A hybrid between the white form of *G. banksii* and *G. bipinnatifida*, from Western Australia, with pendent spikes of flowers. Easily grown, especially in subtropical gardens. Min. –3°C.

Grevillea thelemanniana Huegel ex Endl. A very variable dwarf or spreading shrub, native of W Australia, growing in various soils, flowering mostly in May–October. Shrub to 2.5m; leaves usually pinnate with linear segments. Flower spikes 2.5–3.5cm long, umbel-like; flowers red or pinkish. Min. –5°C. The pale-flowered form (*shown here*) is grown as *Grevillea thelemanniana* in W England.

Grevillea whiteana McGillivray A tall shrub or small tree, native of Queensland, growing in sandy and stony soils in open forests, flowering mostly in April–October. Shrub or tree to 7m; leaves pinnate with linear lobes 3mm wide. Flower spikes 3–15cm long, cylindrical, upright; flowers waxy, cream to pale yellow. Min. –5°C.

Grevillea wilsonii Gunn A small spreading shrub with prickly leaves and intense scarlet flowers, native of Western Australia, growing in sandy gravelly soils in the Darling Range, flowering mostly in August–January. Shrub to 2m; leaves 6cm long and wide, pinnate with flat linear lobes. Flower spikes to 7cm long and wide, cylindrical, upright; flowers waxy. Needs well-drained soil and tolerates light shade. Min. –3°C.

Grevillea whiteana

Grevillea robusta

Grevillea 'Superb'

Grevillea longistyla hybrid

Banksia speciosa in Perth

Banksia victoriae in King's Park Botanic Garden, Perth

Banksia marginata on Tresco

Banksia media in the Moore River National Park

Dryandra formosa in Abbey Gardens, Tresco

Banksia media

Lomatia tinctoria at Trebah, Cornwall

Lomatia ferruginea in Cornwall

Banksia marginata Cav. (*Proteaceae*)
A shrub or small tree with brown furry young shoots and heads of yellow flowers, native of New South Wales, Victoria, South Australia and Tasmania, usually growing in sclerophyll forest from coasts into the mountains, flowering in September–April (summer). Stems to 10m, but often much less. Branches stiff. Leaves 2–10cm, silvery beneath, entire or with short teeth, especially in young plants. Flower heads 4–10cm, bright or pale yellow. Cone covered with dead flowers. Easily grown and tolerant of damp soil and sea winds. Min. –5°C, perhaps less.

Banksia media R. Br. A shrub with white furry young shoots and heads of yellow flowers, native of Western Australia, growing on sandy plains near Perth, flowering in February–October (winter). Stems to 6m. Branches stiff. Leaves 6–15cm, silvery beneath, wavy, with sharp teeth. Flower heads 10–20cm, yellow or orange, strongly scented. Cone covered with dead flowers. Easily grown and tolerant of alkaline soil and sea winds. Min. –5°C.

Banksia speciosa R. Br. A shrub with white furry young shoots, deeply toothed leaves and heads of yellow flowers, native of Western Australia, growing on sandy plains in the Eyre District, flowering in December–September. Stems to 6m. Leaves 20–40cm, green, hairy beneath with triangular teeth reaching the midrib. Flower heads 12–15cm, yellow from grey buds. Cone covered with dead flowers. Easily grown; tolerant of some frost and drought. Min. –3°C.

Banksia victoriae Meisn. A shrub with white silky young shoots, deeply toothed leaves and heads of orange flowers, native of Western Australia, growing on sandy plains in the Irwin District, flowering in January–April. Stems to 5m. Leaves 15–30cm, hairy above and beneath with sharp triangular teeth nearly reaching the midrib. Flower heads 8–15cm, tapering at the apex, orange from grey buds. Cone covered with dead flowers. Needs very well-drained light soil; tolerant of heat and drought. Min. –3°C.

Dryandra formosa R. Br. A shrub or small tree with deeply toothed leaves and numerous heads of yellow or orange flowers, native of Western Australia, growing on stony or peaty soils, flowering in September–November. Stems to 8m. Leaves 5–20cm, soft, hairy beneath, with triangular teeth reaching the midrib. Flower heads to 10cm, yellow or orange. Grows best in partial shade in hot areas. Min. –3°C. *Dryandra* is close to *Banksia* but often has *Protea*-like bracts around the flower head. Its seeds are dispersed when ripe, and not, as in *Banksia*, held in a cone-like head until released by fire.

Isopogon dawsonii R. Baker (*Proteaceae*)
A low shrub with feathery leaves surrounding a head of white flowers, native of New South Wales, growing in dry sclerophyll forest and heathland, flowering in August–November. Stems to 3m. Leaves 8–12cm long with flat segments 1–3mm wide. Min. –5°C.

Isopogon prostratus McGillivray A low prostrate shrub with carroty leaves and heads of yellow flowers, native of New South Wales and Victoria, growing in dry sclerophyll forest and heathland, flowering in October–January.

Isopogon dawsonii in Edinburgh

Stems to 2m long. Leaves 4–10cm long with flat segments 1–2mm wide. For well-drained soil; tolerant of drought. Min. –5°C.

Lomatia ferruginea (Cav.) R. Br (*Proteaceae*) A shrub or small tree with evergreen ferny leaves and brownish-orange flowers, native of Chile and Argentina, growing in wet rainforest, flowering in summer. Tree to 25m, but usually a dense shrub. Leaves velvety when young, 8–20cm long; flower spikes to 4cm long. Needs a moist mild climate. Min. –5°C if sheltered.

Lomatia tinctoria (Labill.) R. Br. A low spreading and suckering shrub with pinnate leaves and small pale yellow flowers, native of much of Tasmania, usually in dry places at up to 1000m, flowering in late summer. Stems to 1m. Leaves dark green, glabrous, 5–8cm long. Flower spikes 10–20cm long with a scent of heliotrope. Min. –5°C if sheltered.

Macadamia integrifolia Maiden & E. Betche (*Proteaceae*) Macadamia Nut
A small tree with narrow dark green leaves and hanging spikes of white or pinkish flowers, native of N Queensland, growing in dry rainforest but widely cultivated elsewhere in Australia, California, Hawaii and Malawi where it is an important crop. Tree to 6m, bushy when young. Leaves in whorls of 3, 7–15cm long, tapering at the base into a short stalk, often toothed and wavy-edged. Spikes 10–20cm long. Fruit 25–30mm across with a very hard shell, so the edible nut is difficult to extract whole. *Macadamia tetraphylla* L. Johnson from Queensland and NSW, has stiffer, sharply toothed leaves with a rounded base; it is also edible.

Persoonia pinifolius R. Br. (*Proteaceae*)
An upright shrub with thin narrow leaves and a many-flowered spike-like inflorescence of yellow flowers, native of New South Wales, growing on heaths and in sclerophyll forest, flowering in spring. Stems to 3m; leaves terete, to 7cm long. Tepals 8–9mm long. Min. –3°C. The genus *Persoonia* has around 90 species in Australia. Most have small yellow flowers in the leaf axils.

Isopogon prostratus

Persoonia pinifolius fruits in Melbourne

Macadamia integrifolia

Protea roupelliae at 2000m on Mike's Pass in the Natal Drakensberg

Protea aurea at Kew

Protea cynaroides pink form

Protea aurea (Burm. fil.) Rourke subsp. **aurea** (*Proteaceae*)   An upright shrub or small tree with short broad leaves and creamy-white or sometimes crimson flowers with a single whorl of styles much longer than the bracts, native of South Africa in the S Cape, growing in cool places in mountain fynbos at 150–800m, flowering mainly in January–June. Stems 3–5m; leaves leathery, 4–9cm long and 1.5–4cm wide, truncate to cordate at the base. Inner bracts 4–9cm, with long white silky margins. Styles 8.5–10cm long. Easy and quick-growing in peaty sandy soil. Min. –5°C.

Protea cynaroides (L.) L. King Protea An upright or spreading shrub with long-stalked leaves and huge heads of creamy-white flowers surrounded by pointed red or pink bracts, native of South Africa in the Cape from the Cedarberg east to Grahamstown, growing in moist areas on poor sandy soils at 100–1000m (and even in rock crevices at 1500m), flowering all year. Stems ½–2m; leaves leathery, oval to elliptic, 8–14cm long, narrowing at the base into a long stalk. Flower heads to 30cm across; inner bracts 8–12cm, with incurved margins, pale pink to bright red. Styles 8–9.5cm long. A widespread, variable and tolerant plant, commonly cultivated and good under glass in peaty sandy soil in good light. As with most *Proteaceae*, avoid fertilisers containing phosphate, but fertilise with potash and a little nitrogen. Min. –5°C.

Protea eximia (Salisb. ex J. Knight) Fourc. A shrub or small tree with upward-curving sessile leaves and heads of black-tipped flowers surrounded by pointed red or pink bracts, native of South Africa in the S Cape, growing in mountain fynbos at 200–1600m, flowering mainly in August–October. Stems 2–5m; leaves leathery, ovate, cordate, 6–10cm

Protea subvestita in the Natal Drakensberg

Protea lepidocarpodendron on Tresco, Isles of Scilly

Protea grandiceps at Kirstenbosch Botanic Garden, South Africa

Protea cynaroides red form

Protea obtusifolia on Tresco, Isles of Scilly

Protea eximia in Australia

long. Inner bracts 4–10cm, spathulate, with incurved silky margins, pale pink to bright red. Styles 8–9.5cm long. A tolerant, easily cultivated plant that may need pruning to keep it compact. Min. −5°C.

Protea grandiceps Tratt.   A stiff low shrub with broad leaves and red rounded white-bearded bracts, native of South Africa in the S Cape, growing in mountain fynbos at 1200–1700m, flowering mainly in August–October. Stems ½–2m; leaves stiff and leathery, obovate, 8–13cm long, sessile. Inner bracts 7–8cm, spathulate, rounded and incurved with long silky margins, bright red. Styles hidden. A tolerant plant, easily cultivated and long-lived, but slow-growing and needing moisture throughout the year. Min. −10°C for short periods.

Protea lepidocarpodendron (L.) L. A tall erect shrub with long narrow leaves and black-bearded bracts, native of South Africa in the SW Cape on the peninsula east to Hermanus, growing on sheltered slopes at up to 300m, flowering mainly in April–August.

Stems to 3m; leaves linear-oblong, 8–13cm long, 1–2cm wide, sessile. Inner bracts 7–8cm, spathulate, rounded and incurved with black tips and beard. Styles hidden. A tolerant plant, easily cultivated, needing moisture throughout the year and best near the coast. Min. −5°C.

Protea obtusifolia Buek ex Meisn. A tall shrub or small tree with narrow leaves and pointed pink bracts, native of South Africa in the S Cape along the coast from Caledon to Riversdale, growing on limestone flats and hills near the sea, flowering mainly in April–September. Stems to 4m; leaves oblanceolate-elliptic, 10–15cm long, 1–2cm wide, tapering towards the base. Outer bracts with brown scarious tips; inner 4–10cm, spathulate, pointed, fringed with white hairs. Styles 6–7cm. One of the few lime-tolerant *proteas*, needing moisture throughout the year and best near the coast. Min. −5°C.

Protea roupelliae Meisn.   A small stout tree with narrow leaves and spoon-shaped pink bracts, native of South Africa in the Transvaal, Natal and the NE Cape, growing in veldt at

up to 2400m in the Drakensberg, flowering mainly in February–April. Old trees can reach 8m; leaves oblanceolate to obovate, 8–17cm long, sometimes silky-hairy. Outer bracts with brown ragged tips, reflexed at flowering; inner 5–10cm, spathulate with a narrow stem, pointed, fringed with white hairs. Styles 5–6.5cm. Forms from the high Drakensberg should be among the hardiest *proteas*, suited to a summer-rainfall climate. Min. −10°C for short periods.

Protea subvestita N. E. Br.   An upright shrub or small tree with silky leaves and creamy-white or sometimes pink flowers, native of South Africa in the Drakensberg, the S Transvaal, Natal and the NE Cape, growing in veldt at 1200–2300m, flowering mainly in January–March. Stems 2–5m; leaves leathery, 5–11cm long, oblanceolate. Inner bracts 3.5–4cm, with white silky margins, tips often reflexed. Styles 5–6cm long. This makes a very attractive shrub where it has been planted in the Natal highlands and should be cold-tolerant. Min. −10°C perhaps, for short periods.

LEUCOSPERMUM

Leucospermum reflexum 'Chittick Red'

Leucodendron argenteum at Kirstenbosch with Table Mountain in the background

Leucospermum cuneiforme

Leucospermum cordifolium 'Riverlea'

Leucospermum cordifolium at Kirstenbosch

Leucospermum oleifolium at Kirstenbosch

Leucospermum praecox at Mossel Bay, SW Cape in October

Leucospermum conocarpodendron on the slopes of Table Mountain

Leucospermum conocarpodendron

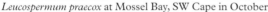

Leucodendron argenteum (L.) R. Br. (*Proteaceae*) Silver Tree A large shrub or tree with narrow silvery leaves and insignificant flowers, native of South Africa from the Cape Peninsula to Paarl and Stellenbosch, growing on rocky slopes, flowering in September. Old trees to 10m; leaves lanceolate, densely covering the twigs. Attractive especially when young, but difficult to grow except in poor sandy soils near the coast where it can stand full exposure. Min. −3°C.

Leucospermum conocarpodendron (L.) Buek (*Proteaceae*) Tree Pincushion A large rounded shrub or small tree with yellow flower heads, native of South Africa from Paarl and the Cape Peninsula to Caledon, growing on lower slopes of mountains, flowering in August–January. Tree to 5m; leaves obovate to oblanceolate, with 4–9 teeth near apex, 5–10cm long. Flower heads 5–7cm across. Styles 5cm long. Sandy acid soil. Min. −3°C.

Leucospermum cordifolium (Salisb. ex J. Knight) Fourc. A low rounded shrub with orange-red or rarely yellow flower heads, native of South Africa from Caledon to Bredasdorp, growing on the lower and middle slopes of the mountains, flowering in August–January. Shrub to 1.5m; leaves ovate, cordate, entire or with 3–6 teeth near apex, 2–8cm long. Flower heads to 12cm across. Needs sandy acid soil. Min. -3°C. **'Riverlea'** is a prostrate variety.

Leucospermum cuneiforme (Burm. fil.) Rourke A many-stemmed rounded shrub with yellow flower heads fading to red, native of South Africa from Caledon to the E Cape and Transkei, growing on hills and flats near the coast, flowering in August–February. Shrub to 3m, with lignotuber; leaves linear to lanceolate, with 3–11 teeth near apex, 5–10cm long. Flower heads about 9cm across. Needs sandy soil. Min. −3°C.

Leucospermum oleifolium (Bergius) R. Br. A many-stemmed rounded shrub with groups of yellow or orange flower heads fading to red, native of South Africa from Paarl to Caledon and Worcester, growing on hillsides from near the coast into the mountains, flowering in August–January. Shrub to 1m; leaves ovate, without teeth, 5–8cm long. Flower heads about 3cm across. Needs well-drained sandy soil. Min. −5°C or perhaps less for short periods.

Leucospermum praecox Rourke A many-stemmed rounded shrub with yellow flower heads fading to orange, native of South Africa from Albertinia to Mossel Bay, growing on sandy heathy flats near the coast, flowering in April–October. Shrub to 3m; leaves obovate, without teeth, 5–8cm long. Flower heads about 3cm across. Needs sandy soil. Min. −3°C.

Leucospermum reflexum Buek ex Meissn. A many-stemmed erect or spreading shrub with bright red or rarely yellow flower heads with long deflexed styles, native of South Africa in the Cedarberg, growing in wet places in the mountains, flowering in August–December. Shrub to 3m; leaves silky, oblong to oblanceolate, obtuse, sometimes with 3 teeth, 2–4cm long. Flower heads about 6cm across. Needs sandy peaty soil. Min. −5°C or less for short spells. **'Chittick Red'** is a low-growing variety.

Spatella species (*Proteaceae*) A low spreading shrub with feathery leaves and upright spikes of hairy grey buds opening pink, native of South Africa on the Cedarberg, growing in rocky places in the mountains, flowering in August–December. Shrub to 1.5m; leaves twice divided into narrow segments. Flower spikes about 8cm high. Needs sandy peaty soil. Min. −5°C or less for short spells.

Spatella species on the Cedarberg, NW Cape

CHRISTMAS CACTUS

Schlumbergera 'Stephanie'

Schlumbergera 'Ilona'

Schlumbergera 'Buckleyi'

Schlumbergera 'Sonja'

Schlumbergera 'Eva'

Schlumbergera 'Yantra'

Specimens from Westfield Cacti, Exeter, 25 January, ½ life-size

Schlumbergera 'Apricot'

Schlumbergera 'Jaffa'

Schlumbergera 'Gina'

Schlumbergera 'Gold Charm'

Schlumbergera 'Altensteinii'

Hatoria 'Red Pride' at Westfield Cacti

'Buckleyi', an old plant in full flower in December in Devon

An old plant of *Hatiora gaertneri*

Hatoria 'Purple Pride' at Westfield Cacti

Hatoria 'City of Aberdeen' at Westfield Cacti

Schlumbergera (Moore) Tjaden, syn. *Zygocactus × buckleyi* Christmas Cactus A familiar winter-flowering cactus forming pendulous chains of flat scalloped leaves terminated by pinkish-red flowers. *S. × buckleyi* is named after W. Buckley, an early breeder who, in the 1840s, crossed *S. russelliana* (Hook.) Britton & Rose with *S. truncata* (Haw.) Moran 'Ruckerianum'. The 6 known species of *Schlumbergera* are all native of the mountains near Rio de Janiero, growing as epiphytes in the forest, flowering in autumn–winter. They are pollinated by hummingbirds. Recent hybrids have extended the colour range which now includes white, pale yellow and orange. All Christmas cacti require a well-drained acid peaty soil, watered and kept shaded in summer and kept drier in winter. Min. 10°C, but the flowers only appear in their ideal colours when the temperature is above 15°C; below this the flowers produce more magenta pigments and the whites become pinkish. Plants may not flower if kept

too dark or if they get artificial light in autumn. Christmas cacti need over 12 hours of darkness to initiate flower buds. Shown here are:
'Altensteinii' An early variety with reddish flowers.
'Apricot' Orange and purple flowers.
'Buckleyi' The original clone with reddish-purple flowers and petals in two whorls.
'Eva' Magenta flowers with a white centre. Raised by Poul Madsen Gartner in Denmark.
'Gina' White or pale pink flowers with a magenta style.
'Gold Charm' The first 'yellow', raised by B. L. Cobia in Florida. A large flower, 5–8cm long. Keep above 15°C for the best colour.
'Ilona' Orange flowers.
'Jaffa' Pale lilac flowers with recurved petals.
'Sonja' Mauve-pink flowers.
'Stephanie' Pale orange flowers; stems with long teeth.
'Yantra' Mauve-pink flowers with a pale centre.

Hatiora gaertneri (Regel) Barthl., syn. *Rhipsalidopsis gaertneri* (Regel) Moran (*Cactaceae*) Easter Cactus A much-branched, upright or spreading cactus with flat stems and masses of bright red flowers, native of E Brazil in the Minas Gerais, growing on trees and rocks flowering in spring. Old stems becoming woody and thickened. Young stems 4–7cm long, 2–3cm wide; flowers 4–7cm long. Min. 5°C.

Hatiora × graeseri (Wederm.) Barthl., syn. *Rhipsalidopsis × graeseri* (Wederm.) Moran A group of hybrids similar to Easter cactus but with smaller stems and flowers. The parents are *Hatiora rosea* (Lagerh.) Barthl. with small pink flowers, native of SE Brazil in the Parana, and *H. gaertneri*. They need the same culture as Christmas cactus. Shown here are:
'City of Aberdeen' Pale orange flowers.
'Purple Pride' Purplish-pink flowers.
'Red Pride' Crimson flowers.

Epiphyllum 'Red Seedling' in Devon

Nopalxochia ackermannii at Holly Gate Cactus Nursery

Epiphyllum 'Pink Seedling' in Devon

Epiphyllum 'Fantasy'

Epiphyllum 'King Midas'

Epiphyllum 'Orange Princess'

Epiphyllum 'Moonlight Sonata'

Epiphyllum 'Clarence Wright'

Hylocereus undatus in a garden in Malawi

Epiphyllum crenatum, an old plant in Kent

×*Aporophyllum* 'Dawn' at Holly Gate Cactus Nursery

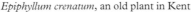

Aporocactus flagelliformis (L.) Lemaire (*Cactaceae*) An epiphytic cactus with long hanging stems and bright pinkish-red flowers, native of Mexico in Hidalgo Province, growing on rocks and trees, flowering in spring. The stems up to 1m long, only 1cm in diameter, covered with bristles. Flowers 5–8cm long. Min. 0°C.

×*Aporophyllum* 'Dawn' A hybrid between *Aporocactus* and *Epiphyllum* with flowers that are between the parents in size and colour.

Epiphyllum crenatum (Lindl.) G. Don. (*Cactaceae*) An epiphytic cactus with clumps of upright or arching stems and large white flowers, so fragrant in the evening that they scent the whole room. A native of Mexico and Honduras, growing on rocks and trees, flowering in spring. Stems to 50cm long, cylindrical below, flattened above, to 3.5cm wide, edges with shallow indentations. Flowers usually near the base of the plant, 20–29cm long and 10–20cm across the inner petals. Min. 0°C.

Epiphyllum oxypetalum (DC.) Haw. A tall epiphytic cactus with upright or arching stems and large white flowers, fragrant in the evening, native of Mexico and Honduras, growing on rocks and trees, flowering in spring. Main stems 2–3m, cylindrical and woody below, side branches thin and flattened, to 12cm wide, edges wavy. Flowers with a very long narrow tube, usually near the top of the plant, 25–30cm long and 12–17cm across. In the tropics this species is reported to initiate its flower buds after a sudden drop in temperature. Min. 10°C.

Epiphyllum hybrids These spectacular and commonly cultivated orchid cacti can now be found in a wide variety of colours. They flower in spring–early summer, each flower lasting only a few days. These hybrids need compost suitable for epiphytes, well-drained, with leaf mould or rough peat, bark or stones. They need water in summer, but should be drier in winter and kept frost-free; around 10°C is ideal. Most are complex hybrids between *Epiphyllum crenatum*, *Nopalxochia ackermannii* and the smaller-flowered pink *Nopalxochia phyllanthoides*. The specimens shown here are:
'Clarence Wright' Flowers very large and loose.
'Fantasy' Flowers 20cm long, 18cm across.
'King Midas' Flowers 20cm long, 20cm across.
'Moonlight Sonata' Flowers about 20cm across, orange with a purple flare.
'Orange Princess' Flowers 20cm long, 24cm across.
'Pink Seedling' and **'Red Seedling'** Two of the seedlings I have raised between *E. crenatum* and an old red hybrid of *N. ackermannii*. They make compact, free-flowering plants, with the long tube and some of the scent of the *Epiphyllum*, ranging in colour from pale pink to red with purplish inner petals, around 15cm across.

Hylocereus undatus (Haw.) Britton & Rose An epiphytic cactus with sprawling or climbing stems and large white flowers that open at night, native of Brazil, growing on rocks and trees, flowering in summer. Stems to 5m or more long, cylindrical, 3-winged, with scalloped edges to the wings, 4–7.5cm wide. Flowers 25–27cm long, 15–25cm wide, scented, lasting one night. Commonly cultivated in the tropics. Min. 10°C.

Nopalxochia ackermannii (Haw.) F. Kunth (*Cactaceae*) An epiphytic cactus with clumps of hanging or arching stems and large red scentless flowers, native of S Mexico, growing on rocks and trees, flowering in spring. Stems to 70cm long, flattened above, 5–7cm wide, edges with shallow indentations. Flowers usually near middle of the stems, 12–14cm long and 10–14cm across the inner petals. There is doubt as to whether this well-known cactus is a true species or an ancient Mexican garden hybrid. Min. 0°C.

Aporocactus flagelliformis

Epiphyllum oxypetalum in a garden in Malawi

Aristolochia grandiflora in the Leiden Botanic Garden

Aristolochia trilobata

Cuphea hookeriana at Tequila

Aristolochia labiata at Wisley

Aristolochia gigantea at Kew

Combretum paniculatum in Madeira in March

Aristolochia gigantea Mart. & Zucc.
(*Aristolochiaceae*)   A strong woody climber
with leaves tomentose beneath and large
chocolate-purple netted flowers, native of
Brazil to Panama, growing in forests,
flowering in summer. Climber to 10m or
more; leaves acuminate, with 2 shallow
rounded lobes at the base, 10–15cm across.
Flowers borne on the old stems, whitish
outside, with a heart-shaped lip, 14mm across
and no tail. An unusual climber for a warm
greenhouse. Min. 5°C.

Aristolochia grandiflora Schwartz
A deciduous climber with downy or glabrous
leaves and huge greyish netted flowers, native
of Mexico to Panama and the West Indies,
growing in forests, flowering in summer.
Climber to 3m or more; leaves ovate, acute,
cordate, 10–20cm across. Flowers with a foul
smell, attracting flies and wasps, opening at
dawn, dead by dusk, whitish, netted outside,
with a heart-shaped lip, 20–50cm across and a
tail up to 3m long. An unusual climber for a
greenhouse; dormant in winter. Min. 3°C.

Aristolochia labiata Willd., syn.
A. brasiliensis Mart. & Zucc.   A tall evergreen
climber with cordate glaucous leaves and

strange flowers with a narrow beak and a hanging flap, native of Crato, Brazil, flowering in late summer. Climber to 10m or more; stipules conspicuous; leaves broadly ovate, rounded, cordate, 10–20cm across. Flowers 20–30cm long. Another curiosity. Min. 3°C.

Aristolochia trilobata L. A slender climber with passion flower-like veined leaves and tubular flowers with a long red-brown twisted tail, native of E Costa Rica to Brazil and the West Indies, flowering in summer. Climber to 3m or more; leaves 3-lobed, truncate at base, 3–15cm across. Flowers about 6cm long, with 10cm-long tail. Sometimes grown as food for tropical swallowtail butterflies. Min. 10°C, for growth.

Combretum paniculatum Vent. (*Combretaceae*) A large woody climber with simple leaves and masses of small red flowers, native from West Africa to Ethiopia, south to the Transvaal, growing on hot savannahs, flowering in the cool dry season (winter–early spring). Stems to 10m or more, with short thorns. Leaves to 20cm long and 10cm wide. Flowers with 4–5 small petals and 8–10 red stamens; fruits red or orange, 4-winged, to 4cm long. A spectacular climber for a warm climate or large conservatory. Min. 0°C, for the hardier forms such as var. *microphyllum* (Klotsch) from Mozambique and the Transvaal, which has smaller rounded leaves.

Cuphea cyanea Moc. & Sesse. ex DC. (*Lythraceae*) A low sub-shrub with masses of small red and orange flowers, native of Mexico, flowering in late summer–winter. Stems to 2m, but usually around 80cm. Leaves ovate, stalked to 3cm long. Flowers about 1cm long, glandular-hairy, with small blackish-purple recurved petals. For a dry sunny position. Min. –5°C.

Cuphea hyssopifolia H. B. & K. A spreading evergreen sub-shrub with dark green linear-lanceolate leaves and masses of small lilac, pink or white flowers, native of Mexico and Guatemala, flowering most of the year. Stems to 60cm, more across. Leaves to 2cm long; flowers around 7mm across. Min. –0°C. A popular small shrub used as an edging in large greenhouses.

Cuphea hookeriana Walpers An elegant perennial with narrowly elliptic leaves and spikes of red and green flowers, native of Mexico, growing in damp open woods in the mountains, flowering in late summer–autumn. Stems to 1m; flowers 1–2cm long, with 2 reflexed red petals, nearly as long as the tube. For any good soil. Min. –3°C.

Cuphea micropetala H. B. & K. A branching perennial, woody at the base with crowded leaves and masses of reddish tubular flowers, native of Mexico, flowering in late summer. Stems to 1m; flowers around 3cm with minute petals. Min. –3°C.

Lagerstroemeria indica L. (*Lythraceae*) Crepe Myrtle A shrub or small tree with lovely smooth flaking bark, privet-like leaves and frilly pinkish, red or white flowers, native of China and Korea, growing in grassland and on cliffs at up to 800m, flowering in summer. Tree to 8m; leaves 3–5cm long; flowers to 4cm across. Min. –10°C. It requires hot and humid summers to grow and flower well. Many colours and sizes are available in California.

Cuphea cyanea   *Cuphea hyssopifolia* at Knightshayes

Lagerstroemeria indica in Grasse, S France

Cuphea micropetala   *Lagerstroemeria indica*

25

Tibouchina organensis at the Royal Botanic Garden, Edinburgh

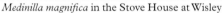

Medinilla magnifica in the Stove House at Wisley

Medinilla fuchsiodes in Newara Eliya, Sri Lanka

Heterocentron elegans (Schldl.) Kuntze, syn. *Schizocentron elegans* Schldl. (*Melastomataceae*) A creeping and mat-forming sub-shrub with opposite leaves and magenta or mauve flowers, native of Mexico, Guatemala and Honduras, growing on shady rocks, flowering mainly in late summer–autumn. Mats to 2m across; leaves ovate 1–2.5cm long; flowers solitary, to 5cm across. A pretty plant for a shady place in summer-dry climates, sunny position in humid areas or in the greenhouse. Min. −3°C.

Medinilla fuchsiodes Gardn. (*Melastomataceae*) An epiphytic shrub with thick evergreen leaves and pink waxy flowers hanging from bare twigs, native of the southern mountains of Sri Lanka, where it is common in Horton Plains and Hagkala, growing on trees in mossy forest, flowering in October–December. Shrub to 2m across. Leaves 3.5–9.5cm long, 1.5–4.5cm wide, 5-nerved. Pedicels 3–7mm. Flowers 16–22mm long, with translucent petals. For cool humid conditions. Min. 5°C.

Medinilla magnifica Lindl. A stout shrub with square winged stems, thick 5-ribbed leaves and pendulous heads of small flowers with large pink bracts, native of the Philippines, growing as an epiphyte in forests, flowering much of the year. Stems to 3m; leaves 20–30cm; bracts 20cm; flowers to 2.5cm across, pink to red. A striking tropical shrub needing heat and humidity to grow; flowering is encouraged by a cooler drier

period in winter. Needs open peaty compost. Min. 10°C.

Osbeckia capitata Walp. (*Melastomataceae*) A perennial with spreading stems and purplish flowers, native of the Himalayan foothills from Bhutan to Yunnan, growing in grassy places or open pine forest at 1500–3050m, flowering in July–October. Stems to 30cm; leaves 1–3cm, sessile; petals 4, 12–14mm; stamens 8. An attractive small perennial for a sunny place. Min. −5°C. Should be one of the hardier species of this tropical family.

Osbeckia stellata Ker-Gawl. A variable perennial or sub-shrub with upright stems and pinkish or purplish flowers, native of the Himalayan foothills from Bhutan and to China from Yunnan to Sichuan and Hubei, growing in grassy places or open pine forest at 1500–2000m, flowering in July–October. Stems to 60cm; leaves 1–3cm, sessile; calyx bristly with stellate hairs; petals 4, 16–25mm; stamens 8. An attractive small perennial for well-drained peaty soil. Min. −5°C. (*Shown here*) var. **yunnanensis** (Franch.) C. Hansen.

Punica granatum L. (*Punicaceae*) Pomegranate A shrub or small tree with small shiny leaves, bright red flowers and large pinkish-brown fruit, native of NE Turkey eastwards to the W Himalayas and widely naturalised around the Mediterranean, growing on limestone hills and cliffs at up to 2700m in Pakistan, flowering in May–June. Tree to 7m; leaves 2.5–7cm, lanceolate to

obovate. Petals 15–20mm long; fruit 5–8cm across. Easily grown in well-drained soil in areas with hot dry summers and mild winters. Min. −10°C. In dry areas of W North America this is grown for its fruit and the variety 'Wonderful', with its large red fruit, is recommended. Ornamental varieties include **'Legrellei'**, syn. 'Mme Legrelle' (*shown here*), with double-veined flowers; var. *nana*, a dwarf with red flowers but dry fruit, is good for pots; 'Chico' is a dwarf with double orange flowers. There are also white 'Albescens' and yellow 'Flavescens' singles, double-flowered white 'Multiplex' and a red double 'Pleniflora'.

Tibouchina organensis Cogn. (*Melastomataceae*) A tall slender shrub with deep purple flowers, native of the Organ Mountains in Brazil, flowering much of the year. Stems to 5m; leaves around 8cm; flowers 11cm across. Min. 0°C. A larger deeper purple version of *T. urvilleana*.

Tibouchina urvilleana (DC) Cogn., syn. *T. semidecandra* hort. A slender upright shrub with rich purple flowers, native of Brazil, flowering March–May in Brazil. Stems to 8m; leaves 10cm, softly hairy, with the 5 strong ribs from base to apex, 5–10cm long, typical of the family *Melastomataceae*. Flowers 7–10cm across with silky petals and 10 purple stamens with characteristic crooked anthers and a yellow sterile zone mimicking the true anther. A popular conservatory plant; prune in early spring. For any good slightly acid soil. Min. −3°C.

Punica granatum

Punica granatum 'Legrelliei' at the Alhambra, Granada

Tibouchina urvilleana

Osbeckia capitata above Dali in September

Heterocentron elegans

Osbeckia stellata var. *yunnanensis* above Dali

Heterocentron elegans in a garden in Natal

Syzygium oleosum

Syzygium paniculatum

Calothamnus
validus

Chamelaucium uncinatum
'University'

Metrosideros carminea

Metrosideros perforata

Specimens from the old Australia House at the Royal Botanic Gardens, Kew, February, ½ life-size

Metrosideros robusta 'Aureovariegata'

Lophomyrtus bullata

Calothamnus gilesii in Perth Botanic Garden

Calothamnus quadrifidus

Calothamnus gilesii F. Muell. (*Myrtaceae*)
An open upright shrub with long narrow
leaves and red flowers with brush-like
stamens, native of Western Australia, growing
in dry sandy areas, flowering July–February.
Shrub to 4m high and wide. Leaves glandular,
terete, to 20cm long. Calyx glandular,
glabrous; stamens 3–4cm long. Tough,
drought- and cold-tolerant. Min. –3°C.

Calothamnus quadrifidus R. Br.
An upright or spreading shrub with narrow
leaves and red flowers with brush-like
stamens, native of Western Australia, usually
growing in sandy heathy places, flowering in
October–March. Shrub to 4m high and wide.
Leaves glabrous or rarely grey and hairy, to
3cm long. Calyx glabrous or hairy; stamens
2.5cm long. Tough, drought- and cold-
tolerant. Min. –3°C. **'Special Form'** (*shown
here*) is a commonly cultivated variety with
many flowers all round the stem, not all on
one side as is normal.

Calothamnus validus S. Moore   A stiff
upright or rounded shrub with narrow leaves
and sparse red flowers with stamens divided

Rhodomyrtus tomentosa growing wild in Hong Kong in June

Metrosideros excelsa on Tresco in July

Metrosideros excelsa

only near the anthers, native of Western Australia, growing in rocky areas, flowering in July–February. Shrub to 3m high and wide. Leaves terete, rigid, incurved, 4cm long. Calyx glabrous; stamens 3–4cm long. Tough, drought- and cold-tolerant; needs well-drained soil. Min. –3°C. *Calothamnus pinifolius* F. Muell. differs in its hairy calyx and slightly shorter leaves and flowers.

Chamelaucium uncinatum Schauer **'University'** (*Myrtaceae*) Geraldton Wax An upright shrub with thin leaves and masses of small purple flowers, native of Western Australia, growing in dry sandy plains north of Perth, flowering in August–January. Shrub to 5m high and wide. Leaves almost terete, to 4cm long. Flowers 1.25–2.5cm across, red, purple, mauve, pink or white in different cultivars. Tough, drought- and cold-tolerant. Min. –3°C. Much grown as a cut flower in arid areas. 'University' is sometimes sold as 'University Red' or 'University Rubrum'.

Lophomyrtus bullata (Sol. ex A. Cunn.) Burret (*Myrtaceae*) A spreading shrub or small tree with rounded puckered leaves and small pale pink or white flowers, native of New Zealand on North Island and near Nelson on South Island, growing on the margins of lowland forest, flowering in November–February. Tree to 6m. Leaves 1.5–5cm long, usually brownish or yellowish. Flowers 12mm; petals 4. A modest shrub, grown for its unusual foliage. Min. –5°C in a sheltered spot.

Metrosideros carminea W. R. B. Oliver (*Myrtaceae*) A liane with elliptic to ovate leaves and heads of crimson flowers with numerous stamens, native of New Zealand in N of North Island, growing in coastal and lowland forests, flowering in August–October. Climber to 15m or more. Leaves leathery, 1.5–3.5cm long. Petals 5mm, stamens

10–15mm long. Needs a moist shady position to get established. Min. –3°C.

Metrosideros excelsa Sol. ex Gaertn., syn. *M. tomentosa* A. Rich. A large evergreen tree with leaves silvery beneath, spectacular when in flower with its crimson stamens, native of New Zealand on North Island south to Poverty Bay, growing in coastal and lowland forests, flowering in December–January (midsummer). Tree to 30m. Leaves leathery, 5–10cm long, elliptic to oblong, glabrous beneath. Petals 3mm, stamens 3–4cm long. A splendid wind-tolerant tree for a mild coastal climate; the fine trees on Tresco are damaged by cold about every 20 years, but sprout again from the thick branches. Min. –3°C.

Metrosideros perforata (J. R. & G. Forst.) A. Rich. A slender liane with small broad leaves and white, yellowish or pink flower heads with numerous stamens, native of New Zealand on North and N South Islands, growing in coastal and lowland forests, flowers January–March. Climber to 15m or a bushy shrub in the open. Leaves leathery, 6–12mm long. Petals 4mm, stamens 8–10mm long. Needs a moist shady site. Min. –3°C.

Metrosideros robusta A. Cunn. An evergreen from North Island and N South Island to Nelson, differs in its smaller broader leaves, glabrous beneath and brighter red flowers; **'Aureovariegata'** has yellowish-variegated leaves. Min. –5°C.

Rhodomyrtus tomentosa (Ait.) Hassk. (*Myrtaceae*) A shrub or small tree with leathery leaves and pink, rose-like flowers, native of China and SE Asia to the Philippines and Sulawesi (and said to be naturalised in Florida), growing on low grassy hills and scrub, flowering in April–June. Tree to 4m; leaves white or yellow, hairy beneath, 4.5–8cm long. Flowers 3–5cm across and the fruits are

purplish-black. Tender, needing deep lime-free soil. Min. 0°C.

Syzygium oleosum (F. Muell.) B. Hyland (*Myrtaceae*) Blue Lilly Pilly A dense evergreen shrub or small tree with flaky bark, white flowers and blue or magenta fruit, native of Queensland and New South Wales, growing in subtropical rainforest, flowering in November–August. Tree to 20m. Leaves lanceolate to elliptic, 3–12cm long, acuminate, with numerous oil glands. Petals to 3.5mm; stamens 6–15mm. Fruit 1–2.5cm across. For any good soil. Min. –3°C. The dried buds of *S. aromaticum* (L.) Herr. & Perry, from the Moluccas, are cloves.

Syzygium paniculatum Gaertn., syn. *Eugenia myrtifolia* An evergreen that grows on sandy soils by the sea in New South Wales, differs in its broader leaves that are without oil glands. For any good well-drained soil. Min. –3°C. Commonly planted for hedging in frost-free parts of California; fruit edible. 'Red Flame' has bright red new growth.

Eucalyptus coccifera, a shrubby form at Marwood Hill, Devon

Eucalyptus ficifolia in the S Cape, South Africa

Eucalyptus macrocarpa in the King's Park Botanic Gardens in Perth

Eucalyptus nitens at Marwood Hill, Devon

Eucalyptus radiata at Marwood Hill, Devon

Eucalyptus coccifera Hook. fil. (*Myrtaceae*)
A large shrub or tall tree with smooth grey
bark, bluish elliptic leaves and small cream
flowers, native of C and SE Tasmania, growing
at 600–1360m, flowering in October–March.
Tree to 40m in the lowlands, shrubby at high
altitudes; leaves to 10cm long and 2cm wide.
Flowers 1.5cm across; fruit 1.4cm in diameter.
One of the hardier species for a moist climate
and good as a specimen indoors. Min. −12°C.

Eucalyptus ficifolia F. Muell.   A large
shrub or small tree with green broadly
lanceolate leaves and large red flowers, native
of SW Western Australia, growing in acid
sandy soil, flowering in January–March.
Tree to 15m; leaves 7–14cm long, 3–5cm
wide. Flowers to 4cm across, sometimes
white, pink or cream; fruit 3cm in diameter.
A spectacular specimen for a mild
Mediterranean climate. Seedlings vary in
colour but good forms can be grafted. Best
on the coast in California. Min. −3°C.

Eucalyptus leucoxylon F. Muell.
A slender tree with flaking bark, long narrow
hanging leaves and white to red flowers, native
of New South Wales, South Australia and
Victoria, growing in open forest on good soil,
flowering in May–September. Tree to 30m;
leaves 7–20cm long, to 3.5cm wide, usually
greyish. Flowers in threes, pendulous, 3cm
across; fruit 1.2cm across. A graceful tree with
lovely flowers, especially in red and pink
forms. Min. −8°C. *E. sideroxylon* A. Cunn. is
similar, but has persistant bark and smaller
flowers in umbels of 7. Both are much planted
in dry-summer climates.

Eucalyptus macrocarpa Hook.   A large
sprawling shrub with broad pale grey leaves
and large red flowers, native of Western
Australia north of Perth, growing in acid
sandy soil, flowering in September–December.
Stems to 4m; leaves broadly ovate, sessile, to

Eucalyptus leucoxylon in California

12cm long, 8cm across. Flowers to 10cm
across; fruit 9cm in diameter, sessile. A
spectacular shrub for a mild Mediterranean
climate with the largest flowers of all
eucalypts. Min. −3°C.

Eucalyptus nitens Dean & Maiden
A tall tree with shredding bark, long narrow
hanging leaves and small flowers, native of
New South Wales and Victoria, growing in wet
forest on good soils at up to 1200m, flowering
in October–March. Tree to 60m; leaves
15–25cm long, 1.5–2.5cm wide, green, glossy.
Flowers white to cream; fruit 4–6mm in

diameter. A fine fast-growing specimen for a
mild moist climate; good in SW England.
Min. −10°C.

Eucalyptus radiata Sieber ex DC   A wide
tree with fibrous bark, narrow aromatic leaves
and tight heads of small flowers, native of New
South Wales and Victoria, growing in open
forests, flowering in October–January. Tree to
30m; leaves to 15cm long, 1.5cm wide, green,
thin-textured. Flowers white to cream, 1.5cm
across; fruit 6mm in diameter. A good
specimen tree for a mild climate such as SW
England. Min. −10°C.

LEPTOSPERMUM

Leptospermum morrisonii growing wild in alpine eucalypt forest in the Blue Mountains near Sydney

Leptospermum grandifolium

Leptospermum 'Kea'

Leptospermum scoparium 'Kiwi'

Leptospermum ericoides A. Rich. (*Myrtaceae*)   A shrub or small tree with narrow-lanceolate or linear leaves and masses of small white flowers with long stamens, native of New Zealand, growing in scrub and on the edges of forest, flowering in September–February. Tree to 15m in New Zealand; leaves 4–12mm long, 1–2mm wide, usually glabrous. Flowers 3–5mm across. Capsule 2–4mm across. For acid sandy soil. Min. –5°C, perhaps less for montane forms.

Leptospermum erubescens Schauer A spreading shrub with obovate leaves and masses of pink or white flowers, native of Western Australia, in sandy heathland, flowering July–December. Shrub to 3m high, 2m across; leaves to 6mm long. Flowers to 1cm across. Capsule 5mm across, hairy. Best in moist acid sandy soil. Min. –5°C.

Leptospermum grandifolium Smith A shrub or small tree with peeling bark, elliptic to obovate leaves, often silky beneath,

and masses of small white flowers, native of New South Wales and Victoria, growing in wet heathland and by streams up into the Snowy Mountains, flowering in October–January. Tree to 6m; leaves usually glossy above, 0.8–3cm long, 3–7mm wide. Flowers 1.5cm across. Capsule 8–10mm across, with a flaking surface. Best in acid sandy soil. Min. –10°C.

Leptospermum lanigerum (Ait.) Smith A shrub or small tree with oblong to narrow-oblanceolate silky leaves and masses of small white flowers, native of New South Wales, South Australia, Victoria and Tasmania, growing in wet heathland, open eucalypt forest and by streams, flowering in October–January. Tree to 18m in Tasmania. Leaves 3–15mm long, 2–4mm wide. Flowers 1.5cm. Capsule 5–10mm across, woolly when young. Best in acid sandy soil. Min. –10°C.

Leptospermum macrocarpum (Maiden & E. Betche) J. Thompson   A shrub with broadly elliptic leaves, silky when young, and

masses of white, pink or red flowers with a conspicuous green centre, native of New South Wales, found on rocks and sandstone in the Blue Mountains, flowering October–December. Shrub to 2m; leaves glabrous when mature, 1–2cm long, 5–10mm wide. Flowers 1.5–3cm across. Capsule 1.5–2cm across. Best in acid stony soil. Min. –5°C. Formerly a variety of *L. lanigerum*.

Leptospermum morrisonii J. Thompson A shrub or small tree with narrowly elliptic to oblanceolate leaves and masses of greenish cream or white flowers, native of New South Wales from the Blue Mountains southwards, growing among rocks in open forest and edges of mountain streams, flowering in December–January. Tree to 5m or more; leaves 1.5–3.5cm long, 2–8mm wide. Flowers 12–15mm across. Capsule 6–10mm across. Best in moist acid sandy soil. Min. –10°C. Close to the widespread *L. polygalifolium* Salisb. (syn. *L. flavescens* Smith) but with larger flowers and larger aromatic leaves.

Leptospermum obovatum

Leptospermum scoparium 'Fascination'

Leptospermum scoparium 'Crimson Glory'

Leptospermum lanigerum

Leptospermum obovatum Sweet   A shrub with oblanceolate to obovate leaves and masses of small white flowers, native of New South Wales and Victoria, growing among rocks along the edges of mountain streams, flowering in November–January. Shrub to 3m or more; leaves 5–20mm long, 2–8mm wide, apex often retuse. Flowers 8–12mm across. Capsule 5–8mm across. Best in moist acid sandy soil. Min. –10°C.

Leptospermum scoparium Forster & Forster fil. Manuka or Tea Tree   A shrub or small tree with narrow-lanceolate or ovate leaves and masses of white, pink or red flowers, native of New South Wales, Victoria, Tasmania and New Zealand, growing in rocky and sandy heathland, often by streams, flowering in September–June. Tree to 4m in New Zealand; leaves 4–15mm long, 1–6mm wide, silky when young. Flowers 8–12mm across in the wild, to 20mm in 'Keatleyi'. Capsule 6–9mm across. Best in well-drained acid sandy soil. Min. –5°C.
The dwarf forms make attractive pot plants for a cold greenhouse. Numerous cultivars are grown in Australia, New Zealand and California, including:
'Crimson Glory'   A tall shrub with double red flowers.
'Kea'   A dwarf with small white flowers.
'Kiwi'   A dwarf with small red flowers.
'Fascination'   A tall shrub with double pink flowers.

Leptospermum squarrosum Gaertner A spreading shrub with broadly elliptic to ovate or lanceolate leaves and masses of pink or white flowers, native of New South Wales, especially around Sydney, growing in open scrub, flowering mainly in March–May. Shrub to 4m; leaves 5–15mm long, 2–8mm wide. Flowers 10–20mm across. Capsule 8–12mm across. Best in dry sandy soil. Min. –5°C. Good for autumn and winter flowering.

Leptospermum ericoides

Leptospermum erubescens

Leptospermum macrocarpum

Leptospermum squarrosum

33

Callistemon citrinus 'Splendens' in northern California

Callistemon citrinus 'Jeffersii' in the Huntington Gardens

Callistemon phoeniceus

Callistemon phoeniceus in a desert garden in Palm Springs, California

Callistemon viminalis 'McGaskilli'

Callistemon citrinus (Curtis) Skeels
(*Myrtaceae*) Crimson Bottlebrush
A spreading or weeping shrub or small tree
with stiff leaves and red bottlebrush flowers,
native of Queensland, Victoria and New South
Wales, growing in swamps and along rocky
streams, flowering in September–December
(spring) and again in March (late summer).
Stems to 8m; leaves 3–7cm long and to 2cm
wide, elliptic. Flowers red, rarely lilac or
white, the spikes 4–7cm in diameter. Stamens
with dark anthers. For any soil; withstands
waterlogging and drought. Min. –10°C in the
hardiest small-leaved forms. The name *citrinus*
refers to the lemony scent of the leaves when
crushed.
'Jeffersi' A Californian variety with short
broad leaves and reddish flowers fading
purplish. It forms a large shrub.
'Splendens' A much-planted variety, first
selected in New Zealand, with large broad
leaves 8–10cm long, 2–2.5cm wide; deep red
flower spikes to 8cm long. Good in desert and
coastal areas. Flowers all year. Min. –5°C.

Callistemon phoeniceus Lindl.
A spreading shrub with narrow curved leaves
and bright red bottlebrush flowers, native of
Western Australia, growing along streams and
in depressions, flowering in August–January.
Stems to 4m; leaves greyish-green, 4–10cm
long, 5–10mm wide, linear, with thickened
edges. Flower spikes about 5cm in diameter,
to 12cm long. For any soil and tolerant of
wind and drought. Min. –3°C.

Callistemon viminalis (Soland. ex Gaertn.)
G. Don ex Loud.   A spreading or weeping
shrub or small tree with lanceolate leaves and
red bottlebrush flowers, native of Queensland
and New South Wales, common along streams
from the Cape York Peninsula southwards,
flowering in September–December. Tree to
12m; leaves 3–6.5cm long, to 1cm wide.
Flower spikes 36cm in diameter, 5–20cm long.
Stamens joined in a ring at the base. For any
soil and tolerant of some shade. Good in the
tropics. Min. –5°C for the hardier forms.
'Balboa' A tall-growing Californian variety.
'McGaskilli' A Californian variety forming
a small dense weeping tree.

Callistemon viminalis 'McGaskilli' in the Huntington Gardens

Callistemon citrinus

Callistemon flavovirens in Perth Botanic Garden

Callistemon linearis

Callistemon rigidus in Sydney Botanic Garden

Callistemon 'Demesne Reliance'

Callistemon viridiflorus

Callistemon 'John Mashlan'

Callistemon pallidus at Marwood Hill, Devon

Callistemon 'Demesne Reliance'
A cultivar with bottlebrushes in groups at the ends of hanging branches. This is one of the varieties raised by Harry Infield of Demesne Farm, Coomba Park, NSW. A shrub to 2m with narrow leaves to 5cm long, 5mm wide. Min. −5°C.

Callistemon 'John Mashlan'   A variety with purplish-pink flowers.

Callistemon flavovirens (Cheel) Cheel
A spreading or weeping shrub or small tree with stiff leaves, silvery when young and greenish bottlebrush flowers, native of Queensland, Northern Territory and New South Wales, growing on granite in crevices and along rocky streams, flowering in

November–January. Stems to 3m; leaves 3–6cm long, to 1cm wide, narrowly oblanceolate. Flower spikes 2.5–5.5cm in diameter, 2–8cm long. For any soil and tolerant of some shade. Min. −3°C.

Callistemon linearis DC   A spreading or dense shrub with narrow stiff leaves and deep red bottlebrush flowers, native of New South Wales and Queensland, growing in damp areas from the coast to the mountains, flowering in October–Febuary. Stems to 4m; leaves 4–10cm long, 1–3mm wide, linear. Flower spikes 5–6cm in diameter, 6–12cm long. For any soil and tolerant of wind and drought. Min. −5°C.

Callistemon pallidus (Bonpl.) DC
An upright shrub with flat leaves and cream to yellow bottlebrush flowers, native of New South Wales, Queensland, Victoria and Tasmania, growing by streams and in wet rocky areas in the mountains, flowering in October–February. Stems to 8m; leaves 3–7cm long, 9–15mm wide, narrowly elliptic to oblanceolate. Flower spikes 2.5–5cm in diameter, 3–7cm long. For any soil; tolerant of wind and waterlogging. Min. −5°C.

Callistemon rigidus R. Br.   A stiff erect or spreading shrub with narrow stiff flat leaves and deep red bottlebrush flowers, native of New South Wales, especially around Sydney, growing in damp places from the coast to the mountains, flowering in November–January. Stems to 3m; leaves dull green, 5–7cm long, 3–4mm wide, linear to narrowly oblanceolate, with thickened edges. Flower spikes 4–6cm in diameter, 7–10cm long. Stands wind, rain or drought. Min. −5°C.

Callistemon viridiflorus (Sims) Sweet
A low upright or spreading shrub with sharp leaves and yellowish-green bottlebrush flowers, native of Tasmania, growing by streams and in wet rocky places in the mountains, flowering in November–January. Stems to 3m; leaves 3cm long, 1cm wide, narrowly elliptic, reddish when young. Flower spikes 4cm in diameter, 8cm long. For

Melaleuca thymifolia

Melaleuca coccinea near Perth

peaty sandy soil; tolerant of wind and wet.
Min. −10°C.

Melaleuca coccinea A. S. George
(*Myrtaceae*)   A spreading shrub with short
stiff leaves and red to crimson feathery flowers
in spikes, native of Western Australia, growing
in sandy granitic soil, flowering in
September–January. Stems to 2m; leaves
6–8mm long, ovate, cordate, decussate.
Flowers terminal. Stamen bundles with 9–18
stamens, the united part 9–12mm long. For
well-drained sandy soil; drought-tolerant.
Min. −3°C.

Melaleuca hypericifolia Smith
A *Callistemon*-like shrub with flat leaves and
dense spikes of red flowers, native of New
South Wales, growing in wet places in open
forest on the coast and into the Blue
Mountains, flowering in September–January.
Stems to 6m; leaves 1–4cm long, up to 10mm
wide. Stamen bundles with 16–20 stamens,
the united part 12–16mm long. For well-
drained acid soil. Min. −5°C.

Melaleuca linariifolia Smith   A spreading
tree with soft papery bark, narrow flat leaves
and white feathery flowers, native of New
South Wales and Queensland, growing in
damp places in heaths and open forest,
flowering in September–January. Tree to 10m
with weeping branches; leaves opposite,
2–4.5cm long, 2–3.5mm wide, narrowly
elliptic to linear-lanceolate. Stamen bundles
with 30–60 stamens, the united part 8–15mm
long. For moist acid soil. Min. −5°C. The stem
needs training to form a good tree.

Melaleuca thymifolia Smith   A low
spreading shrub with flat leaves and pink to
deep mauve feathery flowers, native of
New South Wales and Queensland, growing
in damp heathy places and open scrub,
flowering in September–January. Stems to 1m;
leaves 1–1.5cm long, 1–3mm wide, elliptic.
Flowers on the older stems. Stamen bundles
of 40–60, 4–6mm long. For moist acid soil.
Min. −5°C. Many different colour forms are
grown in Australia.

Melaleuca linariifolia in Auckland Botanic Garden

Melaleuca hypericifolia in Tresco Abbey Garden

Darwinia porteri in Melbourne Botanic Garden

Verticordia grandis in King's Park Botanic Garden, Perth

Kunzea ambigua in the Abbey Gardens, Tresco

Verticordia pennigera in Perth Botanic Garden

Beaufortia squarrosa Schauer (*Myrtaceae*) A spreading shrub with stiff recurved overlapping leaves and red feathery flowers in upright heads, native of Western Australia, growing in sandy soils, flowering in September–April. Stems usually 1–1.5m; leaves bright green, 5mm long, ovate, cordate, decussate. Flower heads terminal, 3cm across, rarely yellow or orange. Stamens united at the base. For dry well-drained sandy soil; very drought-tolerant and hates wet. Min. –3°C.

Darwinia porteri C. White (*Myrtaceae*) A dwarf shrub with heath-like leaves and purplish and salmon-pink flower heads with 2 long styles, native of Queensland, growing in sandy rocky hills, flowering in September–May. Stems to 1m; leaves greyish-green, 1cm long, linear to falcate, in tufts at the ends of the branchlets. Flower 2.5cm long, heads in pairs, nodding. For dry well-drained sandy soil; very drought-tolerant. Min. –3°C. *Darwinia oxylepis* and other species from Western Australia have lovely hanging bells formed by coloured bracts.

Eremaea ebracteata F. Muell. (*Myrtaceae*) A heath-like shrub with flowers mainly composed of tufts of orange stamens, native of Western Australia, growing in sandy heaths, flowering in September–February. Stems to 1.5m; leaves hairy, 1cm long, linear. Flowers about 1cm across, 2–3 per head. For dry well-drained sandy soil and full sun; very drought-tolerant. Min. –3°C.

Homoranthus papillatus N. Byrnes (*Myrtaceae*) Mouse and Honey Plant A wide spreading shrub with green upright flowers, each with a long style, native of Queensland, growing in sandy places among granite boulders, flowering in November–February. Shrubs to 2m high, 2.5m wide; leaves glaucous, 1cm long, linear, incurved. Flowers unpleasantly scented, with a tube 4mm long, style 1.2cm long. For dry sandy soil and full sun; drought-tolerant. Min.–3°C.

Kunzea ambigua (Smith) Druce (*Myrtaceae*) A spreading shrub with small narrow leaves and white flowers with stamens longer than the petals, native of New South Wales, Victoria and Tasmania, growing in heaths and dry open forest, flowering in September–March. Shrub to 3.5m; leaves bright green, 4–12mm long, linear, sometimes pubescent. Petals 1.5–2mm, rarely pink; stamens 3–5mm. For well-drained sandy soil. Min. –8°C.

Kunzea baxteri (Klotz) Schauer A rounded shrub with bottlebrush-like flowers with long red stamens, native of Western Australia, growing in sandy heaths, flowering in September–February. Shrubs to 3m across; leaves oblong, 2cm long, 4mm wide. Flower heads 8–9cm across. For dry well-drained sandy soil and full sun. Min. –3°C.

Verticordia grandis J. L. Drumm. ex Meissn. (*Myrtaceae*) A low shrub with rounded leaves and red flowers with feathery petals and a long red style, native of Western Australia, growing in sandy heaths, flowering in September–November. Shrubs to 1m tall; leaves 1.5cm across. Flowers 2.5cm across. For dry well-drained sandy soil and full sun. Min. –3°C.

Verticordia mitchelliana C. A. Gardner A low spreading shrub with narrow grey leaves and red flowers with a distinct ruff of petals and a long red style, native of Western Australia, growing in sandy heaths, flowering in October– November. Shrubs to 50cm tall, 1m across; leaves 1.2cm long. The flowers are 1.5cm across. Best for dry well-drained sandy soil and full sun. Min. –3°C.

Verticordia monadelpha Turcz A low spreading shrub with needle-like leaves and masses of fluffy pale mauve flowers, native of Western Australia, growing in sandy heaths, flowering in October–November. Shrubs to 50cm tall, 2m across; leaves 1.5cm long.

Verticordia plumosa in King's Park Botanic Garden, Perth

Eremaea ebracteata in King's Park Botanic Garden, Perth

Beaufortia squarrosa in King's Park

Kunzea baxteri in King's Park

Verticordia mitchelliana in King's Park

Verticordia monadelpha in King's Park Botanic Garden, Perth

Flowers 1cm across. For dry well-drained sandy soil and full sun. Min. −3°C.

Verticordia pennigera Endl.   A creeping shrub with pale pink flowers, feathery sepals and fringed petals, native of Western Australia, growing in rocky places, flowering in September–February. Shrubs to 1m across; leaves oblong, 2mm long, 0.5mm wide. Flower heads 1cm across. For dry well-drained sandy soil and full sun. Min. −3°C.

Verticordia plumosa (Desf.) Druce A low rounded shrub with heath-like leaves, masses of small pale pink flowers, native of Western Australia, growing in sandy heaths, flowering in October–November. Shrub to 50cm tall and wide; leaves to 6mm long. Flowers clustered, 5mm across. For dry well-drained sandy soil and full sun. Min. −3°C.

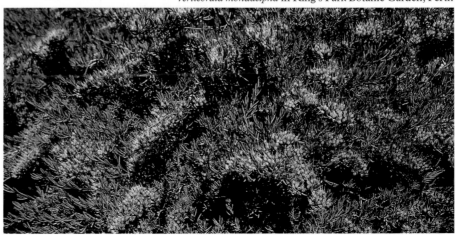

Homoranthus papillatus in Perth Botanic Garden, Perth

Fuchsia boliviana

'Loxensis'

Fuchsia boliviana
'Alba'

Fuchsia denticulata

Fuchsia sanctae-rosae

Fuchsia boliviana

'Wurdackii'

'Highland Pipes'

'Space Shuttle'

Fuchsia fulgens

Specimens from Clay Lane Nursery near Redhill, Surrey, 28 July, ½ life-size

Fuchsia boliviana in a cool greenhouse in Kent

Fuchsia denticulata

Fuchsia 'Loxensis' growing outdoors

Fuchsia boliviana Carr., syn. *F. corymbiflora* hort. non Ruiz & Pavon. (s. *Fuchsia*) (*Onagraceae*)   A large shrub or small tree, native of S Peru to N Argentina mainly on the E slope of the Andes (and naturalised elsewhere in Central America), growing in cool mossy forest, with orchids, bromeliads and peperomias at 1000–4000m, flowering most of the summer. Plants to 6m, but usually fast-growing to 2m under glass. Leaves with a velvety surface, narrowly ovate, or elliptic, 5–15cm long. Flowers in large leafless corymbs at the end of the stems, all crimson, 4–6cm long excluding ovary, sepals reflexed, petals slightly twisted, falling before the rest of the flower. Fruit cylindrical, dark red, 1–2cm long. Easily grown in cool moist partially shaded conditions, in very open leafy soil. A splendid plant when allowed to grow to its full size. Cultivated in early times by the Incas. Min. 0°C.

Fuchsia boliviana Carr. **'Alba'**, syn. var. *luxurians* Johnston   In this variety, which has been found wild in Colombia, the flower is even larger, 7–8cm long; the tube is white or pale pink, the base of the sepals and petals deeper pink. In the cultivars 'Pink Cornet' and 'Pink Trumpet' the tubes are pink.

Fuchsia denticulata Ruiz & Pavon., syn. *F. serratifolia* Ruiz & Pavon. (s. *Fuchsia*) A partially climbing shrub or small tree to 12m, but usually a small shrub under glass, native of Peru and Bolivia, growing in moist canyons in cloud forest and mountain scrub, at 2000–3600m, flowering in summer. Young twigs rather thick, 3–5mm in diameter; leaves opposite or in threes, 4–11cm long, elliptic to oblong, finely hairy to almost smooth. Flowers in upper leaf axils, 7–9.5cm long, tube red, sepals red, tipped green; petals crimson to scarlet, 15–17mm long, 4–6mm wide. Easily grown in cool conditions, kept moist

especially in summer, to flower in early autumn. All the fuchsias of this section are pollinated by hummingbirds, which continue to feed in the mountain cloud forests on days which are too cold for most insects. Min. 5°C.

Fuchsia fulgens DC. (s. *Ellobium*) A tuberous-rooted low shrub, native of Mexico in Michoacan, Morelia and Jalisco, growing on trees, usually oaks, on rock ledges, old walls or clearings in the forest, at 1600–2200m, flowering in late summer. Stems to 120cm, but usually about 40cm, softly woody. Leaves broadly ovate, cordate, 5–17cm long, finely pubescent, bluish-green. Flowers 6–10cm in long racemes, only the lower bracts somewhat leafy, with tube 5–8.5cm, dull scarlet or orange; sepals yellow or red at the base with green tips; petals scarlet. Fruit warty, purplish-red when ripe. Easily grown and free-flowering in warm sunny humid conditions and rich well-drained soil. Can be left dry and leafless in winter. Two other commonly grown clones are illustrated (*see pages 42–3*).

Fuchsia 'Highland Pipes'   An unusual hybrid between *Fuchsia magdalenae* and *F. excorticata*, raised by Herman de Graaff near Lisse in 1983. The plant is lax and upright. Flowers similar to *F. magdalenae*, but about 4cm long, with a purple tube and green-tipped sepals; leaves narrow, dark green. 'Lechlade Rajah' (*not shown*) with deep purple flowers and shorter, broader green-tipped sepals is rather similar (*F. boliviana* × *F. excorticata*).

Fuchsia 'Loxensis'   Probably a hybrid between *F. splendens* and *F. fulgens*; an upright vigorous grower that will form a good standard. Flowers about 5cm long, long tube deep orange, sepals slightly paler, spreading,

and petals orange also. Appreciates plenty of sun and will tolerate dry conditions. RHS Award of Garden Merit. The true *Fuchsia loxensis* H. B. & K. with much smaller flowers and narrow leaves on a small bushy plant is illustrated (*see page 43*).

Fuchsia sanctae-rosae O. Kuntze (s. *Fuchsia*)   A soft sub-shrub with narrow leaves and small bright orange flowers, native of S Peru and Bolivia, growing in cloud forest or in the open among rocks at 1400–3000m, flowering in October. Stems upright or spreading 20–50cm tall. Leaves mostly in whorls of 3–4, elliptic-lanceolate to obovate, glabrous except on the midrib beneath, 3–10cm long. Flowers 20–40mm long, in the axils of the upper reduced leaves; tube red, sepals scarlet, 8–10mm long; petals orange-red to scarlet, oblong-obovate. In temperate climates this only begins to form buds in September, so needs to be kept growing into winter if it is to flower properly. It is seen growing on the ruins of Machu Picchu. Hardy to 0°C., perhaps less.

Fuchsia 'Space Shuttle'   A hybrid between *F. splendens* and *F. fulgens* forming an upright vigorous lax bush with large leaves. Flowers about 3.5cm long, freely produced over a long season. Their special feature is the colour of the petals, which is cream with an orange base that fades to a pale orange-pink (sometimes erroneously described as yellow). Raised by de Graaff in 1981.

Fuchsia 'Wurdackii'   This is a name used for the plant shown here, which is not *F. wurdackii*. This plant is possibly a hybrid and is like a small and bushy form of *F. boliviana*, with dark green purple-veined oblanceolate leaves and dark red flowers, the sepals spreading, not reflexed. The tube and sepals are a reddish-orange.

Fuchsia fulgens 'Rubra Grandiflora'

Fuchsia splendens

Fuchsia vulcanica in Berkeley Botanic Garden

Fuchsia splendens 'Karl Hartweg'

Fuchsia coccinea Soland. (s. *Quelusia*)
A bushy upright shrub or scrambler with small red and purple flowers, native of S Brazil growing in the state of Minas Gerais, flowering in spring. Stems to 3m when supported. Young twigs hairy. Leaves 1.5–4.5cm long, sepal tube 4–6mm long. A subtropical plant, similar to a small *F. magellanica*. The plant shown here was named *F. glazoviana* Taub., which is considered a synonym of *F. coccinea*.

Fuchsia 'Dominiana' (s. *Fuchsia*)
An early hybrid raised by John Dominy in England in 1852. Thought to be a cross between *F. denticulata* and *F. macrostigma* Benth. A tall shrub with leaves dark purple beneath and large flowers with green-tipped sepals. I found this plant to be strong-growing but difficult to flower well; the flowers do not hang gracefully. Dominy worked at Veitch's Chelsea nursery and was the first man to hybridise orchids and *Nepenthes*.

Fuchsia fulgens DC. **'Rubra Grandiflora'**
(s. *Ellobium*) A clone of *F. fulgens* (*see page 40*) which has leaves with purplish veins at the base and flowers 8.5cm long, with a pale orange tube. A second clone 'Gesneriana' (*not shown*) is commonly grown. It has leaves with red veins, purple beneath and flowers about 8cm long, with a bright orange-red tube and redder petals. A third clone (*shown here*) has a slightly shorter redder flower with a distinctly ribbed tube.

Fuchsia hartwegii Benth. (s. *Fuchsia*)
A shrub or small tree with softly hairy leaves and masses of small orange to scarlet flowers in a spreading or pendulous panicle, native of S Colombia, in the C Andes, growing in scrub and cloud forest at 2000–3000m, flowering in spring. Leaves in threes or fours, elliptic-oblong, 4–10cm long. Flowers in a panicle 5–15cm long; the tube 1.4–2cm long; sepals 8–9mm. Fruit to 7mm long. Easily grown, but flowering best on old plants which have not been pruned during winter. Min. 5°C, perhaps less for short spells.

Fuchsia loxensis H. B. & K. (s. *Fuchsia*)
A shrub with shiny leaves and small scarlet flowers in the leaf axils, native of Ecuador mainly from Loja to Pichincha at 2500–3500m, growing in hedges and scrub, flowering in spring. Leaves in threes or fours, elliptic to elliptic-oblong, 2.5–7cm long. Flowers solitary; tube 2–3cm long; sepals 8–10mm. Fruit to 8–15mm long. An attractive plant, flowering well as a dwarf specimen in a pot. Min. 5°C or less for short spells, but said to be susceptible to sudden cold shocks. More tolerant of drought than most of this section.

Fuchsia 'Speciosa' (s. *Ellobium*) This is possibly a hybrid between *Fuchsia splendens* and *F. fulgens*, with broad leaves, almost cordate at the base and flowers about 3.5cm long, orange sepals tipped with green and orange petals. Easy and fast-growing in warm sunny conditions and well-drained rich soil. Min. 0°C. Similar to, but paler than 'Space Shuttle'.

Fuchsia splendens Zucc. (s. *Ellobium*)
A shrub with broad heart-shaped leaves and short red and green flowers, native of Mexico in Chiapas, of Guatemala and Costa Rica, growing in cloud forest and moist oak and pine woods, at 2000–3400m, flowering in summer–autumn. A shrub or small tree to 2.5m, often hanging down. Leaves ovate, usually cordate, 3–10cm long, 2–8cm wide. Flowers with a red or orange tube 17–20mm long, pubescent inside and green sepals 8–15mm long; the tube flattened and constricted above a slightly swollen base. Petals green. Fruit cylindrical, 3–4cm long, 5mm thick, swelling towards the apex, sour and juicy. Easily grown in open peaty soil; free-flowering. May be grown as a climber if given sufficient root room. Min. 0°C. Two forms are shown here: one with a pale orange tube; the other with a red tube.
'Karl Hartweg' is a clone with a slightly longer paler tube, leaves cordate at the base and purplish stems. A plant often sold as *cordifolia* is very similar, but has an even paler yellowish tube. The true *Fuchsia cordifolia*

Fuchsia 'Dominiana'

Fuchsia 'Speciosa'

Fuchsia coccinea in California

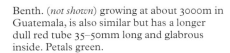

Fuchsia fulgens with ribbed tube

Fuchsia loxensis in California

Benth. (*not shown*) growing at about 3000m in Guatemala, is also similar but has a longer dull red tube 35–50mm long and glabrous inside. Petals green.

Fuchsia vulcanica André, syn. *F. canescens* Benth. *F. ayavacensis* sensu Munz (s. *Fuchsia*) A shrub with whorls of leaves and long-tubed red flowers, native of S Colombia and Ecuador, growing in cloud and elphin forests at 2800–4000m, flowering in winter and spring. An upright or scrambling shrub to 3m. Leaves rather thick, elliptic-ovate, 2–4cm long, 1–2cm wide, opposite or in whorls of four or more. Flowers with a red tube 3.5–4.5cm long, purplish and bulbous at the base, pilose inside; sepals red, 10–12mm, not reflexed; petals red, almost as long as the sepals, about 10mm. Not one of the easiest to grow, flowering in winter–spring in warm climates. Min. 5°C. The closely related *F. ampliata* Benth. appears to have more reflexing sepals and longer petals.

Fuchsia hartwegii at Quince House in Devon

Fuchsia × bacillaris 'Bacillaris'

Fuchsia ravenii

Fuchsia hemsleyana

Fuchsia procumbens

'Wapenfeld's Bloei'

'Lechlade Gorgon'

Specimens from Clay Lane Nursery, Redhill, Surrey, 28 July, ½ life-size

Fuchsia arborescens in the Royal Botanic Garden, Edinburgh

Fuchsia arborescens Sims (s. *Schufia*)
A large shrub or small tree with much-branched inflorescences of small pinkish flowers, native of Mexico from Morelos and Guerrero southwards to Guatemala, Costa Rica and Panama, growing in woods in moist ravines at 1000–2500m, flowering most of the year. A tree to 8m, sometimes epiphytic. Leaves glossy above, ovate to oblanceolate, 3–20cm long. Flowers numerous, in a rather broad inflorescence, all hermaphrodite. Each flower with the tube 5–8mm, the sepals 4.5–7mm long, pale mauve pink, with spreading sepals and petals and conspicuous style and stamens. Fruit purplish, subglobose, 7–10mm across. Easily grown in good moist soil, forming a large upright bush under glass. Can be pruned hard in spring and grows easily from cuttings. *Fuchsia paniculata* Lindley is similar but differs in its dull green leaves and smaller flowers, the tube 3–4mm, the sepals 3–4mm long. Male, female and hermaphrodite flowers are all formed by *F. paniculata*.

'Lechlade Gorgon' A hybrid between *F. arborescens* and *F. paniculata* raised in England by J. O. Wright in 1985. It is a robust grower, said to be easier than its parents, with flowers as large as *F. arborescens* and abundant fruit.

'Wapenfeld's Bloei' A hybrid between *F. arborescens* and another species, raised by Kamphuis in 1991. The plant is robust and much-branched, with flowers larger than *F. arborescens*, and orange, not pink petals.

Fuchsia × bacillaris Lindley **'Bacillaris'** (s. *Encliandra*) This was originally described as a wild species but is now considered a hybrid between *F. microphylla* and *F. thymifolia*. It forms a small much branched shrub with rather small leaves and a profusion of tiny pinkish-orange flowers. Min. –5°C.

Fuchsia cylindracea Lindley (s. *Encliandra*) A medium-sized twiggy small-leaved shrub with numerous bright scarlet tubular flowers, native of Mexico, growing in hedges and on the edges of woods, flowering September–November. Stems to 5m, young shoots pubescent. Leaves 2–5cm long. Flowers dioecious, the male about 15mm long; sepals 3–3.5mm, bright red; female flower with a tube 4–5mm long. This species should be easy in a sunny position in well-drained soil. Hardy to –5°C, perhaps.

Fuchsia hemsleyana Woodson & Siebert (s. *Encliandra*) A rather open shrub with small toothed leaves and tiny purplish-pink flowers, native of Costa Rica and Panama. The plants grow to 3m; leaves 7–15mm, serrulate to sinuate-dentate. Flowers with the tube 5–7mm long, sepals 3.5–4mm; petals 2.5–4mm. Berries small, 4–5mm across. For good soil in a cool light position. Min. –3°C, perhaps less.

Fuchsia microphylla H. B. & K. subsp. ***microphylla*** (s. *Encliandra*) An upright very twiggy shrub with numerous bright purplish flowers, native of Mexico in the states of Hidalgo, México, Michoacan and Jalisco, growing in open places in oak and pine woods, flowering in summer–autumn. Stems to 2m,

Fuchsia microphylla subsp. *microphylla* in open montane oak forest near Morelia, Mexico

Fuchsia cylindracea in open scrub near Conception des Buenos Aires, Jalisco, Mexico

woody at the base. Leaves rather leathery, with small teeth, 5–20mm long. The flowers are deep pinkish-red, the glabrous tubes are 7–9mm long and the sepals 2.5–5mm, acuminate; the petals almost round, usually toothed, 3–5mm long. Smaller, female-only flowers are also formed. Easily grown in cool conditions in good light and in cold climates best grown outdoors in summer. Min. –3°C, perhaps less. Subsp. *aprica* (Lundell) from S Mexico and Guatemala has a minutely puberulent tube and often larger flowers and leaves.

Fuchsia procumbens R. Cunningham (s. *Skinnera*) A creeping shrub with slender stems and small purplish flowers, native of North Island, New Zealand, growing on dunes, shingle and rocks by the sea around high-water mark, flowering from December–February. Stems to 50cm or so; leaves 6–12mm long, 7–10mm wide, subcordate. Flowers erect, 12–20mm long; tube dark red, purple or yellowish, 7–8mm, dark sepals reflexed, narrow-lanceolate, about 6mm. Petals absent. Smaller female-only flowers are also formed. Fruit red to magenta, 2cm long. A good plant for a hanging basket in cool conditions with good light. Min. 0°C. The closely related tree-forming New Zealand species *F. excorticata* is shown in *Shrubs* (*see page 245*).

Fuchsia ravenii Breedlove (s. *Encliandra*) A tall upright bush with relatively large leaves and flowers for the section, native of Mexico in the Sierra Madre near San Miguel Suchixtepec, growing in pine, oak and alder forest at 2600m, flowering in August. Leaves about 4.5cm long; flowers with red tube about 10mm long and red spreading sepals 8mm long; petals pink. Needs well-drained peaty compost and cool conditions with good light. Hardy to –3°C.

Fuchsia cylindracea in Mexico

'Heinrich Henkel'

'Obergärtner Koch'

'Stella Ann'

'Trumpeter'

'Leverhulme'

'Walz Tuba'

Specimens from Oldbury Nurseries, Bethersden, Kent, 20 July, ½ life-size

FUCHSIA TRIPHYLLA HYBRIDS

Specimens from Oldbury Nurseries, Bethersden, Kent, 20 July, ⅓ life-size

Cultivation of Fuchsias Fuchsias are native of Central and South America, Mexico, the West Indies and northern New Zealand; it is evident that they generally prefer a warm climate, making them especially suitable for the greenhouse or conservatory.

Many varieties will survive the winter outside in southern England, but for the purposes of this book we have concentrated on the more tender varieties which require protection from all but the slightest frost. Never allow the plants to dry out in the winter; trim off old growth and repot in a snug-fitting pot with new compost, as fuchsias do not thrive in pots that are too big. As the pot fills with roots during the growing season, pot on to the next size. Propagate by cuttings taken during late winter or early spring, rooted in a mixture of half peat and half sand; spray occasionally with water and provide with bottom heat of 15–20°C. The white and pastel-shaded cultivars tend to be susceptible to botrytis; use a soil-based compost in preference to a peat compost for these types.

Most of the fuchsias on this page have *Fuchsia triphylla* as one parent; others look similar in that they produce long tubular flowers in terminal racemes. Those cultivars closest to the type are more difficult to overwinter and need careful treatment and are also more prone to whitefly. As the original species *Fuchsia triphylla* comes from Haiti and the Dominican Republic, these need a minimum temperature of 5–10°C to grow and flower well.

'Heinrich Henkel' syn. 'Andenken an Heinrich Henkel' An upright though slightly lax *triphylla* hybrid with single flowers in terminal racemes borne almost continuously through the year. Long tube is rosy crimson; sepals and petals are a bright crimson. Foliage dark green with a red midrib. Raised in Germany by Rehnelt in 1897 and introduced into the trade by Henkel of Darmstadt, hence the name.

'Jackqueline' A *triphylla*-type. Sepals blood red, petals mandarin red. Raised by Oxtobey in 1987.

'Koralle' syn 'Coralle' A cross between *F. triphylla* and *F. fulgens* with upright vigorous growth. Flowers single, tube and sepals orange-red. Tends to wilt in very hot sun. Raised in Germany by Bonstedt in 1905.

'Leverhulme' syn. 'Leverkusen' An upright, spreading vigorous and bushy grower, good for hanging baskets. Easy to overwinter. It has single flowers with cerise tube, sepals and petals. Raised by Rehnelt in Germany in 1928.

'Mary' A hybrid of *F. triphylla* and either *F. corymbiflora* or *F. boliviana*, this upright plant requires careful treatment as it does not like either low temperatures or overwatering. The long tube and reflexed sepals are bright scarlet; the foliage sage green, veined with dark purple. Raised by Bonstedt in 1894.

'Obergärtner Koch' Plant upright, similar to the better-known 'Gärtenmeister Bonstedt'. This *triphylla* hybrid is easy to grow and free-flowering. The long tube, sepals and petals are a bright orange. Raised by Schauer in Germany in 1912.

'Stella Ann' An upright very bushy growth and a very prolific flowerer. Long salmon-pink tube and sepals, with darker pink petals. Dark green foliage with a purple midrib. Needs plenty of sun. Raised by Baker and introduced by Dunnett in England in 1974.

'Thalia' One of the best known of the *triphylla* hybrids. A vigorous upright bushy plant with large numbers of orange flowers borne in terminal racemes. Similar in appearance to 'Gärtenmeister Bonstedt', with which it is often confused. This hybrid's tube is straight-sided, whereas that of 'Gärtenmeister Bonstedt' has a bulbous end. Often used as a summer bedding plant outside in England. Very susceptible to frost and draught. Raised by Bonstedt in Germany in 1905.

'Trumpeter' A vigorous trailing plant of the *triphylla* type with a long carmine pink tube and pink sepals, the colour often darkening with age. Lush foliage which needs pinching back when young to obtain a good shape. Good for hanging baskets. Raised by Reiter in San Francisco in 1946.

'Walz Tuba' A *triphylla* type. Long tube and red sepals; petals deep magenta. Raised by Waldermaier in 1985.

Fuchsia 'Leverhulme'

Fuchsia 'Thalia'

'Gärtenmeister Bonstedt' in New Zealand

'Orient Express' on the patio in Eccleston Square

'Lee Anthony'

'Peter Crooks'

'Georg Börnemann' syn. 'Börnemann's Beste'   A strong-growing bushy plant with single flowers. Orange-red tube, sepals and petals. Probably raised by Bonstedt in Germany.

'Gärtenmeister Bonstedt'   An upright vigorous grower, this single-flowered plant has a long bright orange-red tube, sepals and petals of the same colour. A popular, attractive and easy-to-grow plant. Raised by Bonstedt in Germany in 1906.

'John Maynard Scales'   A vigorous strong-growing upright variety, suitable for use as a standard. The single flowers have a long orange tube and short sepals tipped with green; petals are a brighter shade of orange. Flowers well into the winter. Raised by Gouldings in England in 1985.

'Lee Anthony'   An upright grower with rose-pink flowers, long tubes, short sepals and petals. Raised by Gouldings in England in 1994.

'Orient Express'   An upright grower that needs plenty of pinching in order to avoid becoming leggy. The tube is deep pink, slightly darker at the base, sepals are pale pink with stripes of deep pink and a green tip; petals are deep rose pink. Raised by Gouldings in England in 1985.

'Peter Crooks'   Lax grower, good in hanging baskets. The single flowers have a long bright red tube and sepals and darker red petals. Needs plenty of pinching back when young and fairly warm conditions to perform well. Raised by Gouldings in England in 1985.

'Roos Breytenbach'   Single flowers. Tube and sepals pale orange with darker petals. Raised by Stannard in 1993.

'John Maynard Scales'

'Roos Breytenbach'

'Peter Crooks'

'Orient Express'

'Georg Börnemann'

'Roos Breytenbach'

Specimens from Oldbury Nurseries, Bethersden, Kent, 20 July, ½ life-size

'Brighton Belle'

'Lark'

'General Charles de Gaulle'

'Vivienne Davis'

'Fuchsiarama '91'

Specimens from Gouldings Fuchsias, 10 August, ⅔ life-size

'Pan' grown in a shady position outdoors in Devon, with *Adiantum formosum* behind

'Brighton Belle' A spreading plant if pinched when young, good for hanging baskets. The long tube and sepals are rose red with a salmon pink corolla. Easy to grow. Raised by Gouldings in 1985.

'Fuchsiarama '91' An upright-growing single-flowered variety with a long tube and short sepals and petals, all of which are pink. Responds well to pinching out. Raised by Stannard in 1991.

'General Charles de Gaulle' An upright grower with single flowers. Long tubes and short recurved sepals, all rose pink.

'Golden Arrow' A single-flowered cultivar with long slender orange tubes with unusual spurs and greenish or red sepals. Flowers much paler in cool weather. Raised by Gouldings Fuchsias in 1985.

'Lark' A spectacular variety with large single flowers. Our plant has long slender tubes and sepals, both of which are bright pink and an even brighter rose pink corolla. Raised in 1988 by Gouldings, who describe the flowers as orange, so it may be variable in colour according to temperature.

'Lechlade Apache' A large plant with a long flowering season. Flowers with long thin red tubes and short recurved sepals, both red. A cross between *F. boliviana* and *F. simplicaulis* and similar to *F. boliviana* except for its larger petals. Raised by J. O. Wright in 1984.

'Pan' An upright grower, fruiting freely. Flowers spreading, not hanging, on rather stiff stalks. Tube longer than the spreading sepals; these and petals all bright magenta pink, even in cool weather. A distinct and striking plant raised by de Graaff; a cross between 'Small Pipes' (*F. paniculata* × *triphylla*) and *F. magdalenae*.

'Piper's Vale' A strong grower suitable for hanging baskets. Single flowers with long tubes and short sepals, both pink; corolla darker pink. Raised by Stannard in 1992.

'Vivienne Davis' An upright grower with single flowers. Fairly broad tube and sepals, both pink. Raised by Stannard in 1993.

'Golden Arrow' 'Lechlade Apache'

'Pan'

'Piper's Vale'

Specimens from Gouldings Fuchsias, 10 August, ⅓ life-size

'Brighton Belle'

'Lechlade Apache'

'Troika' at Wisley

'Daisy Bell' at Wisley

'Haute Cuisine' from Oldbury Nurseries

'My Dear'

'Chaos' at Quince House

'Jomam'

'Beacon Rosa'

'Pink Cloud'

'Beacon Rosa' Upright bushy growth. Medium-sized single flowers. Tube dark pink, sepals pink-red, petals pink with darker pink veining. Raised by Bürgi-Ott. in Switzerland in 1972.

'Chaos' A very bushy spreading plant with rather small single flowers in great profusion. Tube and sepals rose-red; petals purplish. Good for large pots or hanging baskets. Raised by de Graaff in 1989.

'Checkerboard' Pendulous growth makes this hybrid suitable for growing in a hanging basket; it can also be trained to make a standard. Elegant flowers with slender red-pink tubes 3cm long, white long-pointed sepals, 3cm, and purple corolla. Raised by Walker & Jones in 1948.

'Haute Cuisine' An elegant trailing variety with double flowers. Tube and sepals reddish-purple, petals a darker shade of same colour. Raised by de Graaff in 1989.

FUCHSIA HYBRIDS

'Daisy Bell' Free-flowering with pendulous growth. Tube longer than the green-tinted sepals. Good for a hanging basket. Raiser unknown, in around 1977.

'Jim Coleman' Very free-flowering with single flowers. Tube and sepals crimson; petals light violet veined with crimson. Raised by Holms in 1987.

'Jomam' Upright bushy growth, quite small. Medium-sized single flowers with rose-pink tube and sepals and pale violet petals, lightly veined with pink. Does well in cool conditions, away from direct sunlight. Raised by Hall in England in 1984.

'My Dear' Upright growth. Double flowers with a short white tube and recurved sepals; petals mauve.

'Pink Cloud' Upright bushy growth, suitable for use as a standard. Large flowers with a short white tube, recurved pale pink sepals, tipped with green and pink petals, veined with deep pink. Raised by Waltz in USA in 1956.

'Troika' Makes a rather lax bush. Medium-sized double flowers with reddish-pink tube and white sepals; petals lavender. Appreciates cool conditions. Raised by de Graaff in Holland in 1976.

'Winston Churchill' Upright bushy grower. Medium-sized flowers with pink tube and sepals, tipped green; petals silvery-blue. Raised by Garson in USA in 1942.

'Checkerboard' in the conservatory at Glenbervie, Stonehaven

'Jim Coleman' at Wisley

'Winston Churchill' at Wisley

FUCHSIA HYBRIDS

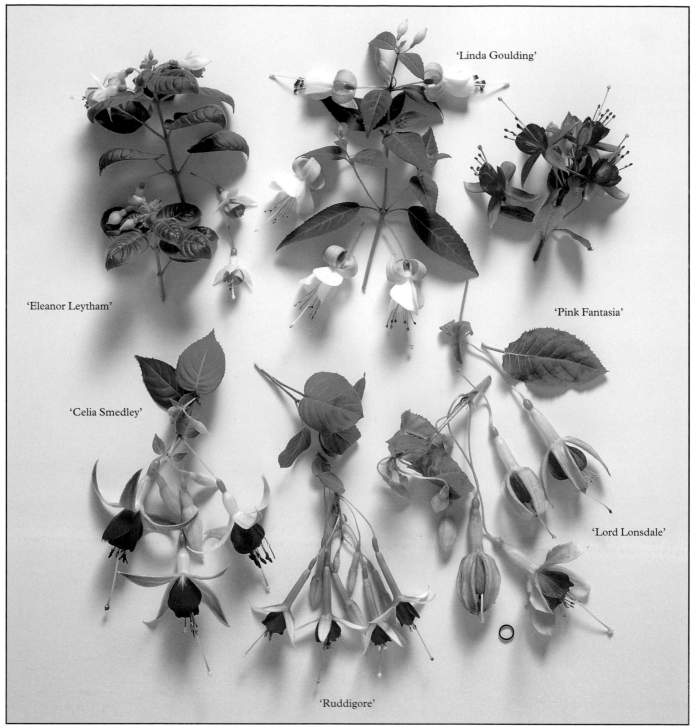

'Linda Goulding'

'Eleanor Leytham'

'Pink Fantasia'

'Celia Smedley'

'Lord Lonsdale'

'Ruddigore'

Specimens from Oldbury Nurseries, Bethersden, Kent, 20 July, ½ life-size

'Celia Smedley' Vigorous bushy growth. Medium-sized single flowers, freely borne. Tube and sepals rose-pink; petals red. Responds well to pinching back. Roots easily. Raised by Roe in UK in 1970.

'Dirk van Deelen' syn. 'Delen' Upright bushy growth with medium-sized flowers. Tube pink, sepals pink with green tips and petals light purple-pink. Raised by Steevens in Holland in 1971.

'Eleanor Leytham' Upright bushy compact growth. Small flowers freely produced. Tube and sepals white, flushed with pink; petals pink edged with deep pink. Raised by Roe in UK 1973.

'Linda Goulding' Upright bushy growth. Medium-sized single flowers. Short white tube, reflexed pink sepals; petals white with pale pink veining. Raised by Goulding in UK in 1981.

'Lord Lonsdale' Bushy but lax. Medium-sized single flowers. Tube and sepals apricot; petals orangey-apricot. Often confused with 'Aurora Superba', but has lighter green foliage and petals are larger and lighter in colour. Raised by Howlett in UK.

'Mazda' Vigorous upright grower which appreciates early pinching out. Medium-sized single flowers with orange-pink tube and sepals, carmine-orange petals. Raised by Reiter in USA in 1947.

'Orange Mirage' Trailing growth. Small single flowers with salmon-pink tube and sepals and pinky-orange petals. Raised by Tiret in USA in 1970.

'Pink Fantasia' A bushy plant with single flowers held erect. Tube and sepals pink, petals purple shading to dark purple edges. Raised by Webb in 1988.

'Swanley Yellow'

'Dirk van Deelen' in a Cretan pot

'Mazda'

'Mrs W. Rundle'

Mrs W. Rundle' Lax habit, suitable for a hanging basket. Single flowers with a long thin pale rose tube and recurving sepals tipped with green; petals vermilion. Raised by Rundle in UK in 1896.

'Ruddigore' A bushy plant with single flowers. Long tube and sepals salmon-orange; petals bright orange. Raised by Goulding in UK in 1987.

'Swanley Yellow' Upright bushy growth. Medium-sized flowers; despite the name, are not yellow. Long orange-pink tube and sepals, petals orange-vermilion. Foliage slightly bronzed. Raised by Cannell in UK in 1900.

'Orange Mirage'

'Celia Smedley'

'Quasar'

'Voodoo'

'Dark Eyes'

'Oldbury Gem'

'Oldbury Delight'

Specimens from Oldbury Nurseries, Bethersden, Kent, 20 July, ½ life-size

'Cascade'

'Rose of Denmark'

'Cascade' Trailing growth in a cascade as the name implies. Medium-sized single blooms with tube and sepals white, flushed carmine. Petals deep carmine. Raised by Lagen in USA in 1937.

'Dancing Flame' Lax upright growth with medium-sized double and semi-double flowers. Short thick tube and sepals, both pinky-orange; petals pale magenta. Raised by Stubbs in USA in 1981.

'Dark Eyes' Upright bushy growth. Medium-sized double blooms with short tube and reflexed sepals, both deep red; petals violet-blue. Raised by Erickson in USA in 1958. One of the hardier varieties. Min. –5°C.

'Golden La Campanella' Lax growth, suitable for baskets. The semi-double flowers are freely borne early in the season. White tube and sepals, the latter slightly flushed with pink; petals purple fading to lavender-blue. A variegated sport of 'La Campanella'. Raised in England in 1981, introduced by Fountains Nurseries of Ripon in 1981.

'Jack Shahan' (also listed incorrectly as 'Sharon' or 'Sharron') Lax bushy plant with large single flowers. Tube, sepals and petals rose pink. Raised by Tiret in USA in 1948.

'Oldbury Delight' A trailing variety with double flowers. Tube and sepals pale pink, flushed with green; petals magenta. Raised by Dresman in England in 1990.

'Oldbury Gem' A trailer with very large double flowers. Tube and sepals bright red, petals purple. Raised by Dresman in England in 1986.

'Pink Galore' Long trailing growth making this very suitable for baskets. Delicate double flowers. Long tube and sepals soft rose-pink; petals similar colour but slightly lighter. Raised by Fuchsia-La in USA in 1958.

'Quasar' A free-flowering trailing plant with very large double flowers. Tube and sepals creamy white; petals violet. Raised by Walker in USA in 1974.

'Voodoo' An upright bushy grower which sometimes needs staking as the blooms can be heavy; good in a basket. The large double flowers have a short tube and long sepals, both dark red; petals are deep purple. Raised by Tiret in USA in 1953.

'Rose of Denmark' Tube short, greenish; sepals pale-lilac pink, reflexed; petals lilac pink, loose, single or semi-double. Free-flowering and good in a hanging basket.

'Golden La Campanella'

'Dancing Flame'

'Jack Shahan'

'Pink Galore'

Specimens from Oldbury Nurseries, Bethersden, Kent, 20 July, ⅓ life-size

'Jack Shahan' at Wisley

Oenothera deltoides wild on dunes in the Anza Borrego Desert

Oenothera deltoides subsp. *howellii* in Berkeley Botanic Garden

Lopezia racemosa in Mexico

Lopezia racemosa near Conception de Buenos Aires in W Mexico

Oenothera speciosa . 'Childsii' in California

Blumenbachia insignis Schräd. (*Loasaceae*)   A climbing or scrambling annual or biennial with stinging leaves and white flowers with unusual bag-like petals, native of Brazil and Argentina, flowering in summer. Stems to 70cm; leaves lobed or pinnatifid to 7.5cm long. Flowers 2.5cm across. A winter-growing annual in frost-free climates or can be started under glass and planted out in early summer. Min. 5°C.

Caiophora lateritia Benth. (*Loasaceae*) A biennial or perennial climber that has greyish leaves with stinging hairs and nodding orange-yellow to reddish flowers, native of Argentina, flowering in summer. Stems twining to 3m; leaves 8–18cm long, cordate, lobed or deeply toothed. Flowers to 6cm across, bag-like petals with a crested keel along the back. Capsules curiously twisted in fruit. Can be grown as a tender annual, though the rootstock may survive the winter if kept dry and protected from frost. Min. 0°C. Many members of the *Loasaceae*, a mainly South American family, have stinging hairs and unusual flowers with bag-like petals and curved staminodes and nectaries. *Mentzelia* is a mainly Californian genus of showy yellow-flowered annuals.

Lopezia racemosa Cav. Mosquito Flower (*Onagraceae*)   A very variable annual or perennial with masses of small flowers like hovering mosquitos, native of C Mexico and El Salvador, growing in damp places along ditches and near waterfalls, flowering in October–December. Stems to 1.5m, but usually around 50cm. Leaves ovate to lanceolate. Flowers white to purple, pink or red; petals 4–10mm long, the lower wing-like, with a long claw. Anthers blue or greenish; staminode white. Capsules globose. For any good, moist but well-drained soil. Min. –3°C. This is commonly grown along the French Riviera for its very long flowering period, from late summer to winter and spring.

Oenothera deltoides Torr. & Frém. (*Onagraceae*)   An annual with a short central stem and a few spreading branches with large white flowers, native of the deserts of California to Arizona and Baja California, growing on dunes, grassy places and desert scrub below 1000m, flowering in March–May. Plants to 1m across, though usually much less, about 30cm. Leaves greyish hairy, lanceolate, 2–8cm long. Flowers in the axils of the upper leaves, opening at dusk; tube 2–4cm; petals 2–4cm long, fading pink. A winter-growing annual. Min. –3°C. Suitable for desert gardens or a pot in a cool dry greenhouse.

Oenothera deltoides Torr. & Frém. subsp. **howellii** Munz   A perennial with greyish leaves and white flowers, native of California in Contra Costa Co. near San Francisco, growing on dunes near Antioch, flowering in summer. Leaves runcinate-pinnatifid, 8–12cm long. Petals 2–3cm long, emarginate. Thompson and Morgan's seed catalogue of 1996 reports that the last wild site for this subspecies has been levelled to make a motorcycle scramble track, so the plant may be extinct in the wild. Needs very well-drained soil. Min. –5°C.

Oenothera macrosteles A. Gray A biennial or short-lived perennial with a carrot-like root, a basal rosette of shiny leaves and short flowering shoots, native of Mexico in the Sierra Madre Oriental near Los Lirios, growing on roadside banks and dry ditches, flowering in July–September. Leaves lanceolate, with shallow teeth, around 10cm long on the main rosettes, shorter on runners. Flowers opening in the evening, fading orange in the day, sessile in the leaf axils; tube around 10cm long; petals almost round, up to 4cm across. Tenderer than the similar *O. stubbii* and less rampant. Min. –3°C.

Oenothera speciosa Nutt. **'Childsii'**, syn. *O. berlandieri* (Spach) Walp.   A perennial with running underground roots and loose clumps of upright stems, native of S Texas and NE Mexico, growing in open stony places, flowering in March–May and

Zauschneria californica subsp. *cana* 'Dublin' at Knighthayes Court, Devon,

Caiophora lateritia at Harry Hay's, Surrey

Oenothera stubbii from Cerro Potosi

Oenothera macrosteles from Los Lirios, Mexico

October–November. Stems to 30cm; leaves silky, narrowly ovate, the lower pinnatifid. Petals 2–3cm long. A very attractive plant for a warm dry climate. Min. –5°C, perhaps. 'Childsii' is the form commonly cultivated in California. 'Siskyou' has slightly paler flowers. Other forms from Texas have almost white flowers and some Mexican forms have smaller deep pink flowers.

Oenothera stubbii Dietr., Raven & W. L. Wagner   A creeping perennial with narrow leaves, long rooting runners and stemless yellow flowers, native of NE Mexico in the Sierra Madre Oriental, growing on cliffs and steep slopes of gypsum, flowering in July–October. Stems trailing to 1.5m or more in a season. Leaves shortly pubescent, linear-lanceolate, with shallow teeth, around 12cm long on the main rosettes, shorter on the runners. Flowers opening in the evening, fading orange on hot days, sessile in the leaf axils; tube 10–15cm long; petals almost round, up to 5cm across. A lovely plant for ground-cover in a sunny position and tolerant of great heat. Min. –5°C, perhaps less.

Zauschneria californica C. Presl. subsp. **cana** Greene **'Dublin'** (*Onagraceae*) Californian Fuchsia   A perennial with a creeping underground rootstock and scarlet tubular flowers, native of California from Sonoma and Lake Counties, southwards to Baja California, growing on dry rocky slopes, usually below 1200m, flowering in June–October. Subsp. *cana* (Greene) is a southern subspecies found near the coast from Monterey Co. to Los Angeles Co. 'Dublin' is a good form of this subspecies and was probably selected at the National Botanic Garden, Glasnevin. It has narrow greenish leaves, broader and less silky than typical subsp. *cana*. For very well-drained soil; it will do best in a wall or rock crevice. Min. –5°C. *Zauschneria* is one of the best perennials for late flowering in dry climates or situations. Other forms are shown in our book *Perennials* (*see pages 202–3*).

Blumenbachia insignis

Tetrapanax papyrifer on Tresco

Schefflera actinophylla in Nairobi

Pseudopanax lineare on Tresco

Pseudopanax laetus on Tresco

Actinotus helianthi wild near Sydney

Oreopanax epremesnilianus

Schefflera elegantissima in Durango, Mexico

Pseudopanax lessonii 'Gold Splash'

Schefflera arboricola

Melanoselinum decipiens in northern Madeira

Actinotus helianthi Labill. (*Umbelliferae*)
Flannel Flower   A sub-shrubby perennial
or annual with yellowish flower heads
surrounded by soft white woolly bracts, native
of Queensland and New South Wales
especially around Sydney, growing in rocky
sandy soils in open forest, flowering in
August–February. Stems to 1.5m; leaves to
10cm with 3 deeply lobed segments. Flower
heads 5–8cm across; flowers without petals.
This attractive plant needs very well-drained
sandy soil in dappled shade or full sun with
some shade and moisture at the root.
Propagate by cuttings or fresh seed; stored
seed may take a year to germinate and may be
stimulated by passing over a flame to scorch
the outer seed coat. Min. –3°C.

Melanoselinum decipiens (Shrad. &
Wendl.) Hoffm. (*Umbelliferae*)   A large sub-
shrubby perennial with purplish-white
flowers, native of Madeira and the Azores,
growing on moist grassy banks, flowering in
March–July. Stems to 2m; umbels to 20cm
across. Fruits pubescent, blackish. For a well-
drained position in moist sun or partial shade.
Min. –3°C.

Oreopanax epremesnilianus (André)
André   A shrub or small tree with 7–9 leaflets
and a stiff pyramidal compound inflorescence,
native of South America but not known in the
wild, flowering in autumn. Stems to 3m or
more. Leaflets oblong to lanccolate, the
middle often with a few lobes. For a sheltered
spot. Min. –3°C.

Pseudopanax laetus (Kirk) W. R. Philipson,
syn. *Neopanax laetum* (Kirk) Allan (*Araliaceae*)
A dioecious shrub or small tree with 5–7
stalked leathery leaflets and flowers in
compound umbels, native of New Zealand in
the northern part of North Island, growing in

subtropical forest, flowering in late summer.
Tree to 5m or more. The leaflets are 12–25cm
long, ovate and toothed when mature; the
petioles are dark reddish-purple. The fruit
dark purple. For a sheltered shady position.
Min. –3°C. *P. arboreus* (L.fil.) W. R. Philipson
from most of New Zealand has narrower
coarsely toothed leaflets and is hardier.
Min. –10°C.

Pseudopanax lessonii (DC) C. Koch
'Gold Splash'   A dioecious shrub or small
tree with 3–5 subsessile leathery leaflets and
flowers in compound umbels, native of New
Zealand, from Three Kings Island to Poverty
Bay, growing in coastal scrub and forest,
flowering in December–February (summer).
Tree to 6m. Leaflets 5–10cm long,
oblanceolate, toothed, with golden veins in
'Gold Splash'. For a mild sheltered position in
sun or shade. Min. –3°C.

Pseudopanax lineare (Hook. fil.) C. Koch
A dioecious shrub with 3–5 sessile narrow
leathery leaflets the flowers are in compound
umbels, native of New Zealand in the W of
South Island, growing in subalpine scrub and
montane forest, flowering in January–
February (summer). Shrub to 3m. The leaflets
are 5–10cm long, 1cm wide, linear and
toothed. For a moist position in sun or shade.
Min. –10°C.

Schefflera actinophylla (Endl.) Harms.,
syn. *Brassaia actinophylla* Endl. (*Araliaceae*)
A many-stemmed large shrub with 7–16
deflexed stalked leaflets and stiff upright
spikes of red flowers and fruit, native of New
Guinea, Queensland and the Northern
Territories, growing in tropical forest, often as
an epiphyte or on rocks, flowering in summer.
Shrub to 12m or more. Leaflets to 30cm long,
10cm wide, oblong, shiny dark green. Fruit in

upright or spreading bunches, pink to red
before turning black. For a tropical climate or
can be grown in a pot. Min. 0°C.

Schefflera arboricola (Hayata) Hayata
An epiphytic shrub or large liane with 7–11
stalked leathery leaflets and flowers in small
umbels along the main inflorescence
branches, a native of Taiwan, growing in
subtropical forest and climbing up into the
treetops, flowering in late summer. Shrub to
4m or more. Leaflets up to 11cm long, 4.5cm
wide, obovate, not toothed. Fruit in nodding
bunches, orange before turning black. For a
sheltered shady position. Min. –3°C.

Schefflera elegantissima (Veitch ex Mast.)
Lowry & Frodin, syn. *Dizygotheca
elegantissima* Veitch ex Mast.   A many-
stemmed shrub or small tree with 7–11
narrow, jagged-toothed leaflets and a
compound umbellate inflorescence, native of
New Caledonia, growing in tropical forest,
often as an epiphyte or on rocks, flowering in
autumn. Tree to 15m or more. Leaflets of
juvenile plants to 23cm long, 3cm wide, linear-
oblong, dark green with a white midrib;
mature leaflets oblong, 25cm long, 8cm wide.
Commonly grown as a houseplant. Min. 5°C.

Tetrapanax papyrifer (Hook.) K. Koch
(*Araliaceae*)   Chinese Rice-paper Plant
A shrub with huge lobed leaves and a loose
long-branching rusty-hairy inflorescence,
native of Taiwan, growing in subtropical
forest, flowering in late summer. Stems to 7m.
Leaves 50cm or more across, orbicular,
whitish when young. For a sheltered position.
This noble plant survives outside in the
warmest gardens in SW England and can
regenerate from underground running
branches if cut back by frost. The stem pith is
used for rice-paper. Min. –3°C.

DAPHNE

Gnidia squarrosa in Madeira

Daphne bholua in the greenhouse at Quince House in Devon

Dais cotinifolia L. (*Thymelaeaceae*)
A rounded shrub or small tree with scented flowers in round heads, and long narrow pink petals, native of SE Africa from Natal to Madagascar, flowering in midsummer. Stems to 4m. Leaves bluish-green, deciduous in cold climates, opposite or alternate, ovate to obovate, to 7cm long. Flower heads around 4cm across, of up to 15 flowers, each 15mm across. Easily grown in sun in well-drained soil. Min. −3°C or less for short periods.

Daphne bholua Buch. Ham.
(*Thymelaeaceae*)   An upright shrub with sweetly scented pink or white flowers in winter, native of the Himalayas from E Nepal to NE Assam, growing on mountain ridges in *Rhododendron arboreum* forest and scrub, at 1600–3500m, flowering in October–April. Stems to 4m. Leaves elliptic to oblanceolate, 4–10cm long, usually evergreen, but deciduous in var. *glacialis* (W.W. Smith & Cave) Burtt. Flowers with 4 lobes, 6–8mm long. Fruit black. Min. −8°C for short periods. An excellent plant for the conservatory where its flowers are enjoyed on the coldest days in winter. Grows well in a large pot or planted in well-drained soil. Though it survives hot summers, potted specimens are better put outside in a partly shaded place in summer and kept watered.

Daphne bholua var. *glacialis*

Daphne bholua 'Alba'

'Jacqueline Postill' is one the best forms. **'Alba'** is white. All are ideal for the California fog belt.

Daphne odora Thunb. **'Aureomarginata'**
A low spreading shrub with evergreen yellowish-edged leaves and scented pink flowers, native of China and Taiwan, and cultivated in Japan and China since ancient times, flowering in early spring or winter under glass. Shrub about 1m high and wide. Leaves leathery, oblanceolate, 4–8cm long. Flowers 12–14mm across, mostly in heads at the ends of branches. Easily grown in well-drained soil. Min. –8°C. The form with a gold edge is reported to be the hardiest.

Daphne sureil W. W. Smith & Cave
An upright evergreen shrub with small scented white flowers, native of the Himalayas from E Nepal to N Assam, growing in scrub and rainforest with oaks and magnolias, at 1500–2200m, flowering October–January. Shrub to 2.5m. Leaves pale shiny green, ovate-elliptic to oblanceolate, 6–17cm long. Flowers 5–15 in a head, white, scented. Fruits reddish-orange. For a moist sheltered position. Min. –3°C.

Edgeworthia chrysantha Lindl. **'Rubra'**,
syn. *E. papyrifera* Sieb. & Zucc.
(*Thymelaeaceae*) A many-stemmed shrub with nodding umbels of flowers, native of C China especially Kiangsi and commonly cultivated elsewhere in China and Japan for paper-making, growing by streams at 300–1600m, flowering in February–April. Deciduous shrub to 1.6m; leaves narrowly ovate, silky; flower clusters 2.5–5cm across; flowers slightly scented, silky outside, inside usually pale yellow, red-orange in **'Rubra'**. Fruits dry, in a cluster. For a sheltered position. Min. –10°C. In cold areas it can be planted against a warm wall or in a pot and brought inside in winter to flower. *E. gardneri* (Wall.) Meissner from evergreen forest in the Eastern Himalayas, differs in its semi-evergreen leaves.

Gnidia squarrosa (L.) Druce, syn.
G. polystachya Bergius (*Thymelaeaceae*)
A many-stemmed shrub with yellowish-green flowers, sometimes flushed pink, native of South Africa from the Cape Peninsula east to Natal, growing on sandy slopes, often on limestone near the sea, flowering in June–October (early spring). Stems to 1.5m; leaves stiff, pointed; flowers with 8 petals, in clusters at the ends of the branches. For well-drained soil and a sunny position. Min. –3°C. *G. polyantha* Gilg. from the Drakensberg is similar and might be hardier.

Griselinia lucida Forst. fil. (*Cornaceae*)
A shrub or small tree with large leaves, very unequal-sided at the base, and small green flowers, native of New Zealand, especially on North Island, growing usually as an epiphyte in lowland forest, flowering in October–December. Tree to 8m; leaves 7–18cm, very glossy above. Inflorescence 7–15cm long. Female flowers without petals. For a moist sheltered position. Min. –5°C. The commoner *G. littoralis* makes a taller tree to 15m with small leaves, 3–12cm and female flowers with petals.

Edgeworthia chrysantha in Nairobi

Edgeworthia chrysantha 'Rubra' in Devon

Griselinia lucida on Tresco

Daphne odora 'Aureomarginata'

Daphne sureil at Sandling Park

Dais cotinifolia in Madeira

Begonia 'Arthur Mallet' at Wisley

Begonia 'Tingley Mallet'

Begonia stipulacea

Begonia × *corallina* 'Lucerna' at Wisley

Begonia aconitifolia 'Metallica'

stems to 20cm, the male opening first on a spreading inflorescence, the female opening later in a large hanging bunch. Min. 5°C. A commonly grown plant in the tropics as well as a houseplant, a hybrid of *B. coccinea* Hook. from Brazil, raised in Lucerne in 1903.

Begonia isoptera Dryand. An arching sub-shrub with bright green, sharply toothed leaves with a red edge and masses of small greenish-white male flowers, native of Malaysia and Java, growing on mossy logs and rocks in the forest, flowering in spring. Stems to 60cm; leaves ovate-oblong, glabrous, 8.5cm long. Male flowers 1cm across, on stems to 10cm; female 2–3 in the leaf axils. Min. 5°C.

***Begonia* 'Orange Rubra'** An upright sub-shrub with green cane-like stems and bright green angel-wing leaves paler beneath, flowering in summer. Stems to 1m; leaves lanceolate, glabrous, 10–15cm long, faintly spotted when young. Flowers bright orange, 3cm across, on stems to 20cm, the male opening first on a spreading inflorescence, the female opening later in a hanging bunch. Min. 5°C. An old cross between *B. dichroa* Sprague from Brazil and 'Coral Rubra'.

Begonia maculata Raddi **'Wightii'** An upright sub-shrub with green cane-like stems and olive-green angel-wing white-spotted leaves crimson beneath, native of Brazil, near Rio de Janeiro, growing on mossy logs and rocks in the forest, flowering in summer. Stems to 2.5m; leaves lanceolate, glabrous, 15–25cm long. Flowers white, 3cm across, on stems to 20cm, the male opening first on a spreading inflorescence, the female opening later in a hanging bunch. Min. 5°C. *B. maculata* Raddi has smaller leaves and pale pink or white flowers.

Begonia radicans Vellozo, syn. *B. sandersii* Hort. Kean ex A. DC. A low sub-shrub with bright green leaves, paler beneath, and small white flowers, native of Brazil, growing on mossy logs and rocks in the forest, flowering in early spring. Stems to 45cm; leaves ovate, glabrous, shallowly scalloped 8–12cm long. Flowers 3cm across, on stems to 20cm. Min. 5°C.

Begonia sanguinea Raddi A spreading sub-shrub with thick, fleshy leaves of dark olive-green, backed with crimson, and masses of small white flowers, native of Brazil, growing on mossy logs and rocks in the forest, flowering in early spring. Stems to 45cm; leaves ovate, glabrous, 10–15cm long, with a recurved and minutely toothed rim. Flowers 2cm across, on stems to 30cm. Min. 10°C.

Begonia stipulacea Willd., syn. *B. angularis* hort. An arching and spreading sub-shrub with green cane-like stems and grey-green, angel-wing white-veined leaves and masses of small white flowers, native of Brazil, growing on mossy logs and rocks in the forest, flowering in winter. Stems to 2.5m; leaves lanceolate, glabrous, 15–25cm long, reddish beneath. Flowers white or pink, to 1.5cm across on upright stems to 20cm. Min. 5°C.

***Begonia* 'Tingley Mallet'** Hybrid between *B. incarnata* f. *purpurea* and *B. rex* 'Eldorado', makes upright stems with hairy maroon leaves and pink flowers. Min. 10°C.

Most begonias prefer a soil composed mainly of leaf mould or moss peat and sand, which forms a well-drained but moisture-retentive compost. They also prefer shade, particularly in summer, and are tolerant of dryness in winter. Vine weevil grubs are a great danger to the fleshy roots and may eat the resting tubers. Mildew can be a problem on the leaves, especially in a dry poorly ventilated greenhouse. It can be controlled with systemic fungicide.

Begonia aconitifolia A. DC **'Metallica'**, syn. *B. sceptrum* hort. 'Hildegard Schneider' (*Begoniaceae*) An upright sub-shrub with cane-like stems and palmately lobed leaves, native of Brazil, growing near Rio de Janeiro, flowering in autumn. Stems to 1.2m; leaves 4–6-lobed, 12–18cm wide, with white streaks. Flowers white or pale pink, to 5cm across. Min. 5°C.

***Begonia* 'Arthur Mallet'** This interesting hybrid between *B. subpeltata* and *B. rex* 'Eldorado' makes upright stems with purple leaves covered in pinkish spots. The flowers are large and rose pink. Min. 10°C.

***Begonia* × *corallina* 'Lucerna'**, syn. 'Corallina de Lucerna' An upright sub-shrub with stout cane-like stems and olive-green angel-wing white-spotted leaves, reddish beneath, flowering in summer. Stems to 3m; leaves broadly lanceolate, glabrous, 15–25cm long. Flowers pink, 3cm across, on

Begonia radicans

Begonia 'Orange Rubra'

Begonia maculata 'Wightii'

Begonia isoptera

Begonia sanguinea

Specimens from the Royal Botanic Gardens, Kew, 3 October, ⅓ life-size

Begonia subvillosa

Begonia × ingramii

Begonia × richmondensis

Begonia schmidtiana

Begonia hirtella var. nana

Begonia thelmiae

Specimens from the Royal Botanic Gardens, Kew, 3 October, ⅓ life-size

Begonia metallica

Begonia minor 'Rosea' in Madeira in March

Begonia × credneri hort. (*Begoniaceae*) The hybrid between *B. metallica* (*see below*) and *B. scharffii*. It has less distinctly veined leaves than *B. metallica* and has upright flowers, more numerous than usual in *B. scharfii*. *Begonia × credneri* has stems to 1.2m; leaves with angular lobes, to 15cm long, reddish beneath. Flowers pale pink, to 3.5cm across. Min. 5°C. A very popular houseplant.

Begonia hirtella Link var. **nana** A. DC. A spreading plant with hairy stems and shiny green ciliate leaves, native of Brazil, growing on rocks in the forest and shady banks, flowering most of the year. Stems to 30cm; leaves around 5cm long; flowers pink. Min. 10°C.

Begonia × ingramii A hybrid between *B. minor* and *B. fuchsioides* Hook. raised in 1849, with narrow shiny green leaves, toothed and only slightly unequal at the base. A hardy plant which can be put outdoors in summer in England, it will make a tall upright plant to 1.5m with drooping deep pink flowers. Min. 0°C.

Begonia luxurians Scheidw. Palm-leaf Begonia A tall sub-shrub with thick red fleshy stems, palmate leaves and frothy masses of minute white flowers, native of Brazil, in the Organ Mountains, flowering in summer. Stems to 1.5m; leaves to 30cm across, with 7–17 narrow lobes. Flowers 6mm across in a large upright raceme. Min. 5°C.

Begonia metallica W. G. Sm. Metallic-leaf Begonia A tall sub-shrub with thick red hairy stems, olive-green leaves with purple veins and pink and white flowers, native of Brazil, growing among rocks in the forest, flowering in summer. Stems to 1.2m; leaves to 15cm long, with angled or shallowly lobed margins. Flowers to 3.5cm across in a large upright raceme. Min. 5°C.

Begonia minor Jacq., syn. *B. nitida* Ait. A tall slender-stemmed sub-shrub with shiny green leaves and white to bright pink flowers, native of Jamaica, growing on shady banks, flowering most of the year. Stems to 2m; leaves ovate, wavy edged, pale green beneath, to 15cm long, reddish beneath. Flowers pale or bright pink, to 5cm across on a tall raceme. Min. 5°C. **'Rosea'** (*shown here*) is a tall form with bright pink flowers; a beautiful garden plant, grown for its showy scented flowers, commonly seen in warm-temperate frost-free climates such as Madeira and Bermuda. *B. minor* was the earliest *Begonia* to be introduced to England, in 1577, but now seldom seen there.

Begonia × richmondensis A free-flowering hybrid between the small-leaved *B. fuchsioides* Hook. and the commonly cultivated *B. semperflorens*. Stems upright or sprawling to 60cm. Leaves ciliate and variably toothed, shiny on both sides. Flowers pink, produced all year. Easily grown. Min. 5°C.

Begonia scharffii Hook. fil., syn. *B. haageana* hort. An upright sub-shrub with hairy stems and rounded hairy leaves reddish beneath, native of Brazil, growing on mossy logs and rocks in the forest, flowering mainly in summer–autumn. Stems to 1.2m; leaves to

Begonia luxurians in the intermediate house at Wisley

Begonia × credneri in a mixed collection

Begonia luxurians

Begonia scharffii at Wisley

25cm long, green when grown in shade, reddening in sunlight. Flowers pale pink with red hairs, to 4cm across. Min. 5°C. A lovely and popular houseplant.

Begonia schmidtiana Reg.   A small plant with much-branched white-haired stems and coarsely toothed leaves, native of Brazil, growing on logs and rocks in the forest, flowering in winter. Stems to 30cm; leaves to 7.5cm long. Flowers numerous, white or pale pink, in drooping panicles. Min. 10°C.

Begonia subvillosa Klotsch.   An upright plant with reddish haired stems and coarsely toothed leaves, hairy above, native of Brazil, flowering mainly in summer. Stems to 60cm; leaves to 3.5–12.5cm long. Flowers hanging white or pale pink, to 2.5cm across. Min. 10°C. This species is usually hairier and more sharply toothed than the specimen shown here.

Begonia thelmae L. B. Sm. & Wassh. A dwarf trailing plant with leaves 2-ranked, with pale veins, native of Sao Tomé in SE Brazil, growing over rocks and trees in the forest, flowering in winter. Leaves around 3cm long. Flowers white, on a slender peduncle.

Begonia subvillosa

67

Begonia masoniana

Begonia soli - mutata

Begonia sharpeana

Begonia goegensis

Begonia ficicola

Begonia pruinata

Begonia olsoniae

Begonia acida

Specimens from the Royal Botanic Gardens, Kew, 3 October, ⅓ life-size

Begonia acida

Begonia limprichtii on Min Shan, SW Sichuan in the Tea Gardens

Begonia sharpeana

Begonia pustulata

Begonia 'Tiger Paws' at Wisley

Begonia acida Vell. (*Begoniaceae*) A tufted perennial with bright pale green suborbicular rugose leaves, native of Brazil, growing on rocks in the forest, flowering in winter–spring. Leaves to 23cm across, with white hairs beneath and on the petioles. Flowering stems to 45cm; flowers white to pale pink, to 1.5cm across. Min. 10°C.

Begonia ficicola Irmsch. A rhizomatous perennial with bullate, bright green peltate, ovate-elliptic leaves, native of Fernando Poo, growing on trees in the forest, flowering in winter–spring. Leaves 8–10cm across, with glabrous petioles. Flowers few, small, yellow, shaded red outside, barely reaching above the leaves. Min. 15°C.

Begonia goegensis N.E.Br. A tufted perennial with suborbicular, peltate leaves, brownish when young, native of Sumatra in Goego Island, growing on rocks in the forest, flowering in winter–spring. Leaves to 15–25cm across, with pale green veins, red beneath. Flowering stems to 15cm; flowers white to pale pink, to 1.5cm across. Min. 10°C.

Begonia limprichtii Irmsch. A tufted perennial with suborbicular, cordate leaves, with scattered bristly hairs, native of SW China in SW Sichuan, growing on moist shady banks in evergreen forest and in tea gardens at 300–1000m, flowering in September–October. Leaves to 10cm across. Flowering stems to 15cm; flowers white to pale pink, to 2.5cm across. Min. 0°C. *B. pedatifida* Lévl. has deeply laciniate leaves.

Begonia masoniana Irmsch., syn. 'Iron Cross' A tufted perennial with suborbicular cordate leaves, bullate with bristly red hairs and brownish around the main veins, native of New Guinea, growing on rocks in the forest, flowering in spring–summer. Leaves to 20cm across. Flowering stems to 15cm; flowers numerous, small, greenish-white. Min. 10°C. Introduced from Singapore in 1952 by L. Maurice-Mason and for long unknown in the wild.

Begonia olsoniae L. B. Sm. & Schubert A low perennial with suborbicular cordate leaves, dark green with paler pink or white veins, native of Brazil, growing on moist shady banks in evergreen forest, flowering in winter. Leaves 12–20cm across. Inflorescence to 15cm; flowers white to pale pink, to 3cm across. Min. 10°C.

Begonia pruinata A. DC. A short-stemmed perennial with ovate cordate leaves, with white hairs beneath on the veins and edge, native of Costa Rica and Nicaragua, growing on moist shady banks in evergreen forest, flowering in winter. The leaves are up to 7.5cm across. Flowering stems to 30cm; flowers many, small, white, in a tight flat-topped cluster. Min. 10°C. *B. acetosa* Vell. from Brazil is similar, but has much larger leaves.

Begonia pustulata Liebm. A shortly creeping perennial with broadly ovate, cordate leaves, bullate and green with silver veins above, pinkish beneath, native of Mexico and Guatemala, growing on trees and rocks in the forest, flowering in summer. Leaves to 15cm across. Flowering stems to 15cm; flowers few, small, bright pink. Min. 10°C. 'Argentea' has leaves with more silvery markings and greenish flowers.

Begonia sharpeana F. Muell. A tufted perennial with ovate cordate leaves and white hairs beneath on the veins and edge, native of New Guinea growing on moist shady banks in evergreen forest, flowering in winter. Leaves to 10cm across. Flowering stems to 30cm; flowers many, small, bright pink in a loose flat-topped inflorescence. Min. 10°C.

Begonia soli-mutata L.B.Smith & D.C.Warshausen A tufted perennial with broadly ovate, cordate leaves, bullate and brown with green veins above, reddish beneath, native of Brazil, growing on trees and rocks in the forest, flowering in summer. Leaves to 15cm across, with blunt angles. Flowering stems to 25cm; flowers many, small, white. Min. 10°C. *B. imperialis* Lem. from Mexico, is similar but has ovate, acuminate, red-brown leaves with bright green veins.

Begonia 'Tiger Paws' A small plant with a creeping and rooting rhizome, the leaves on stalks to 10cm, the blade cordate, to 6cm long. This is one of many hybrids of the Mexican *Begonia bowerae* from Chiapas and Oaxaca, which has similar leaves with brownish markings around the rim. 'Tiger Paws' is good as a houseplant or in a warm greenhouse. Min. 5°C.

Begonia 'Freddie'

Begonia × *ricinifolia* in the Quinta da Palheiro Gardens in Madeira

Begonia 'Marmaduke' at Wisley

Begonia 'Beatrice Haddrell'

Begonia nelumbiifolia in the Botanic Gardens in Hamilton, Bermuda

Begonia 'Black Velvet' in the Fairchild Botanic Garden, Florida

Rhizomatous begonias flowering in the intermediate house at Wisley

Begonia 'Beatrice Haddrell'
A rhizomatous hybrid with star-shaped leaves marked with bright green on brown. A hybrid between *B. bowerae* and *B. × sunderbruchii* (*B × ricinifolia × B. heracleifolia*). Min. 10°C.

Begonia 'Black Velvet' Leaves black, shallowly lobed; flowers pink.

Begonia 'Caina' Leaves green, wavy-edged and ciliate; flowers pink.

Begonia 'Freddie' A rhizomatous hybrid with dark green shiny cordate leaves around 20cm across.

Begonia × erythrophylla J. Neumann
A large plant with almost round leaves, deeply cordate and overlapping at the base, with pink flowers. An old hybrid between *B. manicata* and *B. hydrocotylifolia*, both from Mexico, known since 1847. Leaves to 11cm long, 14cm wide; flowering stems to 30cm. Min. 5°C.

Begonia × erythrophylla 'Helix' Leaves make an extra spiral at the sinus in this form.

Begonia 'Marmaduke' A rhizomatous hybrid with toothed and slightly bullate leaves, pale green with brownish markings, around 20cm across.

Begonia nelumbiifolia Cham. & Schldl.
Lily-pad Begonia A very large plant with a short upright rhizome, huge round peltate leaves and masses of small white or pale-pink flowers, native of S Mexico to Colombia, flowering in winter–spring. Leaves to 45cm across with a serrulate, ciliate margin. Inflorescence to 60cm; flowers 1.5cm across. Min. 10°C.

Begonia × ricinifolia A. Dietr. A large plant with deeply divided leaves and tall inflorescences of pink flowers, flowering in winter–spring. An old hybrid between *B. heracleifolia* and *B. peponifolia*, both from Mexico, known since 1847. Leaves to 30cm long, 20cm wide; flowering stems to 125cm. Min. 5°C. A common garden plant in frost-free climates.

Begonia 'Texas Star' Leaves black, deeply lobed, around 10cm wide.

Begonia × erythrophylla

Begonia 'Caina'

Begonia 'Texas Star'

Begonia × erythrophylla 'Helix'

Begonia 'Fireflush' at Kew

Begonia 'Fireflush' showing the scented flowers

Begonia 'Fireflush' the red hairs catch the light

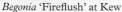

Begonia 'Rapsberry Swirl' at Wisley

Begonia 'Benitochiba' in the National Botanic Garden, Washington DC

Begonia 'de Elegans' at Wisley

Begonia 'Bodnant' at Wisley

The original wild species *Begonia rex* Putzeys was introduced into cultivation in Europe from Assam in 1858. Its leaves are heart-shaped, blue-green with a silvery-white zone near the margin. This was soon crossed with other rhizomatous species to form the beginning of the present race; red hairy forms such as 'Fireflush' appeared with the introduction of *B. decora* from Penang in around 1895. Most varieties are still dwarf and stemless, but crosses with *B. grandis* produced plants with upright stems, such as

'L. R. Russell', which required less heat. Miniatures were raised using *B. imperialis* and small-leaved upright varieties using the African *B. dregei*. Spiral-leaved varieties originated with 'Comtesse Louise d'Erdody' in 1883. This is a very simplified outline of some of the complex ancestry behind this group. Most require shade and humidity in summer. Min. 10°C. Compost should be very open with leaf mould or coarse peat, bark and sand. Mildew on the leaves can be a serious problem in dry conditions; all plants should

be sprayed at the first sign of disease. Vine weevil grubs are very fond of the juicy roots and rhizomes.

Begonia '**Benitochiba**' Tall with deeply dissected purplish leaves overlaid with silver.

Begonia '**Bodnant**' A heart-shaped leaf, mainly green-veined overlaid with silver; with pinkish hairs and a crimson centre and edge.

Begonia '**de Elegans**' A rather upright

Begonia 'Yuletide' at Wisley

Begonia 'Fireworks' at Wisley

Begonia 'Happy New Year' in the old vinery at Sellindge, Kent

Begonia 'Salamander' at Wisley

small-leaved plant with green veined silver spotted leaves, each spot topped with a hair. Raised by Ashizawa in 1969. Parentage said to be *B. decora* × *B. deliciosa*.

Begonia **'Fireflush'**   Leaves large, olive green covered with crimson hairs; flowers white, waxy, scented. 'Bettina Rothschild' is generally considered to be the same.

Begonia **'Fireworks'**   Leaves strongly veined, almost bullate with a dark centre, a pink and silver zone and a wide purple edge.

Begonia **'Happy New Year'**   A striking leaf with clear zones of black, silver and green with silver spots, with a toothed purple edge. An old variety which Martyn rescued from the rubbish heap at Cambridge Botanic Gardens in 1968. 'Merry Christmas' is similar but without the spotting.

Begonia **'Lilian'**   A spiral leaf with a big gap between the spirals, mostly silver, with a dark centre and edge.

Begonia **'Raspberry Swirl'**   A ruffled leaf of crushed raspberry, with a silver border.

Begonia **'Salamander'**   One of several mainly silver varieties with a sharply toothed edge.

Begonia **'Yuletide'**   Similar to 'Happy New Year, but with less distinct zoning.

Begonia 'Lilian' at Wisley

Begonia gracilis wild in pine forests on the flanks of Volcan Collima, W Mexico

Begonia sutherlandii

Begonia gracilis on Volcan Collima, W Mexico

Begonia gracilis H. B. & K.   An upright plant with lightly spotted leaves and pink flowers, native of Mexico, growing on shady rocks and mossy banks in pine forest, at around 2000m, flowering in September–November. Tuber small, about 2cm across; stems annual, to 100cm, usually about 30cm. Leaves shallowly cordate, the lower stalked, crenate, to 10cm across; the upper sessile, with shallow teeth, a hair on each spot. Flowers 3.5–4cm across, faintly scented, the tepals with shallow teeth near the apex. As the stems fade, bunches of tiny bulbils appear in the leaf axils. Min. 5°C or less if dormant. Var. *martiana* A. DC. is said to have entire leaves, shorter stems and flowers to 5cm across.

Begonia uniflora S Wats.   A delicate creeping plant with almost round leaves and small pink flowers, native of Mexico, in the Sierra Madre Orientale, growing on moist limestone rocks, flowering in October. Stems far-creeping; leaves crenate, around 3cm across. Flowers 2cm across. Min. 5°C.

Begonia grandis Dryand. subsp. *evansiana* (Andr.) Irmsch., syn. *B. evansiana* Andr. An upright plant with large ovate, cordate leaves and pink flowers, native of Malaysia and China and cultivated in Japan, growing on shady banks, flowering in summer. Root tuberous. Stems to 100cm, forming bulbils in autumn. Leaves to 15cm long; flowers scented, in hanging cymes, to 3cm across, usually pinkish, but white in 'Alba' and larger in 'Simsii'. One of the hardiest species, surviving −5°C when dormant.

Begonia sutherlandii Hooker fil. A small spreading and pendulous plant with thin bright green acuminate leaves and orange flowers, native of South Africa from Natal north to Tanzania, growing on rocks along streams in humid forests, flowering in January–February (summer). Tubers to 5cm across; stems red, to 80cm. Leaves toothed, cordate at the base, to 15cm long; flowers 2–2.5cm across. Easily grown, the tubers kept dry in winter. Min. 0°C. The hybrid between *B. sutherlandii* and *B. dregei*, called *B.* × *weltonensis* is now seldom seen; it is a most attractive and graceful plant with heart-shaped leaves and masses of bright pink flowers on a bushy plant to 60cm across.

Begonia sutherlandii wild on mossy rocks by a stream in the Weza Forest, Natal

Begonia uniflora on shady limestone rocks above Linares, NE Mexico

Begonia grandis subsp. *evansiana* at Kew

Begonia 'Pendula'

Mixed large-flowered tuberous *Begonias* in Golden Gate Park, San Francisco

Winter-flowering *Begonia* 'Elatior'

Begonia 'Giant Pendula' in Golden Gate Park

Begonia 'Falstaff'

Begonia 'Mr Steve'

Begonia 'Ophelia'

Large-flowered Tuberous Begonias
(*Begonia tuberhybrida*) It is in this group
of tuberous begonias from the Andes that the
most spectacular garden plants have been
bred. The first of these tuberous species,
Begonia boliviana, was introduced from
Bolivia in 1864; its pendulous red flowers with
long narrow tepals are recognisable in the
modern 'Giant Pendula' varieties used for
hanging baskets.

Other species with dwarf upright stems and
the yellow-flowered *B. pearcei* soon followed,
mostly collected by Richard Pearce for the
great nursery firm Messrs Veitch and
hybridised by John Seden. His first cross
appeared in 1868, and by 1876 the variety
'Acme' had orange-pink flowers 10cm across.
Victor Lémoine of Nancy produced the first
good double, 'Gloire de Nancy', in 1875. The
famous variety 'Viscountess Doneraile' with
large red single flowers was listed by Veitch in
1881. Frilled and ruffled varieties soon
followed. Double varieties were improved and
refined by C. F. Langdon of Bath from 1885
onwards; Blackmore and Langdon's hybrids
are still famous, combining perfection of
form, size, a wide colour range and sturdy
stems.

Other modern developments have been the
F1 hybrids such as 'Pin-up' which can be
easily raised from seed, and the dwarf, early-
flowering 'Non Stop'. These begonias do best
in cool conditions such as suit the more
delicate fuchsias, and thrive outside in
summer in a sheltered position. The tubers
only need to be protected from winter frost
and kept rather dry. Plant the tubers so that
they can root over all their surface.

These are now sold either as seed-raised
strains, or more rarely as named varieties
which are single clones. Blackmore and
Langdon's Giant named varieties are still the
finest of all tuberous begonias. Numerous
named varieties are available in a wide range
of colours. Shown here are:

'Falstaff' A new bright red large-flowered
perfect double from Blackmore and Langdon.

'Mr Steve' A pure white with a fine pink
picotee edge.

'Non-stop' An early-flowering double-
flowered strain available in selected colours
such as orange, pink, salmon, scarlet, yellow
and white, or in mixed colours; available as
tubers or as seeds. Stems around 20cm.

'Pin-Up' An F1 single-flowered strain
which can be raised from seed to flower the
same year. Flowers white with a pink frilly
edge.

'Picotee' These are usually sold separately,
with a pink edge on a white or apricot ground.
Sometimes frilled. Modern strains include
'Giant Trumpet Picotees' and 'Picotee Giant
Primadonnas' which are frilled.

'Pendula' A group of hybrids with lax stems
and long-stalked flowers which are usually
single or semi-double; suitable for hanging
baskets or the edges of large urns. The older
varieties had the lovely narrow curved tepals
of *B. boliviana*. 'Chanson', a strain from
Unwins, can be raised from seed sown early in
heat. The finest named varieties such as the

Winter-flowering *Begonia* close to
'Emily Clibran'

white 'Crystal Cascade' are available from
Blackmore and Langdon. Shown here are:

'Firedance' Bright orange, from Blackmore
and Langdon.

'Giant Pendula' A strain combining the
hanging habit with large double flowers;
available in separate colours or mixed.
'Hanging Sensation' is similar.

'Ophelia' Creamy white with an apricot
centre, from Blackmore and Longdon;
photographed in their nursery.

Winter-flowering *Begonias*
The interesting winter-flowering species,
Begonia socotrana Hook. fil. from the island of
Socotra off the coast of Somalia, was
introduced by Professor I. Bayley-Balfour to
Kew in 1880. Initially, it was considered a
mere curiosity, but in 1883, John Heal of
Veitch's succeeded in raising a single seedling
with 'Viscountess Doneraile' to produce 'John
Heal', the first of the winter-flowering
hybrids, now known as Hiemalis begonias. At
the same time Lémoine produced 'Gloire de
Lorraine' (*B. socotrana* × *B. dregei*), a winter-
flowering type with masses of small pink
flowers and nearly round leaves, generally
called the Cheimantha group. Another hybrid
between *B. socotrana* and *B. subpeltata* was
raised by Lémoine in 1885 and named 'Gloire
de Sceaux'.

These winter-flowering varieties need
temperatures around 12–15°C for good
growth and flowering and so are ideal for an
airy conservatory attached to the house. They
are liable to mildew in a wet cold atmosphere.
The plant shown here which is close to
'Emily Clibran', one of the Hiemalis group,
shows the round leaves typical of *B. socotrana*
and has no tuber. Flowers pink and orange.
Nowadays these traditional varieties are
seldom seen, having been replaced by the
more compact Elatior varieties, hybrids
between large-flowered tuberous hybrids and
B. socotrana, which can be produced as winter
pot plants.

'Elatior' A strain with bushy stems and
masses of double flowers, used as winter-
flowering pot plants or for autumn bedding
outside. The plants I have seen of this type
lack any grace of form or subtlety of colour.

Begonia 'Picotee'

Begonia 'Pin-Up'

Begonia 'Firedance'

Begonia 'Non-stop Salmon Pink'

77

Primula verticillata in the Alpine House at Kew

Primula floribunda in Devon

Primula forbesii in an old temple near Lijiang

Primula obconica 'Salmon' at Wisley

Primula × *kewensis* at Kew

Primula boveana in Devon

Primula species in temperate rainforest at the foot of Omei Shan

Primula boveana Dcne. (*Primulaceae*) A perennial with narrow leaves, farinose beneath and whorls of long-tubed small yellow flowers, native of Mount Sinai, Mount St Catherine and near Raphidim, growing on shady rocks below 2800m, flowering in March–May. Plant slender; bracts broader than *P. verticillata*; flowers small, pale yellow with crenate petals and usually serrate sepals. For a shady position in the greenhouse, with careful watering. Min. –3°C. Sometimes considered a subspecies of *P. verticillata* as is the rather similar *P. simensis* Hochst. from Tigre in Ethiopia.

Primula floribunda Wall. A perennial with hairy leaves and yellow flowers, native of the Himalayas from Afghanistan on the Khyber Pass to W Nepal, growing on damp shady cliffs and by mountain streams at 500–2000m, flowering in April–July. Leaves ovate to elliptic; flowering stem 5–15cm, with 2–6 whorls of 3–6 scented flowers, each around 1.5cm across. For well-drained leafy soil and shade, kept rather dry in winter. Min. –3°C. Leaves usually without farina, but apparently farinose in the plant shown here.

Primula forbesii Franch. A very variable annual with a rosette of short-stalked leaves and whorls of lilac flowers, native of SW China in Yunnan from Kunming west to Dali and in SW Sichuan, growing in marshes, by rice fields and canals at 2000–3000m, and cultivated in village and temple gardens in the Lijiang valley, flowering in January–April. Leaf blade 2–5cm long; flowering stems 10–30cm with 1–4 tiers of 4–8 flowers, each around 1cm across. Calyx lobes acute, somewhat spreading. This species was formerly cultivated but is now seldom seen. Min. –3°C, perhaps less.

Primula malacoides Franch. A graceful hairy annual with a rosette of long-stalked leaves and several stems bearing whorls of lilac flowers, native of SW China in Yunnan, Guizhou and N Burma, growing as a weed in bean fields, on sunny and shady banks and common in the Dali Valley, flowering in January–April. Leaf blade 3–10cm long; flowering stems 10–40cm, with 1–6 tiers of 4–20 flowers, each around 5–15mm across. Calyx lobes blunt, somewhat reflexed. Min. –3°C, perhaps less. This species was introduced by George Forrest from the Dali area in 1906. It very soon became the subject of intense breeding, producing larger flowers, semi-double and frilled petals and a greater range of colours. Tetraploid strains were also selected for their greater size and recently the trend has been towards chunkier plants with dense whorls of flowers. One of these, **'Lilac Queen'** is shown here.

Primula obconica Hance A softly hairy short-lived perennial with lavender, pink or white flowers, native of W China from Hubei to Guizhou and Yunnan, growing on shady rocks and in woods, flowering in March–May. In the wild form the leaf blades are up to 17cm long and the flowers 1.5–2.5cm across. The cultivated forms have much larger flowers; the original collection from which the cultivated plants were raised was made by Maries in the Ichang Gorges, collecting for Messrs. Veitch in 1879. Veitch soon realised

Primula malacoides

Primula malacoides 'Lilac Queen' at Wisley

Primula sinensis on the sides of an old tank in the garden of a temple on Omei Shan

the potential of the plant for winter-flowering in the greenhouse and raised plants with larger, more rounded flowers and fimbriated petals, in a range of colours.

'Salmon' (*shown here*) is one of the more recent colour strains which come true from seed. There is also a good blue, 'Blue Agate', and a strain 'Freedom', which is free of the irritants which can cause skin rashes when the plant is touched.

Primula × kewensis hort.   A hybrid between *P. verticillata* and *P. floribunda*, found at Kew among plants of *P. floribunda*. At first it was sterile but spontaneously became fertile by the doubling of its chromosomes, thereby forming a new species. Leaves obovate, usually farinose beneath. Flowers around 1.5cm across. 'Thurgold' is a recent cultivar name given to a stock of this species.

Primula species close to *obconica*
A delicate perennial with stalked leaves and umbels of pure white flowers, native of SW Sichuan and particularly common on the lower slopes of Omei Shan, growing on mossy banks among ferns in subtropical forest, flowering in April–May. Leaf blades around 7cm long and the flowers 1.5cm across. An attractive species for a moist mild climate. Min. 0°C.

Primula sinensis Lindl.   A softly hairy perennial with deeply lobed leaf blades and rounded flowers with a very large calyx in an umbel among the leaves, not known in the wild.

This species was one of the ancient garden plants grown by the Chinese. It was introduced to Europe from Canton in 1821, along with China and Tea roses, camellias and chrysanthemums, having been illustrated in John Reeves' drawings sent to the Horticultural Society in 1819. Its cultivation reached a peak in the late-19th century and continued until the 1930s. Since then it has declined in popularity and is now seldom seen or offered for sale. It is shown here growing in the stones of an old tank in the garden of a temple on Omei Shan in Sichuan.

The wild form of this species is probably that called *P. rupestris* Balf. fil. & Farrer, collected by Farrer on hot dry limestone cliffs on the Shensi-Sichuan border and graphically described in *Rainbow Bridge*. Wilson, Delavay and Henry collected it on the limestone cliffs of Ichang. It has thin petioles and pink flowers 2–3cm across.

Primula verticillata Forsk.   A perennial covered with farina, with long-tubed yellow flowers, native of Yemen, growing by streams on limestone on Mount Kurma or Kierma near Menacha, at 2200–3000m. Leaves oblanceolate to 30cm long; flowering stem 10–60cm, with several whorls of scented flowers, each 1.5–2.5cm across, with a very long tube. For well-drained leafy soil and shade from full sun in summer. Min. –3°C.

Limonium perezii naturalised on the coast of California south of Los Angeles near Laguna Beach

Plumbago indica

Limonium arborescens

Limonium redivivum

Limonium spectabile in the Canary Island House at Kew

Ceratostigma griffithii C. B. Clarke
A spreading sub-shrub with obovate leaves
and bright blue flowers, native of S Yunnan
and the E Himalayas, growing on sunny rocks
in dry valleys at 1500m, flowering in
August–November. Stems to 1m, with rufous
hairs; leaves 1.5–3cm long, bristly-hairy on the
margins. Flowers 12–25mm across. For a
warm dry climate, with water in summer.
Min. –3°C.

Limonium arborescens (Brouss)
O. Kuntze   A large perennial, shrubby at the
base, with glaucous leaves and masses of blue
calyces and white flowers, native of Tenerife
where it is rare and endangered, growing on
cliffs on the north coast, flowering in winter.
Stems to 1.8m. Leaves ovate with a long stalk;
flowering stem and branches narrowly
winged. For well-drained soil. Min. –3°C.
There are around 15 species of Sea Lavender
found only on the Canary Islands confined to
small areas of mountain or cliff.

Limonium perezii (Stapf) Hubb.   A large
perennial with dark green leaves and masses of
deep blue calyces and white flowers, native of
Tenerife where it is confined to the west,
flowering in winter–spring. Stems to 10cm.
Leaves wavy, tapering into a long stalk;
flowering stem and branches not winged.
For well-drained sandy soil. Min. –3°C.
According to the Bramwells' flora, this species
is poorly known on Tenerife, but it is
commonly cultivated in California and has
become naturalised in a few places along the
coast. The flowers are generally described as
pale yellow, but are white in California.

Limonium redivivum (Svent.) Kunkel &
Sund.   A large perennial, stems shrubby at
the base, with dark green leaves and masses of
pale blue calyces and white flowers, native of
Gomera where it is found on cliffs at 1000m
near Chipude and in the E of the island at
800m, flowering in winter–spring. Stems to
20cm. Leaves obovate to spathulate, tapering

into a long stalk; flowering stem and branches broadly winged. For well-drained soil. Min −3°C

Limonium spectabile (Svent.) Kunkel & Sund.   A large perennial, stems shrubby at the base, with dark green pinnate leaves and masses of purple calyces and white flowers, native of Tenerife where it is known only from the sea cliffs of the Barranco de Masca, flowering in winter–spring. Stems to 30cm. Leaf lobes linear-lanceolate; flowering stem and branches not winged. For well-drained sandy soil. Min. −3°C.

Plumbago auriculata Lam., syn. *Plumbago capensis* Thunb. Plumbago (*Plumbaginaceae*) A scrambling or loose-growing shrub with masses of lovely pale blue flowers, native of South Africa from Knysna to the E Cape, Natal and E Transvaal, growing in hedges and open scrub in hot dry areas, flowering mostly in November–May. Shrub to 2m or more if supported; leaves around 5cm long with auricles at the base. Flowers 2cm across with a very sticky glandular calyx. Heat- and drought-tolerant; will survive −8°C overnight and sprout from old wood. An excellent hedge plant when clipped and standards can be used for summer bedding. One of the best and most trouble-free plants for the greenhouse. **'Chessington Blue'**, syn. 'Bleu Foncée' in France or 'Royal Cape' in Australia is a deeper blue form. We found acres of *P. auriculata* in flower near Somerset East in the E Cape, but there was almost no variation in colour or size of flower. This slightly deeper blue and the white are the only colour forms available. ***Plumbago auriculata*** var. ***alba,*** the white-flowered form, is sometimes found in the wild.

Plumbago indica L., syn. *Plumbago rosea* L. A perennial or low shrub, sometimes almost climbing, with long spikes of flowers from deep pink to scarlet or purple, native perhaps of India and Sikkim, but widely cultivated in SE Asia, flowering in winter. Stems to 2m, usually around 1m; leaves 5–11cm long; flower spikes to 30cm long, corolla tube to 5cm. A beautiful plant, as difficult as *P. auriculata* is easy, needing ample heat, light and feeding to thrive and flower well. Min. 15°C. Said to be propagated by root cuttings.

Plumbago auriculata at Le Clos du Peyronnet, Menton

Plumbago auriculata

Ceratostigma griffithii

Plumbago auriculata 'Chessington Blue'

Plumbago auriculata var. *alba*

Rhododendron 'Phoeniceum' seedlings naturalised in Bermuda

Rhododendron simsii double red, in a monastery courtyard on Min Shan near Ya-an, flowering in April

Rhododendron 'Concinnum' in a garden in Malawi

Rhododendron 'Phoeniceum'

Rhododendron simsii wild on Victoria Peak in Hong Kong in April

'Leopold-Astrid'

'Aquarell'

Rhododendron 'Phoeniceum'

An evergreen azalea with pinkish-purple, very open flowers and rather narrow lobes, often used as an understock for the double winter-flowering azaleas. It grows well in subtropical climates where it is often seen in old gardens. It was introduced from Japan in 1824. It is probably a hybrid, with *Rhododendron scabrum* as one of the parents. Min. −3°C.

Rhododendron 'Concinnum' Very similar to 'Phoeniceum' but has brighter redder flowers with broader, more rounded lobes on a faster growing shrub. This is also used as an understock and has replaced 'Phoeniceum'. It is commonly seen in gardens with little frost and is shown here in Malawi, though we have seen it at the Descanso Gardens in southern California too.

Rhododendron simsii Planch. (*Ericaceae*)

A spreading evergreen shrub with bright red flowers, native of S China from Hong Kong and Taiwan, to Hubei, Sichuan and Yunnan, and in Burma and N Thailand at up to 2900m, growing on cliffs and rocks, in open woods and by streams, flowering in February–May. Shrub 1–2.5m; leaves to 5cm long, 12mm wide, obovate to oblanceolate or elliptic; flowers to 5cm across; stamens 10; style glabrous. Min. −3°C or perhaps less in plants from high altitudes.

Rhododendron simsii double red

The plant shown here growing in a temple courtyard in SW China is almost certainly a double-flowered form of *R. simsii*. It is a very slow-growing plant in cultivation; indeed the specimen here has a label on it stating that it is 500–600 years old. This double red form is very similar to *Rhododendron indicum* (L.) Sweet 'Balsaminiflorum' an ancient cultivar of the Japanese species *R. indicum*. This is close to *R. simsii*, but has only 5, not 10 stamens. It was introduced to Europe in 1833 and widely grown as a greenhouse shrub until it was pushed out by the more showy *R. simsii* and its hybrids from 1850 onwards.

Winter-flowering azaleas *Rhododendron simsii* The original species from which the winter-flowering azaleas were developed, it was introduced to Europe before 1812, when it was illustrated in Curtis's *Botanical Magazine* under the name *Azalea indica*, almost certainly from plants brought from Canton or Hong Kong. Chinese garden varieties were introduced and then developed, mainly in Belgium but also in France and Germany, into a range of colours from red to pink and white, and variously striped and frilled. These are long-lived pot plants for a cool greenhouse and can be grown into large specimens if a few rules are kept. Plants should not be allowed to dry out, or be waterlogged either; water with neutral or acid water; they should be put outdoors in shade in summer and brought in before the first hard frost in autumn. Watch for greenfly on new leaves in early spring. Shown here are:

'Leopold-Astrid' A double white with a red frilly edge introduced in 1933. Flowers 8cm across. A sport from 'Vervaeneana' which is a double pink with a white margin, itself a sport from var. *vittatum* Wilson, a white striped with lilac-purple, an old Chinese variety, recorded by Fortune in a garden in Canton. 'Albert-Elizabeth' is another with a dark reddish-pink edge to a white flower, but that has distinct green spots on the upper corolla lobe.

'Aquarell' A sport of 'Hellmut Vogel' detected by Gartenbau Verheyen-Baetcke in 1992 in Germany. The spots distinguish it from the very familiar 'Sima' which also has a smaller red edge.

Rhododendron formosum at Savill Gardens, Windsor

Rhododendron 'Fragrantissimum' outside in S Devon

Rhododendron 'Countess of Haddington' at Quince House, Devon

Rhododendron ovatum at the Royal Botanic Garden, Edinburgh

Rhododendron konorii from New Guinea, at the Royal Botanic Garden, Edinburgh

All the Rhododendrons on this page are excellent plants for the frost-free greenhouse and respond well to the treatment described on the previous page for winter-flowering azaleas. They will also do well in warm climates, being more tolerant of heat than most of the hardy species. They do particularly well along the fog belt of coastal California from Golden Gate Park, San Francisco, south to Beverley Hills.

Rhododendron championae Hook.
An evergreen shrub or small tree with white scented flowers, sometimes pale pink in bud, native of SE China from S Zhejiang and Hong Kong west to Guangdong, growing on rocky hills and ravines, flowering in April–May. Tree to 7.6m. Leaves oblong-oblanceolate, 7.5–15cm long. Flowers around 11cm across. Stamens 10. A pretty shrub with flowers like a fine large azalea. Min. 3°C.

Rhododendron 'Countess of Haddington'
An evergreen shrub with large white scented flowers, pale pink outside, flowering in April–May. Shrub to 2m. Leaves oblong-oblanceolate, 10–15cm long. Flowers about 7cm across, trumpet-shaped. The easiest and most free-flowering of the group. Min. –5°C. Raised before 1862; parentage: R. ciliatum × R. dalhousiae var. dalhousiae.

Rhododendron formosum Wall., syn. R. iteophyllum Hutch.   An evergreen shrub with white, pink or yellowish scented flowers, sometimes striped in bud, native of NE India in the Khasia Hills at 600–1800m, growing on rocky hills and river banks, flowering in April–June. Shrub to 3m. Leaves linear to obovate, 3–7cm long. Flowers around 8cm across. Stamens 10. Min. –3°C. The larger tenderer var. inaequale (Hutch.) Cullen has particularly good scent. R. iteophyllum Hutch. was the name given to narrow-leaved forms (shown here).

Rhododendron 'Fragrantissimum'
An evergreen shrub with white scented flowers, yellowish in the throat, flowering in April–May. A lax shrub to 2m. Leaves ovate-elliptic to obovate, around 8cm long, scaly beneath. Flowers 7.5–10cm across, widely funnel-shaped. Min. –5°C. Raised before 1868; parentage R. edgeworthii × R. formosum.

Rhododendron jasminiflorum Hook.
A dwarf evergreen shrub with long-tubed white scented flowers, native of Malaysia in the Cameron Highlands, Philippines and Sumatra, growing in forests in the hills at 1200-1500m, flowering in winter. Shrub to 2.5m. Leaves 2.5–6cm, obovate-elliptic to almost round, in whorls at the ends of the season's growth. Flowers 3.5–4.5cm long, sometimes pinkish in the throat. Min. 5°C. This was one of the first members of the tropical Vireya section to be introduced by Thomas Lobb for Veitch in 1848. It became one of the parents of the javanico-jasminiflorum hybrids which were popular in greenhouses from the 1850s to around 1910 and are now popular again in Australia.

Rhododendron konorii Becc.   An evergreen shrub or small tree with elliptic leaves and white carnation-scented flowers, native of New Guinea, growing on cliffs and grassland at 750–2400m, flowering in

Rhododendron championae wild on Victoria Peak, Hong Kong, by the peak path in late April

Rhododendron veitchianum in the Temperate House at Kew

Rhododendron championae

August–September. Shrub to 4m. Leaves 10–18cm, in whorls of 3–5. Flowers 12–16cm long, 5–8 in an umbel, rarely pinkish. Min. 0°C. One of the largest-flowered of the Vireya section.

Rhododendron ovatum Maxim.
An evergreen shrub with flat white spotted flowers, native of Taiwan and SE China from Jiangsu and Anhui south to Hong Kong and west to Guangdong and the warmer parts of Hubei and Sichuan, growing in shade of forests or by streams, flowering in March–June. Shrub to 4m. Leaves broadly ovate to elliptic, 2.5–5cm long. Flowers around 5–7.5cm across, with spots on the upper three

petals, sometimes pale pink in bud. Stamens 5. Min. –3°C. This species is said to be particularly heat-tolerant and suitable for the southeastern states of USA.

Rhododendron veitchianum Hook.
A spreading evergreen shrub with white frilled scented flowers, native of S and C Burma and Thailand at 900–2400m, usually growing as an epiphyte on birch, oak or in evergreen forest, flowering in February–July. Shrub to 3m. Leaves broadly elliptic to obovate, 5–10cm long. Flowers to 12.5cm across, frilled petals, sometimes with a yellow throat, stamens 10. Min. 0°C. Introduced by Thomas Lobb for Veitch in 1848.

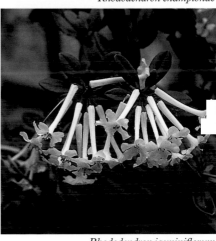

Rhododendron jasminiflorum

Rhododendron macgregoriae hybrid

Rhododendron christianae

Rhododendron orbiculatum

'Pink Delight'

Rhododendron commonae × *lochiae*

Rhododendron zoelleri × *jasminiflorum*

Specimens from the Temperate House at the Royal Botanic Gardens, Kew, 7 February, ½ life-size

Rhododendron 'Princess Frederica' in the
Temperate House at Kew

Rhododendron lochiae × javanicum in the
Temperate House at Kew

Rhododendron laetum

Rhododendron macgregoriae

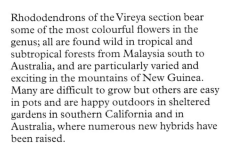

Rhododendron zoelleri

Rhododendron 'Donald Stanton'

Rhododendrons of the Vireya section bear some of the most colourful flowers in the genus; all are found wild in tropical and subtropical forests from Malaysia south to Australia, and are particularly varied and exciting in the mountains of New Guinea. Many are difficult to grow but others are easy in pots and are happy outdoors in sheltered gardens in southern California and in Australia, where numerous new hybrids have been raised.

Rhododendron christianae Sleumer
An evergreen shrub with pointed leaves and yellow to deep red flowers with a yellow centre and long greenish tube, native of SE New Guinea, growing on cliffs and mountain grassland at 600–1500m, flowering in April in the wild, but winter under glass. Shrub to 6m. Leaves 4.5–7.5cm, broadly elliptic, in whorls of 3. Flowers 3–4cm long, 3–4 in an umbel. Min. 0°C. Named after the mother of Canon N. E. G. Crutwell, a botanist-missionary in Highland New Guinea.

Rhododendron commonae × lochiae
A low-growing hybrid with an umbel of waxy, deep red flowers on slender stalks. In *R. lochiae* F. V. Muell. from NE Queensland, the flowers are 3–5cm long, scarlet or bright red. In *R. commonae* Foerster, from high in the mountains of New Guinea, the flowers are deep crimson or purplish, tubular, to 3cm long. Min. 0°C.

Rhododendron 'Donald Stanton', syn. 'D. B. Stanton' A hybrid between *R. lochiae* and *R. laetum* with an umbel of 9–12 bright red flowers.

Rhododendron laetum J. J. Sm.
An evergreen shrub with wide open yellow scented flowers, native of NW New Guinea, growing in wet places by lakes at 1800–2300m, flowering in winter. Shrub to 2m. Leaves 10–20cm, lanceolate to oblong-lanceolate, in whorls of 5. Flowers 6–8cm long, 6–8 in an umbel. Min. 5°C. One of the largest flowered of the Vireya section.

Rhododendron lochiae × javanicum
A fine hybrid with umbels of intense red

trumpet-shaped flowers. 'Fire Plum' is a similar Australian variety.

Rhododendron macgregoriae F. V. Muell.
An evergreen shrub or small tree with short tubed orange flowers, native of New Guinea, on mountain slopes, open grassland and on margins of forest at up to 3200m, flowering in winter. Shrub to 5m. Leaves 5–7.5cm, ovate-lanceolate to elliptic-oblong, in whorls at the ends of the season's growth. Flowers 2.5cm long, with a narrow tube red, orange or yellow and spreading reddish-orange lobes, 8–15 in an umbel. Min. 0°C.

Rhododendron orbiculatum Ridl.
An evergreen shrub or small tree with long-tubed pink scented flowers, native of Borneo in Sabah and Brunei, growing as an epiphyte in forest at 800–1700m, flowering in winter. Shrub to 3m. Leaves 3–4.5cm, broadly elliptic to almost round, in whorls of 4, 3 or 2. Flowers 6–7.5cm long, with a narrow curved tube and spreading obovate lobes, up to 5 in an umbel. Min. 0°C.

Rhododendron 'Pink Delight' Flowers long-tubed pink, on a sparse shrub.

Rhododendron 'Princess Frederica'
An old hybrid raised by Messrs Veitch before 1882. Parentage 'Princess Royal' × *R. brookeanum* . The parentage of the pale pink 'Princess Royal' was *R. jasminiflorum* × a yellow *R. javanicum*.

Rhododendron zoelleri Warb.
An evergreen shrub or small tree with wide open salmon-red or yellow and orange often scented flowers, native of NW New Guinea and the Moluccas, growing on the sides of gorges or epiphytic in mossy forest at up to 2000m, flowering in winter. Shrub to 2m. Leaves 6–12cm, broadly elliptic to oblong-elliptic, in whorls of 4–5. Flowers 6–8cm long, 5–8 in an umbel. Min. 0°C.

Rhododendron zoelleri × jasminiflorum
A hybrid with the palest pink flowers around 5cm long, with a slender tube. 'Highland White Jade' is a very similar Australian variety.

Rhododendron retusum

Rhododendron loranthiflorum from New Britain and the Solomon Islands

Rhododendron crassifolium from Sarawak

Rhododendron leptanthum from New Guinea

Rhododendron aurigerianum Sleumer
An evergreen shrub or small tree with oblong leaves and orange or yellow waxy flowers, native of New Guinea, growing on cliffs and mountain grassland at 1000–1800m, flowering in winter. Shrub to 2.5m. Leaves 7.5–10cm, in whorls of around 5. Flowers 6.5–7cm long, 8–10 in an umbel. Min. 5°C.

Rhododendron burttii P. Woods   A dwarf evergreen shrub with small shiny oblanceolate leaves and deep crimson hairy hanging flowers, native of Borneo in Sabah, growing on mossy trees at around 1500m, flowering in winter. Shrub to 45cm. Leaves 20–25mm, in whorls of 5–9.Flowers 2.5cm long, solitary or in pairs. A charming miniature for a cool moist situation. Min. 5°C.

Rhododendron crassifolium Stapf
An evergreen shrub with strongly ribbed

elliptic-obovate leaves and red, orange, apricot or bright pink flowers, native of Borneo in Sabah, growing on cliffs and mountain grassland at 1200–3000m, flowering in July–August. Shrub to 4m. Leaves 7.5–10cm, in whorls of 3–5. Flowers 2.5–3cm long, 10–14 in an umbel. Min. 5°C.

Rhododendron leptanthum F. V. Muell.
A low evergreen shrub with ovate or oblong-ovate leaves and pink to salmon or carmine flowers, nodding, with a curved tube, native of E New Guinea, growing on cliffs and mountain grassland at 1300–2200m, flowering in September. Shrub to 2m. Leaves 3–6.5cm, in whorls of 3. Flowers 2.5–3cm long, 2–3 in an umbel. Said to be one of the easier vireyas in cultivation. Min. 0°C.

Rhododendron loranthiflorum Sleumer
An evergreen shrub with shiny obovate leaves

and narrow-tubed scented white flowers, native of New Britain and the Solomon Islands on Bougainville, growing in forests and on cliffs at 200–1000m, flowering in September. Shrub to 2m. Leaves 3–6.5cm, in whorls of 3–5. Flowers 4–8 in an umbel, the tube 2–2.5cm long. Min. 0°C.

Rhododendron polyanthemum Sleumer
An evergreen shrub with elliptic pointed leaves and funnel-shaped orange flowers, native of Borneo, growing as an epiphyte in the forest at 1200–2000m, flowering in winter. Shrub to 3m. Leaves 8–15cm, in whorls of 5. Flowers 3–4cm long, around 20 in an umbel. Min. 0°C.

Rhododendron retusum (Blume) Benn.
An evergreen shrub with small obovate, retuse leaves and small, tubular red flowers, native of Sumatra and Java growing as an epiphyte in the forest and on cliffs at 1300–3200m, flowering in winter. Shrub to 3m. Leaves 2.5–4cm, in whorls of 4–7. Flowers 2–2.5cm long, 4–10 in an umbel. Min. –4°C.

Rhododendron sessilifolium J. J. Sm.
An evergreen shrub with wide open yellow or orange-yellow flowers, native of Sumatra, growing as an epiphyte in the forest and on cliffs at 1200–2000m, flowering in winter. Shrub to 3m. The leaves are 10–20cm long, lanceolate to oblong-lanceolate in shape, in whorls of 5. The flowers are 3–4cm long, 6–8 in an umbel. Min. 0°C.

Rhododendron polyanthemum from Borneo, in the RBG, Edinburgh

Rhododendron suaveolens from N Borneo

Rhododendron burttii from Borneo, in the RBG, Edinburgh

Rhododendron sessilifolium from Sumatra in the RBG, Edinburgh

Rhododendron suaveolens Sleumer
An evergreen shrub or small tree with narrow-tubed white scented flowers, native of N Borneo, growing in forests and on cliffs at 1500–2000m, flowering in March–July. The shrubs grow to 3m. The leaves are from 6–12cm, broadly elliptic to oblong-obovate, in whorls of 3–5. The flowers are 15–25 in an umbel and the tube is 4–6cm long. Min. 0°C.

Rhododendron vitis-idaea Sleumer
An evergreen shrub with small shiny obovate-elliptic leaves and tubular red flowers, native of E New Guinea, growing on open hillsides and as an epiphyte in mossy forest at 2200–2600m, flowering in September. Shrub to 0.6–2m. The leaves are 1.5–2.5cm long, in whorls of 3–5. The flowers are 1.5–2cm long and solitary. Min. –4°C. Named because of the close similarity of the leaves to those of the Cowberry, *Vaccinium vitis-idaea* L.

Rhododendron vitis-idaea

Rhododendron aurigerianum

Erica longifolia pink form

Erica vestita on Tradouws Pass in October

Erica longifolia red form

Erica densifolia on Tradouws Pass

Erica curviflora on Tradouws Pass

Erica discolor in the Abbey Gardens, Tresco, Isles of Scilly, in July

Erica (*Ericaceae*)   The greatest number and diversity of species of heathers is found in the Cape region of South Africa; no fewer than 526 species are known from this area. The richest area is a rough circle of about 80km (50 miles) around the town of Caledon which is east of Cape Town, where 220 species are recorded. The genus is divided into 41 sections, the names of which appear in brackets below after the Latin names of the species. These Cape heathers were very popular in greenhouses during the first half of the 19th century; many flower in winter and merely need protection from frost, and a poor acid soil. Min. −3°C for most Cape heathers.

Erica bauera Andr. (Pleurocallis)   An erect shrub with large tubular pink or white flowers, native of the S Cape in the Riversdale and Albertinia districts, growing on damp sandy flats, flowering in November–May. Stems to 1m; leaves 4–5mm, oblong to lanceolate, spreading or recurved. Flowers 16–20mm long, inflated with a narrow mouth. A commonly cultivated species *E. mammosa* L. with similar red, pink, purple, green or white flowers, is native of most of the W Cape from Clanwilliam to Caledon; it has narrower, erect, more scattered leaves 6–10mm long and flowers with four dents or furrows at the base.

Erica curviflora L. (Evanthe)   A spreading shrub with long curved tubular red, orange or yellow flowers, native of the S Cape from Vanrhynsdorp to the Cape Peninsula and east to Grahamstown, growing in wet places on flats and in the mountains by streams and waterfalls, flowering most of the year. Stems hairy, to 1.6m; leaves 3–7mm, erect, incurved or spreading. Flowers 20–38mm long, hairy outside in the W Cape, often glabrous in the east, usually solitary on short side shoots, but rarely with up to 4 flowers together. Anthers often slightly exserted. Alway found near water.

Erica densifolia Willd. (Evanthe)   An erect shrub with long curved tubular red flowers with greenish lobes, native of the S Cape coast from Riversdale to Humansdorp and on the Swartberg, growing on flats and among rocks in the mountains, flowering in September–March. Stems to 1m; leaves 3–5mm, incurved or spreading. Flowers 4–30mm long, sticky below, sometimes hairy, with a wide mouth.

Erica discolor Andr. (Evanthe)
A spreading shrub with long curved tubular red, pink or white flowers with greenish lobes, native of the S Cape from Stellenbosch to Swellendam and on the Witteberg, growing on lower slopes in the mountains, flowering most of the year. Stems hairy, to 1.5m; leaves 4–12mm. Flowers 15–20mm long, in twos and threes on short side shoots.

Erica longifolia Ait. (Pleurocallis)   An erect shrub with large tubular crimson, pink, yellow, orange, green or white flowers, native of the S Cape from Paarl to Bredasdorp, where it is common, growing on flats, hills and mountains, flowering most of the year. Stems to 1m; leaves very slender, 8–20mm long, 0.7–1mm wide, erect, spreading or rarely squarrose. Flowers 12–22mm long, straight or curved, pubescent, usually sticky. Sepals narrow and leaf-like.

SOUTH AFRICAN HEATHERS

Erica bauera pink form in Australia

Erica patersonia on flats near Betty's Bay in October

Erica bauera white form at the Huntington Gardens, Pasadena in April

Erica versicolor above Swellendam

Erica plukeneti on Franshoek Pass in October

Erica patersonia Andr. (Evanthe)
An erect shrub with long curved tubular yellow flowers, native of the S Cape coast, growing on sandy, boggy flats of the Cape of Good Hope Nature Reserve and at Betty's Bay, flowering mainly in April–August (winter). Stems to 90cm; leaves 8–12mm, incurved. Flowers 14–18mm long, smooth, not sticky, with a slightly contracted mouth, on very short side branches.

Erica plukeneti L. (Gigandra)
An erect shrub with large tubular pink or red flowers and large exserted stamens, native of much of the Cape from Nieuwoudtville to Mossel Bay, growing on flats and peaty places in the mountains, flowering most of the year. Stems to 1m; leaves 12–16mm. Flowers 13–18mm long, sometimes white, green or yellow; anthers 12mm long. *E. coccinea* L. with similar flowers but shorter, stiffer leaves in tufts, grows in dry, sandy or rocky places.

Erica versicolor Wendl. (Evanthe)
An upright shrub with long curved tubular red and green flowers, native of the S Cape from Swellendam to Knysna, growing in rocky places in the mountains, flowering from March–November. The stems are hairy, to 1.6m; leaves 4–8mm, in threes, sometimes they are also hairy or ciliate. The sepals are red. Flowers 20–25mm long, usually in threes on short leafy shoots.

Erica vestita Thunb. (Pleurocallis)
An erect shrub with large tubular crimson, pink, yellow or white flowers, native of the S Cape from Worcester to Bredasdorp and Riversdale, growing on dry or damp mountains and hills, flowering from August–May. Stems to 1m; leaves very slender, 12–33mm long, 0.5mm wide, crowded. Flowers 17–25mm long, straight or curved, pubescent but not sticky. A popular species in cultivation.

Erica daphniflora (pink) above Swellandam

Erica pectinifolia on the Swartberg Pass

Erica pectinifolia (pink form)

Erica glauca near the summit of
Franshoek Pass, October

Erica daphniflora in a wet sandy spot near
Ceres, W Cape in October

Erica arborea L . A large shrub or small
tree with masses of small tubular white
flowers, native of S Europe from Portugal to
Turkey, Madeira and the Canaries, Tibesti,
Yemen and mountains of E Africa to S
Tanzania, growing in dry or moist peaty soils,
flowering in winter–spring. Tree to 7m; leaves
3–5mm, soft, linear, in fours. Sepals ovate,
saccate at the base. Corolla 2.5–4mm long;
stigma white. A tall sturdy heather, remarkable for its occurence on mountains in the
tropics and in the middle of the Sahara.

Erica canaliculata Andr. (Gamochlamys)
A tall upright shrub with masses of small bell-
shaped pink or white flowers, native of the
Cape from George to Humansdorp, growing
at low altitudes in damp open ground or on
forest edges, flowering most of the year,
mainly in summer in the wild, during winter
in cultivation. Stems to 2m or more. Leaves
4–10mm, erect or spreading, in threes. Sepals
red inside. Flowers 3–3.5mm long, anthers
slightly protruding. One of the South African
species more commonly grown in Europe,
persisting outside in SW England where it can
reach 5m. Min. –10°C.

Erica cerinthoides L. (Dasyanthes) Fire
Heath   A dwarf shrub with inflated tubular
red, pink or white flowers, native of the Cape
from Vanrhynsdorp to the Cape Peninsula and
east to Swaziland and the N Transvaal,
growing on dry flats and in the mountains,
flowering at any time of year, usually after fire.
Stems hairy, usually less than 30cm, from a
fire-resistant rootstock. Leaves 6–16mm,
erect, spreading or recurved, in whorls of 4, 5
or 6. Flowers 22–34mm long, hairy outside
and sometimes glandular, in terminal umbels.
Baker and Oliver record that this species
needs regular burning to stay floriferous and
healthy. In cultivation this can be done by
regular hard pruning accompanied by a light
dressing of bonfire soil.

Erica cubica L. (Melastemon)   A low stiff
shrub with masses of small bell-shaped bright
pink or red flowers on woolly stalks, native of

the Cape from Swellendam to Uitenhage and
Natal near Pietermaritzberg, growing in wet
peaty places on the mountains and on flats,
flowering mainly in September–November.
Stems to 45cm. Leaves 4–10mm, incurved or
very stiff, in fours. Bracts 2; sepals with keel
and scarious margins, forming a square cup at
the base of a deeply 4-lobed corolla which is
3.5–4mm long.

Erica daphniflora Salisb. (Callista)
An upright shrub with masses of small bottle-
shaped white, pink, red, vinous or yellow
flowers, native of the Cape from the
Cedarberg and Tulbagh east to Swellendam,
growing on sandy flats and mountain slopes,
flowering mainly in July–March. Stems to 1m.
Leaves 4–6mm, erect or spreading. Bracts and
sepals leaf-like. Flowers 6–14mm long, with
reflexed lobes. A very variable species with
several varieties described.

Erica glauca Andr. var. **elegans** (Andr.)
Bolus (Eurystegia)   A stout erect shrub with
pink tubular green-tipped flowers almost
hidden by the large pink bracts and sepals,
native of the Cape in the Langeberg from
Robertson to Knysna and on the Swartberg,
growing on moist slopes facing south,
flowering in June–October. Stems to 60cm.
Leaves 6–12mm, glaucous, mostly incurved,
in threes. Sepals nearly as long as the corolla.
Flowers 8–12mm long, in a nodding umbel of
around 8. In var. *glauca* from around Ceres,
the flowers are deep purple on longer pedicels
with shorter bracts.

Erica melanthera L. (Gamochlamys)
An upright shrub with masses of small bell-
shaped bright pink or red flowers, native of the
Cape in the Langeberg from Robertson to
Knysna and on the Swartberg, growing on
moist slopes facing south, flowering in
June–October. Stems to 60cm. Leaves
2–4mm, spreading or very stiff, in threes.
Sepals forming a cone at the base of the
flower. Flowers 3.5–4mm long, deeply
4-lobed. Anthers nearly black. A very
floriferous species, like a bright version of
common *Calluna*.

Erica pectinifolia Salisb. (Dasyanthes)
An upright shrub with inflated tubular white
flowers, native of the Cape from the Swartberg
and Uniondale east to Port Elizabeth, growing
on dry hills and on the lower slopes of the
mountains, flowering mainly in October–
November. Stems to 1.5m. Leaves 3–6mm,
rigid, ciliate, in whorls of 4. Bracts and sepals
deeply pectinate. Flowers 14–18mm long,
hairy outside, in terminal umbels of 4, with
spreading lobes. *E. strigillifolia* Salisb., found
near the summits of mountains from Montagu
to Uniondale, is similar but has broader, less
deeply divided sepals and usually pale pink
flowers.

Erica ventricosa Thunb. (Ceramus)
A small shrub with bottle-shaped pink shiny
waxy flowers, native of the Cape in the high
mountains around Paarl, Franshoek and
Stellenbosch, growing on rocky peaty slopes,
flowering mainly in October–January. Stems
to 90cm. Leaves 12–16mm, thin, needle-like.
Sepals linear-lanceolate, ciliate. Flowers
12–16mm long, in dense terminal clusters,
pink in bud, with white spreading lobes. One
of the hardier species and once commonly
cultivated; in 'Grandiflora' the flowers are
rosy-purple, over 25mm long.

Gnarled trees of *Erica arborea* high in Madeira in March

Erica arborea

Erica cubica

Erica canaliculata at Cedar Tree Cottage, Sussex in February

Erica melanthera
on Tradouws Pass in October

Erica ventricosa near the summit of Franshoek
Pass in October

Erica cerinthoides flowering shortly after a fire

95

Agapetes serpens

Agapetes obovata

Agapetes incurvata var. *incurvata*

Agapetes buxifolia

Specimens from the Temperate House at the Royal Botanic Gardens, Kew, 7 February, ⅝ life-size

Agapetes 'Ludgvan Cross' at the Royal Botanic Garden, Edinburgh

Agapetes incurvata var. *hookeri*
at Sandling Park

Agapetes buxifolia Hook. fil. (*Ericaceae*)
A spreading shrub with small leaves and
tubular red flowers, native of Assam and
Bhutan, growing in forest at 600–1350m,
flowering in February–April under glass.
Shrub to 1m high and wide; young stems
bristly; leaves 2–3cm, elliptic, shallowly
toothed and glandular towards the obtuse
apex. Flowers to 2.5cm long. Free-flowering
and easily grown in a pot in acid soil or on a
raised peat bed. Min. –3°C.

Agapetes incurvata (Griffith) Sleumer var.
incurvata An erect shrub with narrow
leaves and tubular white or pink, purple-
barred flowers, native of Assam to Bhutan,
growing as an epiphyte at 2100–1900m,
flowering in June–July. Shrub to 1m high;
young stems with short white hairs; leaves
7.5–10cm long, 1.6–2.2cm wide, narrowly
elliptic, shallowly toothed and glandular from
base to apex. Calyx-lobes triangular. Flowers
to 2.2cm long. Perhaps the hardiest species,
grown outside in Cornwall. Min. –5°C.

Agapetes incurvata var. **hookeri** (C. B. Cl.)
Airy-Shaw, syn. *A. hookeri* (C. B. Cl.) Sleumer
An erect shrub with bullate leaves and tubular
yellow flowers, native of E Nepal to Assam,
growing as an epiphyte at 2100–1900m,
flowering in June–July. Shrub to 1m high;
young stems with short erect hairs; leaves
7–10cm long, 2.2–3.5cm wide, elliptic,
shallowly toothed and glandular from base to
apex. Calyx-lobes ovate, winged with a dark
nectariferous gland at the apex. Flowers to
1.9cm long. A rare species in cultivation.
Min. –5°C, perhaps.

Agapetes 'Ludgvan Cross' An arching
leafy shrub with hanging pinkish flowers
barred with crimson; a hybrid between
A. incurvata and *A. serpens*, raised by Miss G.
Talbot at Ludgvan in Cornwall around 1946.
Stems to 1.5m; leaves 4–4.7cm long, 1–1.3cm
wide, finely toothed. Calyx red. Flowers about
2.5cm long. Less colourful than *A. serpens* but
said to be hardier and easier to grow than
either parent. For moist but well-drained
peaty soil in shade and shelter. Min. –5°C.

Agapetes moorei Hemsl. An erect shrub
with leathery leaves and tubular orange-red
flowers with recurved green tips to the lobes,
native of Burma, growing as an epiphyte,
flowering in March–April under glass. Shrub
to 2.5m high; stems glabrous; leaves
6.5–7.5cm long, 2.5–3.2cm wide, elliptic,
acute, not toothed. Calyx-lobes short,
triangular. Flowers in erect groups of 12–20,
to 2.4cm long, the green lobes becoming
yellow and finally red. Cultivated before 1895.
Min. –5°C.

Agapetes obovata (Wight) Hook. fil. A low
spreading shrub with small obovate leaves and
bell-shaped greenish flowers, native of Assam
in Khasia Hills, flowering in February–April
under glass. Shrub to 60cm high and wide;
young stems bristly; leaves 1.4–1.8cm long,
not toothed with 1–2 pairs of small glands
near base. Flowers 5–7mm long. Min. 0°C.

Agapetes serpens (Wight) Sleumer
A scrambling or pendulous shrub with long
bristly shoots, small leaves and red flowers
barred with crimson, native of E Nepal to
Bhutan and N Assam, growing on mossy
banks or as an epiphyte in the forest at 1500–

3000m, flowering in February–June.
Rootstock a woody tuber; stems to 2m; leaves
1.5–2.2cm long, lanceolate to oblong-ovate.
Flowers 2.5cm long. 'Nepal Cream'
introduced by Roy Lancaster has pale
yellowish flowers. Easily grown, but tender;
grows well in a pot or hanging basket, put out
in a shady place in summer. Min. –3°C.

Agapetes variegata (Roxb.) G. Don var.
macrantha (Hook. fil.) Airy Shaw, syn.
A. macrantha Hook. fil. An erect shrub with
narrow leaves and tubular pinkish or red
flowers barred with red, with recurved green
or white tips to the lobes, native of the Khasia
Hills at 900–1500m, the Chittagong Hills and
of S Burma in the Kola Mountains near
Moulmein, probably growing as an epiphyte,
flowering in March–April under glass. Shrub
to 2m high; stems minutely hairy when young;
leaves 8–12cm long, 2–2.8cm wide, narrowly
elliptic, acute, not toothed. Pedicels red to
pink. Calyx-lobes short, white, triangular.
Flowers to 4.6cm long, in groups of 3–7,
hanging from old branches. Min. 5°C.

Macleania insignis M. Martens & Gal.
(*Ericaceae*) A scrambling or pendulous shrub
with long slender shoots, leathery leaves and
tubular red flowers, native of S Mexico in the
state of Vera Cruz, of Guatamala and
Honduras, growing as an epiphyte in the
forest, flowering in spring–summer. Stems
glabrous, to 2m; leaves 4–10cm long, 2–4cm
wide, ovate-elliptic. Calyx shortly winged.
Flowers 2.2–3.7cm long, with blunt angles.
For moist peaty soil in a humid position.
Min. 10°C.

Agapetes moorei in the Temperate House at Kew

Agapetes variegata var. *macrantha*

Macleania insignis in the Temperate House at Kew

Epacris longiflora in Sydney Botanic Garden

Habitat of *Epacris longiflora* on misty cliffs in the Blue Mountains

Clethra arborea in the garden at Portmeirion in North Wales

Epacris impressa in Sydney Botanic Garden

Dracophyllum townsoni in Christchurch Botanic Garden

Richea dracophylla in the Alpine House at Kew

Arctostaphylos pringlei in the San Jacinto Mountains near Riverside, S California

Arbutus xalepensis in fruit in NE Mexico, near Saltillo in October

Arbutus menziesii near Black Butte, N California

Arbutus menziesii Pursh Madroño
A large shrub to tall tree with smooth reddish bark and white or pink flowers, native of coastal California and Baja California, north to British Colombia, growing in Redwood forest and inland to open oak woodland below 1500m, flowering in March–May. Tree to 40m; leaves 5–12cm long, smooth or finely toothed. Flowers 6–8mm long; fruit 8–10mm across. For well-drained, preferably acid soil. Min. –10°C in a sheltered position away from freezing wind.

Arbutus xalepensis H. B. & K. (*Ericaceae*)
An evergreen shrub or small tree with peeling red bark, reddish flowers and red strawberry-like fruit, native of E and C Mexico, usually growing on limestone at up to 3000m, flowering in spring. Tree to 5m; young shoots hairy, the bark peeling in the second year; leaves ovate to elliptic, rounded at the base, variable on the same tree from coarsely to very finely toothed. Flowers red in an upright branching inflorescence. For well-drained dry soil; thrives on limestone. Min. –5°C.

Arctostaphylos pringlei Parry var. **drupacea** Parry (*Ericaceae*) A spreading shrub with reddish smooth bark, grey leaves and heads of pink flowers, native of the San Bernadino Mountains to Baja California, growing on dry slopes in chaparral at 1200–2000m, flowering in Febuary–April. Stems to 4m; leaves minutely glandular pubescent. Bracts and pedicels pinkish. Flowers 7–8mm long. This is only one of the 40 or more species of *Arctostaphylos* in California, most of which are lovely greyish-leaved shrubs with pink flowers. Few are cultivated, mainly because they are not easy to propagate; seed, which may need fire to germinate, and cuttings taken in late summer, are worth trying.

Clethra arborea Ait. (*Ericaceae*) A tree with shiny evergreen leaves and spikes of scented white cup-shaped flowers, native of Madeira, growing in dense laurel forests and ravines at up to 1500m, flowering in August–October. Tree to 10m. Leaves 8–15cm. Spikes to 15cm, each flower 6cm long. This lovely tree survives outside only on the mildest coasts of California and the British Isles, but can be grown and will flower in a large pot brought under cover in winter. Peaty soil. Min. –3°C.

Dracophyllum townsoni Cheeseman (*Epacridaceae*) A many-stemmed grass-like shrub or small tree with reflexed leaves and small white flowers on a drooping spike below the leaves, native of New Zealand on South Island, growing in lowland to montane forest and scrub, flowering in January–February. Trunk to 6m with smooth bark; leaves 15–30cm long, 8–15mm wide; flowers broadly bell-shaped. For a moist sheltered position. Min. –5°C.

Epacris impressa Labill. (*Epacridaceae*)
An upright heath-like shrub with pointed leaves and tubular white, pink or red flowers, native of South Australia, New South Wales, Victoria and Tasmania, growing in coastal heathland and forest, flowering mainly in February–November (summer). Stems to 2.5m; leaves 8–15mm long, lanceolate. Flowers to 2cm long with 5 dents near the base. Formerly much grown in greenhouses in Europe and popular for native gardens in Australia. 'Bega' is a selection with orange-red flowers. Var. *grandiflora* Benth., of which a double form is known, comes from moist cliffs and shady rocks in the Grampians in Victoria. Min. –5°C.

Epacris longiflora Cav. Fuchsia Heath
A dwarf or spreading heath-like shrub with pointed leaves and tubular red flowers with white tips, native of Queensland and New South Wales, growing in coastal heathland, dry forest, and on cliffs and rocks in the mountains, flowering most of the year. Stems to 2.5m; leaves 5–12mm long, ovate-cordate to lanceolate. Flowers to 4cm long. Best in well-drained sandy soil in sun or shade. Min. –5°C. The most spectacular of all the *Epacris* species, most of which have starry white flowers.

Richea dracophylla R. Br. (*Epacridaceae*)
A many-stemmed grass-like shrub smelling of kerosene with small white flowers crowded onto a stout spike, native of Tasmania and of New Zealand on North Island, growing in forest and scrub, flowering in January–February. Stems to 3m, with reddish flaky bark; leaves to 20cm long, 1–2cm wide; flowers with purplish-brown bracts, the petals falling as the flowers open. For a moist sheltered position. Min. –5°C.

BUDDLEIA

Buddleia asiatica

Buddleia auriculata at Quince House in Devon in October

Buddleia salviifolia on Tresco

Buddleia cordata in forest on the lower slopes of Volcan Colima, SW Mexico

Buddleia asiatica Lour. (Loganiaceae)
A shrub or small tree with thin narrow leaves and long drooping spikes of wonderfully scented white flowers, native of the foothills of the Himalayas from Pakistan to Hubei, Taiwan and SE Asia, growing on sandy river banks, in scrub and waste places at 300–1800m, flowering in November–April. Tree to 5m; leaves to 200m long, almost sessile, narrowly lanceolate, white beneath; inflorescence to 25cm; flowers 6–10mm long. For any soil in a sheltered spot, but very frost-tender. Lovely to bring into a conservatory in winter where its freesia-like scent will fill the house; liable to attack by red spider mite if kept indoors in summer. Min. 0°C.

Buddleia asiatica × officinalis
This hybrid is found in several gardens along the French Riviera. It flowers throughout the winter with long spikes of pale flowers with a good sweet scent. A large upright shrub to 3m, intermediate between the parents. Prune hard after flowering. Min. –5°C.

Buddleia auriculata Benth. A lax arching shrub with thin leaves and a large branching inflorescence of small but spicily scented creamy-white flowers, the tube fading orange, native of Natal, growing on river banks and on the margins of forest, flowering in April–June (autumn). Shrub to 3m; leaves 5–10cm long, broadly lanceolate, acuminate, white beneath. Flowers with the tube 9mm, the lobes 1mm long. Min. –5°C. Often grown on a wall for its autumn scent, but good in the greenhouse too, where it flowers throughout the winter.

Buddleia cordata H. B. & K. A large shrub or small tree with heart-shaped leaves and white, yellow or orange short-tubed flowers, native of Mexico and Guatemala, growing in ravines and rocky openings in oak and pine forest at 1500–3000m, flowering in October–December. Tree to 12m; leaves thin, to 20cm

long; inflorescence to 30cm, much broader than long; flowers around 5mm across, with little scent. For any soil in a sheltered spot. Min. –3°C. A frequent coloniser of areas with recent volcanic activity.

Buddleia madagascariensis Lam. A lax arching and scrambling shrub with narrow leaves and a long spike of small scented orange flowers, native of Madagascar, growing on the margins of forest, flowering from autumn–spring. Scrambler to 10m; leaves 15cm long, white, tomentose beneath. Flowers with tube 12mm, lobes 4mm long. Min. –3°C. A very rampant plant, interesting and unusual for its fleshy orange or purple fruit.

Buddleia × lewisiana Everett A hybrid between B. madagascariensis and B. asiatica, like a slender version of B. madagascariensis with slightly paler flowers on spikes around 20cm long. 'Margaret Pike' is a clone of this hybrid, raised in around 1950 by V. A. Pike, head gardener at Heathfield Park, Sussex, Hever Castle, Kent and Tresco Abbey, Isles of Scilly. Flowering in winter, with a good scent. Min. –3°C.

Buddleia 'Nicodemus' This hybrid, which is probably B. madagascariensis × B. officinalis, is a good plant for the greenhouse or mild garden, flowering from autumn–spring. A shrub to 6m, but can be kept smaller by pruning. Leaves soft and white beneath; inflorescence solid towards the tip, branched at the base, the flowers honey-scented, opening creamy, becoming orange and dying brown. Of unrecorded origin. The name 'Nicodemus', by which this hybrid is known at Read's Nursery, appears to be a corruption of B. nicodemia, a synonym of B. madagascariensis.

Buddleia officinalis Maxim. A stiff shrub with lanceolate leaves and an upright pyramidal inflorescence of honey-scented, pale mauve flowers with an orange eye, native of W China, growing on cliffs, in scrub and waste places up to 1000m in Hubei, flowering in March–May. Shrub to 3m; leaves to 15cm long, soft, greyish or tawny-woolly beneath; inflorescence to 15cm; flowers 9–13mm long. For any soil in a sunny sheltered spot as the leaves are easily torn by wind. Buds formed in autumn withstand –5°C.

Buddleia salviifolia (L.) Lam. A large shrub or small tree with blue, purplish or white flowers, native of South Africa from the W Cape to Natal and north to Tanzania, growing in scrub and on forest margins, at up to 2425m in the Drakensberg, flowering in August–October (late spring). Tree to 8m; leaves thick and felted, to 15cm long, almost sessile, tapering from a broad base. Inflorescence to 15cm, broader than long; flowers 6–9mm long, with a sweetish, spermatic scent. For any soil in a sheltered spot. Min. –5°C.

Buddleia tubiflora Benth. An upright shrub with narrow leaves and a long spike with whorls of tubular, scented orange flowers, native of S Paraguay, Brazil and Argentina, flowering in autumn–early spring. Shrub to 2m; leaves 10cm long, greyish or reddish-tomentose beneath. Flowers with the tube 15–20mm, the lobes 2mm long. Min. 0°C. An unusual species but not easy to grow well.

Buddleia 'Nicodemus'

Buddleia officinalis

Specimens from Sellindge, Kent, 18 February, ¼ life-size

Buddleia × *lewisiana* in the Temperate House at Kew

Buddleia *madagascariensis* naturalised in Bermuda

Buddleia *tubiflora* at Read's Nursery, Loddon, Norfolk

Buddleia *asiatica* × *officinalis* at Serre de la Madonne

Jasminum polyanthum in Madeira in March

Jasminum subhumile var. *glabricorymbosum* wild above the Butterfly Spring near Dali, Yunnan in late April

Jasminum mesnyi in a hedge near Ronda, Spain in March

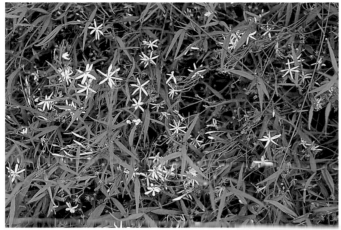

Jasminum simplicifolium subsp. *suavissimum* in Ventnor, Isle of Wight

Jasminum volubile in the Royal Botanic Garden, Edinburgh

Jasminum grandiflorum L. Spanish Jasmine, 'de Grasse'   A lax or scrambling evergreen shrub with leathery leaves and wonderfully scented white flowers, of uncertain origin, but long cultivated by the Moors in Spain, and from there reaching S Europe, flowering in summer–autumn. Wild possibly in Arabia or SW China, but a very similar species, *J. floribundum* R. Br. ex Fresenius, is found on stream banks in E Africa and Ethiopia. Shrub to 3m, but usually pruned to less, as it forms a good hedge. Leaflets usually 7, the side lobes ovate, blunt. Flowers in a cyme (the later ones overtopping those that opened first), tube 15–23mm long, lobes 12–20mm long, reddish outside when grown in full light. Min. −3°C. This species is now commonly sold in pots of around 5 rooted cuttings, 20cm tall, in flower in late autumn. The deciduous and hardy *J. officinale* L., native of the Himalayas and its variety 'Affine', syn. 'Grandiflorum' are twining climbers with acuminate leaflets and smaller flowers; both are commonly cultivated in Europe.

Jasminum grandiflorum in the greenhouse at Quince House in Devon

Jasminum nitidum in Bermuda

Jasminum mesnyi Hance, syn. *J. primulinum* Hemsl.   A tall climbing and smothering shrub with long arching branches and large semi-double yellow flowers, probably native of SW China, but known only in cultivation in China, flowering in January–March. Stems to 4m or more when supported, but best when allowed to cascade down from around 3m. Leaves opposite, trifoliate. Flowers 3.8–5cm across, not scented. An excellent winter-flowering shrub for a cool conservatory or mild garden. Min. −5°C.

Jasminum nitidum Skan   A much-branched shrub with shiny leaves and well-scented starry white flowers from crimson buds, native of the Admiralty Islands, N of New Guinea, flowering in spring. Shrub to 1.5m, usually pruned to form a hedge. Leaves simple, ovate, acuminate, to 10cm long. Flowers in cymes in the upper leaf axils, with around 5 flowers. Calyx lobes reflexed; flowers with tube 20mm long, lobes 6–11, 20mm long, reddish outside. Easily grown in sun in a mild climate. Good in S California. Min. −3°C.

Jasminum polyanthum Franch.
A climbing shrub with 5–7 foliolate leaves and masses of scented white flowers from crimson buds, native of SW China in Yunnan and Guizhou, flowering in March–April. Climber to 6m. Leaves to 10cm long, leaflets short-stalked with a rounded base. Flowers in terminal cymes and in upper leaf axils. Calyx lobes very small; flowers 3.2–3.8cm across. Easily grown in good soil and needs full sun to flower freely, even in S California. Can be forced to flower under glass in mid-winter; but flowers are then pure white. Min. −5°C.

Jasminum simplicifolium G. Forst. subsp. **suavissimum** (Lindl.) P. S. Green
A scrambling or weakly climbing shrub with narrow simple leaves and scented starry white flowers, native of Queensland and New South Wales, growing in open forest and rocky slopes, flowering in August–January (summer). Climber to 2m, with wiry green stems. Leaves to 7cm long, linear, linear-lanceolate to narrowly elliptical. The flowers are around 3cm across, with 5–8 narrow lobes in terminal cymes of 1–9. It is drought-tolerant and easy to grow in full sun, it has a

good scent. Min. −5°C overnight.

Jasminum subhumile W. W. Sm. var. **glabricorymbosum** W. W. Sm., syn. *J. heterophyllum* Roxb.   A lax or scrambling shrub with glossy evergreen leaves and branching heads of rich yellow scented flowers, native of SW China in Yunnan, growing on sunny slopes in scrub at around 2000m, flowering in April–May. Shrub to 3m; stems purplish; leaves usually simple, sometimes trifoliate. Flowers around 2cm across. For a warm well-drained position. Min. −3°C.

Jasminum volubile Jacq., syn. *J. gracile* Andr.   A scrambling or twining shrub with ovate simple leaves and scented white flowers, native of Queensland, New South Wales, Northern Territory and Western Australia, growing by streams in open forest, flowering in August–January (summer). Climber to 2m. Leaves to 7cm long, lanceolate to broadly ovate. Flowers around 2cm across, with 5–6 lobes. Easy to grow in full sun but it will need plenty of water and very good drainage. Min. −5°C overnight.

Jasminum sambac 'Grand Duke of Tuscany'

Jasminum sambac 'Maid of Orleans' in Bermuda

Melodinus suaveolens wild in Hong Kong

Trachelospermum asiaticum showing the bean-like fruits

Jasminum abyssinicum Hochst. ex DC.(*Oleaceae*) A strong climber with 3-foliolate leaves, masses of pink buds and heavily scented white flowers, native of Africa from Ethiopia to Tanzania and Zaire, growing by streams and on the edges of forest at 1650–2830m, flowering in January–March. Stems climbing to 15m. Leaflets ovate, the largest to 10cm, with tufts of hairs beneath. Flowers 2.5–3cm across, with 5–6 ovate lobes, in terminal cymes of 30–50 and cymes of around 20 in the upper leaf axils. Fruits small, black. Easily grown in good soil and very floriferous even under glass. This has one of the best and heaviest scents of all the species. Min. –5°C.

Jasminum angulare Vahl A scrambling shrub with 3-foliolate leaves and scented white flowers, native of South Africa, growing in scrub near the coast from the S Cape near Humansdorp to Natal, flowering in November–January. Stems to 7m. Twigs angular. Leaflets ovate, the largest to 6cm, with tufts of hairs beneath. Flowers 2.5–3cm across, with 5–6 narrow lobes each 5–7mm wide, in terminal cymes of around 9 and cymes of around 3 in the upper leaf axils. Will

grow outdoors in warm coastal gardens in W Europe. Min. –5°C.

Jasminum azoricum L. A scrambling shrub with 3-foliolate leaves and scented white flowers, native of Madeira, growing in scrub in the hills above 1000m, flowering for much of the year. Stems to 7m. Twigs rounded. Leaflets ovate-lanceolate, largest to 7cm, with tufts of hairs beneath. Flowers 2.5–3cm across with 5–6 narrow lobes, each 3–4mm wide, in terminal cymes of around 9. Min. –5°C.

Jasminum sambac (L.) Ait. Arabian Jasmine A spreading shrub with simple broad leaves and a tight terminal head of heavily scented white flowers, native of India, Burma and Sri Lanka, growing at up to 600m, flowering for much of the year. Stems to 3m. Leaflets ovate-lanceolate, the largest to 12cm long. Calyx lobes long and narrow. Flowers 2.5–3cm across, with 7 wide lobes in terminal cymes of around 3 or more. Min. –2°C. This jasmine is sacred to Vishnu and is used to flavour jasmine tea. Shown here are two cultivars:
'Maid of Orleans' with large single flowers and the double **'Grand Duke of Tuscany'**, syn. 'Flore Pleno'.

Jasminum tortuosum Willd. A tall climber with 3-foliolate leaves and sharply scented white flowers, native of South Africa in the S Cape from Caledon and Mossel Bay to Oudtshoorn, flowering in November–December (summer). Stems to 5m. Leaflets diamond-shaped, the largest to 10cm, with slender stalks. Flowers 2.5–3cm across, with 5–6 narrow lobes each 5–7mm wide, in terminal cymes of around 9. Should grow outdoors in warm coastal gardens in W Europe. Min. –5°C.

Melodinus suaveolens Champ. (*Apocynaceae*) An evergreen climber with simple leaves and scented white propeller-like flowers, native of S China and the Philippines, growing in scrub and forest, flowering in April–May. Stems to 6m. Leaves ovate-lanceolate, the largest to 9.5cm long. Flowers around 2cm across, with 5 lobes in a rather flat head. Young fruit like small oranges, but dry and inedible. Min. –2°C.

Trachelospermum asiaticum (Sieb. & Zucc.) Nak. (*Apocynaceae*) An evergreen

climbing shrub with simple leaves and scented, white to pale yellow jasmine-like flowers, native of S Japan, and Korea, growing in scrub and climbing up trees in the forest, flowering in April–May. Stems to 8m. Leaves ovate-lanceolate, 3–6cm long. Calyx lobes spreading only at the tip. Flowers 2–2.5cm across, with 5 lobes. Fruit long, narrow and bean-like, pinkish-red. Min. –10°C. Jasmine-like members of the Periwinkle (*Vinca*) family *Apocynaceae*, can be recognised by a milky latex and often large paired seed pods with silky seeds, in contrast with the small juicy fruit of the Olive family *Oleaceae*.

Trachelospermum jasminoides (Lindl.) Lemaire Star Jasmine An evergreen climbing shrub with simple leaves and scented white to pale yellow jasmine-like flowers, native of S China, Vietnam, S Japan, and Korea, growing in scrub and climbing on trees in the forest, flowering in April–May. Stems to 3m. Leaves elliptic to lanceolate, 4–8cm long. Calyx lobes spreading or reflexed. Flowers 2–2.5cm across, with 5 wavy lobes. Fruit, long, narrow and bean-like, pinkish-red. Min. –10°C. An attractive plant for a large pot, pruned as a shrub and brought under cover in winter.

Jasminum tortuosum

Jasminum azoricum

Jasminum abyssinicum

Jasminum angulare

Trachelospermum asiaticum

Trachelospermum jasminoides

Specimens from the Temperate House at the Royal Botanic Gardens, Kew, 19 June, ⅜ life-size

Vinca difformis

Mandevilla × amoena 'Alice Dupont' at Longwood Gardens, Pennsylvania

Catharanthus roseus in Nairobi, Kenya

Tabernaemontana pandacaqui

Catharanthus roseus in Bermuda

Tabernaemontana divaricata in Hong Kong

Mandevilla sanderi 'Rosea'

Mandevilla sanderi in Australia

Mandevilla laxa at Ventnor Botanic Garden

Mandevilla boliviensis

Catharanthus roseus (L.) G. Don, syn. *Vinca rosea* L. (*Apocynaceae*) A perennial with bright pink periwinkle-like flowers, native of Madagascar, but now found naturalised over most of the tropics, flowering most of the year. Stems to 60cm. Leaves 2.5–5cm, oblong, shiny green. Flowers around 3cm across, generally pink, but also pure white and in 'Ocellatus', white or pink with a red eye. Min. 5°C. Formerly required temperatures above 15°C to grow and flower, but some modern varieties are cold-tolerant enough to be used outdoors in summer in temperate areas. Contains alkaloids which are used in the treatment of leukemia.

Mandevilla × amoena hort. **'Alice Dupont'** (*Apocynaceae*) A twining climber with dark green shiny leaves and rich pink flowers with a deep red-lined throat, thought to be a hybrid between *M. splendens* (Hook. fil.) Woodson, a native of Brazil, in the Organ Mountains at 900m and *M. × amabilis*. Stems to 4m; leaves 10–20cm long, shiny dark green, the veins impressed above. Flowers without scent, on short branches of 4–6 in the leaf axils, 10–13cm across, the tube 10cm long. A most attractive free-flowering clone, named after one of the Dupont family of Longwood Gardens, Pennsylvania, where this clone originated. Spray regularly in warm weather to keep red spider at bay. Min. 5°C.

Mandevilla boliviensis (Hook. fil.) Woodson A twining evergreen climber with dark green shiny leaves and white flowers with a yellow throat, native of Ecuador and Bolivia, flowering in summer. Stems to 4m; leaves around 10cm long, 4cm wide. Flowers without scent, on short branches of 3–7 in the leaf axils, 6cm across, the tube 4cm long. An attractive free-flowering species. Min. 2°C.

Mandevilla laxa (R. & P.) Woodson, syn. *M. suaveolens* Lindl. Chilean Jasmine (though not native of Chile) An often deciduous twining climber with cordate leaves and pure white scented flowers, native of Argentina (Tucuman province) and Bolivia, flowering in summer. Stems to 5m; leaves thin, around 6–15cm long, 3–6cm wide. Flowers on short branches of 5–15 in the leaf axils, 7.5cm across, the tube 2.5cm long. A beautiful fast-growing climber for a mild garden or cool greenhouse. Min. –10°C.

Mandevilla sanderi (Hemsl.) Woodson, syn. *Dipladenia sanderi* Hemsl. A twining climber with dark green shiny leaves and pink flowers with a yellow throat, native of Brazil, flowering in summer. Stems to 5m; leaves to 6cm long, 3cm wide. Flowers without scent, on short branches of 3–5 in the leaf axils, 8cm across, the tube 4.5cm long. An attractive, free-flowering species. Min. 2°C. **'Rosea'** is a clone with flowers that open deep pink; 'Scarlet Pimpernel' (*not shown*) has bright red flowers and 'Summer Snow' is very pale pink.

Tabernaemontana divaricata (L.) R. Br. (*Apocynaceae*) A shrub with shiny dark green leaves and pure white jasmine-like flowers, scented at night, native of N India to Thailand and Yunnan, flowering in summer. Shrub to 1.75m, forking regularly. Leaves thin, 7–10cm long. Flowers in groups of 4–6 in the upper leaf axils, with a tube 15–27mm, the lobes oblong, 0.7–1 3 times as long as the tube. For a warm climate, tolerating some shade. Min. 0°C.

Tabernaemontana pandacaqui Lam A shrub or small tree with shiny dark green leaves and pure white jasmine-like flowers, scented at night, native of SE Asia to Australia, flowering in summer. Tree to 14m. Leaves thin, 3–25cm long. Flowers solitary or paired in the upper leaf axils, with a slightly twisted tube 8–22mm, the lobes overlapping, 0.25–1 times as long as the tube. The distinction between these species seems unclear, but the larger and fewer-flowered plants grown in Hong Kong seem to belong to this species. In the double-flowered form the flowers are like small gardenias; the plants are easier to grow and can be stood outside in summer. Min. 0°C

Vinca difformis Pourret (*Apocynaceae*) A creeping ground-covering perennial with pale blue flowers, native of Spain, Portugal, the Azores, Italy and N Africa, growing in woods and on shady banks, flowering in November–April. Flowering shoots 10–30cm tall. Leaves 2.5–7cm, ovate to lanceolate. Calyx lobes glabrous. Flowers 3–4.5cm across. One of the tenderer species of *Vinca*, good for growing under shrubs in Mediterranean gardens. Min. –5°C. The large-flowered subsp. *sardoa* Stearn, from Sardinia, has flowers 6–7cm across and minutely ciliate calyx lobes.

Allamanda cathartica 'Hendersonii' in the warm glasshouse at Wisley

Allamanda blanchetii in Florida

Allamanda 'Cherry's Jubilee' in Florida

Cryptostegia grandiflora naturalised in Mexico

Beaumontia grandiflora

Beaumontia grandiflora in Malawi

Thevetia peruviana in Bermuda

Urechites lutea at the Plantsman Nursery, Devon

Thevetia thevetioides in Australia

Allamanda blanchetii A. DC., syn.
A. violacea Gardn. & Fielding (*Apocynaceae*)
An evergreen shrub or weak scrambling
climber with leaves hairy, especially beneath
and pinkish-purple flowers, native of Brazil
growing along lowland streams and on the
edges of forest, flowering most of the summer.
Stems to 3m or more; leaves 3–5 in a whorl,
8–12cm long, ovate. Flowers on short
branches in the leaf axils; calyx lobes large,
ovate, hairy; corolla around 7cm across, the
tube 7cm long. For a warm moist climate.
Min. 5°C.

Allamanda cathartica L. (*Apocynaceae*)
A strong climber with shiny leaves and bright
yellow scented flowers, native of NE South
America, Trinidad (rare) and especially
abundant in Guyana, growing in mangrove
swamps and along lowland streams, flowering
most of the year. Stems to 6m or more; leaves
to 6cm long, 3cm wide. Flowers, around 12
(in a raceme) on short branches on the ends
of shoots or in the leaf axils. An attractive free-
flowering species, commonly planted in the
tropics and very good in a warm conservatory.
Min. 5°C. **'Hendersonii'**, the form
commonly grown in Europe, has larger
flowers 12.5cm across; tube 9cm long. Buds
can be brownish and the throat has reddish-
brown veins; introduced to Europe from
Guyana in 1865.
The smaller-flowered *A. schottii* Pohl has a
much shorter (12mm long) narrow portion of
the floral tube and shorter lobes, which gives
the flower a more trumpet-like shape.

Allamanda 'Cherry's Jubilee', syn.
'Caribbean Sunrise' has pinkish flowers; in
'Jamaica Sunset' (*not shown*) the flowers are
more purplish.

Beaumontia grandiflora (Roxb.) Wall.
(*Apocynaceae*)   A very large and robust
climber with large white scented trumpet-
shaped flowers, native of Nepal to Assam,
Burma, SE Tibet and Yunnan, growing in
scrub and on rocks and climbing up trees in
the forest at 300–1500m, just below the winter
frost level, flowering in March–April. Stems
climbing in coils to 10m or more. Leaves
elliptic to obovate, 18–30cm long. Flowers 6–8
on a cyme in the leaf axils, with a leafy calyx to
5cm long and corolla 12–13cm long, 8–10cm
across. A wonderful climber for a climate with
a cool dry winter and warm wet summer.
Min. –2°C. The closely-related *B. murtonii*
Craib has wider open flowers; it needs a more
tropical climate.

Cryptostegia grandiflora R. Br.
(*Apocynaceae*)   A tall twining climber with
leathery opposite leaves and lilac-purple
flowers, native of Madagascar and East
Africa, but now a pest in other parts of the
world from Mexico and the West Indies to
India and N Australia, often growing on
coasts and the edges of mangrove swamps,
flowering much of the year. Leaves 7.5–10cm
long. Flowers to 9cm across, with forked

filiform lobes inside the corolla. (The very
similar *C. madagascariensis* Bojer has simple
lobes.) Can be pruned and trained as a shrub.
Min. 5°C.

Thevetia peruviana (Pers.) Schum., syn.
A. neriifolia A Juss. (*Apocynaceae*) Yellow
Oleander   A shrub with evergreen narrow
shiny leaves and nodding yellow or pale
orange flowers, native of the West Indies,
Mexico and tropical America, flowering most
of the year. Shrub to 8m; leaves alternate,
linear-lanceolate, to 15cm; flowers scented, to
7cm long, 5cm across, white in 'Alba'. Fruits
like small apples, green then red, opening
black. For a hot sunny position. Min. –2°C.

Thevetia thevetioides   A shrub or small
tree with narrow dark green evergreen leaves
and heads of deep yellow flowers, native of
Mexico, from Michoacan to Vera Cruz,
flowering most of the year. Tree to 8m; leaves
alternate, linear-lanceolate, to 10cm; flowers
scented, to 7cm long, 7cm across. For any
sunny position. Min. –2°C.

Urechites lutea (L.) Britt. (*Apocynaceae*)
A twining perennial with yellow or pale yellow
flowers, native of SE Florida, the West Indies
south to Virgin Islands, growing on the edges
of mangrove swamps, flowering all year. Stems
to 2m; leaves shiny, ovate, opposite. Flowers
trumpet-shaped with the throat 1.5–3.5cm
long, 4–6cm across at the mouth. For good
rich soil and sun. Min. 5°C.

Nerium oleander growing wild in a stream near Antalya in Turkey

Nerium oleander

Oleander 'Doctor Golfin'

Oleander 'Luteum Plenum'

Oleander 'Maria Gambetta'

Oleander 'Papa Gambetta'

Oleander 'Splendens'

Oleander 'Souvenir d'Auguste Roger' at Hadrian's Villa, Frascati

Oleander 'Tito Poggi'

Oleander 'Mlle Dubois'

Nerium oleander L., syn. *Nerium indicum* Mill. *N. odorum* Soland. (*Apocynaceae*) Oleander A shrub or small tree with dull green narrow evergreen leaves and pink flowers, native of the Mediterranean area from S Spain to Syria and Jordan, growing by or in streams and watercourses, at up to 800m in Turkey, and of Iran to the Himalayas, at up to 1500m, flowering in April–September. Tree to 8m; leaves narrowly elliptic, to 30cm long, usually in whorls of 3. Flowers in loose heads, pink or reddish, with a short tube, 3–5cm across. Min. −5°C or less for short periods. Needs full sun. Planted everywhere in subtropical areas and good in pots brought indoors in winter. Good in desert areas and drought-resistant once established, but needs ample water in summer if grown in pots. All parts of the plant are very poisonous; do not even make a kebab skewer with the sticks. *Nerium indicum* Mill. native from Iran to India is now regarded as *N. oleander*, differing in its scented flowers in larger heads. Numerous colour forms of Oleander have been named including the following shown here:

'Doctor Golfin' Flowers bright red.

'Luteum Plenum' Flowers double, pale yellow.

'Maria Gambetta' Flowers pale yellow.

'Mlle Dubois' Flowers white with a yellow throat, sometimes semi-double.

'Papa Gambetta' Flowers large, reddish-pink.

'Petite Salmon' A dwarf compact variety with pale salmon-pink flowers.

'Souvenir d'Auguste Roger' Flowers pale pink, with lines in the throat.

'Splendens' Flowers large, double, rich pink. There is a variegated form of this with yellow-edged leaves. An old variety, but still commonly grown.

'Tito Poggi' Flowers single, apricot.

Oleander 'Petite Salmon' in California

Carissa macrocarpa at Elbow Beach, Bermuda

Adenium obesum

Plumeria alba wild in the British Virgin Islands in November

Pachypodium succulentum near Oudtshoorn

Acokanthera opposotifolia in the Huntington Gardens, California

Pachypodium succulentum showing the underground tuber exposed

Acokanthera oblongifolia (Hochst.) Codd (*Apocynaceae*) An evergreen shrub with alternate leaves and very well-scented white starry long-tubed flowers, native of the Natal coast to Mozambique, growing in scrub, flowering in April–December (mainly in early spring). Shrub to 6m; leaves to 6–12cm long; flowers 6–15mm across, the tube to 2cm long. Fruits blackish-purple, very poisonous. For a sunny position. Min. –3°C.

Acokanthera oppositifolia (Lam.) Codd Bushman's Poison A shrub or small tree with alternate leaves and white starry long-tubed flowers, native of S Africa from the SE Cape to N Natal, growing in scrub, flowering in April–December (mainly in early spring). Tree to 6m; leaves to 13cm long, often tinged reddish; flowers 5mm across, the tube pinkish, to 2cm long. Fruits blackish-purple, very poisonous. For a sunny position. Min. –3°C.

Adenium obesum (Forssk.) Roem. & Schult. (*Apocynaceae*) A succulent shrub with thick grey stems, obovate leaves and pink, red or white flowers, native of the dry parts of East Africa, from Socotra S to Natal, growing in dry rocky and sandy areas, flowering in summer. Stems to 2 m, sometimes partly underground; leaves to 15cm. Flowers 2–5cm long. A lovely shrub for a hot dry climate, difficult but not impossible in a pot, given little water, and then only in summer. Min 5°C.

Carissa macrocarpa (Eckl.) A. DC. (*Apocynaceae*) Natal Plum A dense evergreen shrub with forked spines, opposite ovate, shiny leaves and white scented flowers, native of Natal, growing in coastal scrub, flowering and fruiting much of the year. Shrub to 2m, rarely to 9m; leaves 3–6.5cm long. Flowers to 5cm across; fruit bright red, becoming black, like a small plum. For any good soil. Min. –3°C. Salt- and wind-tolerant, so much planted in Bermuda as a windbreak and in East Africa as a thief-proof thorny hedge. Many cultivars are grown in southern California.

Pachypodium succulentum (L. fil.) A. DC. (*Apocynaceae*) A spiny shrublet with a large mainly subterranean rootstock, narrow leaves and pink flowers, native of the dry parts of the E and N Cape, north to Orange Free State, growing in dry rocky and sandy areas, flowering in September–December. Stems to 60cm, fleshy, little branched; leaves oblong-lanceolate to oblanceolate, with a pair of 2.5cm long spines at their base. Flowers 1–2cm long, 2–4cm across, red, pink or white. For dry sandy soil. Min. –3°C. Other species, especially those from Madagascar, are more tender.

Plumeria alba L. (*Apocynaceae*) A spreading deciduous tree with thick succulent twigs, terminal leaves and yellow, white-centred flowers, native of Puerto Rico and the S West Indian islands, growing in dry rocky places, flowering much of the year. Tree to 6m; shoots with milky juice. Leaves to 30cm, lanceolate, often bullate. Flowers to 6cm across, with a short tube 2–2.5cm. For any well-drained soil. Min. 0°C.

Plumeria rubra in Nairobi

Plumeria rubra, a white variety in Nairobi

Plumeria rubra L. Frangipani
A spreading deciduous tree with thick succulent grey twigs, terminal leaves and flat heads of pinkish, white, yellow or striped flowers, native of Mexico to Panama, growing in dry rocky places, flowering much of the year, mainly June–November. Tree to 6m; shoots with milky juice. Leaves to 30cm, lanceolate, often bullate. Flowers to 6cm across, with short tube 2–2.5cm. For any well-drained soil in a hot position, though with afternoon shade in desert areas. Commonly planted in the tropics for its waxy, wonderfully scented flowers. Can be grown in a pot if kept dry and frost-free in winter. Min. 0°C.

Strophanthus divaricatus (Lour.) Hook. & Arn. (*Apocynaceae*) A shrub or climber with opposite leaves and smelly greenish flowers with long tail-like tips to the lobes, native of SE China and Vietnam, growing in scrub and forest, flowering in March–May. Stems climbing to 10m; leaves elliptic, to 9cm long. Flower lobes around 9cm long, streaked

Acokanthera oblongifolia at Kew

Strophanthus speciosus

Strophanthus divaricatus wild in Hong Kong

with red at the base; fruits a pair of large, beak-like capsules to 23cm across, full of silky seeds. For any good soil. Min. –3°C.

Strophanthus speciosus (Ward & Harv.) Reber A shrub or climber with whorled leaves and creamy-yellow flowers with long twisted tail-like tips to the lobes, native of Natal, growing in bush and forest, flowering in March–May. Stems climbing to 10m; leaves narrowly elliptic to lanceolate, to 11cm long. Flower lobes 2–5cm long, blotched with red at the base; fruits a pair of slender capsules to 22cm across, full of silky seeds. For any good soil. Min. –3°C.

Hoya macgillivrayi at Kew

Hoya longifolia in Devon

Hoya lanceolata subsp. *bella* from the vinery at Sellindge, Kent

Hoya pauciflora in forest by a stream in the hills south of Periyar, Kerala, SW India

Marsdenia oreophila at the Plantsman Nursery, Throwleigh, Devon

Hoya carnosa at Quince House in Devon

Dregea sinensis wild near Baoxing, Sichuan

Marsdenia oreophila W. W. Sm., syn.
Cionura oreophila hort. A slender climber
with opposite stalked leaves and *Hoya*-like
umbels of white flowers, native of SW China,
in Yunnan, growing in hedges and scrub,
flowering in May–August. Stems to 2m;
leaves to 6cm long. Flowers 1cm across, in
umbels of around 10. For any good soil with
ample water in summer, drier in winter.
Min. –5°C.

Dregea sinensis Hemsl., syn. *Watakaka
sinensis* (Hemsl.) Stapf (*Asclepiadaceae*)
A deciduous climber with heart-shaped leaves
and hanging umbels of scented pink or white
flowers, native of W China in W Hubei,
Sichuan and Yunnan, growing in scrub in
rocky places at 40–2400m, flowering in
May–July. Climber to 2.5m; leaves softly
greyish-hairy beneath, to 10cm long. Flowers
1.5cm across, in umbels to 8cm across. For
any good soil in sun or partial shade. Min.
15°C, perhaps with protection for the root.
A nearly hardy *Hoya*-like climber.

Hoya carnosa (L. fil.) R. Br.
(*Asclepiadaceae*) A shrubby evergreen
climber with thick waxy leaves and tight round
umbels of icing-sugar pink scented flowers,
native of India to SE China, climbing like ivy,
on rocks in ravines and in the forest, flowering
in April–October. Stems to 5m or more.

Leaves ovate, to 8cm. Flowers 1.5cm across, in
umbels to 8cm across, white to pink; corona
waxy white with a red centre, scenting the
whole area in the evening. Needs open sandy
soil. Min –4°C. In S Japan *Hoya carnosa* is also
found in Kyushu, on Yakusima, S to the
Ryukyu Islands; there it has been named var.
japonica Sieb. ex Maxim. and *H. motoskei*
Teijsm. & Binnend.

Hoya lanceolata Wall. ex D. Don subsp.
bella (Hook.) D. H. Kent A pendulous
succulent shrub with diamond-shaped leaves
and flat umbels of white scented flowers,
native of N India, Nepal, Bhutan and N
Burma, growing on trees in forests at
1000–1800m, flowering in May–June. Stems
to 45cm; leaves to 4cm; flowers in umbels of
8–14, each 1.5cm across, with a violet corona.
Easily grown in a hanging basket, in compost
suitable for orchids, such as bark and moss.
If the plant fails to thrive the roots may have
rotted or been eaten by vine weevils.
Min. 0°C. Geoffrey Herklots records that
Hoya bella is plentiful in the wet hills above
Dharan in E Nepal.

Hoya macgillivrayi Bailey An evergreen
climber with ovate waxy leaves and large
umbels of red, purple or chesnut-brown
flowers, native of the C Cape York Peninsula,
growing as an epiphyte in the rainforest,

flowering in September–November (spring).
Stems to 1m. Leaves to 6–18cm. Flowers
4–5cm across, in umbels of 4–15, fragrant in
the evening; corona pinkish. Needs a compost
suitable for epiphytes. A tropical species,
requiring ample water in summer, but little
in winter. Good light assists flowering.
Min. 8–10°C.

Hoya pauciflora Wight An evergreen
climber with narrow waxy leaves and solitary
or few large whitish scented flowers, native of
S India in Kerala, and of Ceylon, around
Kandy and Newara Eliya, growing as an
epiphyte in moist montane forest at 400–
1700m, flowering in March and
September–November. Stems to 1m. Leaves
around 2–5.5cm, lanceolate to narrowly ovate-
lanceolate. Flowers 1–2cm across, almost
glabrous; corona small, purplish. Needs a
compost suitable for epiphytes. Min. 0°C.

Hoya shepherdii Short ex Hook., syn *H.
longifolia* Wall. var. *shepherdii* An evergreen
climber with long narrow waxy leaves and
small umbels of whitish scented flowers,
native of India, growing as an epiphyte in the
forest, flowering in April–June. Stems to 1m.
Leaves to 15cm, linear, pendent. Flowers 1cm
across, in umbels to 5cm across; corona
pinkish. Needs a compost suitable for
epiphytes. Min. 0°C.

Asclepias pinifolia in NE Mexico, near Saltillo

Calotropus gigantea in the Botanic Gardens, Bermuda

Araujia sericofera at the Plantsman Nursery, Throwleigh, Devon

Araujia sericofera Brot. (*Asclepiadaceae*)
Cruel Plant   A twining woody climber with
softly hairy stalked leaves and loose cymes of
whitish flowers which trap the tongues of
moths, native of Brazil and Peru, flowering in
late summer. Climber to 10m. Leaves
opposite, tapering from the base, 5–10cm
long. Flowers scented, with 5 leafy calyx lobes
and 5 corolla lobes on a short tube, 2.5cm
across. Easily grown in a frost-free area. Min.
0°C. Naturalised in N Australia.

Asclepias curassavica Brot.
(*Asclepiadaceae*)   An annual or shrubby
perennial with opposite leaves and umbels of
reddish flowers, native of S America, but now
found throughout the tropics and subtropics,
including S Europe, growing on roadsides and
waste places, flowering in summer. Stems to
1m. Leaves to 15cm long. Flowers 1cm across.
Capsules 15cm long. Min. –5°C. A good food
plant for Monarch butterflies.

Asclepias pinifolia Greene   A tufted
perennial with narrow needle-like leaves and
white flowers, native of E Mexico in the Sierra
Madre Oriental, growing in dry places and
rock crevices on limestone, flowering in
June–November. Stems 10–40cm; leaves
linear, around 8cm long. Flowers 1cm across,
white with reddish-purple flecks. For a dry hot
position, watered in summer. Min. –5°C.

Asclepias speciosa Torr.   A perennial with
greyish-hairy stems and leaves and purplish-
pink flowers, native of California in the
foothills of the Sierra Nevada, to Washington

and Nevada, growing in dry stony places
below 1800m, flowering in May–July. Stems to
120cm; leaves 8–15cm; flowers 1.5–2cm
across, woolly on the back. A good food plant
for Monarch butterflies.

Calotropis gigantea (L.) Dryander
(*Asclepiadaceae*)   A large shrubby perennial
with opposite leathery leaves and umbels of
pinkish, purple or white flowers, native of
India, China and SE Asia, growing in river
gravels, on roadsides and waste places,
flowering in March–October. Stems to 2m.
Leaves 10–20cm long, white beneath. Flowers
1.2–2.5cm across. Capsules 8–10cm long,
curved. This plant has many uses; the hairs of
the seeds are used as stuffing; the stem fibres
are used for fishing lines; the poisonous juice
is used medicinally. Min. 0°C. The closely
related *C. procera* (Ait.) Ait. fil., is often seen
on roadsides in E Africa.

Ceropegia sandersoniae Decne. ex Hook.
(*Asclepiadaceae*)   A twining perennial with
fleshy stems, small opposite leaves and upright
flat-topped flowers, native of Mozambique
and South Africa in Natal, growing in stony
soil by streams, flowering in summer. Stems to
2m or more. Leaves heart-shaped to 2cm
long. Flowers 4.5–5cm tall, trumpet-shaded
with 5 lobes which form an umbrella-like cap.
For well-drained soil, well watered in summer,
dry in winter. Min. 0°C. *Ceropegia linearis*
subsp. *woodii* (Schltr.) H. Huber (*not shown*)
from SE Africa, is a commonly grown
houseplant. It has hanging or twining thin
stems, with small heart-shaped variegated

leaves and tubular flowers. Rounded tubers
are formed at the nodes.

Sarcostemma viminale (L.) R. Br.
(*Asclepiadaceae*)   A shrubby scrambler with
green succulent stems, no leaves and masses
of yellowish-green flowers, native of South
Africa from the E Cape to Natal and Transvaal
to Namibia, growing in dry scrub, flowering at
any time of year. Stems to 1m, around 5mm in
diameter. Flowers to 1.5cm across. For dry
sandy soil. Min. 0°C.

Stephanotis floribunda (R. Br.) Brongn.
(*Asclepiadaceae*) Madagascar Jasmine,
Wax Flower   A twining climber with opposite
leaves and pure white scented flowers, native
of Madagascar, flowering in summer. Stems
to 4m; leaves to 15cm long, usually around
10cm. Flowers 6cm long, waxy, fading to
creamy white, in large clusters. A lovely and
popular plant, needing warm humid
conditions to thrive. Min. 15°C or less in
winter if kept dry.

Tweedia caerulea D. Don ex Sweet., syn.
Oxypetalum caeruleum (D. Don) Decne
(*Asclepiadaceae*)   A twining or scrambling
subshrub with softly hairy elongated heart-
shaped leaves and pale blue starry flowers,
native of S Brazil and Uruguay, flowering in
summer. Stems to 80cm; leaves to 10cm;
flowers 2.5–4.5cm across, opening greenish-
blue, pinkish as they fade. An attractive
perennial for a frost-free greenhouse or mild
garden outdoors. In frosty areas it may also be
grown as an annual.

Sarcostemma viminale on a rocky bank in the SE Cape near Port Elizabeth

Tweedia caerulea

Asclepias curassavica naturalised near Seville, Spain

Asclepias speciosa

Stephanotis floribunda

Ceropegia sandersoniae

Ipomoea lobata in the cool conservatory
at Wisley

Operculina alatipes below Copala in Mazatlán, SW Mexico in late October

Ipomoea alba L., syn. *Calonyction aculeatum*
House (*Convolvulaceae*) Moonflower
A rampant climbing annual or perennial with
long-stalked heart-shaped leaves and large
white flowers with a long narrow tube, native
of tropical America, but now widely cultivated
and naturalised throughout the tropics.
Climber to 5m, with tubercules on the stem;
leaves 6–20cm long, usually entire, but
sometimes deeply 3-lobed. Outer sepals
awned. Flowers opening in early evening,
scented, 11–16cm across, with the tube
7–12cm long. Capsule with 4 large seeds of
various colours. A lovely plant in a tropical
climate, but not easy in a greenhouse as it
needs a long period of growth to reach
flowering size. Sow early in heat and keep
humid. Watch especially for attacks by red
spider which seems to love all *Ipomoeas*.
Min. 5°C, to overwinter.

Ipomoea cairica (L.) Sweet (s. *Leiocalyx*)
The Railway Creeper   A climbing perennial
with deeply 7-lobed leaves and purplish-pink
flowers, native distribution unknown, but
now found everywhere in tropical and
subtropical climates. Climber to 5m, the stems
rooting; leaves to 10cm across, the 3 central
lobes divided to the base, the outer pairs
attached. Flowers 3–6cm across, sometimes
red, purple or white. Seeds hairy with longer
hairs on the axils. A common but pretty weed.
Min. 5°C.

Ipomoea lobata (Cerv.) Thell., syn. *Mina
lobata* (Cerv.) *Quamoclit lobata* (Cerv.) House
A climbing perennial, often grown as an
annual, with a forked upright inflorescence of
many small flowers, red in bud, becoming
orange and yellow, before opening nearly
white, native of Mexico to South America,
flowering in summer–autumn. Stems to 5m;
leaves deeply lobed, somewhat maple-like.
Flowers tubular, 1.8–2.2cm long, with
exserted style and stamens. Easily grown as
an annual in warm seasons. Min. 5°C, to
overwinter.

Ipomoea mauritiana Jacq. (s. *Eriospermum*)
A rampant climbing perennial with deeply
7-lobed fleshy leaves and large reddish-purple
or purplish-pink flowers, native throughout
the tropics, usually in forest by rivers or near
the sea in mangrove swamps, flowering all

Ipomoea alba at Clos du Peyronnet, Menton

Ipomoea pandurata

Ipomoea cairica wild in Hong Kong

summer–autumn in subtropical climates. Tuberous-rooted climber to 10m, woody at the base; leaves around 20cm across. Flowers in branched heads, lasting more than a day, 4–8cm across, with a pale tube. Capsule with 4 large black seeds tufted with silky hairs. A lovely plant in a tropical climate or heated greenhouse, needing moist rich soil. Min. 15°C, to overwinter.

Ipomoea pandurata (L.) G. Mey. Wild Potato Vine   A perennial climber from a huge tuber, native of E North America from Ontario south to Florida and Texas, growing in dry fields, flowering in May–September. Climber to 10m; leaves to 15cm, ovate, sometimes 3-lobed. Flowers to 10cm across, white with a purple throat. Seeds woolly on the margins. The hardiest *Ipomoea*, surviving frozen soil. Min. –10°C at least.

Operculina alatipes (Hook.) House (*Convolvulaceae*)   A rampant climber with heart-shaped leaves and masses of orange-pink to purplish flowers emerging from a thickened calyx, native of SW Mexico to Colombia, Venezuela, Ecuador and Trinidad, growing in scrub and roadsides in warm moist areas, flowering in September–December. Perennial climber to 8m; leaves around 6cm long. Calyx reddish. Flowers 6–8cm across. A lovely climber of an unusual colour, seen in western Mexico, but without ripe seed. Min. 10°C, to overwinter.
Operculina alata (Ham.) Urban, from the West Indies and tropical America, is striking with its clear yellow flowers which open in the morning, and in its winged flower stalk.

Stictocardia beraviensis (Vatke) Hall, syn. *Ipomoea beraviensis* Vatke (*Convolvulaceae*) A rampant climber with broad heart-shaped leaves and masses of upright crimson flowers with an orange throat, native of C Africa from Madagascar to Ethiopia and Zimbabwe and in West Africa, growing in open bush and forest along rivers at 900–1800m, flowering in July–October. Perennial woody climber to 10m; leaves around 20cm long and wide. Flowers around 4.5–5.5cm long. A striking climber seen here in Malawi. Min. 10°C, to overwinter. *Stictocardia campanulata* (L.) Merrill, found throughout the tropics, is cultivated in Australia.

Stictocardia beraviensis in Malawi

Ipomoea mauritiana in the Waterlily House at Kew

Ipomoea tricolor by Lake Chapala, SW Mexico in late October

Ipomoea hederifolia L. (*Convolvulaceae*) (s. *Quamoclit*)   A climbing annual that has small bright scarlet flowers with curved tube and exserted style and stamens, native of Mexico to South America, but now found throughout the tropics, flowering in summer–autumn. Stems to 2m; leaves heart-shaped or shallowly 5–7 lobed, to 10cm across. Flowers tubular, 2.5–4.5cm long, to 2.5cm across, with exserted style and stamens. Easily grown as an annual in warm seasons. This and other members of section *Quamoclit* are typical hummingbird-pollinated flowers.

Ipomoea × imperialis hort. **'Early Call Mixed'**   A group of hybrids between *I. nil* and other species. These need heat and humidity to grow and flower satisfactorily. 'Early Call' is one of the first to flower from seed. In 'Scarlet O'Hara' the flowers are bright purple.

Ipomoea indica (Burm.) Merrill, syn. *I. acuminata* (Vahl) Roem. & Schult. (s. *Ipomoea*)   A perennial climber native of tropical America and the West Indies, but now found throughout the tropics, growing in scrub and waste places. Climber to 10m; leaves 5–17cm, ovate, often 3-lobed. Sepals acuminate, 1.4–2.2cm long. Flowers 6–8cm across, blue or purplish, then pinker through the day, in few or several-flowered heads.

Ipomoea purpurea (L.) Roth. (s. *Ipomoea*) An annual climber, native of Mexico and the West Indies now found further north in America and throughout the tropics, growing in scrub and waste places. Climber to 3m, with bristly and hairy stems; leaves hairy, 2–10cm, ovate, often 3-lobed. Sepals lanceolate, bristly-hairy at the base. Flowers 3 5cm across, blue or purplish, becoming pinker through the day, red, pink, white or striped, in cultivars, with up to seven flowers in a loose head. The third species in this group, *Ipomoea nil* (L.) Roth. has very narrow sepals 2.2–2.5cm long and a flower similar to *I. purpurea*.

Ipomoea quamoclit L., syn. *Quamoclit pennata* (Descr.) Boj. (s.*Quamoclit*) A climbing annual that has small bright scarlet flowers with a straight tube and 5-lobed

Ipomoea tricolor wild seedlings in Mexico showing colour variations

Ipomoea indica naturalised in Moore River National Park, Western Australia

mouth, native of Mexico to South America, and now found throughout the tropics, flowering in summer–autumn. Stems to 2m; leaves pinnate with linear lobes. Flowers tubular, 2.5cm long, 1.5cm across; there is a rare white form. Easily grown as an annual in warm seasons.

Ipomoea × ***sloteri*** (House) Ooststr. (s. *Quamoclit*)   A hybrid between *I. hederifolia* and *I. quamoclit*, raised by Mr L. Sloter in around 1910. This cross was the culmination of 11 years work, only one seedling was raised. The leaves have long narrow lobes, 7–15cm long; flowers 4–5cm long, 3.5–4cm across, shallowly lobed at the mouth. Min. 5°C.

Ipomoea tricolor Cav. (s. *Leiocalyx*)
Morning Glory, Heavenly Blue   An annual climber, native of Mexico and the West Indies to tropical South America, growing in scrub and waste places, flowering in late summer to winter. Climber to 3m, with glabrous stems; leaves hairless, 4–10cm, ovate, cordate. Sepals lanceolate, smooth at the base. Flowers to 6–10cm across, pale sky blue, greenish or blue and white striped, becoming pinker as they fade. This is the most commonly grown morning glory. The leaves are very prone to attack by red spider mite, so the plants should be kept very humid and warm while growing up, then cooler while they are in flower in late summer and autumn.

Ipomoea purpurea in the garden of the Elbow Beach Hotel, Bermuda

Ipomoea × *imperialis* 'Early Call Mixed'

Ipomoea hederifolia near Copala in Mazatlan, SW Mexico

Ipomoea × *sloteri* at the Plantsman Nursery, Throwleigh, Devon

Ipomoea quamoclit in Mexico, by Lake Chapala in late October

Ipomoea arborea wild in Mexico

Ipomoea arborea wild in Mexico

Convolvulus cantabrica

Convolvulus cneorum, an old plant in a wall at Sissinghurst Castle, Kent

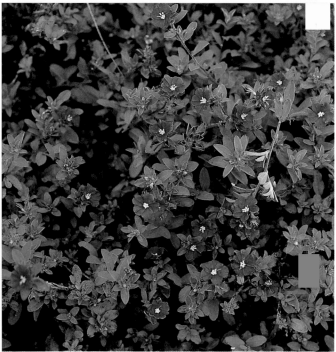

Convolvulus canariensis in Madeira

Evolvulus pilosus 'Blue Daze' in California

Convolvulus sabatius hanging over a wall at M. Pellizzaro's nursery in Vallauris, S France

Ipomoea arborea (*Convolvulaceae*)
A spreading tree with sparse heart-shaped leaves and white flowers with a dark centre, native of C Mexico, growing in desert and semi-desert scrub, flowering in October–March. Tree to 4m high and across. Leaves to 20cm long, heart-shaped; flowers around 8cm across. A conspicuous tree in the arid regions of Mexico. Min. –3°C.

Convolvulus canariensis L.
(*Convolvulaceae*)   A climbing shrub, woody below with hairy ovoid-oblong leaves and clusters of small pale bluish flowers, native of the Canary Islands, growing in the laurel forest zone at 600–800m, flowering in March–September. Climber to 10m; leaves 4–9cm long; flowers around 3cm across. Easy in frost-free conditions. Min. –3°C.

Convolvulus cantabrica L.   A perennial with narrow grey leaves and pink flowers, native of the Mediterranean area and E Europe to Iran, growing on dry banks and in rocky open woods, flowering in April–August. Stems 10–50cm from a woody base. Leaves to 4cm long, oblanceolate to linear. Flowers pink, 1.5–2.5cm across. An attractive perennial for a dry position. Min. –10°C.

Convolvulus cneorum L.   A silvery shrub with white or pale pink flowers, native of Italy, Sicily, Albania and the former Yugoslavia, growing on limestone rocks near the sea, flowering March–June. Plant to 50cm tall and

Dichondra micrantha used as a lawn in S France

wide. Leaves linear to oblanceolate, to 4cm long. Flowers 15–25mm, usually white with a pink flush outside. The closely-related *C. oleifolius* Desr. from Malta, Sicily, Crete, Greece, Turkey and Syria has narrower leaves and smaller, usually pink flowers. Both are good plants for a dry crevice or rocky slope in full sun. Min. –8 to –10°C if the rootstock is kept very dry.

Convolvulus sabatius Viv., syn. *C. mauritanicus* Boiss.   A spreading perennial with silvery leaves and bluish-mauve flowers, native of NW Italy, Sicily and NW Africa, growing on dry limestone rocks near the sea,

flowering in April–October. Stems to 50cm, from a woody rootstock. Leaves oblong to almost round, to 3cm long. Flowers 1.5–2.2cm across, sometimes pink in the wild. A beautiful and easy plant for summer bedding, to hang over a wall or edge a large pot. The rootstock will survive underground in a dry frost-free position. Min. –5°C.

Dichondra micrantha Urban
(*Convolvulaceae*)   A dwarf creeping perennial with round shiny leaves, often used as a lawn in dry climates, native of E Asia. Stems to 15cm in moist shade, but usually much less. Leaves 5–30mm across, on stalks to 5cm. Flowers inconspicuous, 2–2.5mm, white or yellow-green, in summer–autumn. Can be grown from seed or planted out as plugs. Good in areas where the ground never freezes, needing little mowing in sunny spots. Keep well watered in summer. Min. –3°C overnight

Evolvulus pilosus Nutt. **'Blue Daze'**, syn. *Evolvulus glomeratus* hort. (*Convolvulaceae*) A sub-shrub with silver-backed leaves and bright blue white-centred flowers, native of S Dakota and Montana to Texas and Arizona, growing in dry places, at 100–1800m, flowering in March–July. Stems to 15cm; leaves to 15mm, narrowly ovate, green above. Flowers around 1.5cm across. *E. pilosus* is the name commonly given to this plant; *E. arizonicus* Gray, is said to be a finer plant, with flowers to 2cm across. Min. –5°C, in a dry position in full sun.

Cobaea species from Mexico, in Devon

Cobaea species in a limestone gorge SE of Saltillo, in NW Mexico

Ipomopsis aggregata in NE Mexico

Loeselia mexicana near Durango in NW Mexico in October

Loeselia mexicana flowering in the greenhouse in Devon

Cantua buxifolia in the greenhouse at Quince, Devon

Leptodactylon californicum above Santa Barbara in late February

Cantua buxifolia

Leptodactylon californicum

1800m, climbing into trees, flowering in August–October. Perennial with fleshy roots and annual stems to 10m. Leaves with ovate leaflets to 9cm. Pedicels to 30cm. Calyx lobes lanceolate, appressed, 3cm long. Corolla 7.5cm long, expanded at the mouth. For any good soil. Min. –3°C. This species is close to and possibly the same as *Cobaea trianti* Hemsl. recorded from Colombia and Ecuador. Both resemble the familiar *Cobaea scandens* Cav. but in this species the flowers become purple and it has larger, leafier calyx lobes.

Several other exciting species are not in cultivation at present; *C. minor* Mart. & Gal. from Orizaba, Mexico and Costa Rica has deeply-lobed pale violet corollas with a darker eye, and in several species such as *C. penduliflora* (Karst.) Hook. the corolla of the hanging flower is split almost to the base.

Cantua buxifolia Juss. ex Lam Sacred Flower of the Incas   An arching shrub weighed down by its lovely crimson flowers with an orange tube, native of Peru, Bolivia and N Chile, reaching 4000m in the Andes, flowering in spring. Stems to 2.5m; leaves 2.5–5cm long, lanceolate, with blunt teeth. Flowers 6–8cm long. A most beautiful plant needing careful treatment to flower well. Plant in good soil and water well in summer; keep drier in winter when the plant will lose some leaves and increase watering again as the buds appear in spring. Prune lightly and repot after flowering. Can be grown outside in warm climates and is best stood outside in summer as it is prone to attack by red spider. Min. –3°C. *C. bicolor* from Bolivia, has smaller flowers with the tube white to yellow and with orange-red lobes. Both are easy from cuttings.

Cobaea species (*Cobaeaceae*)   A rampant climber with masses of pale greenish-yellow trumpet-shaped flowers, native of NE Mexico in the limestone gorges near Saltillo, at around

Ipomopsis aggregata (Pursh) V. Grant (*Polemoniaceae*)   A biennial with narrow thread-like leaves and spikes of tubular red flowers, native of Montana and British Columbia south to California and N Mexico, growing in open pine forests, on dry rocky banks and roadsides at 1000–3000m, flowering in June–October. Stems to 80cm, from a rosette of finely dissected leaves. Flowers 2.9–3.5cm long, usually red with yellow mottling, rarely all yellow, (or pinkish-purple with purple spots in var. *macrosiphon* Kearney & Peebles from Arizona which has flowers to 4cm long). All are attractive plants but the rosettes need to be overwintered under glass in damp climates. Min. –5°C or less in alpine forms.

Leptodactylon californicum Hook. & Arn. (*Polemoniaceae*)   A bristly shrub with pink, white or lavender phlox-like flowers, native of S California from St Luis Obispo Co. southwards, growing on dry shady rocks in the mountains below 1500m, flowering in

February–June. Shrub to 60cm high and wide. Leaves 5–9-lobed with narrow segments to 12mm long. Flowers 2–3cm across. An attractive shrub for a dry position or large pot but difficult to establish as the roots resent disturbance. Min. –3°C.

Loeselia mexicana (Lam.) Brand, syn. *L. coccinea* G. Don (*Polemoniaceae*) A sub-shrub with upright stems and masses of tubular red flowers, native of Mexico, from Chihuahua and Sinaloa to Puebla and Oaxaca, growing in dry rocky places at around 2000m, flowering in August–December. Stems to 1.5m from a woody base. Leaves lanceolate, 2–3cm long, with spine-tipped teeth. Flowers 2.5–2.8cm long, usually bright red, but a yellow form is known. A hummingbird-pollinated flower, full of thick sugary nectar which can go mouldy in damp weather if the dead flowers are not removed. An easy plant for a dry sunny position or cool conservatory. Min. –5°C if kept dry in winter. Take cuttings of new shoots in late spring.

Echium callithyrsum on Tresco

Echium nervosum wild on coastal cliffs in Madeira

Echium candicans in a garden near Los Angeles, California

Echium callithyrsum Webb ex Bolle (*Boraginaceae*) A spreading shrub with lanceolate to ovate leaves and short dense ovate spikes of deep blue flowers, native of Gran Canaria, growing on cliffs at 800–1500m, flowering in May–July. Shrub to 1.5m high and wide. Leaves with large-based setae on the upper surface, with simple hairs and prominant pubescent veins on the lower surface. The rather similar *E. webbii* Coincy from La Palma has laxer spikes and leaves with similar hairs on both surfaces. Needs sun and well-drained soil. Min. -3°C.

Echium candicans L. fil., syn. *E. fastuosum* Jacq. Pride of Madeira A large spreading shrub with lanceolate leaves and long dense spikes of purplish-blue flowers, native of Madeira, growing on cliffs in the laurel forest zone, flowering in April–June. Shrub to 2.5m high and wide. Leaves silvery. Flower spikes to around 60cm long, elongating during flowering. Needs sun and well-drained soil.

Fast-growing in fertile soil so suited only for the largest greenhouse, unless planted in a large tub. The best coloured forms may be propagated by cuttings. Min. –3°C.

Echium nervosum Ait. A large spreading shrub with broadly lanceolate leaves and broad dense spikes of pale blue flowers, native of Madeira, growing on cliffs near the sea, flowering in March–June. Shrub to 1.5m high and wide. Leaves silvery. Flower spikes to around 20cm long. Needs full sun and moist but well-drained soil to stay compact and healthy. Min. 0°C.

Echium × scilloniense hort. Probably a hybrid between *E. callithyrsum* and *E. pininana*. A branching shrub with tall narrow spikes around 1m long, in size and shape between those of the parents. Raised (or possibly self-seeded) at Tresco and illustrated in the *Journal of the Royal Horticultural Society* in 1947.

Echium candicans from Madeira, naturalised on the Cape Peninsula in South Africa

Echium × scilloniense and *Echium callithyrsum,* flowering with *Puya chilesis* in the garden at Tresco Abbey, Isles of Scilly

Echium pininana

Echium pininana with *Euphorbia mellifera* in the garden at Tresco Abbey, Isles of Scilly

Echium aculeatum on dry rocky hills near Masca, Tenerife

Lobostemon fruticosus at the National Botanic Gardens, Kirstenbosch, Cape Town

Echium aculeatum Poiret (*Boraginaceae*) A low shrub with linear spiny leaves and short conical spikes of white flowers, native of Tenerife, Gomera and Hierro, growing on cliffs and dry rocky places at up to 1000m, flowering in March–May. Shrub to 1.5m high and wide. Leaves with margins and midrib densely spiny. Calyx lobes as long as the corolla. Needs sun and well-drained soil. Min. 0°C.
E. giganteum L. fil. (*not shown*) from forest areas in N Tenerife is larger with broader lanceolate or oblanceolate leaves and would be better in cooler wetter climates.

Echium leucophaeum Webb ex Spr. & Hutch.   A rounded shrub with linear-lanceolate leaves and rather flat heads of white flowers, native of Tenerife, growing on cliffs and dry rocky places at 300–600m, flowering in March–May. Shrub to 2m high and wide. Leaves with short stiff hairs, but few or no marginal spines, less than 1.5cm wide. Inflorescence branched at the base. Needs sun and well-drained soil. Min. 0°C. Seen here in the nursery of Dino Pellizaro, S France.

Echium pininana Webb & Berth.   A short-lived shrub with a large rosette on a stout stalk, developing into a massive spike of bluish flowers, native of La Palma, growing at around 600m in laurel forests in the NE part of the island where it is very rare, flowering in April–July. Stem to 4m; leaves elliptic-lanceolate, rough, green. A spectacular plant for a mild garden and partial shade in hot areas. Min. −3°C. The hybrid between this species and *E. wildpretii* has rich purple flowers on a spike to around 3m. It is common on Tresco.

Echium virescens DC   A dense shrub with linear spiny leaves and long rather loose spikes of pink or bluish flowers, native of Tenerife, growing on cliffs and dry rocky places in the forest and lower pine zone at 500–1900m, flowering in March–May. Shrub to 2m high and wide. Leaves silvery. Needs sun and well-drained soil. Min. −3°C.

Echium virescens

Echium virescens on a rocky roadside on the lower southern slopes of Mount Teide, Tenerife

Echium wildpretii on Tresco

Echium wildpretii in Las Cañadas, Tenerife

Echium wildpretii Pearson ex Hook. fil. A spectacular biennial, in the first year forming a large rosette of narrow silver leaves and in the second year a tall spike of crimson flowers, native of Tenerife, growing in dry rocky places in the subalpine zone at around 2000m and in the mountains of La Palma at 1600–1800m, flowering in May–June. Flowering stem to 2m. Leaves linear, with long dense setae. For a dry very sunny climate; easy to grow but resents winter damp under glass. Min. −5°C if dry. On bare ground near the Parador at Las Cañadas, I found the rosettes coated with ice in the early morning; they would then have been scorched by the sun all day.

Lobostemon fruticosus (L.) Buek (*Boraginaceae*)   A rounded shrub with silvery leaves and short leafy spikes of pink and blue flowers, native of South Africa, in W and S Cape Province, growing in sandy places, flowering in August–October (spring). Shrub to 80cm; leaves 15–60mm long. Flowers to 2.5cm long, changing colour after opening. For sun and sandy soil. Min. −3°C.

Echium leucophaeum at M. Pellizaro's, Vallauris

Mallotonia gnaphalodes in Bermuda

Cordia boissieri near Saltillo, NE Mexico

Heliotropium arborescens in Auckland Botanic Garden, New Zealand

Cordia sebestena in Yucatan, Mexico

Myosotidium hortensia in Otari, New Zealand

Wigandia urens in Menton, S France

Cordia boissieri A. DC. (*Boraginaceae*) A shrub or small tree with large evergreen leaves and small heads of white, yellow- and orange-throated flowers, native of Texas and Mexico, growing on dry rocky hills, flowering mainly in spring and autumn. Small tree to 6m. Leaves roughly hairy, to 15cm; flowers to 2.5cm across. For dry well-drained soil, with water in midsummer. Min. −6°C, for short periods.

Cordia sebestena L. Geiger Tree A shrub or small tree with large broad leaves and rounded heads of bright orange frilly flowers, native of Mexico to Venezuela and the West Indies, growing on rocky hills and coasts, flowering mainly in spring. Small tree to 8m. Leaves rough, pointed, to 20cm; flowers around 5cm across. Fruits becoming white and fleshy. For dry well-drained soil, with water in midsummer. Min. −6°C, for short periods.

Heliotropium arborescens L., syn. *H. peruvianum* L. (*Boraginaceae*) Cherry Pie, Common Heliotrope A shrubby perennial with hairy leaves and masses of small sweetly scented white flowers, becoming purple as they age, native of Peru, flowering most of the year. Stems to 2m; leaves to 8cm; flowers to 5mm across, varying in different cultivars from white to dark blue and purple. This was a very popular plant in Victorian conservatories, where the plants were trained and pinched to shape and brought indoors for their sweet rich scent. Sandy loamy soils are best, and plants need a winter minimum of 5°C at night to continue growing. Prune in spring and water and feed well in summer. Many of the old varieties are now available again in England. Outdoors the plant survives −2°C and prefers a little shade in hot climates.

Lithodora fruticosa (L.) Griseb. (*Boraginaceae*) A sprawling sub-shrub with narrow leaves and bright blue or purplish flowers, native of S France and Spain, growing in dry places on limestone, flowering in March–June. Stems ascending to 60cm; leaves linear, to 2cm long. Flowers 10–15mm long with rounded lobes. An attractive plant for a warm position in sun or partial shade, flowering very early in warm gardens, as shown here in Menton. Min. −8°C.

Mallotonia gnaphalodes (R. Br.) Britton (*Boraginaceae*) A soft silvery shrub with narrow leaves and pinkish-purple flowers, native of Bermuda, growing on coral rocks and cliffs, flowering in March–May. Shrub to 1.5m; leaves to 4cm long; flowers 8mm across. An attractive neat shrub for dry places exposed to the sea. Min. 0°C.

Myosotidium hortensia (Decne) Baill. (*Boraginaceae*) Chatham Island Forget-me-not A large perennial with shiny ribbed leaves and heads of blue or white flowers, native of the Chatham Islands, east of New Zealand, growing in rocky, sandy and peaty places near the shore, even on the high tide line among cockleshell deposits, flowering in September–November (spring). Leaves to 1m long, the blades 20–40cm across. Flowering stems elongating during flowering and

Lithodora fruticosa in Clos du Peyronnet, Menton

sprawling to 60cm. Flowers 15–20mm across.
Easily grown in peaty soil with sea sand
added, fed well with manure or liquid feed.
Plants will grow well and flower in large pots
and should be kept cool and shaded around
midday in summer but with good light,
protected in winter in cold areas. Min. –5°C.
Slugs and hot dry air are its main enemies, so
it is best in cool coastal gardens.

Wigandia caracasana Kunth, syn.
W. macrophylla Cham. & Schldl.
(*Hydrophyllaceae*)   A coarse shrubby plant
with large rounded leaves and large branched
heads of small purplish-blue flowers, native
from Mexico to Colombia and naturalised in
the W Mediterranean, growing in rocky places
and ravines, flowering in winter–spring. Stems
to 4m, little branched; leaves 45–60cm long,
cordate at the base. Flowers around 2cm
across. A striking plant whose large leaves give
a tropical effect. It needs a sheltered position,
as the leaves easily become tatty. Good soil
and free drainage, with ample water in
summer. Min. –3°C.

Wigandia urens (Ruiz. & Pav.) H. B.& K.
A branching shrub with rounded leaves and
branched heads of purplish-blue flowers,
native of Peru, flowering in autumn. Shrub to
5m tall and wide. Leaves 15–30cm long,
obovate, tapering towards the base. Flowers
around 2cm across. For mild climates, with
water in summer. Min. –3°C.

Wigandia caracasana in the Huntington Gardens, California

Solanum wallacei

Solanum rantonnetii at Tourettes-sur-Loup, Alpes Maritimes

Cyphomandra crassicaulis fruit in the conservatory at Wisley

Solanum jasminoides 'Album' near San Francisco

Solanum wendlandii at the Plantsman Nursery, Throwleigh, Devon

Cyphomandra crassicaulis (Ortega) Kuntze, syn. *C. betacea* (Cav.) Sendtn. (*Solanaceae*) Tree Tomato   An evergreen or semi-evergreen shrub with small creamy-pink or buff flowers and tomato-like edible fruits, native of Peru, growing in open forest at medium to high altitudes, flowering in spring and summer. Open-branched tree-like shrub to 4m. Leaves to 15cm, ovate and often heart-shaped at the base, downy and slightly fleshy. Flowers 2.5cm wide, star-shaped, long-stalked, borne in axillary clusters. Fruit a fleshy ovate orange-red berry up to 8cm long; edible either fresh or cooked when fully ripe. Min. 5°C. Grown for its bold foliage and long-lasting fruits.

Solanum aculeatissimum Jacq.   A spiny evergreen sub-shrub with small clusters of white flowers, native of tropical America and southern North America and commonly naturalised elsewhere in the tropics, growing in waste places and roadside scrub, flowering in summer. Shrub to 1m with spiny branches. Leaves to 15cm, ovate but with deep rounded lobes and prominent yellow-brown spines in the main veins above and below. Flowers 2.5cm wide, star-shaped, white, flushed lavender, with a conspicuous yellow staminal boss, followed by globose, orange-brown fleshy fruits 3–5cm in diameter. Min. 5°C. A weed in the tropics but cultivated for its striking foliage as well as the flowers.

Solanum hispidum Pers., syn. *S. warscewiczii* hort ex Lambertye (*Solanaceae*) Devil's Fig

A stocky spiny evergreen shrub with handsome foliage and star-shaped white flowers, native of Mexico and Guatemala, growing in open dry places, flowering in late summer–autumn. Shrub to 2m with spiny branches. Leaves 20–30cm, ovate, deeply pinnately lobed, the lower surface spiny on the midrib and covered with coarse brownish hairs. Flowers 3–4cm wide, in dense racemes at the ends of the branches, sometimes followed by small globose yellow or brownish fruits. Min. 5°C.

Solanum jasminoides Paxt. **'Album'**
A deciduous shrubby climber with pure white flowers, a selection from a species native of Brazil, growing in cool submontane forest, flowering over a long period in summer–autumn. Scandent shrub to 6m. Leaves mostly simple, ovate or lanceolate, occasionally lobed at the base, tinged with purple. Flowers star-shaped, white with a prominent yellow boss of stamens, opening from pale mauve buds. Min. –5°C. Needs tying in to wires or other support. The wild form has blue-tinged flowers. In **Solanum jasminoides 'Album Variegatum'**, the flowers are the same as 'Album' but the leaves are boldly margined with bright yellow.

Solanum laciniatum Ait. Kangaroo Apple
A vigorous evergreen shrub with attractively divided foliage and deep violet-blue flowers, native of Australia and New Zealand, growing in coastal areas in open scrub and forest margins at low altitudes, flowering in summer

SOLANUM

and autumn. Shrub to 3m, with purple stems.
Leaves to 30cm, pinnately divided into up to 9
narrow dark green lobes. Flowers 2.5cm wide,
3–8 in axillary clusters, followed by ovoid
yellowish berries 2.5cm long. Min. –5°C.
Handsome shrub of distinctive appearance
with attractive fingered leaves and richly
coloured flowers.

Solanum marginatum L. fil.   A somewhat
prickly evergreen shrub with striking foliage
and white flowers, native of Ethiopia, growing
in dry scrubby places at low altitudes. A
biennial or short-lived shrub to 1.5m. Leaves
to 20cm, ovate with sinuately lobed margins,
spiny on the midribs; at first covered with
white hairs, these persisting only on the
margins and underside. Flowers 3cm wide, in
few-flowered terminal clusters, white, often
veined with purple. Fruit a globose yellow
berry 4cm wide with a persistent prickly calyx.
Min. 5°C. A handsome foliage shrub.

Solanum rantonnetii Lescuyer, syn.
Lycianthes rantonnetii (Lescuyer) Bitter
An open evergreen shrub with rounded violet-
blue flowers, native of Argentina and
Paraguay, growing in open habitats at low to
medium altitudes, flowering over a long
period in summer–autumn. Shrub to 1.8m.
Leaves 6–10cm, ovate or lanceolate, with
undulate margins. Flowers 10–20mm wide, in
small clusters, often with a yellow zone
around the stamens. Min. –3°C. Some named
selections, such as the deep violet 'Royal
Robe', are fragrant.

Solanum seaforthianum Andrews
A slender hairless evergreen climber with
starry light violet-blue flowers, native of
Trinidad and South America, growing in dry
conditions in woodland margins at low to
medium altitudes, flowering in summer.
Scrambling shrub to 6m. Leaves to 10cm,
entire or more often pinnatifid with 3–9 lance-
shaped lobes. Flowers 12–20mm wide, with
spreading oblong lobes, in pendulous
branched clusters. Min. 5°C. The starry
flowers and divided leaves give this species the
appearance of a jasmine.

Solanum wallacei Andrews (A. Gray) Parish
A low sparsely branched evergreen sub-shrub
with large violet flowers, native of California,
growing in open arid places, flowering in
summer. Shrub of variable habit, up to 1.7m,
but usually low and spreading to 1m tall.
Leaves 5–12cm, rather leathery, oblong-ovate
and covered with brownish glandular hairs.
Flowers 4cm wide, 2–6 in clusters at the ends
of the stems. Fruit a globose purple berry
2.5cm across. Min. 5°C. The large flowers and
greyish foliage compensate for the untidy
habit. *S. xantii* A. Gray is a close ally, but has
smaller flowers and green berries.

Solanum wendlandii Hook. fil. Potato Vine,
Paradise Flower   A vigorous, more or less
evergreen hairless climber with rounded lilac-
blue flowers, native of Costa Rica, growing in
montane forest at about 1500m, flowering in
summer. Scrambling climber with spiny
branches, to 5m tall. Lower leaves 10–25cm
long, pinnate with a large terminal leaflet and
smaller lateral leaflets; upper leaves simple
and ovate. Flowers 4–5cm wide, in branched
clusters to 50cm across, occasionally followed
by ovoid orange fruits 8–10cm long. Min. 5°C.
A magnificent large climber with a long
flowering season.

Solanum aculeatissimum

Solanum seaforthianum at Throwleigh, Devon

Solanum jasminoides 'Album Variegatum'

Solanum laciniatum

Solanum hispidum at the Jardin Exotique de
Val Rahmeh, Menton, S France

Solanum marginatum at the Giardino Botanico
Hanbury, La Mortola, Italy

133

SOLANACEAE

Cestrum nocturnum in a garden in Malawi

Nicotiana cordifolia at Berkeley Botanic Garden

Nicotiana tabacum var. *macrophylla* at Ventnor

Cestrum aurantiacum wild in Mexico

Cestrum elegans 'Smithii' in a garden in Malawi

Cestrum anagyris in wet mountain woods, above Anguangeo, Mexico

Nicotiana tomentosa var. *leguiana* in a coastal garden near San Francisco

Cestrum anagyris Dunn. (*Solanaceae*)
A large evergreen shrub with creamy or greenish-white flowers, native of Mexico, growing in open places within and on the margins of evergreen forests, flowering in October–December. Shrub to 3m tall and wide. Leaves to 10cm, oblong-elliptic, leathery, rather blunt. Flowers 20–25mm long, narrowly funnel-shaped, borne in drooping spikes in the upper leaf axils. Fruit a shiny black berry. Min. 5°C. Similar and closely related species include *C. laurifolium* and *C. nocturnum* which are scented only at night, and *C. diurnum* which is scented in the day. Min. –3°C.

Cestrum aurantiacum Lindl.
An evergreen shrub with small bright orange flowers, native of Central America, growing in clearings in evergreen forest at low altitudes, flowering in spring and early summer. Shrub to 3m or more, often developing long scandent shoots. Leaves to 15cm, lanceolate or ovate, untoothed and somewhat leathery. Flowers to 25mm long, tubular with spreading lobes, borne in terminal and axillary clusters, slightly fragrant at night. Fruit a spongy white berry 6–8mm across. Min. 5°C.

Cestrum × cultum Francey   A more-or-less evergreen shrub with narrowly funnel-shaped pinkish or dull purple flowers, a hybrid between *C. elegans* and *C. parqui* known only from cultivation, and flowering in late summer. Lax shrub to 3m. Leaves 5–10cm long, lanceolate, slender-pointed. Flowers about 25mm long, variable in colour, borne in rounded mostly terminal clusters and slightly fragrant at night. Min. 5°C. Several shrubs in cultivation appear to belong to this or a similar hybrid.

Cestrum elegans (Brongn.) Schlechtend. (*not illustrated*)   An evergreen shrub with nodding terminal clusters of reddish-purple flowers, native of Mexico, growing in open scrubby places at altitudes to 1000m, flowering in summer–autumn. Shrub of lax, arching growth, to 3m. Leaves to 12cm long, narrowly ovate, dark green. Flowers 20mm long, tubular, constricted just below the five small lobes, borne in clusters and sometimes followed by showy deep purple berries. Most often grown is the cultivar **'Smithii'** (*shown here*), which has attractive pink flowers borne over a long period.

Cestrum 'Newellii'   A lax evergreen shrub with bright red flowers, known only from cultivation but closely allied to the Mexican *C. fasciculatum*, flowering in late summer and autumn. Shrub to 3m. Leaves ovate to lanceolate, slightly leathery, dark green. Flowers 25mm long, rich crimson, broadly tubular with a constriction just below the lobes, carried in dense rounded terminal clusters. Min. 5°C. A very showy and free-flowering plant, probably of hybrid origin, differing from *C. fasciculatum* mainly in having glabrous corollas.

Cestrum nocturnum L.   An evergreen shrub with greenish-white flowers strongly scented at night, native of the West Indies, growing in open places in evergreen forests, flowering in summer–autumn. Lax shrub to 4m. Leaves to 20cm long, oblong-elliptic or narrowly ovate, thin-textured. Flowers 25mm long, narrowly funnel-shaped with erect rather than spreading lobes, borne in long elegant clusters. Fruit a small white berry. Min. 5°C. Although the flowers are less showy than those of other species, they compensate for this by their powerful scent.

Cestrum parqui L'Hérit. A deciduous shrub with greenish-yellow flowers, fragrant at night, native of Chile, growing on forest margins, flowering in summer–autumn. Shrub to 3m. Leaves 5–14cm, narrowly lanceolate, dark green and unpleasantly scented when bruised. Flowers 2.5cm long, narrowly funnel-shaped with 5 spreading lobes in large axillary and terminal clusters. Fruit a small blackish berry. Min. 0°C. Probably the hardiest species. All parts are poisonous to animals

Nicotiana cordifolia Philippi An evergreen shrub with night-scented white flowers, endemic to the Island of Juan Fernandez in the Pacific Ocean, 750km off C Chile, growing in areas of scrub, flowering in late summer–autumn. Shrub to 3m. Leaves to 20cm, elliptic, tapering at the base into an indistinct, winged petiole which runs a short distance down the stem. Flowers 3–4cm long, with a short tube widening abruptly into a bowl-shaped mouth which has 5 short, spreading or recurved lobes, borne in short terminal panicles. Min. 10°C, perhaps lower. An interesting species, probably allied to *N. tomentosa*, with some potential as an ornamental.

Nicotiana glauca Graham (*Solanaceae*) A fast-growing evergreen shrub with tubular yellow or greenish-yellow flowers, native of South America from Bolivia to Argentina and naturalised in S North America, Africa and elsewhere in mild areas, growing in open dry places, flowering in autumn. Lax shrub to 6m or more, occasionally a small tree. Leaves 6–25cm, ovate to lanceolate, glaucous and rubbery in texture. Flowers 3–4cm long, narrowly tubular, abruptly expanded then constricted just beneath the 5 very short spreading lobes, borne in usually lax panicles. Min. –5°C. Well-suited to a cool conservatory and may be grown outside in mild climates.

Nicotiana tabacum L. var. **macrophylla** Schrank A robust annual or biennial with night-scented flowers in shades of pink or dull red, native of Bolivia and adjacent Argentina, growing in open sunny places, perhaps always as a relic of cultivation, and flowering in summer. Annual or biennial to 1.2m, stems and leaves covered with sticky hairs. Leaves 20–40cm long, broadly ovate, usually cordate at the base, entire but with a wavy margin. Flowers 4–5cm long with a short tube, suddenly expanded into a bowl-shaped mouth with 5 spreading or reflexed lobes. Min. –5°C. A close ally of smoking tobacco.

Nicotiana tomentosa Ruiz & Pavon var. **leguiana** (J. F. Macbr.) Goodspeed A large-leaved evergreen shrub with pink and white flowers, endemic to S Peru, growing in half-shaded places, flowering in late summer. Shrub to 7m with white-woolly stems. Leaves to 50cm, ovate-elliptic, tapering at the base to a winged stalk which is expanded at the base to clasp the stem, the lower surface hairy at least on the veins. Flowers to 3.5cm long, with a stout whitish tube, spreading pink lobes and exserted stamens, carried in short panicles at the ends of the stems. Min. 5°C. A robust shrub with striking foliage and attractive flowers.

Cestrum 'Newellii' in the Generalife, Granada, Spain in April

Cestrum 'Newellii' in the greenhouse

Cestrum × *cultum*

Nicotiana glauca on the Swartberg Pass, South Africa in November

Cestrum parqui at Clos du Peyronnet

Iochroma australis at Gorwell House, Barnstaple

Streptosolen jamesonii

Iochroma australis Griseb., syn. *Dunalia australis* (Griseb.) Sleumer, *Acnistus australis* (Griseb.) Griseb. (*Solanaceae*)   An evergreen or semi-evergreen shrub with pendent violet-purple flowers, native of N Argentina, growing in montane forest to about 3000m, flowering in late spring and early summer. Spreading shrub to 3m or more, developing long leafy branches. Leaves 5–10cm, elliptic or oblong, rather leathery. Flowers 3–6cm long, narrowly trumpet-shaped with 5 shallow triangular lobes, borne in small clusters in the upper leaf axils. Min. −5°C or lower in a sheltered site. A most elegant shrub when the arching branches are hung with flowers. *Iochroma cyaneum* (Lindl.) Green, differs mainly in the shorter stamens, each with a pair of lateral cusps from the filament.

Iochroma coccineum Scheidw. (*Solanaceae*) An evergreen shrub with scarlet flowers, creamy-yellow in the throat, native of Mexico and Central America, growing in partially shaded places such as open woodland, flowering in summer. Shrub of open growth, to 4m. Leaves to 12cm, ovate or elliptic and shortly pointed, slightly lustrous on the upper surface, hairy on the veins beneath. Flowers 4–5cm long, narrowly tubular and slightly curved, flared at the mouth with 5 small recurved teeth, borne in small terminal clusters. Min. 5°C. A showy shrub, best tied in to some support. The flowers are variable in shade.

Iochroma grandiflorum Benth.
An evergreen shrub with trumpet-shaped rich violet flowers, native of Ecuador and Peru, growing in open forest conditions, flowering in summer–autumn. Shrub to 4m, rather lax in habit. Leaves to 13cm, broadly ovate, often cordate at the base, hairy on both surfaces. Flowers about 4cm long, flared at the mouth into 5 large triangular lobes and borne up to 8 together in nodding clusters at the tips of the shoots. Min. 5°C. One of the showiest species, valued for its rich colour.

Iochroma purpureum hort.   An evergreen shrub with rosy or magenta-purple flowers, apparently known only from cultivation, flowering in summer–autumn. Shrub to 3m, the young growth downy. Leaves 8–20cm, elliptic or ovate, downy beneath. Flowers in terminal clusters of up to 25, narrowly tubular with a slightly flared mouth, 3.5cm long. Min. 5°C. The status of this plant is uncertain but some authors consider it to be a colour variant of the deep blue-flowered *I. cyaneum*, native of Ecuador and Colombia.

Juanulloa mexicana (Schldl.) Miers, syn. *J. aurantiaca* Otto & Dietr. (*Solanaceae*) A scrambling evergreen shrub with short racemes of bright orange flowers, native of S Mexico, C America and N Peru, growing as an epiphyte in rainforest, flowering in summer. Shrub to 2m, with grey-tomentose stems. Leaves 10–20cm, ovate to oblong, rather leathery and covered with felty hairs beneath. Flowers with a waxy bright orange, tubular corolla 4–5cm long, with 5 short rounded lobes; calyx about two-thirds as long, tubular, 5-ribbed, waxy, paler orange. Min. 10°C. Like other epiphytes, needs a free-draining compost and shade from direct sun.

Streptosolen jamesonii (Benth.) Miers (*Solanaceae*) Marmalade Bush   A lax evergreen shrub with bright orange flowers, native of Colombia, Peru and Ecuador, flowering in late spring–summer. Shrub to 1.8m, developing long scandent shoots unless trimmed regularly. Leaves 3–4cm, ovate, deep green and prominently veined. Flowers 3–4cm long, with a yellow or pale orange twisted tube, with 5 spreading rounded deep reddish-orange lobes, borne in large terminal panicles up to 20cm long. A spectacular shrub for a conservatory or cool greenhouse. Min. 5°C. It can be kept quite compact by shortening the older growth in late winter.

Vestia foetida (Ruiz & Pavon) Hoffsgg., syn. *V. lycioides* Willd. (*Solanaceae*)   An evergreen shrub with yellow tubular flowers, native of Chile, growing in woodland, flowering in spring–summer. Erect shrub to 1.8m. Leaves 2–5cm long, elliptic to oblong, bright glossy green, unpleasantly scented when bruised. Flowers nodding, solitary or a few together in the upper leaf axils, 3cm long, tubular with 5 recurved triangular lobes. Min. −5°C.

Iochroma coccineum at the Jardin Exotique de Val Rahmeh, Menton

Vestia foetida at Kew

Iochroma coccineum

Iochroma purpureum in Nairobi

Juanulloa mexicana

Iochroma grandiflorum at La Mortola, NW Italy

Brugmansia × candida 'Knightii' in Menton

Brugmansia × candida 'Knightii' in Dali, Yunnan

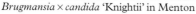

Brugmansia versicolor at Elbow Beach Hotel, Bermuda

Datura inoxia subsp. *inoxia* in Kent

Datura ceratocaula in Copala, Mazatlan, W Mexico in late October

Brugmansia × candida Pers.   An evergreen shrub (a natural hybrid between *B. aurea* and *B. versicolor*) with pendulous fragrant white, rarely yellow or pink flowers, native of Ecuador, growing in open scrub, flowering in summer–autumn. Shrub to 5m. Leaves 30-50 cm long, alternate, ovate, mostly untoothed, with wavy margins. Flowers to 30cm long, rather narrowly trumpet-shaped, with recurved lobes and a spathe-like calyx. Min. 5°C. **'Knightii'** is a selection with longer-lasting hose-in-hose double white flowers.

Brugmansia × candida 'Grand Marnier' An evergreen shrub with large fragrant soft apricot-yellow pendulous flowers, the origin of which is not recorded, although similar colour forms occur in the wild, flowering in summer–autumn. Shrub to 5m. Leaves to 50cm long, ovate, entire or toothed. Flowers trumpet-shaped, with recurved lobes and a spathe-like calyx. Min. 0°C. A beautiful shrub for a frost-free conservatory, but it appears that some plants grown under this name do not belong to *B. × candida*.

Brugmansia suaveolens (Humb. & Bonpl. ex Willd.) Bercht. & J. Presl   A large evergreen shrub with white flowers, scented at night, native of SE Brazil, growing in open forest at up to 3000m, flowering from summer–autumn. Hairless shrub to 5m. Leaves to 20cm, narrowly ovate to elliptic, entire. Flowers to 30cm long, nodding, funnel-shaped but abruptly narrowed just above the 2–5-toothed calyx, white, rarely pale yellow or pink. Min. 5°C. Widely cultivated in the tropics and subtropics, less so elsewhere.

Brugmansia versicolor Lagerh.
An evergreen shrub with very large white flowers, native of Ecuador, growing at low altitudes in the Guayaquil Basin, flowering from summer–autumn. Open-branched shrub to 5m tall. Leaves to 50cm long, oblong-elliptic, entire, hairy or hairless. Flowers up to 45cm long, with a slender tube extending beyond the calyx, then funnel-shaped with recurved teeth, white, often turning yellow or pink with age. Calyx spathe-like. Min. 5°C. The largest flowers in the genus.

Datura ceratocaula Ortega   An annual with erect fragrant white flowers, native of Mexico, growing in seasonally wet open places, flowering in summer–autumn. Bushy annual to 90cm tall, with young stems and foliage greyish-hairy. Leaves to 20cm long, ovate, with a few triangular lobes on each side, grey-hairy beneath. Flowers to 18cm long, trumpet-shaped with 5 shallow lobes alternating with 5 small teeth, white with reddish-purple marks in the throat. Fruit a smooth fleshy nodding capsule. Min. 5°C. Distinguished by its boldly lobed leaves.

Datura inoxia Mill. subsp. *inoxia* (*Solanaceae*)   A finely downy annual with upward-facing fragrant white or violet-tinted flowers, native of SW North America and Mexico, growing in open, scrubby or waste areas, flowering in summer. Bushy annual to 90cm tall, the stems purplish. Leaves to 25cm, ovate, entire or wavy-margined, dark or greyish-green. Flowers funnel-shaped, to 20cm across the rounded, 5-toothed limb, solitary in the angles of the branches. Fruit a nodding spiny capsule. Hardy to −5°C. Like all species of *Datura*, all

Brugmansia × candida double form

Datura inoxia. subsp. *quinquecuspida* by a stream in the semi-desert east of Durango, Mexico

Brugmansia suaveolens

Brugmansia suaveolens in the Botanical Garden in Pietermaritzberg, Natal

parts are toxic. The name is sometimes incorrectly spelt *innoxia*.

Datura inoxia Mill. subsp. **quinquecuspida** (Torr.) A.S. Barcl., syn. *D. wrightii* Regel
An annual or perennial of spreading habit with grey foliage and erect fragrant white or pale violet flowers, native of SW North America and N Mexico, growing in open, scrubby or waste places, flowering in summer. Annual or short-lived perennial to 1m. Leaves to 25cm long, ovate, like the stems, covered with fine grey hairs. Flowers up to 20cm long, erect, tubular with a spreading, shallowly 5-lobed rim, each borne in the axil of a branch and lasting only one night. Fruit a spiny nodding capsule. Hardy to −5°C.

Brugmansia × candida 'Grand Marnier'

Brugmansia × insignis in a cottage garden near Copala, Mazatlan, W Mexico in late October

Brugmansia × insignis in a greenhouse in Devon

Brugmansia sanguinea in California, flowering in spring with wisteria and cinerarias

Brugmansia arborea

Brugmansia arborea (L.) Lagerh., syn.
Datura cornigera Hook. (*Solanaceae*)
An evergreen shrub with fragrant white
flowers, native of the Andes of Ecuador, Peru
and northern Chile, growing at 3000–4000m,
flowering from late spring–summer. Shrub to
4m. Leaves 15–30cm ovate, entire or coarsely
toothed. Flowers 12–16cm long, nodding,
tubular funnel-shaped; calyx spathe-like, often
long pointed. Min. 5°C. Less showy than
other species; *B. × candida* is frequently grown
under this name.

Brugmansia aurea Lagerh.   A small
spreading evergreen tree with night-scented

Brugmansia aurea at Château de la Guaroupe, S France

Brugmansia aurea

Brugmansia sanguinea var. *flava* in the gardens at Quinta da Palheiro, Madeira

Brugmansia sanguinea 'Golden Queen' from Reads' Nursery, Norfolk

white or golden-yellow flowers, native of the Andes from Colombia to Ecuador, growing at around 3000m. Laxly branched tree to 10m. Leaves 15–25cm long, ovate, entire but strongly toothed on young plants, downy or smooth. Flowers 15–25cm long, trumpet-shaped, flaring widely into 5 recurved, long-pointed lobes. Calyx slender, with 2–5 teeth. Min. 5°C. A showy species with elegantly shaped flowers.

Brugmansia × insignis (Barb. Rodr.) Lockwood   An evergreen shrub with large fragrant white, pink or yellow flowers, a backcross of *B. suaveolens × B. versicolor* to the first parent, growing wild in the lower Peruvian Andes and widely cultivated elsewhere in South and Central America, flowering in summer–autumn. Shrub to 4m. Leaves to 25cm, alternate, ovate or elliptic, entire, hairless. Flowers pendent, trumpet-shaped, to 35cm long, with recurved lobes and a slightly inflated, spathe-like, finely downy calyx. Min. 0°C. A showy and variable hybrid with some named colour forms, sometimes sold as *B. versicolor* with pink flowers.

Brugmansia sanguinea (Ruiz & Pavon) D. Don, syn. *D. rosei* Safford   An evergreen shrub with tubular red, orange or yellow flowers, native of an area from Colombia to northern Chile, at altitudes about 3000m, flowering from late spring–autumn. Lax shrub to 10m. Leaves to 20cm long, ovate, entire or coarsely toothed with wavy margins, velvety hairy. Flowers 15–25cm long, scentless, almost cylindrical with a short recurved limb, orange-red with a yellow tube. Calyx inflated, with 1–4 teeth. Min. –3°C. The showiest and most vividly coloured of the species.

Brugmansia sanguinea var. *flava,* syn. *D. chlorantha* Hook.   Flowers yellow. **'Golden Queen'** Flowers orange-yellow; introduced by Reads' Nursery, Norfolk, England.

Solandra grandiflora at the Fairchild Arboretum, Florida

Solandra maxima in the intermediate conservatory at Wisley

Brunfelsia americana in the British Virgin Islands

Brunfelsia pauciflora in Nairobi

Brunfelsia americana in Bermuda

Solandra longiflora in Bermuda

Brunfelsia pauciflora 'Macrantha' in California

Browallia speciosa 'Blue Troll' and 'White Troll'

Petunia axillaris

Brunfelsia pauciflora 'Macrantha' in the Temperate House at Kew

Browallia speciosa Hook. (*Solanaceae*)
A bushy perennial with star-shaped purple, blue or white flowers, native of Colombia, growing in evergreen forest at low altitudes, flowering in summer. Woody-based perennial to 1.5m tall. Leaves 5–9cm, ovate, slightly sticky, with strongly impressed veins. Flowers up to 5cm across the pointed ovate lobes, with a slender tube about 2.5cm long, solitary or in small clusters in the leaf axils. Min. 12°C. Usually grown as an annual in temperate regions, where various selections have been made, varying in habit and flower colour. **'Blue Troll'** and **'White Troll'** are shown here in the same photograph: they are particularly compact cultivars, 25–30cm tall.

Brunfelsia americana L. (*Solanaceae*)
A shrub or small tree with long-tubed white flowers soon fading to creamy yellow and very fragrant at night, native of the West Indies, growing in evergreen forest at low altitudes, flowering in summer. Shrub or small tree to 5m tall. Leaves 5–13cm long, elliptic or obovate, rather leathery. Flowers solitary at the ends of the branches, 4–7cm across, with a slender, slightly curved tube to 7cm long and 5 spreading, wavy-edged lobes; calyx short, bell-shaped. Min. 10°C. Widely cultivated in warm regions for its scented flowers.

Brunfelsia pauciflora (Cham. & Schltdl.) Benth., syn. *B. calycina* Benth. A compact evergreen shrub with flowers that open rich violet-purple, soon fading to near white in the wild type, native of Brazil, flowering in spring–summer. Shrub to 3m. Leaves 7–15cm long, elliptic to oblong-lanceolate, blunt or acute, leathery. Flowers to 7cm across the wavy lobes, with a narrow tube about half as long, mostly within the tubular calyx. Min. 10°C. Deservedly the most popular species. **'Macrantha'** has especially large flowers which fade less than the type.

Petunia axillaris (Lam.) BSP. (*Solanaceae*)
A spreading or erect annual with dull white flowers, scented at night, native of southern Argentina, Brazil and Uruguay, growing in open places, flowering in summer. Annual, variable in habit, to 60cm tall. Leaves to 10cm, ovate, entire, covered with fine sticky hairs. Flowers 5cm across, dull white or buff-white, with a slender tube 5–6cm long. Min. 5°C. Largely supplanted in gardens by the more showy hybrid petunias, but well worth growing for the nocturnally fragrant flowers.

Solandra grandiflora Swartz. (*Solanaceae*)
A rampant evergreen climber with large white to yellow trumpet-shaped scented flowers, native of the West Indies and tropical America, climbing into the tops of huge forest trees, flowering in March–December. Climber to 25m or more. Leaves elliptic to oblong, 10–12cm long. Calyx 7–8cm, sheath-like, with 2–3 lanceolate lobes; corolla 18–20cm long, 8–11cm across at the mouth, opening white,

becoming yellow by the third day. Spectacular where it has enough space. Min. 5°C.

Solandra longiflora Tussac. An evergreen climber with large white to yellow trumpet-shaped flowers, opening and scented in the evening, native of the West Indies, climbing into trees, flowering in March onwards. Climber to 25m, but often less. Leaves elliptic to oblanceolate, 6–10cm long. Calyx 7.5–10cm with 2–3 lanceolate lobes; corolla 20–25cm long, around 13cm across when fully expanded, opening white, becoming yellow by the third day. Corolla tube very long, the narrow part well-exserted from the calyx, the lobes frilled on the margins. A smaller species which can be pruned to make a large wall-shrub. Min. 5°C.

Solandra maxima (Sessé & Mocino) P. S. Green A rampant evergreen climber with large yellow trumpet-shaped scented flowers, native of Mexico, in Guerrero, Oaxaca, Puebla and Vera Cruz states, climbing into the tops of huge forest trees, flowering in March–December. Climber to 50m or more. Leaves broadly elliptic, 10–12cm long. Calyx deeply lobed, 6cm with 5 lanceolate lobes; corolla 16–18cm long, 20–25cm across at the mouth when fully spread, lobes recurving and deepening in colour to brownish-yellow by the third day. The flowers open much wider than those of *S. grandiflora*. Needs a dry winter rest to flower well. Min. 0°C.

Verbena cf. *bipinnatifida*, covering the ground after a forest fire between Linares and Saltillo in NE Mexico

Verbena cf. *bipinnatifida*

Verbena rigida 'Polaris' at Auckland Botanic Garden

Verbena 'Pink Parfait'

Verbena 'Silver Anne'

Verbena scabridoglandulosa at Harry Hay's

Lantana camara 'Arlequin' in the garden at Herrenhausen, Hanover

Lantana camara 'Naide' in the garden at Herrenhausen, Hanover

Lantana montevidensis in Nairobi

Lantana camara 'Spreading Sunset' at Huntington Gardens, Los Angeles

Lantana camara L. (*Verbenaceae*)
An evergreen shrub with small bright yellow to orange flowers, turning to red with age, native of tropical America, growing in open woodland, often colonising disturbed ground, and now found in quantity throughout the tropics, flowering from late spring–autumn. Shrub 1–2m tall, with somewhat prickly stems bearing opposite, finely wrinkled ovate leaves 5–10cm long, the margins slightly toothed. Flowers salver-shaped, 8–10mm wide, carried in rounded terminal clusters 3–5cm across. Min. 5°C. Long cultivated, this species has given rise to many cultivars in a range of colours. All parts are considered toxic if eaten, but the flowers are greatly loved by butterflies. The following cultivars are shown here:
'Arlequin' Flowers opening pale yellow from pink buds and ageing abruptly to pink.
'Naide' Flowers creamy-yellow, fading to almost white.
'Spreading Sunset' Flowers opening deep yellow from red buds and ageing abruptly to cerise-pink.

Lantana montevidensis Briq. A spreading and scrambling sub-shrub, with pale magenta flowers, not changing colour, native of Uruguay and naturalised in California, growing in dry sunny places, flowering in summer. Stems to 1m or more; leaves ovate, 2–5cm long. Flowerheads 2.5–3cm across. A good and easily grown plant for sprawling over a bank or sunny slope. Min. –8°C. There is also a white form.

Verbena bipinnatifida Nutt. (*Verbenaceae*)
A spreading perennial with vivid magenta flowers in small clusters, native of S North America and Mexico. This photograph, taken between Linares and Saltillo in NE Mexico, in a woodland clearing after a fire, shows the open scrub or wasteland habitat typical of many members of this genus. Perennial forming wide spreading mats to 30cm tall and up to 90cm wide. Leaves deeply dissected and 3–6cm long. Flowers 6–8mm wide, with deep magenta-rose (sometimes pink, purple or violet) notched petals, over a long period in summer and early autumn. Min. –3°C.

Verbena × hybrida 'Pink Parfait'
A compact low-growing perennial to 60cm across with sweetly fragrant pink and white flowers in rounded clusters over much of the summer and early autumn. A selection of *V. × hybrida*, a complex group derived from *V. incisa*, *V. peruviana*, *V. phlogiflora* and *V. teucrioides*. Stems to 30 cm tall. Leaves 3–6cm long, ovate, regularly and deeply toothed or lobed. Flowers 8mm wide, opening from red buds to light crimson with a white eye, but quickly fading almost to white, giving a distinct bicolored effect. Hardy to –3°C.

Verbena × hybrida 'Silver Anne'
Low-growing perennial usually grown as an annual and tending to legginess in its second and subsequent years, producing an abundance of deep rosy-pink flowers that fade to pale pink in summer and early autumn.

Perennial to 30cm tall, making a mat to 90cm wide. Leaves 8cm long, ovate, deeply toothed, borne in pairs on the wiry stems. Flowers fragrant, 12mm across, with 5 notched petals in flat corymbs to 5cm wide. Min. –3°C. Somewhat susceptible to mildew.

Verbena rigida Spreng., syn. *V. venosa* Gillies & Hook. A bushy tuberous-rooted perennial with flat corymbs of fragrant purplish flowers, native of Argentina and S Brazil, growing in open, scrubby places. Several different cultivars have been selected recently, which make good plants in hot summers.
'Polaris' is a compact selection, up to 60cm tall and wide; leaves paired, coarsely toothed oblong, to 7cm long; corymbs of pale lilac-blue flowers 5cm wide, each floret 8mm across, produced from early summer to autumn. Hardy to –5°C, if the roots are not frozen.

Verbena scabridoglandulosa Turrill
A low stiffly branched, open sub-shrub with small heads of sweet-scented pale lilac or white flowers, native of exposed rocky habitats in the Andean foothills of Argentina, at up to 1300m. First introduced by Harold Comber in 1925. Sub-shrub to 45cm tall, with tiny thyme-like entire leaves 5–10mm long. Flowers 8mm wide, with wedge-shaped corolla-lobes, up to 12 in a long-stalked dense raceme which elongates as the seeds develop. Hardy to –5°C, given a sheltered sunny position in a well-drained soil.

Clerodendrum philippinum at Wisley

Clerodendrum × speciosum in Chicago Botanic Garden

Clerodendrum paniculatum

Clerodendrum myricoides 'Ugandense' at Kew

Clerodendrum aculeatum (L.)
Schlechtend. (*Verbenaceae*)   An evergreen
vine-like shrub with small clusters of tubular
white or pink-flushed flowers, native of open
scrub at low altitudes in the West Indies,
flowering in the summer–autumn. Shrub to
3m, climbing with the aid of paired prickles on
the stems. Leaves 4–7cm long, elliptic to
oblong, entire. Flowers 5–10 in axillary cymes,
narrowly trumpet-shaped with a slender tube
to 2cm and five spreading or recurved lobes
8mm long, white with a pink flush on the
tube, with long-exserted pink stamens.
Min. 10°C. Distinct in its climbing habit and
neat foliage.

Clerodendrum myricoides (Hochst.) Vatke
'Ugandense', syn. *C. ugandense* Prain, Blue
Glory Bower   An erect hairless evergreen
shrub with pale or deep violet-blue flowers,
native of tropical West Africa, flowering in
summer–autumn. Shrub to 3m tall, with
opposite, elliptic, slightly toothed leaves
5–10cm long. Panicles terminal, up to 15cm
long. Flowers 2.5cm long, pale or deep violet-
blue or bicolored white and blue, with slender
tubes and 5 irregular lobes, the lowest longer
and deeper coloured than the others. Stamens
as long as corolla, strongly down-curved. Min.
10°C. Valued for its unusual flower colour.

Clerodendrum paniculatum L. Pagoda
Flower   A small evergreen shrub with
spectacular conical panicles of small scarlet or
reddish-orange flowers, native of SE Asia,
growing in woodland margins and clearings,
flowering in summer–autumn. Erect shrub to
1.2m tall. Leaves ovate, 15–25cm long, mostly
3- to 5-lobed, the upper ones often simple.
The flowers are pale or deep scarlet, 10mm
across the lobes, with slender tubes to 15mm
long, and exserted stamens borne in tiers
forming a broad panicle to 30cm long.
Min. 10°C.

Clerodendrum philippinum Schauer, syn.
C. fragrans Willd. 'Pleniflorum'   An evergreen
shrub with fragrant pink-flushed double
flowers, the single form native of S China and
possibly S Japan, but commonly naturalised in
the tropics and subtropics, especially in its
double form which flowers over a long period
in summer. Erect shrub to 3m. Leaves long-
stalked, the blades to 25cm, broadly triangular
or ovate, toothed or entire, softly hairy.
Flowers fragrant, double, pale pink, about
2.5cm wide in dense clusters. Min. 10°C. A
compact and long-flowering shrub well-suited
to a smaller conservatory.

Clerodendrum speciosissimum Van Geert
An evergreen shrub with large panicles of
bright scarlet flowers, native of the island of
Java where it grows in forest clearings in low
mountains, flowering in summer–autumn.
Upright shrub 1–4m tall. Leaves to 30cm
long, ovate, with a slender tapering point and
heart-shaped base, rather hairy on both
surfaces and with a characteristic odour
common in the genus. Panicles to 45cm long.
Flowers with a slender tube 3–5cm long and
about 2.5cm across the 5 spreading lobes,
followed by dark blue berries. Min. 10°C.

Clerodendrum × speciosum Dombr. Java
Glory Bean   An evergreen twining shrub
with dull red flowers, each set in a
conspicuous pinkish calyx, this is a hybrid
between *C. splendens* and *C. thomsoniae*, both
native of tropical Africa, in spite of the
common name. Shrub twining to 4m. Leaves
ovate, to 15cm long, the margins entire.
Flowers dull red, with a slender tube to 2cm
long, about 2cm across the spreading rounded
lobes; stamens long, well exserted from the
tube; calyx bell-shaped, pinkish white,
remaining colourful long after the flowers fall.
Min. 10°C. Less showy than *C. thomsoniae* but
perhaps more easily grown.

Clerodendrum speciosissimum in San Francisco in August

Clerodendrum thomsoniae

Clerodendrum speciosissimum in the Harry P. Leu Gardens, Florida

Clerodendrum thomsoniae Balf. Bleeding Heart   A hairless twining evergreen climber with showy clusters of crimson flowers, each with a contrasting white calyx, native of West Africa from Senegal to Cameroon, growing in clearings in deciduous forest, flowering in summer. Twining shrub to 4m or more. Leaves opposite, 10–15cm long, ovate, with impressed veins and tapering abruptly to a short drip-tip. Flowers 2cm across, with 5 rounded deep crimson lobes and a slender tube 2cm long, equalling the bell-shaped, pure white calyx; borne in terminal and axillary clusters. Fruit a dark red or black berry. Min. 10°C. Needs good drainage and flowers freely when young.

Clerodendrum aculeatum in Bermuda

LABIATAE

Hemiandra pungens in Perth

Westringia fruticosa in Bermuda

Westringia 'Wynyabbie Gem'

Hemiandra pungens R. Br. (*Labiatae*)
A low spreading shrub with linear to linear-lanceolate leaves and white, pink or lilac flowers, conspicuously spotted in the throat, native of Western Australia, growing in heathland on sandy soils, flowering mainly in October–January. A variable plant, usually prostrate, but up to 1.5m in some forms. Leaves 1–3cm long. Flowers to 2cm long. For full sun and well-drained soil, and tolerant of drought. Min. –3°C.
H. linearis Benth. has larger flowers, to 4cm long, with spotting extending onto the lobes of the lower lip. *H. gardneri* O. Sarg. is bright red.

Prostanthera incisa R. Br., syn. *P. sieberi* Benth. An erect open shrub with ovate coarsely toothed, rather thin leaves and purple flowers, native of New South Wales, growing in wet sclerophyll forest and on the edges of rainforest, flowering in spring. Shrub to 3m high. Leaves ovate to oblong, dark green above, paler beneath, to 1.5cm long, cuneate at base. Flowers in short, sometimes leafy spikes of 4–8, with corolla 7–10mm long. For a sunny position and well-drained soil. Min. –5°C.

Prostanthera nivea A.M. Cunn. ex Benth. (*Labiatae*) A loose, erect or spreading shrub with linear leaves and white or rarely mauve flowers, native of Queensland, New South Wales and Victoria, growing in open woodland and heathland, in shallow sandy soils, flowering in spring. Shrub to 4m high and wide. Leaves 1–5cm long, acute, margins inrolled. Flowers with calyx 6–8mm, corolla 14–18mm long, pubescent, pale to deep mauve in var. *induta* Benth. For a sunny position and careful pruning after flowering to prevent the plant becoming straggly. Min. –5°C. The genus *Prostanthera* has around 100 species, all endemic to Australia.

Prostanthera ovalifolia R. Br. An upright shrub with lanceolate to ovate leaves and purple or rarely white flowers shaded with purple, native of Queensland, Victoria and New South Wales, growing in wet or dry sclerophyll forest on sandstone, flowering in August–November (spring). Shrub to 4m high. Leaves to 4cm long, dull green. Flowers with calyx 2–3mm long, corolla 6–10mm long. For a sunny position and well-drained soil. One of the most free-flowering species, but likely to be short-lived in gardens. In Australia many *Prostanthera* species are grafted onto *Westringia fruticosa* at the cutting stage to provide a hardier and more reliable root

system, resistant to root rot in warm, wet conditions. Min. –5°C.

Prostanthera 'Poorinda Ballerina' and **'Poorinda Pixie'** are two good cultivars from Australia.

Prostanthera rotundifolia R. Br. Mint Bush A rounded shrub with almost round, sometimes toothed leaves and purple or rarely pink flowers, native of New South Wales, Victoria and Tasmania, growing in sandy soils over sandstone on rainforest edges and sheltered spots in sclerophyll forest, flowering in September–November (spring). Shrub to 3m high. Leaves dark green above, paler beneath, to 1cm long, rounded at apex, cuneate at base. Flowers with calyx 4–5mm, corolla to 10-15mm long. For a sunny position and well-drained soil. A free-flowering species, differing from *P. ovalifolia* in its smaller rounded leaves. Min. –5°C.

Prostanthera rotundifolia R. Br. f. **rosea**, syn. *P.* 'Chelsea Pink' A beautiful pink form of *Prostanthera rotundifolia*, which occurs wild with the purple one. Leaves grey-green; anthers conspicuously mauve. A lovely plant for spring colour in the conservatory and for its leaf scent throughout the year. Min. –5°C.

Prostanthera rotundifolia R. Br. **'Glen Davis'** A clone of *Prostanthera rotundifolia*, selected in Australia, forming a stronger-growing, more upright shrub than the usual type. Min. –5°C.

Westringia fruticosa (Willd.) Druce, syn. *W. rosmariniformis* Smith (*Labiatae*) Coastal Rosemary A dense rounded shrub, upright when young, with linear leaves and white flowers, native of New South Wales, growing in bare places and cliffs near the sea, flowering most of the year. Shrub to 2m high, 4m across, which can be clipped to shape. Leaves in whorls of 4, 1–3cm long, Flowers with a 5-lobed calyx, which helps to distinguish it from the 2-lobed calyx of *Prostanthera*; corolla 10–14mm across. For a sunny position and well-drained soil. Very tolerant of drought and of salt wind; often used as a rootstock for *Prostanthera*. Min. –5°C, perhaps.

Westringia 'Wynyabbie Gem' A hybrid between *W. fruticosa* and *W. eremicola*, with purple flowers. Plant to 1.3m tall, 1.5m across, with blue-mauve flowers throughout the year. A tough shrub for a sunny position. Min. –3°C.

Prostanthera rotundifolia 'Glen Davis'

Prostanthera rotundifolia at Derry Watkin's

Prostanthera
'Poorinda Ballerina'

Prostanthera
rotundifolia rosea

Prostanthera ovalifolia

Prostanthera incisa

Prostanthera nivea

Prostanthera 'Poorinda Pixie'

Specimens from Green Farm Plants, 20 April, ¾ life-size

LABIATAE

Prostanthera lasianthos in the Dandenong Hills, east of Melbourne

Prostanthera lasianthos

Prostanthera striatiflora

Prostanthera aspalathoides A. M. Cunn. ex Benth. (*Labiatae*)   A rounded shrub with linear sticky glandular leaves and yellow, orange or red tubular flowers, native of Queensland, New South Wales, Victoria and South Australia, growing in sandy and stony, sometimes calcareous soils in low scrub, flowering in spring. Shrub to 70cm high. Leaves to 1.5–6mm long. Flowers with calyx to 5–7mm, corolla to 10–20mm long For a sunny position and well-drained sandy soil. Min. –3°C.

Prostanthera baxteri A. M. Cunn. ex Benth.   An upright shrub with linear, silvery leaves and purple flowers with dark stripes in the throat, native of South Australia and Western Australia, growing in scrub, flowering in spring. Shrub to 2m high. Leaves terete, to 2cm long. Flowers with calyx to 3mm, corolla to 12mm long. For a sunny position and well-drained soil. Min. –3°C.

Prostanthera cuneata   Benth. Alpine Mint Bush   A low rounded shrub with thick dark green crowded leaves and white flowers, native of New South Wales, Victoria and Tasmania growing in subalpine heath and scrub, often under snowgums, in rocky granite soil, flowering mainly in spring. Shrub to 1m high, 1.5m across. Leaves to 4–5mm long, cuneate at base, rounded at apex. Flowers with purple blotches in the throat, to 10–15mm long. For a sunny position and well-drained soil. The hardiest species. Min. –10°C.

Prostanthera lasianthos Labill.
An upright shrub or small tree with lanceolate to ovate leaves and purple or rarely white flowers shaded with purple, native of Queensland, Victoria, New South Wales and Tasmania, growing in rainforest, sclerophyll forest or subalpine forest, mainly in gullies and by streams, flowering in November–March (summer). Tree to 6m high. Leaves 4–12cm long, dark green, paler beneath. Flowers with calyx 3–4mm long, corolla 10–15mm long. For a sunny position and well-drained but moist soil. Min. –3°C.
Prostanthera lasianthos var. **subcoriacea** Has smaller leaves 3–4.5cm long, with toothed margins; it forms a compact shrub in exposed rocky places at 100–1350m in New South Wales and Victoria. Flowers similar to the type variety. Probably hardier, to –5°C.

Prostanthera saxicola R. Br. var. **montana** A. A. Ham.   A low spreading shrub with linear to elliptic leathery leaves and white flowers with purple stripes in the throat, native of New South Wales, growing in heaths or dry sclerophyll forest on sandstone, flowering in September–February (summer). Shrub to 1m high. Leaves to 6–15mm long, 2–6mm wide. Flowers with calyx 5–6mm long, corolla 10–12mm long. For a sunny position and well-drained sandy soil. Min. –5°C.

Prostanthera striatiflora F. Muell.
An upright shrub with narrowly ovate to elliptic leaves and white flowers with purple

Prostanthera cuneata in Devon

Prostanthera baxteri at Bill Grant's, California

Prostanthera lasianthos var. *subcoriacea* near Melbourne

Prostanthera saxicola var. *montana* from Green
Farm Plants

Prostanthera lasianthos var. *subcoriacea*

Prostanthera walteri

lines inside, native of Queensland, Northern
Territories, Western Australia, South Australia
and New South Wales, growing in dry rocky
places in semi-arid areas, flowering in
July–November (spring). Shrub to 2m high.
Leaves to 3cm long, bright green. Flowers
with calyx 6–10mm long, corolla 10–17mm
long. For a sunny position and dry well-
drained soil. Min. 0°C.

Prostanthera walteri F. Muell.   A low
spreading shrub with dark green leaves and
blue-green flowers, veined with purple, native
of New South Wales and Victoria, growing in
Eucalyptus forest on granite soils, at
1000–1400m, flowering in spring. Shrub to
2m and more across. Leaves ovate to almost
rhombic, 1–3cm long. Flowers rather sparse,
in the leaf axils, with calyx 10–12mm long,
corolla 15–26mm long. For sandy well-
drained soil, but often short-lived. Min. –3C.
For some reason the strange blue-green
flowers appear brownish on our colour film.

Prostanthera aspalathoides near Melbourne

Prostanthera aspalathoides red form

Salvia × jamensis, a mixture of red and orange near Los Lirios, NE Mexico

Salvia coccinea Juss. ex J. Murray
A spreading perennial best treated as a showy
annual, originally native of central Mexico,
but now with a cosmopolitan distribution as
an introduced ornamental, growing in open
cultivated places or by roadsides, flowering
throughout summer. Stems spreading to
90cm tall, much-branched, covered in short
and long hairs; leaves smelling like those of
dead nettles, deltoid-ovate, both surfaces
pubescent, lower greyish, margins crenate-
serrate; flowers 3–6 in whorls on interrupted
racemes to 30cm long; corolla tube straight,
to 15mm long, stamens prominently exserted.
Easily cultivated but prone to white fly attack
under glass; plants seldom live tidily for more
than one season. There are many cultivated
varieties in a range of colours from salmon to
scarlet, pink and white. Min. 0°C.

Salvia greggii A. Gray   A short much-
branched shrub with narrow elliptic leaves
and pinkish-red flowers, native to S Texas
south to central Mexico, growing among rocks
in open situations in the mountains, flowering
continuously from mid- to late summer and
into autumn. Stems thin, woody below,
glandular above to 50cm high; leaves to 3cm,
simple, sessile to shortly petiolate, commonly
elliptic to linear, glabrous but glandular

punctate, margin entire; flowers red, pink or
rarely white, borne in pairs on racemes to
15cm long; corolla tube to 22mm long, upper
lip to 13mm long. Easy to grow in dry sunny
positions. Min. –10°C.

Salvia × jamensis J. Compton   A hybrid
between *S. greggii* and *S. microphylla* found
originally by John Fairey of Yucca Do
Nursery, Texas, in a valley near Saltillo in NE
Mexico. Intermediate in leaf between the
parents, with elliptic to ovate leaves often
somewhat serrate-crenate, but exhibiting great
variation in flower colour from yellow and
peach to palest pink. The following are among
several colour forms that have been named:
'La Luna'   Cream coloured flowers and rust
coloured hairs on the upper corolla lip.
'Pat Vlasto'   Apricot-pink flowers.

Salvia microphylla Kunth, syn. *S. grahamii*
Benth. *S. microphylla* Kunth var. *neurepia*
(Fern.) Epling   A spreading shrub with
woody branches and glandular aromatic
leaves and pink or red flowers, native of the
mountains of central and north Mexico,
flowering continuously from early summer to
October. Shrub to 1.2m; leaves variable,
commonly ovate or deltoid-ovate to ovate-
elliptic, apex obtuse, surfaces finely

hispidulous, margin crenate-serrate; flowers
opposite in pairs on elongating racemes to
20cm long; corolla folded below and swollen
near the base; tube 16–22mm long, upper lip
hooded, lower broadly spreading. Easily
cultivated in a well drained compost and full
sun. Min. –10°C. A herbal tea is made from
the leaves which is called *mirto de montes*.
Several selected forms have been named,
including 'Newby Hall' which has leaves to
6cm long, softly pubescent on both surfaces,
with rich scarlet flowers, and 'Cerro Potosi',
with vibrant magenta flowers, which was
collected from the mountain of that name at
3300m in NE Mexico.

Salvia microphylla Kunth var. **wislizenii**
A. Gray, syn. *S. lemmoni* A. Gray   A spreading
shrub to 1m tall, native of S Arizona and New
Mexico and NW Mexico growing in rocky
barren places in the mountains. Differs from
var. *microphylla* in its deltoid acute to
acuminate leaves 2–3cm long, often somewhat
glaucous, and the shorter inflorescences
bearing deep magenta flowers. Needs full sun.
Min. –5°C.
'Raspberry Royale'   An American variety
which makes a neat shrub with a tight habit
and deep magenta flowers. 'Plum Wine' is
similar but has darker flowers.

Salvia × *jamensis* pink form

Salvia × *jamensis* 'Pat Vlasto'

Salvia × *jamensis* 'La Luna'

Salvia coccinea at Harry Hay's

Salvia microphylla var. *wislizenii* 'Raspberry Royale'

Salvia greggii in a hot dry limestone riverbed
in NE Mexico

Salvia microphylla among agaves and dwarf pines near Los Lirios, NE Mexico

161

Salvia involucrata 'Mrs Pope'

Salvia madrensis above Copala, SW Mexico

Salvia madrensis

Salvia involucrata 'Bethellii'

Salvia confertiflora at Home Covert, Roundway, Wiltshire

Salvia leucantha

Salvia confertiflora Pohl.   A large upright perennial with deep tawny red velvety flowers, native of lowland woods in Brazil, flowering in July–October in cultivation. Stems to 1.5m. Leaves broadly ovate to 20cm long, covered on both surfaces with a tawny pubescence, foul-smelling when bruised. Flowers in tight many-flowered whorls borne on long straight inflorescences to 45cms. Calyx and corolla both red, densely pubescent. Prone to whitefly under glass but spectacular when grown well. Min. 0°C.

Salvia fulgens Cav.   A tall upright perennial, woody at base with scarlet velvety flowers, native of C Mexico, growing in forest clearings in the mountains, flowering in midsummer–autumn. Stems to 1.2m, glandular pubescent above; leaves deltoid-ovate, 3–6cm long, margin crenate, surfaces hirtellous, paler beneath; flowers in whorls of 2–6 on lax racemes to 50 cm long; bracts green, often large, 5–30 mm long, acuminate, deciduous; corolla tube folded at base, 20–40mm long, upper lip pilose, lower lip not spreading. A prolific grower needing plenty of space to increase by means of short subterranean rhizomes. Flowering can occur in cultivation in full sun from late summer–autumn. Min. 0°C.

Salvia involucrata Cav., syn. *S. puberula* Fern.   An upright perennial with large ovate or orbicular brightly coloured pink bracts and bright magenta flowers, native of S Mexico, growing in woodland, flowering in August–October. Stems shortly branched to 1.2m. Leaves to 10cm, ovate, glabrous to densely glandular pubescent. Racemes to 30cm. Bracts, soon falling. Corolla to 3cm long. Flowers best in full sun with plenty of water. Can be cut back to the ground each spring. Min –10°C.
'Bethellii'   Produces tight spherical inflorescence buds, bracts orbicular.
'Mrs Pope'   Has elongated loose-flowered inflorescences, bracts ovate, acuminate often curled at apex. 'El Butano' (*not shown*), is a very pubescent elongate flowering form.

Salvia leucantha Cav.   A spreading perennial, quite distinct on account of its densely velvety stems and flowers, native of S Mexico, flowering in July–November or later. Stems to 1m, shortly branched near apex, densely white lanate above. Leaves linear to lanceolate, white pubescent below.

Salvia regla

Inflorescence racemose to 25cm. Calyx tubular with dense violet-purple pubescence. Corolla to 2cm, white, sometimes lilac or purple, pubescent. In frosty climates often put out in spring to flower in summer. Min. 0°C.

Salvia madrensis Seem.   A tall herbaceous perennial with large heart-shaped leaves and very showy golden yellow flowers, native of the warm lower regions of the Sierra Madre Occidentale in NW Mexico, growing in partially shaded forest margins and along cliff bases, flowering in September–October. Vigorous perennial herb to 2m, with prominently quadrangular stems, glandular-hispid on the inflorescence; leaves simple, petiolate, cordate, 8–18cm long, pubescent above, margin serrate-crenate; flowers in whorls of 6–12, on racemes to 50cm long; calyces golden-yellow, densely viscid; corolla tube yellow, 18–20mm long, upper lip golden pubescent. Plants need plenty of pot space, light and heat, especially early in the year, to encourage growth and flowering. Min. 5°C.

Salvia regla Cav.   An erect shrub, often with deep reddish stems and large bright scarlet flowers, native of Texas and E Mexico to Oaxaca, growing in dry scrub in the mountains, flowering in late autumn, in cultivation from October onwards. Stems upright, glabrous, to 2m tall; leaves 2–5cm long, simple, deltoid to subreniform, margin crenate, upper surface glabrous, lower glandular-punctate; corolla tube straight, 3–4cm long; stamens occasionally slightly exserted. The leaves may become deciduous below 4°C, but the plant may survive –5°C.

Salvia fulgens in the wet mountain forests above Anguangueo in C Mexico

Salvia regla among limestone rocks near Los Lirios, NE Mexico

Salvia africana-lutea in Huntington Gardens, San Merino, Los Angeles

Salvia mexicana wild in a hedge south of Lake Chapala, W Mexico

Salvia africana-coerulea L.   A spreading shrub with blue flowers, native of South Africa in the S and E Cape, growing on dry rocky hillsides and sandy flats, flowering in June–January, but mainly late summer–autumn in cultivation. Stems to 2.5m, pungently aromatic, much-branched. Leaves elliptic to obovate strongly sinuate-crenate, glandular pubescent, grey-green below, green above. Flowers in loose whorls. Calyx strongly accrescent, expanding in fruit, campanulate, veins often red. Corolla to 3cm, rarely violet or pink or white with yellow markings; upper lip strongly falcate. Min 0°C.

Salvia africana-lutea L., syn. *S. aurea* L. A spreading shrub with greyish leaves and brownish flowers, native of South Africa in the S and E Cape and in Namaqualand, growing on dry hillsides and fynbos near the sea, flowering in June–December. Stems to 1m tall, pungently aromatic. Leaves suborbicular to obovate, sparsely pubescent, entire or crenulate, white tomentose below. Flowers in short racemes to 10cm. Calyx campanulate, accrescent, purple tinged in fruit. Corolla to 3cm, occasionally mauve, upper lip strongly falcate. Min. 0°C.

Salvia darcyi J. Compton   An upright much-branched, strongly glandular aromatic perennial with bright scarlet flowers, native of Mexico in Nuevo Leon in a deep rocky ravine, flowering in July–October. Plant stoloniferous forming a large spreading clump when well grown; stems rather brittle to 1.5m tall. Leaves deltoid-cordate, bases rounded cordate becoming shallowly cuneate, glandular pubescent, crenate-serrate. Inflorescence racemose to 25cm long. Flowers in whorls of 6; calyx tubular, glandular-pubescent. Corolla to 3cm or more, upper lip longer than lower. A very easy species to cultivate, first found by Compton, d'Arcy and Rix during the autumn of 1991. Ideal in the glasshouse on account of its brittle branches. Full sun. Min −5°C.

Salvia dorisiana at Clos du Peyronnet, Menton, S France

Salvia africana-coerulea in the National Botanic Gardens, Kirstenbosch, Cape Town

Salvia darcyi, the original wild plant in Nuevo Leon, Mexico

Salvia gesneriflora

Salvia darcyi detail at Quince House, Devon

Salvia dorisiana Standl.   A highly aromatic perennial smelling of sweet pineapple, native of Honduras and Central America, growing in forest clearings, flowering in the winter months under glass at 15°C. Stems villose, glandular throughout, to 2m tall. Leaves to 18cm, glandular, villose, cordate, serrate. Inflorescence to 20cm, racemose, flowers in whorls. Corolla 5cm long, villose, magenta. Min 2°C.

Salvia gesneriflora Lindl. & Paxton   A tall perennial, shrubby at the base with bright scarlet densely pubescent flowers, native of upland C Mexico, growing in large clumps in open places, flowering intermittently from March–November. Sprawling vigorous shrub with many soft branches. Stems 1–3m tall, glandular villose. Leaves ovate to cordate, glandular villose. Inflorescence racemose or paniculate, racemes to 20cm long. Flowers to 5cm long. This species can be well trained against a glasshouse wall, pruned hard after flowering to promote plenty of new flowering growth. Full sun is best. Min 0°C.

Salvia mexicana L.   A tall perennial, shrubby at the base, flowers with a green or black calyx and a deep blue corolla, native of Mexico where it is common and variable from the Sierra Madre Occidentale southwards, growing in hedges and open woods, flowering in August–December. Stems 1.5–4m tall. Leaves ovate, dark green and glossy, 6–15cm long. Inflorescence a loose spike to 50cm. Calyx to 17mm; corolla 4–5cm long, the upper lip longer. Best in partial shade in hot areas, sun elsewhere. Late-flowering plants in cultivation need protection from early frosts. Min. −5°C if the roots are protected. When we photographed this plant, a group of hummingbirds were squabbling noisily over it. 'Ocampo' is a fine form introduced by the Yucca Do Nursery from Tamaulipas, in eastern Mexico.

Salvia guaranitica 'Blue Enigma' at the Chelsea Physic Garden

Salvia iodantha at 2400m above Copala in Mazatlan, W Mexico

Salvia guaranitica 'Black and Blue' in the Chelsea Physic Garden, London

Salvia concolor in the cold greenhouse at Quince House, Devon

Salvia atrocyanea in the Chelsea Physic Garden, London

Salvia atrocyanea Epling   A tall-growing perennial, native of forest clearings in the Bolivian mountains, flowering in late summer and autumn, dormant in winter. Upright stems to 2m arising from thick fleshy tubers. Leaves softly pubescent, ovate, 6–10cm long. Inflorescence racemose to 40cm long; flowers in whorls of 3–6; bracts persistent under each flower, large and showy to 2cm, broadly ovate usually tinged deep blue. Corolla deep blue, 2.5cm long. This showy salvia can be left to dry out almost entirely during winter on account of its large tubers. Stems can be cut back to reduce height at flowering. Min. –2°C.

Salvia concolor Benth.   A tall upright perennial with deep blue flowers, native of C Mexico, growing on the lower wooded slopes of volcanoes, flowering from late summer into winter under glass. Stems 1.5–4m with many short side branches. Upper branches blue-violet tinged. Leaves deltoid or cordate, very soft villose, upper petioles blue-violet tinged. Inflorescences 20–40cm long. Calyx blue tinged, pubescent. Corolla 2–5cm long. Under glass this beautiful salvia is very prone to whitefly and red spider mite. Old stems can be cut off completely annually after flowering. Plants can either be cut down for winter dormancy or kept damp and grown continuously throughout winter. Min. –5°C.

Salvia guaranitica Benth., syn. *S. ambigens* Briquet   An upright perennial with flowers that have a green or very dark indigo blue calyx and a blue corolla, native of Brazil, Uruguay and Argentina, growing in grassy clearings. The tallest clone in cultivation, 'Black and Blue', may flower from

Salvia sessei at Clos du Peyronnet, Menton, S France

autumn–winter under glass. Other clones flower from summer–autumn. Stems 1.5–3m tall. Leaves ovate to cordate, 8–12cm long, glabrous or pubescent above. Inflorescences racemose or paniculate; flowers 4–6cm long, in whorls of 2–8, the upper lip longest.
'Black and Blue' This is a robust form but more tender. Leaves pubescent. Flowers deep blue set in almost black calyces, very showy. Min. 0°C.
'Blue Enigma' This is less tall but hardier. Leaves glabrous. Flowers royal blue set into green calyces. Min. –10°C.
'Purple Majesty' (*not shown*) Same height as 'Blue Enigma'. Leaves sparsely pubescent. Flowers dark purple set in purplish black calyces. Min –5°C.

Salvia iodantha Fern. A shrubby perennial with many partly woody branches and dense racemes of rose-purple or wine red flowers, native throughout C and S Mexico, growing in open places, flowering in late summer–autumn. Stems to 2m. Leaves softly puberulous, ovate-lanceolate. Flowers in spicate racemes to 30cm long, sometimes in slender panicles. Calyx short, 4mm long. Corolla 1.5cm long, upper lip softly pubescent. Although smaller than many species, the flowers of *Salvia iodantha* are produced in great numbers creating a superb overall effect. Whitefly can be a problem under glass. Min. 0°C.

Salvia sessei Benth. A huge shrub with intense scarlet flowers, native of central and south Mexico, growing at low elevations in the forest, flowering under glass from autumn–winter at a constant temperature of 15°C. Huge shrub 3–5m tall, spreading. Leaves deltoid-ovate, 5–12cm long, pubescent. Flowers in pairs forming panicles of short racemes. Calyx campanulate, inflated and often scarlet tinged. Corolla 3–4cm long, lower lip slightly deflexed. This is possibly the largest salvia, with immense vigour at warm temperatures. Its distinctive enlarged calyces and robust growth distinguish it. It can be treated as a wall shrub, trained rigorously annually or it can be hard pruned as a pot plant. Whitefly, red spider mite and mealy bug can be a problem. Min. 2°C.

Salvia sessei

Salvia chamaedryoides   *Salvia carduacea* in the Theodore Payne Foundation Reserve, California

Salvia canariensis

Salvia buchananii with *Artemisia* 'Powis Castle'

Salvia apiana Jeps. (*Labiatae*)   A low shrub with long flowering stems topped by whorls of white flowers, native of California from Santa Barbara S to Baja California, growing in dry stony places below 1500m, flowering in March–July. Stems to 1.5m; leaves stalked, oblong-lanceolate, 3cm long. Calyx 5–7mm. Corolla 1.2–2.2cm. An attractive large shrub for a dry climate. Min. –3°C overnight.

Salvia buchananii Hedge   A perennial with shiny dark green leaves and cherry red velvety flowers, unusually large in relation to the plant's size; unknown in the wild, discovered in a garden in Mexico City, flowering from June–September. Stems to 60cm, arising from a stoloniferous rootstock. Leaves ovate-lanceolate to spathulate, thickly coriaceous, serrate or crenate. Flowers in loose racemes to 10cm, often in pairs. Calyx tubular, green, glandular. Corolla densely pubescent to 5cm long. *S. buchananii* thrives in full sun but may attract whitefly under glass. It will survive mild winters outside in a sheltered spot. Min –5°C.

Salvia canariensis L.   A sub-shrub with narrow sagittate leaves and long flowering stems with purple bracts and pinkish flowers, native of the Canary Islands, growing in dry

open places at up to 1600m, flowering in spring–summer. Leaves 5–15cm long. Stems to 2m. Bracts ovate, papery, longer than the calyx. For dry well-drained soil. Min. –3°C for the high-altitude forms.

Salvia carduacea Benth.   An annual with a rosette of silvery leaves and upright woolly stems bearing dense whorls of lilac flowers, native of California from San Francisco S to Baja California, growing in open grassy places below 1400m, flowering in March–June. Stems to 50cm; leaves sinuate-pinnatifid, somewhat spiny. Bracts spiny. Calyx lobes spine-tipped. Corolla 2–2.5cm. A winter annual germinating in autumn rains and growing through the winter. Min. –3°C overnight.

Salvia chamaedryoides Cav.   A sprawling low-growing shrub with blue flowers, native of E and C Mexico, growing in dry rocky mountains at 2000–3000m, flowering throughout the summer. Plant spreading from rhizomatous stems below ground. Stems around 30cm tall, woody. Leaves small, deltoid or elliptic, 1–2cm long, green above, grey pubescent below. Inflorescence a loose raceme; flowers in whorls or pairs. Corolla deep blue; lower lip widely spreading. Upright forms of this small species grow well in pots under glass and are surprisingly free from pests. Good outdoors in California. Min. –10°C.

Salvia lavanduloides Kunth   A lavender-like perennial with spikes of blue flowers, native of Mexico, growing in waste places, abandoned fields and open pine woods above 2000m, flowering in September–November. Stems to 1m or more. Leaves 3–9cm, oblong to elliptic, both surfaces pubescent. Flowers in dense spikes 3–12cm long; corolla around 1cm long, the tube 3–5mm. An attractive perennial when growing well, needing good soil and sun or partial shade. Min. –3°C.

Salvia patens Cav.   One of the most spectacular species in cultivation with enormous blue flowers which are some of the largest in the genus, native of C Mexico, growing in clearings or grassy banks in oak woods, flowering intermittently throughout summer–autumn. This herbaceous species perennates by means of white fleshy tubers. Stems upright 1–2m tall. Leaves ovate or

hastate, petiolate. Inflorescence racemose, sometimes paniculate, 20–40cm long. Flowers in pairs. Corolla usually intense royal blue; upper lip 3–6cm long, strongly falcate, style not branched. Very easy to cultivate; pot-grown plants need to be dried out to resting tubers during winter. Min –5°C. The flowers of 'Chilcombe' are pale lilac, 'Alba' are white and 'Cambridge Blue' very pale blue.
'Guanajuato'   Superb large form collected in the Sierra de Guanajuato in C Mexico by Compton, d'Arcy and Rix in 1991. Grows to 2m tall; flowers 6cm or more long. Good in rich moist soil in sun or partial shade. The tuberous roots can be dug up and brought indoors to overwinter, like a dahlia.

Salvia uliginosa Benth.   A perennial with tall arching stems and small bright blue flowers, native of Brazil, Uruguay and Argentina, growing in damp grassland, flowering in late summer–autumn. Stems to 2m, rising from a fleshy stoloniferous rootstock. Leaves lanceolate to 7cm long, slightly sticky. Flowers in short racemes at the top of each branch. Corolla to 2cm long with a white patch on the lower lip. For moist sandy soil in full sun. The overwintering roots must be protected from freezing and from slugs. Also shown on page 284 with *Canna iridiflora*.

Salvia apiana in the Living Desert Reserve

Salvia lavanduloides on the plateau south of Lake Chapala, Mexico

Salvia uliginosa in a warm damp spot at Greenway Gardens, S Devon

Salvia patens 'Guanajuato' in wet oak woods above Guanajuato, Mexico

SCROPHULARIACEAE

Mimulus longiflorus, a cultivated plant

Mimulus 'Verity Purissima'

Keckiella antirrhinoides

Keckiella cordifolia south of San Luis Obispo in May

Mimulus bifidus subsp. fasciculatus

Mimulus aurantiacus in N California

Mimulus puniceus in the Santa Ana Mountains in March

Galvesia speciosa (Nutt.) Gray (*Scrophulariaceae*)   A spreading shrub with small bright green leaves and bright red snapdragon-like flowers, native of Santa Catalina and San Clemente islands off S California and Guadalupe Island off Baja California, growing in rocky canyons, flowering in February–May. Stems spreading to 2m across; leaves elliptic-ovate, 2–4.5cm long. Flowers 2–2.5cm long. For a warm position, partially shaded in hot climates. Min. 0°C.

Keckiella antirrhinoides (Benth) Straw, syn. *Penstemon antirrhinoides* Benth. (*Scrophulariaceae*)   An upright or arching shrub with small leaves and yellow flowers tinged with red, native of S California from San Bernadino Co., to Baja California, growing on dry rocky slopes, flowering in April–May. Stems to 2.5m, leaves linear to ovate-elliptic, 1–2cm long. Flowers 16–20mm long, 8–10mm across with all the filaments pubescent at the base. For a warm sunny position and dry soil. Min. –5°C.

Keckiella cordifolia (Benth.) Straw, syn. *Penstemon cordifolius* Benth.   A scrambling shrub with short opposite leaves and tubular 2-lipped reddish flowers, native of California from San Luis Obispo Co., S to Baja California, growing in dry rocky canyons, flowering in May–July. Stems to 3m; leaves 2–5cm long. Flowers 3–4cm long. For a warm sunny position and dry soil. Min. –5°C.

Mimulus aurantiacus Curt., syns. *M. glutinosus* Wendl., *Diplacus aurantiacus* Jeps. (*Scrophulariaceae*)   A low spreading shrub with sticky dark green leaves and orange or deep yellowish flowers, native of W Oregon and California, from Del Norte to Santa Barbara Co., growing in rocky places and open woodland, along the coast and in the foothills of the Sierras from Placer to Tuolumne Co., flowering in March–August. Shrub to 1.2m. Leaves 2.5–5cm long, veins impressed above. Flowers with calyx glabrous; corolla 3.5–4.5cm long, the lobes entire, notched or toothed. For dry well-drained soil. The species in this group are not easy to distinguish and appear to hybridise freely in the wild. Min. –5°C.

Mimulus puniceus, a dark red form

Pink seedling This pink-flowered seedling was seen in N Los Angeles at the Theodore Payne Foundation Garden which preserves, raises and sells rare Californian native plants.

Mimulus bifidus Penn. A spreading sub-shrub with buff or creamy white flowers, the lobes deeply notched, native of California in the W foothills of the Sierras from Plumas and Butte to Placer Co., with subsp. **fasciculatus** Penn. (*shown here*), in the Santa Lucia Mountains, growing on dry rocky slopes below 1900m, flowering in April–July. This species is recognised by its deeply notched corolla lobes. Min. –3°C.

M. 'Verity Purissima' A pure white seedling or hybrid of *M. bifidus*, raised by a Mr Verity of Los Angeles. Other Verity colour forms include 'Verity Buff' with creamy buff flowers; 'Verity Caroline' a good yellow; and 'Verity Magenta', flowers 7–7.5cm long, deep purplish-red with very narrow paler margins.

Mimulus longiflorus (Nutt.) Grant A spreading shrub with deep orange to buff and almost white flowers, native of California from San Luis Obispo Co. south to Baja California, mainly along the coast, growing on dry rocky slopes below 1400m, flowering in March–July. This species is recognised by its pubescent and glandular-hairy young shoots, leaves and calyx. Min. –3°C.

Mimulus puniceus (Nutt.) Steud., syn. *M. aurantiacus* var. *puniceus* An erect shrub with linear-lanceolate to elliptic leaves and brick-red to orange-red flowers, native of S California from Laguna Beach and the Santa Ana Mountains to Baja California and Santa Catalina Island, growing in chaparral and coastal scrub, flowering in March–July. Stems to 1.5m; corolla 3–5cm long, 2.5–3cm across. Min. –3°C. *M. longifolius* var. *rutilus* Grant has deep velvety-red flowers and a pubescent and glandular hairy calyx.

Russellia equisetiformis Schldl. & Cham., syn. *R. juncea* Zucc. (*Scrophulariaceae*) A hanging or arching leafless shrub with thin green stems and tubular waxy red flowers, native of Mexico, growing on cliffs, flowering from spring–autumn, and now naturalised in Florida and other subtropical areas. Stems to 1.5m. Flowers to 3cm long. A striking plant when in flower. Good for a hanging basket or on top of a wall. Min. –3°C.

Russellia sarmentosa Jacq. A scrambling or arching sub-shrub with short broad sticky leaves and whorls of tubular red flowers on long spikes, native of C Mexico to Cuba and Colombia, growing in openings and by rocky streams in oak and pine forest at around 2000m, flowering in Oct.–Dec. Stems angled, to 1.8m. Leaves to 8cm, ovate, cordate. Flowers to 4cm long. An attractive plant for a partially shaded position. Min. –3°C.

Scrophularia coccinea Gray A glandular upright perennial with tubular bright red flowers, native of New Mexico where it is rare, growing at the foot of rock ledges in the high mountains, flowering in summer. Stems to 60cm. Leaves softly glandular-pubescent. Flowers 15–20mm long. This grew well in an unheated greenhouse for a few years. Min. –5°C, perhaps less if kept rather dry.

A pink *Mimulus* seedling

Galvesia speciosa

Russellia sarmentosa in woods on Volcan Collima in C Mexico at 1900m

Russellia equisetiformis in Bermuda

Scrophularia coccinea at Harry Hay's

Anemopaegma chamberlaynii in Florida in September

Campsis grandiflora in Tuscany in July

Pyrostegia venusta in Nairobi, Kenya

Tecoma capensis 'Lutea'

Macfadyena unguis-cati in Bermuda

Anemopaegma chamberlaynii (Sims) Bur. & Schum. (*Bignoniaceae*) A slender climber with a pair of thin leaflets, a long trifid tendril and clusters of primrose-yellow flowers, native of Brazil, growing in open forest, flowering sporadically, but mainly in late summer. Climber to 6m or more, flowering best on hanging branches. Leaflets 5–14cm. Flowers 6.3cm long, 3.8cm across. Capsules oblong to orbicular. Min. 0°C. In the paler flowered *A. chrysoleucum* (H. B. & K.) Sandwith, from Trinidad to Brazil and Peru, the flowers are larger and scented of roses.

Campsis grandiflora (Thunb.) K. Schum. (*Bignoniaceae*) A robust deciduous climber with pinnate leaves and large wide-open trumpet-shaped orange or pinkish flowers, native of E China from near Beijing to Hainan Island, climbing into trees and on rocks, flowering in July–September. Climber to 6m, rooting from the shoots. Leaves to 30cm, with 7–9 leaflets. Flowers to 6.3cm long and 7.5–9cm across, in a large usually hanging inflorescence. Pods around 12.5cm long. Although winter hardy to –10°C, this plant flowers well only in warm summer climates. The hybrid with the American *C. radicans*, *C. × tagliabuana* (Vis.) Rehder is hardier with deep apricot-orange flowers to 8cm across in the commonly cultivated variety 'Mme Galen'.

Macfadyena unguis-cati (L.) A. Gentry, syn. *Doxantha unguis-cati* (L.) Miers (*Bignoniaceae*) Cat's Claw A very rampant climber with a pair of thin leaflets, and with a cat's-claw-like trifid tendril and large bright yellow solitary flowers, native of Mexico down to Argentina and across the West Indies, found growing in open forest and scrub, generally flowering in spring and, but also less freely, in autumn. Climber to 6m or more, rooting at the nodes and forming tubers; often festooning large trees. Leaflets 5–16cm, deciduous in cold areas. Flowers 6–9cm across, striped orange in the throat. Capsules to 70cm long. Min. –5°C. Best on a west wall in borderline areas.

Tecoma × smithii in Oudtshoorn, Cape Province in November

Tecoma stans in the Virgin Islands in November

Pyrostegia venusta (Ker-Gawl.) Myers (*Bignoniaceae*)   A rampant climber with a pair of leaflets, a central tendril and masses of pale orange tubular flowers, native of Brazil, but commonly planted wherever the climate has warm summers and cooler winters, generally flowering in winter–early spring. Climber to 6m or more. Leaflets 5–7.5cm; flowers 5–6cm long with exserted style and stamens. Good in warm desert areas of North America and in S California, or climbing to the roof of a tall conservatory and allowed to hang down. Min. 0°C. Best on a west wall in borderline areas.

Tecoma capensis (Thunb.) Lindl., syn. *Tecomaria capensis* (Thunb.) Spach (*Bignoniaceae*)   A sprawling shrub with pinnate leaves and red, orange or yellow upright tubular flowers, native of South Africa from the Cape to Natal, growing in scrub and on the edges of forest, flowering in October–May. Shrub to 2m or more if supported. Leaves with 5,7 or 9 obovate leaflets. Flowers around 4.5cm long with exserted stamens; tube curved. Capsule linear, flat. Commonly cultivated in warm climates and often clipped to form a hedge. Different cultivars are tolerant of dry or wet summers. Min. –3°C.

Tecoma × smithii W.Wats., syn. *T. alata* DC, and probably *T. fulva* G. Don (*Bignoniaceae*) An erect shrub with pinnate leaves and heads of yellow flowers, reddish-brown outside, said to be a hybrid between *T. stans* and the Peruvian *T. arequipensis* (Sprague) Sandwith, but probably native of Peru, flowering in winter–spring. Shrub to 5m; leaves with 8–10 ovate leaflets, the terminal larger and lanceolate. Flowers 5cm long. Good in a dry climate. Min. –3°C. *T. × smithii* is said to have been introduced to cultivation in Europe from Australia and to come true from seed. James

Veitch reported receiving seed of *T. fulva* from Peru, and finding it 'apparently identical with *T. smithii*'.

Tecoma stans (L.) Juss. ex H. B. & K. An erect shrub with narrow pinnate leaves and heads of bright yellow trumpet-shaped flowers, reddish-brown outside, native of Arizona and New Mexico to Mexico, the West Indies, N Venezuela and Argentina, growing on dry stony or gravelly slopes, flowering in June–January. Shrub to 6m; leaves with 8–10 lanceolate, acuminate leaflets. Flowers to 6cm long and 2.5cm across at the mouth. Commonly grown in warm climates. Min. –3°C, will recover from short spells of frost.

Tecoma stans in Bermuda

Clysostoma callistegioides in the Huntington Gardens, San Marino, California

Clytostoma callistegioides (Cham.) Bur. & Schum. (*Bignoniaceae*)   A strong-growing climber with pairs of large leaflets, a simple tendril and pale lilac flowers with a yellow throat, native of S Brazil and Argentina, flowering in spring. Climber to 6m or more. Leaflets 7.5–10cm long, oblong-elliptic. Flowers 6.3–9cm long, around 7cm across. Fruits spiny. Flowers best in areas where the winter is cool and dry, the summer hot and wet. Min. –5°C and will sprout from the ground if cut down by colder temperatures.

Distictis buccinatoria (DC) A. Gentry, syn. *Phaedranthus buccinatorius* (DC) Miers (*Bignoniaceae*)   A rampant climber with a pair of leathery leaflets, often a trifid tendril and large bright red flowers with a long tube, native of Mexico, growing in open forest and scrub, flowering in summer. Climber to 10m or more. Leaflets around 10cm, evergreen, ovate-lanceolate. Flowers 7.5–10cm long, 2cm across, tomentose outside. Min. –3°C. Best on a sunny wall in borderline areas and good in the warmest gardens along the Mediterranean coastline.

Distictis laxiflora (DC) Greenm.
A climber with a pair of leathery leaflets and large violet to magenta flowers fading to white as they age, scented of vanilla, native of Mexico, growing in open forest and scrub, flowering all summer. Climber to 6m or more. Leaflets around 6cm, evergreen, ovate-elliptic. Flowers 4.5–7.5cm long and 3.5cm across, finely hairy outside. Min. –3°C. *D.* 'Mrs Rivers' syn. 'Rivers', *D. riversii*, has deeper purple flowers with an orange centre.

Pandorea jasminoides (Lindl.) K. Schum. (*Bignoniaceae*) Bower Plant   A climber with twining stems, shiny pinnate leaves and terminal inflorescence of white or pale pink flowers, often with a dark throat, native of the coasts of Queensland and New South Wales, growing in open forest, flowering much of the year. Stems to 5m. Leaves dark green, with 5–9 lanceolate leaflets, to 5cm long. Flowers 6–7cm across. Best in rich soil with shade in the hottest part of the day. Good in a large conservatory if allowed to grow up and cascade down. Min. –3°C. Named cultivars include **'Alba'** white; 'Red Eyes', white with a crimson throat; 'Rosea Superba', large flowered, pink with a dark throat.

Pandorea pandorana (Andr.) van Steenis Wonga Wonga Vine   A large climber with twining stems, large pinnate leaves and branched inflorescence of many small cream, buff, pinkish or maroon flowers, native of New Guinea, S through E Australia to Tasmania, growing in open forest, flowering in winter and spring. Stems to 30m. Leaves with 7–19 leaflets, to 10cm long. Flowers scented, 1–3cm long, usually hairy and streaked with red inside. Best in areas with moist summers and cool winters, but tolerant of drought and a minimum of –5°C. Prune after flowering. **'Golden Rain'**, syn. 'Golden Showers' is a selection with golden-yellow flowers. 'Rosea' (*not shown*) is pale pink.

Podranea brycei (N. E. Br.) Sprague (*Bignoniaceae*) Zimbabwe Creeper   A climber with long slender stems, pinnate leaves and hanging bunches of pale pink flowers with a lined throat, native of Zimbabwe and Malawi, growing on rocky hills and kopjes, flowering mainly from autumn–spring. Stems to 5m.

Podranea ricasoliana in the Virgin Islands in November

Pandorea jasminoides 'Alba' in Bermuda

Distictis buccinatoria

Distictis laxiflora growing with a *Passiflora* with 3-lobed leaves

Distictis buccinatoria in the garden at La Mortola, NW Italy in June

Pandorea pandorana 'Golden Rain' from Read's Nursery, Loddon, Norfolk

Pandorea pandorana in the Berkeley Botanic Garden, California in March

Podranea brycei in the garden at Villa Roquebrune, Cap Martin, S France

Leaves with 7–9 lanceolate leaflets, to 4cm long, deciduous in cold weather. Calyx with acuminate lobes. Flowers 8cm across, the throat hairy inside. The very similar and commoner *P. ricasoliana* differs in the broader, shorter calyx lobes, the narrowed base to the corolla tube, which has a glabrous throat. Min. –3°C.

Podranea ricasoliana (Tanf.) Sprague
A climber with long slender stems, pinnate leaves and hanging bunches of pale pink flowers with a lined throat, native of South Africa in E Cape Province near Port St Johns, growing on rocky hills near the coast, flowering in summer–autumn. Stems to 5m. Leaves with 5–11 lanceolate leaflets, to 4cm long,

deciduous in cold weather. Calyx inflated, with blunt lobes. Flowers 8cm across, throat glabrous inside, the margins of the lobes very wavy. In a conservatory this species can make masses of leafy growth and few flowers if the soil is too damp and rich. In the open it flowers well on a sunny wall and is commonly cultivated in subtropical areas. Min. –5°C.

Thunbergia erecta in the British Virgin Islands

Thunbergia grandiflora at Villa Roquebrune, S France

Thunbergia grandiflora 'Alba'

Thunbergia grandiflora

Ruellia macrantha Mart. ex Nees (*Acanthaceae*) Christmas Pride A bushy sub-shrub with showy bright pink flowers, native of Brazil and Venezuela, in the Sierra de Perija Mountains, growing on the forest margins, flowering in winter–early spring. Stems erect, to 2m. Leaves dark green, lanceolate, to 15cm long. Flowers solitary, axillary, to about 9cm long, 6cm across, rose-pink with veined throat; tube narrow at base, widening towards mouth, lobes rounded. Does well as a pot plant in a warm greenhouse. Min. 5°C.

Thunbergia alata Bojer. (*Acanthaceae*) Black-eyed Susan A small perennial twining plant with distinctive dark-centred flowers, native of tropical Africa but is now naturalised in many other countries, including Hong Kong and the Philippines, where it is found from sea level up to 1500m growing in rough grassland, flowering in summer. Stems to 2m. Leaves ovate-elliptic, to 7cm long. Flowers numerous, funnel-shaped, to 4.5 cm long and across, borne singly on long stalks in the leaf axils; usually orange, but also yellow or white, usually with the characteristic very dark purple 'eye'. Good in a light frost-free greenhouse or outside in mild areas; often grown as an annual in cooler climates. Min. 0°C.

Thunbergia battiscombei A variable bushy semi-climbing or climbing perennial, native of Kenya and Uganda where it is found

Thunbergia battiscombei from Kenya and Uganda

Thunbergia kirkiana in Malawii

in a variety of habitats, flowering in summer. Stems usually around 80cm, occasionally to 3m or more. Leaves light green, ovate-elliptic, to 10cm long, 5cm wide. Flowers around 4cm across, borne in axillary inflorescences of 8 or more, bright violet-blue with yellow throat. For good soil in a warm greenhouse or outside in Mediterranean areas. Min. −3°C. Close to *T. cordata* Lindau.

Thunbergia erecta (Benth.) Anderson An erect evergreen shrub, native of tropical West and South Africa, flowering in summer. Stems to 2m. Leaves ovate, glossy, to 6cm long. Flowers solitary, trumpet-shaped, to 7cm long; tube creamy-yellow, lobes violet-blue. Needs a cool greenhouse and may be planted as a hedge in tropical and subtropical gardens. Min. 2°C.

Thunbergia grandiflora (Roxb. ex Rottl.) Roxb. A large variable twining climber with paired or hanging racemes of pale blue flowers, native of Sikkim and Assam to Burma, Cambodia, Thailand and S China, climbing into bushes and trees at up to 1200m, flowering in spring–autumn. Stems to 20m or more. Leaves variable, but usually rough, scalloped, ovate to about 7.5cm long. Flowers bell-shaped, 6–7cm long and wide, usually pale blue with a yellow throat; sometimes solitary on stalks up to 12cm long in leaf axils, sometimes on long pendent racemes on stalks about 5cm long. Good for a cool greenhouse or outside in Mediterranean areas; frequently seen on the Côte d'Azur. Min. −5°C.

Thunbergia grandiflora 'Alba' A form of the above with yellow-throated white flowers.

Thunbergia gregorii S. Moore, syn. *T. gibsonii* S. Moore A twining perennial climber with bright orange flowers, is also grown as an annual, native of tropical Africa from Kenya around Nairobi to S Tanzania, at up to 2350m, flowering in winter–spring. Stems woody, to 4m or more. Leaves bright green, hairy, triangular-ovate, to 8cm long. Flowers solitary to 5cm long and wide, on stalks to 11cm long in leaf axils. Flowers for much of the year in a cool greenhouse or outside in tropical or subtropical areas. Good in California. Min. −2°C.

Thunbergia kirkiana T. Anders. A low-growing climber, native of Malawi and S Tanzania, where it is found hanging over banks and growing in rough grass, flowering in early spring. Leaves sagittate. Flowers large with pure white corolla and narrow yellow tube. Good in a warm greenhouse and in the tropics if there is a cool season. Min. 5°C.

Thunbergia mysorensis T. Anderson ex Bedd. A robust climber with hanging chains of yellow and reddish-brown flowers, native of S India, from the Nilgiris to Cape Cormorin, climbing into forest trees in the hills to 900m, flowering in winter–early spring. Stems to 10m. Leaves ovate, lanceolate, acuminate, to 15cm long. Flowering racemes to 90cm; flowers 3.8cm long, 5–6cm across; tube yellow, lobes red-brown, reflexed; the flowers attract sunbirds. Good in a warm greenhouse and outside in the tropics if there is a cool season. Min. 10°C.
Thunbergia coccinea Wall. from N India has a similer habit, but smaller flowers with bright red lobes. It flowers in winter.

Thunbergia gregorii at the Huntington Gardens

Thunbergia alata in Bermuda

Thunbergia alata mixed colours

Ruellia macrantha, a species from Brazil and Venezuela

Thunbergia mysorensis in the Tropical House at Wisley

Hypoestes aristata in the Temperate House at Wisley in December

Acanthus mollis with palms and tree ferns at Trebah, Cornwall

Crossandra pungens

Crossandra infundibuliformis at Kew

Acanthus mollis L. var. ***latifolius*** hort. (*Acanthaceae*) A large perennial with jagged shiny leaves and spires of white and purplish flowers, native of SW Europe from Portugal to the Balkans and NW Africa, growing in rocky places, flowering in June–August. Leaves emerging in winter, to 45cm long, 30cm across. Flowering stems to 2m. This is a fine foliage plant in a Mediterranean climate with stately spikes of flowers; excellent in California. For a sheltered position. Min. −5°C.

Crossandra infundibuliformis (L.) Nees (*Acanthaceae*) A small evergreen sub-shrub with shiny dark green leaves and orange to salmon pink flowers, native of S India and Ceylon, flowering much of the year. Shrub to 1m; leaves ovate to lanceolate, 5–12cm. Flowers with a narrow tube, 5cm long and wide. For any well-drained soil in sun or part shade. Min. −3°C.

Crossandra pungens Lindau A small evergreen sub-shrub with dull green leaves and orange to yellow flowers, native of Africa from Zululand northwards, flowering much of the year. Shrub to 60cm; leaves oblong, 5–12cm. Bracts spiny. Flowers with a narrow tube, 5cm long and wide. For any well-drained soil in sun or part shade. Min. −3°C.

Hypoestes aristata R. Br. (*Acanthaceae*) A tall evergreen perennial with spikes of purplish-pink flowers, native of South Africa from the S Cape at Cape Infanta, east to Natal and tropical Africa, growing in scrub on the edges of forest, flowering much of the year. Shrub to 1m; leaves ovate, around 8cm. Flowers 2.5cm long, lobes recurved, the upper spotted. For any well-drained soil in sun or part shade; valuable for its winter-flowering under glass. Min. −3°C.

Strobilanthes kunthianus

Peristrophe speciosa in the Temperate House at Wisley in December

Strobilanthes dyerianus in Florida

Mackaya bella in California

Mackaya bella Harv., syn. *Asystasia bella* hort. (*Acanthaceae*)   An evergreen shrub with shiny elliptic leaves and veined pale purplish blue flowers, native of the coast of Natal and Zululand, growing as an understorey shrub in forest, flowering much of the year. Shrub to 1.5m; leaves wavy-toothed to 7.5cm. Flowers 5cm long. For any well-drained soil in sun or part shade. Min.   5°C.

Odontonema strictum (Nees) Kuntze (*Acanthaceae*)   An evergreen sub-shrub with dark green leaves and loose spikes of tubular waxy red flowers, native of C America, growing in forest and along rivers, flowering much of the year. Stems to 1.5m. Leaves to 15cm, glossy, glabrous. Flowers to 2.5cm. For shade, warmth and moisture in summer. Min. 5°C. *Odontonema schomburgkianum* (Nees) Kuntze from Colombia, has flowers in long pendulous racemes.

Otacanthus caeruleus Lindl. (*Acanthaceae*) A small evergreen perennial with toothed leaves and bluish flowers, native of Brazil, flowering much of the year. Stems to 50cm; leaves elliptic, 7.5–10cm. Four bracts small, bristle-like, the fifth large, leafy. Flowers with a narrow curved tube with rounded spreading lobes, around 5cm across. For well-drained soil in sun or part shade. Min. –3°C.

Peristrophe speciosa (Roxb.) Nees (*Acanthaceae*)   An evergreen sub-shrub with loose spikes of bright purplish-pink flowers,

Odontonema strictum in Hong Kong in October

Otacanthus caeruleus at Derry Watkins' Special Plants

native of N India, in the foothills of the Himalayas up to 1600m, flowering mainly in winter. Stems greyish, to 1.2m; leaves elliptic, around 8cm. Flowers to 5cm long, strongly 2–lipped, lobes recurved, the upper blotched at the base. For well-drained soil in sun or part shade; useful for its winter-flowering under glass. Min. –3°C.

Strobilanthes dyerianus Mast. (*Acanthaceae*) Persian Shield   An evergreen sub-shrub with young leaves prettily marked, silver and pale blue flowers, native of Burma and Penang, flowering in winter. Stems to

1.2m; leaves ovate-lanceolate, dark purple beneath, to 15cm. Flowers to 3.2cm long, funnel-shaped, in short spikes. For well-drained soil in sun or part shade. Min. –3°C.

Strobilanthes kunthianus Nees   A clump-forming sub-shrub with tough stems, leathery leaves and dense heads of pale lilac flowers, native of India in the Nilgiri Hills at 1600–2000m, flowering in late summer. Stems to 1m. Leaves 7cm long. Flowers in short spikes, with green overlapping bracts and an almost regular bell-shaped corolla, 2.5cm long. Well-drained soil in full sun. Min. 5°C.

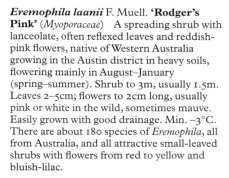

Pachystachys lutea in the greenhouse in Paris

Eremophila laanii F. Muell. **'Rodger's Pink'** (*Myoporaceae*)   A spreading shrub with lanceolate, often reflexed leaves and reddish-pink flowers, native of Western Australia growing in the Austin district in heavy soils, flowering mainly in August–January (spring–summer). Shrub to 3m, usually 1.5m. Leaves 2–5cm; flowers to 2cm long, usually pink or white in the wild, sometimes mauve. Easily grown with good drainage. Min. –3°C. There are about 180 species of *Eremophila*, all from Australia, and all attractive small-leaved shrubs with flowers from red to yellow and bluish-lilac.

Eremophila nivea Chinn.   A spreading shrub with narrow greyish leaves and mauve flowers, native of Western Australia growing in the Irwin district on sandy soils over clay, flowering mainly in August–December. Shrub to 2.5m. Leaves 1.5cm; flowers to 2cm long. Easily grown and tolerant of heavy soil and periodic wet. Min. –3°C.

Justicia adhatoda L., syn. *Adhatoda vasica* Nees (*Acanthaceae*)   An upright evergreen shrub with dark green leaves and spikes of white flowers, native of India and Sri Lanka, flowering in January–March. Stems 2–3m; leaves to 20cm, usually puckered between the sunken veins. Flowers 3cm long, the lower lip veined red. For good moist soil. Min. –4°C.

Justicia californica (Benth.) D. Gibson, syn. *Beloperone californica* Benth. Chuparosa A twiggy shrub with obovate greyish leaves, though often leafless, and upright spikes of 2–lipped dull red flowers, native of S California, S Arizona and NW Mexico, growing on rocky slopes and along watercourses in the desert, at up to 1200m, flowering in March–June. Shrub to 1.5m. Leaves to 1.5cm. Corolla 3–3.5cm, 2-lipped. Min. –3°C. Much loved by hummingbirds. The only member of this mainly tropical family native to California.

Justicia carnea Lindl., syn. *Cyrtanthera magnifica* Nees   An upright evergreen shrub with dark green leaves and dense upright spikes of narrow white, pink, red or purplish flowers, native of Brazil, flowering mainly in summer–autumn. Stems 1–2m; leaves to 25cm, ovate, acuminate. Flower spikes to 10cm, dense with narrow green bracts. Corolla 5cm long, 2–lipped. For good moist soil; it is tolerant of shade but needs summer warmth. Min. –5°C. **'Alba'** is a white form.

Justicia sericea 'Inca Queen'

Justicia carnea 'Alba' in Florida

Justicia rizzinii in the Temperate House at Kew

Eremophila nivea

Justicia leonardii Wassh., syn. *Sericographis incana* Nees   A spreading shrub with leaves silky-hairy beneath and masses of red to orange flowers, native of Mexico, flowering in spring. Stems to 1m; leaves to 15cm, narrowly ovate. Corolla 3–3.5cm, tubular, 2-lipped. For dry well-drained soil and full sun. Min. –3°C.

Justicia rizzinii Wassh., syn. *Jacobinia pauciflora* (Nees) Lindau   A small shrub with masses of nodding red flowers with yellow tips, native of Brazil, flowering through the winter. Plant spreading to 60cm high. Leaves elliptic to obovate, downy. Flowers corolla around 2.5cm long, 2-lipped for 5mm. Easily grown, valued for winter flowering. Min. 5°C.

Justicia sericea 'Inca Queen'   A sub-shrub with numerous upright stems, elliptic leaves and scarlet, 2-lipped flowers, native of Peru, flowering in spring summer. Stems to 1.5m, silky-hairy; leaves around 5cm; flowers 3cm long, the broad lower lip with 3 lobes. For good soil and a sunny position. Min. –3°C.

Pachystachys lutea Nees (*Acanthaceae*) An erect evergreen sub-shrub with dark green leaves, broad overlapping yellow bracts and white flowers, native of Peru, flowering in spring–autumn. Stems 40–100cm; leaves to 12cm, with conspicuous sunken veins; corolla to 4.75cm long, deeply 2-lipped. For good moist soil and shade or partial shade. Min. 5°C. *Pachhysstachys coccinea* (Aubl.) Nees has green bracts and red flowers. The Shrimp Plant, formerly *Beloperone guttata*, now *Justicia brandegeana* from Mexico, has a curving spike of reddish bracts and white flowers.

Eremophila laanii 'Rodger's Pink'

Justicia californica in Palm Springs

Justicia leonardii at the Huntington Gardens

Justicia adhatoda

Justicia carnea in the Harry P. Leu Gardens, Florida

Gardenia augusta 'Veitchii'

Mussaenda pubescens

Luculia gratissima

Gardenia augusta on Victoria Peak, Hong Kong in May

Luculia intermedia in the park in Dali, Yunnan in October

Rondeletia roezlii in Florida

Rondeletia odorata

Lonicera sempervirens clothing a low fence in Bermuda

Gardenia augusta (L.) Merrill, syn.
G. florida L. *G. jasminoides* Ellis (*Rubiaceae*)
An evergreen shrub or small tree with dark
green shiny leaves and wonderfully scented
white flowers, native of SE China from Hong
Kong, where it is common to W Hubei, and of
S Japan, growing in scrub on low hills up to
330m, flowering in April–June. Tree to 12m;
leaves 5–15cm, ovate to lanceolate or oblong.
Flowers around 6cm across, fading to yellow
after one day. Fruit ripening orange, topped
by the persistent narrow calyx lobes.
'Veitchii' The traditional double cultivar
with thick-petalled flowers, 4cm across, with a
particularly rich heavy scent. It makes a low
dense shrub to 2m in diameter, producing
flowers mainly in May–November. Under
glass it needs frequent spraying and humidity
to keep red spider mite at bay, with feeding in
warm weather, kept drier in winter. Shade
from hot sun. Needs acid soil and much the
same climatic conditions as oranges.
Min. –5°C for short periods.

Lonicera hildebrandiana Collett & Hemsl.
(*Caprifoliaceae*) A strong-growing evergreen
climber with leathery leaves and long narrow
scented flowers, native of Manipur to the
Shan states in Burma and east to Yunnan,
flowering in summer. Climber to 25m. Leaves
broadly ovate, to 12cm long, 10cm across.
Flowers 10–16cm long, opening whitish,
changing to yellow and orange as they fade.
Fruit to 2.5cm long. The largest but most
tender honeysuckle, surviving outdoors on
Tresco and the Riviera. Min. –3°C.

Lonicera pilosa Willd. ex H.B.& K. non
Maxim. A rather weak climber with bluish-
green hairy leaves and hanging bunches of
tubular orange flowers, native of NW Mexico
in the Sierra Madre Orientale, scrambling in
scrub on dry limestone slopes, flowering in
summer. Stems to 3m; leaves ovate, around
5cm long. Flowers around 6cm long,
pubescent outside, subtended by hat-like
united bracts. Min. –5°C. C. D. & R 1218
(*shown here*) has been wrongly listed under *L.
pilosa* Maxim., syn. *L. strophiophora* Franch., a
shrubby species from Japan.

Lonicera sempervirens L. A climber with
bluish-green leaves, hairy beneath and
hanging bunches of tubular red flowers, native
of E North America from Connecticut to
Florida and Texas, scrambling in scrub,
flowering in spring–autumn. Stems to 5m;

Lonicera pilosa from Mexico at Hanging
Langford, Wiltshire

Lonicera hildebrandiana in the Conservatory at
the Royal Botanic Garden, Edinburgh

leaves oval to obovate, 8cm long. Flowers 5cm
long, pubescent outside. Min. –15°C. Though
hardy, this species is usually seen in
subtropical gardens, where it grows well.

Luculia gratissima Sweet (*Rubiaceae*)
An evergreen shrub with rounded heads of
scented pale pink flowers, native of the
foothills of the Himalayas from C Nepal to
Yunnan, growing in scrub at 1200–1800m,
flowering in September–January. Shrub to 5m.
Leaves 13–18cm. Flowers with rounded lobes,
2–2.5cm across, in heads 8–15cm across.
Good for a cool greenhouse; put outside in
summer. Min. –3°C.

Luculia intermedia Hutch. An evergreen
shrub with loose heads of scented pink or
reddish flowers with crested flaps between the
lobes, native of N Burma and Yunnan,
growing in mountain forest and scrub at
1600–2600m, flowering in September–April.
Shrub to 3.5m. Leaves 10–15cm, acuminate.
Flowers with rounded lobes, 3–4cm across.
Possibly hardier than *L. gratissima*. Min. –5°C.

Mussaenda pubescens Ait. fil. (*Rubiaceae*)
An evergreen shrub or climber with loose
heads of starry yellow flowers, the outer sepal
of each group becoming white and leaf-like,

native of S China from Taiwan and Hong
Kong to Yunnan, growing in forest and scrub
in the hills to 1500m, flowering in April–May.
Shrub to 2m or more. Leaves 5–8cm, elliptic,
acuminate. White sepal 9cm long, 5cm wide.
Flowers 1.5cm across. Min. –5°C, perhaps.
Mussaenda erythrophylla Schumach. & Thonn.
from tropical West Africa, has a bright red
leafy sepal and hairy pink or red flowers. It has
several spectacular cultivars, raised in Thailand
and the Philippines, in shades of red and pink,
with all the sepals leafy.

Rondeletia odorata Jacq. (*Rubiaceae*)
An evergreen shrub with ovate to oblong
leaves and scented brownish orange flowers,
native of Cuba, the West Indies and Panama,
flowering in late summer. Shrub to 3m,
usually about 1m. Leaves to 10cm. Flowers
orange to red with a yellow eye, the tube
15mm long, with round to elliptic lobes to
5mm and a yellow eye. For slightly acid soil in
part shade. Min. 5°C.

Rondeletia roezlii Hemsl. A large
evergreen shrub with nodding branches and
large heads of pale pinkish flowers, native of
Guatemala, flowering in late summer. Shrub
to 3m. leaves 2.5–10cm long. Flowers around
1cm across. For good sandy soil. Min. –3°C.

CAMPANULACEAE

Azorina vidalii

Azorina vidalii at Marwood Hill, Devon

Trachelium caeruleum

Musschia wollastonii in the conservatory at the
Ventnor Botanic Garden, Isle of Wight in July

Musschia aurea wild in Madeira in March

lanceolate leaves and a branched inflorescence
of yellow starry flowers, native of Madeira,
growing on volcanic cliffs near the sea,
flowering in March–May. Stems to 60cm,
leaves to 30cm. Flowers around 3cm across,
the calyx lobes leafy, yellow, the corolla lobes
reflexed. An unusual plant with similarities to
the Turkish genus *Michauxia*. For well-
drained soil. Min. 5°C.

Musschia wollastonii Lowe   A large
sub-shrubby perennial with a rosette of
oblanceolate leaves and a pyramidal
inflorescence of whitish starry flowers, native
of Madeira, growing on volcanic cliffs near the
sea, flowering in March–May. Stems to 2m,
leaves to 75cm. Flowers to 3cm across, the
corolla lobes reflexed with conspicuous
5-pointed stigmas. Min. 5°C.

Nesocodon mauretanicus (I. K. B.
Richardson) M. Thulin (*Campanulaceae*)
A fleshy evergreen dwarf shrub with long
narrow finely toothed leaves and single large
bell flowers, pale pink netted with purple,
native of Mauritius, growing on sea cliffs,
flowering in June–July. Plant with few
branches, topped by rosettes of 5–10cm long
leaves. Stems to 20cm. Corolla 3.5–5cm. For a
cool partly shaded position. Min. 0°C.

Scabiosa cretica L. (*Dipsacaceae*)   A low
rounded shrub with pale leaves and heads of
pale bluish flowers, in spite of its name, native
of the Balearic Islands, Italy, Sicily and N
Africa, growing in rocky places, flowering in
June–August. Shrub to 25cm. Leaves
oblanceolate, 3½–5 times as long as wide.
Flower heads much above the leaves. For a
dry sheltered position. Min. –5°C. *S. minoana*
(P. H. Davis) W. Greuter, from Crete is also
cultivated. It has broader silvery leaves,
1½–2¾ times as long as wide and slightly
longer stalks to the flower heads.

Trachelium caeruleum L. (*Campanulaceae*)
A perennial with a woody base, toothed leaves
and a flattish inflorescence of very small bluish
flowers, native of Portugal, Spain, Italy, Sicily
and N Africa, growing on shady rocks and
cliffs, flowering in June–August. Stems to 1m;
leaves mostly stalked. Corolla with a very thin
tube 4–6mm long and short lobes. For a warm
position and well-drained soil. Min. –3°C.

Azorina vidalii (H. Wats.) Feer, syn.
Campanula vidalii H. Wats. (*Campanulaceae*)
A fleshy evergreen dwarf shrub with narrow
shiny leaves and spikes of pink or white bell
flowers, native of the Azores, growing on sea
cliffs, flowering in June–July. Plant has few
branches, topped by rosettes of leaves 3–8cm
long. Stems to 30cm. Corolla 2.5–3.5cm. Easy
from seed, but not long lived, tending to rot in
humid conditions. The flowers tend to be
white on all plants grown in the greenhouse,
but pink in plants grown outdoors. Min. 0°C.

Canarina canariensis (L.) Vatke
(*Campanulaceae*)   A perennial with a large
fleshy root, waxy bluish leaves and orange
bells, native of the Canary Islands in Tenerife,

Gran Canaria, La Palma and Gomera,
growing in laurel forests and clambering up
among tree heaths and bracken at
300–1000m, flowering in September–March.
Stems to 3m; leaves triangular with toothed
edges. Flowers 3–6cm long, orange to red with
darker veins and copious watery nectar. Fruits
fig-like, orange to black when ripe, with
numerous small seeds. Easily grown in a frost-
free greenhouse, in sandy leafy soil, kept dry
in summer. Growth starts in August and
flowering will continue through the winter if
the plant has enough warmth and light. The
leaves will survive a little frost. Min. –2°C.

Musschia aurea (L. fil.) Dumort.
(*Campanulaceae*)   A perennial with broadly

Canarina canariensis wild on N Tenerife in March

Canarina canariensis, an unusual striped
flower, growing with *Erica arborea* on Tenerife

Nesocodon mauretanicus

Scabiosa cretica in a garden of the Villa Thuret
in April

Lobelia laxiflora, shrubby form in woods on Nevado di Colima, Mexico

Lobelia laxiflora var. *angustifolia* on Tresco

Laurentia axillaris (Lindl.) E. Wimmer, syn. *Isotoma axillaris* Lindl. (*Campanulaceae*) A perennial with narrow dissected leaves and starry bluish or rarely white flowers, native of Australia in Queensland, New South Wales and Victoria, growing in rocky places on hills and mountains, usually in peaty soil, flowering mainly in September–May (summer). Plant spreading to 1m across. Leaves ovate to obovate in outline. Flowers about 4cm across. This is commonly sold as a plant for hanging baskets, under the name 'Blue Stars'. 'White Stars' with narrower leaves and more 2-lipped flowers probably belongs to a second species, *L. anethifolia*. Both are poisonous and the sap can cause irritation to the skin. Min. –3°C.

Laurentia longiflora (L.) Endl., syn. *Isotoma longiflora* (L.) K. Presl A dwarf perennial with a rosette of rather hairy leaves and long-tubed, scented, white flowers, native of the West Indies and naturalised elsewhere including Hong Kong, growing on shady rocks, flowering in winter. Leaves around 15cm long. Corolla tube around 10cm long and 6cm across the segments. Very poisonous. Min. 0°C.

Lobelia alata Labill. (*Campanulaceae*) An erect or spreading perennial with winged stems and blue, mauve or white flowers, native of South Africa from the Cape Peninsula to Natal, of Chile and the Juan Fernandes Islands, of Australia along the south coast and also of Tasmania and of New Zealand, growing in damp places, flowering mainly in November–June. A very variable plant. Stems to 60cm; leaves obovate to lanceolate, decurrent. Flowers 5–10mm long. Min. 0°C. *Lobelia anceps* L. is sometimes united with this species.

Lobelia anatina in C Mexico, south of Saltillo

Lobelia bridgesii from Trebah, Cornwall

Lobelia anatina Wimmer A slender perennial with spikes of bright blue flowers, native of S New Mexico and Arizona south to Durango, growing in marshy meadows and by streams up to 3000m, flowering in July–October. Stems around 40cm; stem

Laurentia axillaris at Barter's Nursery, Wiltshire

Laurentia longiflora on Victoria Peak, Hong Kong

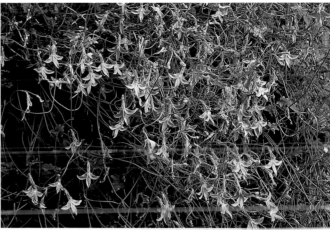

Lobelia preslii in the Royal Botanic Garden, Edinburgh

Lobelia laxiflora in meadows south of Lake Chapala, SW Mexico

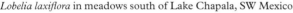

Lobelia alata in Melbourne Botanic Garden

Lobelia tomentosa wild near Mossel Bay

Monopsis lutea in the Temperate House at Kew

leaves shallowly toothed or entire, narrowed to the base. Flowers with the tube 3.5–5mm long, the lobes to 2mm across. For sandy soil in a warm position, dry in winter, wet in summer. Min. –5°C. The similar *L. fenestralis* Cav. is usually annual and has leaves sharply serrate, clasping at the base.

Lobelia bridgesii Hook., syn. *L. excelsa* hort A robust perennial with tall spikes of pinkish flowers, native of Chile, flowering in summer. Stems to 1.5m, several from a stout rootstock. Leaves narrowly lanceolate. Flowers around 4cm long. For good well-drained slightly acid soil and sun. Min. –3°C with protection for the roots. This is like a smaller pinkish version of *L. tupa* which is shown in *Perennials* vol. II, page 135.

Lobelia laxiflora H. B. & K. A very variable perennial or sub-shrub with obovate to linear leaves and orange to red a lipped flowers, native of S Arizona, south to Mexico and Colombia, growing in oak and pine woods, flowering in May–November. Stems to 1m or more. Flowers to 4cm long, both lips recurved. Three distinct forms are shown: var. **angustifolia** DC This is the variety found in Arizona. It forms a mass of stems to 75cm and has very narrow leaves. It is probably the hardiest, surviving –5°C. The second form, from moist oak and pine woods at around 2000m in SW Mexico, is shrubby with short broad leaves and red flowers on very long stalks. The third form from grassy meadows in SW Mexico, is a large herbaceous

plant with upright stems, crowded leaves and yellow-tipped flowers on rather short stalks, approaching *L. tupa* in habit. These Mexican ones are more tender, surviving perhaps –3°C.

Lobelia preslii A. DC An erect or spreading perennial with blue flowers on long slender stalks, native of South Africa from the Natal Drakensberg to the mountains of E Africa, growing in damp shady places by streams and among rocks, flowering much of the year. Stems to 30cm; lower leaves ivy-shaped, toothed. Flowers around 10mm across with the outer lobes curved apart. Min. –3°C.

Lobelia tomentosa L. fil. A small shrub with whitish hairy leaves and blue or purple flowers on long stalks, native of South Africa from Caledon and Oudtshoorn to the E Cape, growing in sandy places and on low hills, flowering most of the year. Shrub to 20cm, usually less. Leaves pinnatifid, with the pinnae forked, the edges rolled. Flower stalks to 20cm; flowers around 1cm across. Unusual in its shrubby habit. Min. –3°C, perhaps.

Monopsis lutea (L.) Urb. (*Campanulaceae*) A straggling perennial with small bright yellow flowers, native of South Africa throughout the W and S Cape, growing in damp places and on lower slopes, flowering in November–April. Stems to 60cm; leaves lanceolate, toothed. Flowers around 1cm across. For moist good soil. Min. –3°C. Many *Monopsis* species have deep violet flowers.

Stylidium graminifolium near Sydney

Dampiera diversifolia

Lechenaultia biloba from Green Farm Plants,
Surrey

206

Goodenia ovata

Goodenia pinnatifida

Lechenaultia floribunda

Lechenaultia laricina in King's Park Botanic
Garden, Perth, Western Australia

Dampiera diversifolia Vriese (*Goodeniaceae*)
A creeping perennial with small oblanceolate
leaves and purplish-blue scented flowers,
native of Western Australia, flowering in
August–December. Plant to 2m across. Stem
leaves 1cm long, 3mm wide. Flowers to 1.5cm
across. An adaptable species, best in moist
clay-loam soils, often suckering. Min. 0°C.

Goodenia ovata Smith (*Goodeniaceae*)
A spreading shrub with ovate to lanceolate
leaves and yellow flowers, native of most of
E Australia, growing in a variety of habitats,
and especially frequent after bushfires,
flowering in August–February. Shrub to 2.5m
high, 3m wide. Leaves to 10cm long, 6cm
wide. Flowers about 2cm across, 3–6 on short
stalks in the leaf axils. Prefers acid soil and is
tolerant of shade and wet soils. Min. –3°C.

Goodenia pinnatifida Schltdl.   A dwarf
annual or perennial with lobed leaves and
yellow flowers, native of most of the arid
regions of S Australia, forming large colonies
after autumn rains, flowering in July–January.
Stems to 50cm tall and more across. Basal
leaves to 10cm, stalked, toothed or lobed.
Flowers 2.5cm across. Easily grown with a
long flowering season if watered. Min. –3°C.

Lechenaultia biloba Lindl. (*Goodeniaceae*)
A spreading shrublet with heath-like greyish
leaves and bright blue flowers, native of
Western Australia, growing in sandy rocky
places, flowering in spring. Stems to around
50cm. Leaves to 10mm long. Flowers to 2cm
across, with a white centre in 'White Flash'.
Needs very well-drained acid sandy soil, so is
best grown in a raised bed or rockery. Not
long-lived in gardens, but easy from cuttings.
Min. –3°C.

Lechenaultia floribunda Benth.
A spreading shrublet with heath-like greyish
leaves and small pale blue or white flowers,
native of Western Australia, growing in sandy
rocky places, flowering in spring–early
summer. Stems to around 60cm. Leaves to
8mm long. Flowers to 16mm across with
narrow lobes. Needs very well-drained acid
sandy soil; easy from cuttings. Min. –3°C.

Lechenaultia laricina Lindl.   An erect
heath-like shrublet with bright scarlet flowers,
native of Western Australia, growing in sandy
rocky places, flowering in spring–early
summer. Stems to around 60cm. Leaves to
12mm long. Flowers to 13mm across. Needs
very well-drained acid sandy soil; easy from
cuttings. Min. –3°C.

Scaevola aemula R. Br. (*Goodeniaceae*)
A spreading, rather fleshy perennial with
toothed leaves and small mauve-blue fan-
shaped flowers, native of Australia from near
Sydney to Western Australia and Tasmania,
growing mainly near the coast, flowering in
spring–summer. Plant very variable but
usually spreading to 1m across. Flowers to
3cm across, sometimes pale blue or white.
'Blue Wonder' and 'Blue Fan' are more
robust and upright, and are among the
varieties sold for growing in hanging baskets.
They need to be propagated from cuttings and
prefer ample water, excellent drainage and full
sun. Min. –3°C.

Scaevola albida (Sm.)Druce   A spreading,
perennial with broad toothed leaves and small
pale blue or white fan-shaped flowers, native

Scaevola crassifolia on coastal dunes near Perth, Western Australia in December

of Australia from Queensland to South Australia, growing in sandy areas, flowering in spring summer. Plant to 1m across. Flowers to 1.3cm across. Needs sun and good drainage. Min. –3°C.

Scaevola crassifolia Labill.   A rounded shrub with stalked finely toothed rounded leaves and pale blue flowers, native of Western Australia, growing in sandy areas, including coastal dunes, flowering in spring. Plant to 1m across. Leaves fleshy to 5cm. Flowers to 1.3cm across with narrow lobes. Needs sun and good drainage. Min. –3°C.

Scaevola gracilis Hook. fil.   A spreading shrub with stalked oblanceolate leaves and pure white flowers, native of Western Australia, growing in sandy areas, flowering in spring. Plant to 1m across. Leaves to 5cm. Flowers to 1.3cm across with narrow, widely spreading lobes. Needs sun and good drainage. Min. –3°C.

Stylidium graminifolium Sweet (*Stylidiaceae*) Trigger Plant   A perennial with a rosette of stiff grassy leaves and a hairy stem with small pinkish to magenta flowers, native of SE Australia and Tasmania, growing in bare sandy places, flowering in spring. Leaves 5–25cm; stem 15–60cm; flowers around 1.5cm across, the anthers and stigma united on a column which bends back to form a trigger. This is sprung by a visiting insect, landing the pollen on the insect's back. For sandy soil and sun. Min. –3°C.

Scaevola albida

Scaevola crassifolia

Scaevola aemula 'Blue Wonder'

Scaevola gracilis

ARGYRANTHEMUM

Argyranthemum foeniculaceum wild on Tenerife

Argyranthemum foeniculaceum

Specimens from Quince House in July, ¼ life-size

Argyranthemum can be planted as annuals for bedding or grown in pots where they will flower profusely whenever they have sufficient water. They will survive drought and soon revive again when rain comes. Apart from the species which mostly have white flowers, many named varieties, in shades of pink and pale yellow, are now grown. All survive a degree or two of frost, provided they are not exposed to freezing wind. If they become straggly they can be pruned and very lovely specimens can be trained as standards or pyramids for pots. All are easily grown from cuttings.

Argyranthemum foeniculaceum (Willd.) Webb ex Schultz Bip. (*Compositae*) A perennial sub-shrub with white daisy flowers, native of Tenerife, found in the south and SW regions, usually on dry cliffs and occasionally on high mountains, flowering mainly in autumn–spring. Stems to 1m. Leaves to 10cm, feathery, bluish-grey, crowded, 4–6-fid, the lobes less than 3mm wide. Flower heads solitary, to 2cm. Min. −3°C or less for short periods.

Argyranthemum frutescens (L.) Webb ex Schultz Bip. A perennial sub-shrub or sometimes creeping mat with white daisy flowers, native of N Gran Canaria, Gomera, and La Palma (very rare), growing mainly around the coast up to 700m, flowering much of the year. Stems to 80cm. Leaves to 8cm, with 2–6 primary lobes which are flat, lanceolate to linear-lanceolate, usually bluish. Flower heads to 2cm across in corymbs. Min. −3°C or less for short periods.

Argyranthemum gracile Webb ex Schultz Bip. A perennial sub-shrub with very thin leaf segments and white daisy flowers, native of Tenerife in the south coast region and common up to 600m, flowering much of the year. Stems to 1.5m, slender, ascending, branched. Leaves 2–10cm, feathery, 3-lobed, or forked, less than 3mm wide. Flower heads small in broad loose clusters. Min. −3°C.

Argyranthemum maderense (D. Don.) Humphries, syn. *A. ochroleucum* Webb ex Schultz-Bip. A small shrub with pale yellow flowers, native of Lanzarote on coastal cliffs and occasionally in inland rocky areas up to 650m. Stems to 1m, slender, usually branched. Leaves 8–10cm, obovate, pinnatifid, soft grey. Flower heads small to 1.5cm across in corymbs. Min. −6°C.

Argyranthemum pinnatifidum (L. fil.) Lowe A perennial sub-shrub with broad divided leaves and small white daisy flowers, native of Madeira in the north and interior, growing on rocks in ravines and on shady cliffs, flowering in April–July. Stems to 1.5m. Leaves with flat overlapping segments. Flowers in corymbs, around 1.8cm across. Min. −3°C.

Argyranthemum 'Gill's Pink' Single pink flowers.

Argyranthemum 'Blizzard' A rounded habit and masses of small white double flowers.

Argyranthemum 'Mary Cheek' A bushy habit and pale pink pom-pom type flowers.

Argyranthemum 'Mary Wooten' Pink semi-double flowers with longer outer florets.

Argyranthemum 'Chelsea Girl' An upright habit with fine foliage and white single flowers. A selection of *A. gracile*.

Tanacetum ferulaceum (Webb & Berth.) Schultz Bip. A shrubby perennial with white flowers, native of Gran Canaria in the S and SW regions from 300–600m, flowering in March–June. Stems to 50cm. Leaves to 10cm, 1–2 pinnatisect, felty to nearly smooth. Flower heads small, in dense clusters. Min. −3°C.

Argyranthemum gracile wild on Tenerife in March

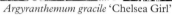

Argyranthemum gracile 'Chelsea Girl'

Argyranthemum pinnatifidum wild on sea cliffs in Madeira

Argyranthemums in Mrs Millar's garden near Grasse, S France

Argyranthemum maderense at Wisley

Tanacetum ferulaceum

Coreopsis gigantea

Coreopsis gigantea in Santa Barbara Botanical Garden, California

Roldana petasitis

Chiliotrichum diffusum

Chiliotrichum diffusum (Forst. f.) Kuntze. (*Compositae*) An erect evergreen shrub with white daisy flowers, native of S Chile, SW Argentina and the Falkland Islands, growing in the Andes down to sea level in the south, on the edges of forests and by streams and bogs, flowering from late spring–summer. Stems to 1m, much-branched with peeling bark, grey-brown when mature, twigs hairy-white. Leaves to 30cm, spear-shaped, dark green, glossy and smooth above, hairy-white below. Flower heads to 3cm; ray florets to 12mm long, white; disc florets yellow, tubular. Min. −12°C. This plant is ideal for growing in coastal gardens.

Coreopsis gigantea (Kellogg) Hall. (*Compositae*) A stout erect perennial with yellow daisy flowers, native of SW California from St Luis Obispo Co. southwards to Baja California, growing on rocky sea cliffs and dunes, flowering from March–May. Stems to 3m, thick and fleshy from a large woody root. Leaves to 20cm, alternate, in dense tufts at the ends of the branches, feathery, bright green. Flowers from 4–8cm across, in clusters on long stems; ray florets yellow; disc florets dark yellow-orange. Min. −3°C. Loved by bees, this plant is excellent for growing in an herbaceous or cut flower border. Its flowers last well in water.

Encelia farinosa A. Gray (*Compositae*)
Brittle-Bush, Incienso   An aromatic rounded
shrub with orange-yellow daisy flowers, native
to SW North America and NE Mexico,
growing on dry stony slopes up to 1000m,
flowering in the spring. Stems to 1m, brittle.
Leaves to 8cm, narrowly or broadly ovoid,
smooth or toothed at the margin, silvery-
green and woolly. Flower heads single or in
small clusters; ray florets up to 12mm long,
orange-yellow; disc florets yellow or red-
brown. Min. 12°C. This plant, which covers
thousands of acres on the dry hills around
Palm Springs, flourishes in very hot dry
conditions similar to its native habitat. It
should be watered moderately when growing
and kept almost dry in winter.

Eriophyllum confertiflorum (DC.) A. Gray
(*Compositae*)   A sub-shrub with yellow starry
daisy flowers, native of California and Baja
California, growing on scrub-covered hillsides
up to 2000m, flowering in spring–summer.
Stems to 60cm, slender, erect at the top,
branched lower down. Leaves 1–4cm,
feathery, silvery green. Flower heads in
clusters with 4–6 ray florets 2–4mm, oval-
shaped, yellow; disc florets yellow. Min.
–12°C. This plant is attractive grown in a
rockery or sunny herbaceous border. Clip
after flowering to maintain a compact shape.

Eriophyllum nevinii A. Gray (*Compositae*)
Catalina Silver Lace   A stout shrubby
perennial with yellow flowers, native of
California on Santa Catalina and San
Clemente islands, growing on rocky
headlands by the sea, flowering from
spring–early autumn. Stems to 2m, stout,
ground-hugging, very hairy. Leaves 8–20cm,
numerous, feathery, silvery, hairy. Flower
heads in clusters; 4–8 ray florets to 2mm,
yellow. Min. –6°C. This plant is grown for its
lovely silver foliage.

Farfugium japonicum '**Aureomaculatum**'
(L.) Kitam., syn. *Ligularia tussilaginea*
'Aureomaculata' (Burm. f.) Mak.
(Composital) Leopard Plant   An evergreen
perennial herb with yellow florets, native of
Japan, growing near the sea, flowering from
October–December. Stems 30–75cm, grey to
brown. Leaves 6–30cm across, kidney-shaped
or heart-shaped, usually in basal tufts, thick
and shiny above, green with irregular round
creamy yellow spots, hence the common
name. Flowers 4–6cm across, growing in
rather flat loose clusters, florets yellow. Min.
–5°C. This plant is grown for its striking,
variegated foliage but should be kept in a
rather cool greenhouse or as a houseplant in
colder climates.

Roldana petasitis (Sims) H. Robinson &
Brettell, syn. *Senecio petasitis* (Sims) DC.
(*Compositae*)   A shrub or perennial herb with
yellow flowers, native of Mexico, naturalised
in Australia from the Hunter Valley to the
Macquarie Pass, flowering mainly in the
spring. Stems 1.5–2m, softly hairy. The leaves
are 10–20cm long and wide, broadly ovate,
clearly veined, margins lobed, softly hairy.
Flower heads 4–5mm, growing in many-
headed clusters; 4–6 ray florets 8–10mm long,
yellow. Min –3°C. Popularly cultivated as an
ornamental.

Encelia farinosa at the Living Desert Museum, Palm Springs, California

Eriophyllum confertiflorum

Eriophyllum nevinii

Farfugium japonicum 'Aureomaculatum'

Senecio johnstonii subsp. *johnstonii* on Mount Meru, Tanzania

Delairea odorata in the south of France

Telanthophora grandifolius in Menton

Pseudogynoxis hoffmannii in the Botanic
Gardens, Menton in April

Pseudogynoxis chenopodioides naturalised
in Bermuda

Delairea odorata Lem., syn. *Senecio
mikanioides* Otto ex Harv. (*Compositae*)
German Ivy, Parlour Ivy   A succulent
climbing herb with masses of tiny yellow
flowers, native of South Africa and naturalised
elsewhere, climbing into shrubs on the edges
of forests, flowering in winter. Stems to 6m,
woody at base. Leaves to 10cm, roundish to
heart-shaped, lobed, bright green. Flower
heads numerous in dense clusters, without
rays. Min. −6°C. In frost-free Mediterranean
climates this plant is used for hedging and
ground-cover or it may be grown as an
attractive climber in a conservatory.

Pericallis cruenta (DC.) Nordenstam, syn.
Senecio cruentus DC. (*Compositae*)
A perennial with rounded leaves and a flattish
head of pale purple flowers, native of Tenerife
along the north coast, growing in shady
places in the laurel forest at 800–1500m,
flowering in February–May. Stems to 60cm.
Leaves with a wavy edge, pinkish and hairy
beneath, to 15cm across. Inflorescence
7–20-flowered; flower heads 2.5–4cm across.
For a moist position in semi-shade.
Min. −3°C.

Pericallis × hybrida Nordenstam Florists'
Cineraria   These gaudy plants originated
from hybrids between *P. cruenta*, *P. lanata* and
other species. They are grown as annuals for
winter-flowering from seed sown in summer.
Modern strains vary from dwarf to large
compact and the more delicate 'Stellata'. All
need excellent drainage and cool airy
conditions. In some gardens old cultivars of
cineraria may self-sow and these can be quite
graceful plants with large heads of mauve-pink
flowers in early spring. Min. −6°C.

Pericallis lanata (L'Hérit.) Nordenstam,
syn. *Senecio heritieri* DC. (*Compositae*)
A rounded sub-shrub with mauve daisy
flowers, native of S Tenerife, growing on rocky
north-facing cliffs and walls at 200–600m,
flowering in winter–spring. Stems to 40cm,
densely covered in short soft hairs. Leaves to
3cm across, roundish, with 5–7 lobes, densely
hairy beneath. The flower heads 3–5cm, are
usually single, with 10–12 mauve ray florets;
the disc florets are purple and violet-scented.
For a dry soil with shade from strong sun.
Min. −6°C.

Pseudogynoxis chenopodioides (Kunth)
Cabr., syn. *Senecio confusus* (DC.) Britten
(*Compositae*)   A twining climber with
coarsely toothed leaves and loose clusters of
orange-red flowers, native of S Mexico in
NW Yucatan and Honduras, growing into
trees, scrub, and hedges, flowering much of
the year, mainly in summer in cultivation.
Stems woody at the base, to 10m or more.
Leaves lanceolate, the lower cordate at the
base. Flower heads to 5cm across. Best in
rather dry conditions. Min. 0°C.

Pseudogynoxis hoffmannii (Klatt) Cuatr.,
syn. *Senecio hoffmannii* Klatt   A climber with
finely toothed leaves and 3–5 brownish-
crimson flowers, native of Costa Rica and
Panama, growing in rough grass, scrub and
hedges, at up to 1500m, flowering in winter.
Climber to 3m. Leaves with an acuminate
apex and cuneate base. Flowers opening in
succession, 4.5cm across, the outer bracts
spreading, curved. For good soil with water in
summer. Min. 0°C.

CINERARIAS

Senecio glastifolius L. A tall multi-stemmed sub-shrub with many leaves becoming progressively smaller towards the top of the stem and loose heads of purplish-pink flowers, native of South Africa in the S Cape from George to Uniondale, growing on the edges of forest, flowering in August–December. Stems to 1m; leaves variably toothed; flower heads to 3cm across. A fine plant for a mild garden. Min. –3°C or less for short periods.

Senecio johnstonii subsp. **johnstonii** A stout little-branched tree with a rosette of cabbage-like leaves on top and a large pyramidal inflorescence of hundreds of small yellow flowers, native of Mount Kilimanjaro and Mount Meru in Tanzania, growing usually above 3000m. These tree senecios are a speciality of the mountains of central Africa. They may reach 10m in height and have leaves to 45cm long. The inflorescence may add another 1.3m. Subspecies of *S. johnstonii* are found on all the taller mountains from Zaire and Rwanda to Tanzania. Giant Lobelias with a similar habit are found over an even wider area, from Fernando Poó to Ethiopia.

Senecio saxifraga hort. A small rounded shrub with evergreen fleshy leaves and small starry yellow flowers, native of Argentina, flowering in spring–autumn. Shrub to 30cm. Leaf blades lobed, around 1cm across. Flower heads around 1.5cm across with about 5 ray florets. For sun and good soil. Min. –5°C.

Telanthophora grandifolius (Less.) Robinson & Brettell, syn. *Senecio grandifolius* Less. (*Compositae*) A shrub or small tree with large leaves and huge heads of small flowers, native of Mexico near Jalapa Enríquez, growing in cloud forests at around 1750m, flowering in autumn–winter. Stems to 3m; leaves entire or lobed. Flowers scented, to 1cm across with around 5 ray florets. A striking plant for a cool conservatory or a mild and sheltered garden in partial shade and good well-drained soil. Min. –2°C.

Pericallis × hybrida, an old variety in California

Cinerarias at Wisley in December

Senecio glastifolius on Tresco, Isles of Scilly

Pericallis cruenta in laurel woods on Tenerife

Senecio saxifraga from M. Pellizzaro, Vallauris

Pericallis lanata wild on Tenerife in March

Pericallis lanata

Brachyglottis hectoris (Buchan)
Nordenstam, syn. *Senecio hectoris* Buchan
A shrub with flat heads of small white flowers,
native of New Zealand in NW South Island,
flowering December–February. Stems to 4m.
Leaves 10–25cm long, 4–12cm across, broadly
oblanceolate, white woolly beneath when
young, finely toothed, with small lobes along
the leaf stalk. Flower heads to 5cm, in a large
flat corymb with 18–12 narrow ray florets.
Min. –5°C.

Brachyglottis huntii (F. Muell.)
Nordenstam (*Compositae*)   A tree or shrub
with yellow flowers, native of Chatham Island
especially Pitt Island, New Zealand, flowering
in summer. Stems to 6m or more. Leaves
5–10cm, spear-shaped to oblong, dense,
woolly beneath when young, more leathery
green above when mature. Flower heads to
2cm, in a dense leafy group, with 15–20 broad
ray florets. Min. –5°C. Because of its excellent
wind resistance this species thrives in coastal
gardens.

Brachyglottis perdicioides (Hook. fil.)
Nordenstam   A shrub with yellow flowers,
native of North Island, New Zealand, growing
in lowland forests, flowering in summer.
Stems to 2m, branches slender, hairy. Leaves
2.5–5cm, oblong to elliptic, wavy, serrated
edges. Flower heads to 1cm, in crowded
clusters; ray florets broad, to 8mm. Min.
–5°C. To gain best foliage effects without
flowers prune hard in spring.

Brachyglottis rotundifolia Forst. & Forst.
fil., syn. *Senecio reinholdii* Endl., syn. *S.
rotundifolius* Hook.   A shrub or small tree

Oldenburgia grandis in Kirstenbosch Botanic Garden, South Africa

Brachyglottis rotundifolia at Eagle's Nest Garden, Zennor, Cornwall

Brachyglottis hectoris with *Astelia* in the Ventnor Botanic Garden, Isle of Wight

Brachyglottis hectoris

Hymenolepsis parviflora

Nauplius sericeus

Brachyglottis perdicioides

with insignificant flowers, native of South Island, New Zealand, south of Jackson's Bay and on Stewart and Solander islands, growing in coastal scrub, flowering in summer. Stems to 6m or more, branches stout, hairy white to buff. Leaves 10cm, oblong to broadly ovoid, entire, densely woolly below, leathery and glossy green above. Flower heads to 1cm, in long panicles up to 20cm in length, greenish, without rays. Min. −5°C.

Chysanthemoides monolifera (L.) Norl, (*Compositae*) Boneseed An erect shrub with yellow flowers and black berry-like fruits, native of South Africa from the E Cape and Natal, north to Malawi and naturalised in Australia and California, growing in rocky places, usually by streams, flowering all year. Stems 1–3m, densely branched, woolly at first; older bark greyish-brown and cracked. Leaves to 7cm, obovate; margin finely toothed and spiny, cobwebby at first, smooth, glossy green later. Flower heads few, in a loose cluster with 7–10 ray florets. About 5 of the outer florets form round juicy berries. Min. −5°C for the hardier forms. Remarkable as one of the only members of the daisy family to have fleshy fruit. Now a serious pest in many parts of Australia.

Hymenolepsis parviflora (L.) DC., syn. *Athanasia parviflora* L. (*Compositae*) A robust shrub with yellow flowers, native of South Africa in the mountains of the SW Cape, flowering in November–December. Stems to over 1m, densely branched. Leaves 3–9cm, very thin, deeply pinnatifid, woolly hairy at first, smooth later. Flower heads 2cm long, 4cm across, numerous in dense, disc-shaped clusters; ray florets sulphur yellow. Min. −6°C.

Nauplius sericeus (L.fil.) Cass., syn. *Asteriscus sericeus* (L. fil.) DC. (*Compositae*) A fragrant sub-shrub with yellow flowers, native of the Canary Islands in Fuertevantura, growing in rocky areas from the coast to 700m, flowering in spring–summer. Stems to 1m, glandular, browny-grey. Leaves to 6cm, broadly oblanceolate, densely crowded, covered in soft silver grey hair becoming yellowy-green in age. Flower heads 3.3–5cm, ray florets to 20mm, numerous, yellow. Min. −6°C. This plant is particularly suitable for growing in a rockery or mixed border if the climate is warm and dry otherwise it can be grown in pots in a cool conservatory and brought out in summer.

Oldenburgia grandis (Thunb.) Baill., syn. *Oldenburgia arbuscula* DC. (*Compositae*) A stiff rounded shrub with purple and white flowers, native of South Africa in the Uitenhage District to the E Cape, growing on rocky mountain ridges, flowering in November–December. Shrub to 3m. Leaves 15–25cm, leathery, long-ovate, crowded, densely white-woolly below and when young, dark green and smooth above on the older leaves. Flower heads to 10cm, large, domed, thistle-like, silver-grey to purple. Min. −10°C. Grown for its striking flowers and felted leaves, this plant thrives best in hot dry positions in, for instance, a rockery. In cooler climates it needs a well-ventilated sunny glasshouse.

Olearia insignis Hook. fil., syn. *Pachystegia* insignis (Hook. fil.) Cheesem A spreading shrub with white flowers, native of New Zealand in the Marlborough District, growing in rocky places from the coast into the mountains, flowering in December–February. Stems to 2m, stout young branches white or light brown, woolly. Leaves 8–16cm, alternate, entire, oval or obovate, , shiny green above except on midrib and margins, woolly white below. Flower heads to 3–8cm, solitary ray florets 12mm, numerous, in two rows, white, disc florets crowded, yellow. Min. −6°C.

Olearia rotundifolia (Less.) DC. (*Compositae*) A stout shrub with white flowers, tinted rose native of E Australia, flowering from spring–summer. Stems to 1m. Leaves 3–6cm, alternate, ovate, dark green, rough and veined above, woolly below. Flower heads 2.5–6cm, 9–12 in a loose cluster, ray florets numerous, rose to white-tinged rose, disc florets yellow. Min. −6°C.

Olearia chathamica T. Kirk A lax shrub with white or pinkish flowers, native of the Chatham Islands, New Zealand, growing in dry or somewhat boggy ground, flowering in early summer. Stems to 2m, densely branched. Leaves 3–8cm, alternate, oblong spear-shaped to elliptic, regularly and finely toothed, shiny green above, woolly below. Flower heads 3.5–4.5cm, solitary; ray florets numerous, white, occasionally tinged purple; disc florets dark purple. Min. −6°C. A very attractive shrub for a mild, moist climate. *Olearia semidentata* Dcne, also from the Chatham Islands, differs in its smaller narrower leaves with smaller teeth and usually purple flowers.

Brachyglottis huntii at Otari Native Botanical Garden in New Zealand

Olearia insignis at Harry Hay's

Olearia rotundifolia

Olearia chathamica in Tresco, Isles of Scilly

Chysanthemoides monolifera wild in Natal

Bidens aurea near Saltillo, NW Mexico in October, showing the extent of different-coloured clones

Bidens aurea at Kew

Montanoa bipinnatifida

Bidens heterophylla at Quince House, Devon

Montanoa bipinnatifida by a stream above Anguangueo, C Mexico in November

Bidens aurea (Ait.) Sherff (*Compositae*)
A suckering perennial with lanceolate toothed leaves and yellow flowers, native of NE Mexico, growing in marshy fields, flowering in October–November. Stems to 1m. Leaves 8–10cm long. Flowers yellow to cream, around 3.5cm across, with 4–5 rays. For good well-drained soil in the garden. Min. −5°C.

Bidens cf heterophylla Orteg.   A spreading and much-branched perennial with a leaf with 3 lanceolate lobes and a bright yellow flower, native of Mexico, flowering in summer–autumn. Plant to 1m high and wide. Leaves around 6cm long, the lobes rounded. Flowers with spreading outer bracts and 5 broadly elliptic rays. For good well-drained soil in the garden. Min. −5°C.

Cosmos atrosanguineus (Hook.) Voss. (*Compositae*)   A tuberous-rooted perennial with narrow leaves and chocolate-coloured flowers with an almost chocolate-like scent, native of Mexico but now rare in the wild, flowering in summer–autumn. Stems to 1m. Leaves with 5–7 leaflets. Flowers around 6cm across, with around 8 rays, 3-toothed at the apex. For good well-drained soil. Min. −5°C.

Cosmos crithmifolius H. B. & K.
A tuberous-rooted perennial that has divided leaves with linear leaflets and pinkish flowers, native of Mexico in Chiapas, flowering in summer–autumn. Stems to 1m. Flowers around 3cm across with around 5 rays, 3–4-toothed at the apex. For good well-drained soil. Min. −5°C.

Cosmos diversifolius Otto   A tuberous-rooted perennial that has divided leaves with linear to oblanceolate leaflets and pinkish flowers, native of Mexico in Durango, growing in open pine woods, flowering in summer–autumn. Stems to 50cm. Flowers around 4cm across with 7–8 twisted elliptic rays, not toothed at apex. For good well-drained soil. Min. −5°C.

Cosmos montanus in oak woods on Volcan Tequila in late October

Cosmos montanus Sherff   A slender
tuberous-rooted perennial that has narrow
pinnate leaves and arching stems with solitary
crimson flowers, native of C Mexico, growing
in wet oak woods at around 2000m, flowering
in October–November. Stems to 1m; leaves
with 2–3 pairs of simple or forked linear
leaflets. Flowers around 4cm across, with 5–6
broad rays, toothed at the apex. For good soil
with ample water in summer, dry in
winter. Min. –3°C. I have found the Mexican
species of Cosmos difficult to identify with
any confidence, though they are varied,
beautiful and a common feature of the
landscape in autumn (*see bibliography*).

Grindelia chiloensis (Corn.) Cabr.
(*Compositae*)   A sub-shrub with clammy
resinous leaves, buds covered with white gum
and yellow flowers, native of Chiloé to
S Argentina, flowering in summer. Stems to
1m; leaves to 10cm long, oblanceolate to
obovate. Flowers 5–7cm across. For well-
drained sandy soil. Min. –5°C. About 12 other
species are native of California.

Montanoa bipinnatifida (Kunth) K. Koch
(*Compositae*)   A large soft thick-stemmed
shrub with jaggedly cut leaves and many white
daisy flowers, native of C Mexico, growing in
scrub and forest by streams at up to 1750m,
flowering in August–December. Stems to
10m; leaves to 30cm long, deeply toothed to
bipinnate. Flowers 5–7.5cm across. Heads
nodding in fruit. Seeds enclosed by a wing-
like scale. For good soil and ample water in
summer. Min. –5°C. This makes a fine
specimen in the warmer parts of California
and on the Côte d'Azur. Two magnificent
climbing species are described by Herklots:
Montanoa schottii Robinson & Greenhan,
from the Yucatan, and *M. pauciflora* Klatt from
Belize. Both climb to around 15m or more and
are supported by the hooked stems of the
fruiting heads.

Cosmos diversifolius

Cosmos crithmifolius

Grindelia chiloensis in Sydney Botanic Garden

Cosmos atrosanguineus at Bloom's Nurseries

Dahlia pinnata in wet oak woods near Anguangueo, C Mexico in November

Dahlia imperialis in a village near Lake Chapala, SW Mexico in late October

Dahlia coccinea Cav. (*Compositae*)   A tall perennial with bright orange-red flowers, native of Mexico and Guatemala, growing in rich open woods at around 2000m, flowering in October–December. Stems to 3m. Leaves simple to pinnate, variably divided. Flowers on long slender stalks, sometimes yellow, around 8cm across. Easily grown and almost hardy. Min. −5°C provided the root is protected from frost. In var. *palmeri* from dry woods in the Sierra Madre Orientale, the leaflets are smaller.

Dahlia excelsa Benth.   A very tall perennial with purplish flowers, native of Mexico. The origin of this plant is doubtful and it may be of hybrid origin between *D. imperialis* and another species, as we saw it only in village gardens. Stems to 6m. Leaves pinnatisect, segments acuminate. Flowers held horizontal, around 10cm across. Easily grown and almost hardy. Min. −5° provided the root is protected from frost.

Dahlia imperialis Roezl ex Ort.   A huge perennial with bamboo-like stems and masses of nodding pale lilac-pink flowers, native of S Mexico and Guatemala to Colombia, flowering in October–March. Stems to 9m, shrubby at the base. Leaves 2–3-pinnate. Flowers slightly cupped, around 15cm across. Easily grown in a frost-free climate, needing shelter, rich soil and ample water in summer. Min. −3°C. This species does well in the hills in India and in the warmest gardens in S France.

Dahlia merkii Lehm.   A slender perennial with lilac-pink or white flowers, native of NE Mexico in the Sierra Madre Orientale, growing in dry open woods and scrub, in loose leafy soil, at around 1600m, flowering in August–September. Stems to 1.5m. Leaves 1- or 2-pinnate, with ovate to obovate segments. Flowers on long slender stalks, 6–7cm across. Easily grown and almost hardy. Min. −5°C if the root is protected from frost.

Dahlia pinnata Cav., syn. *D. rosea* hort. A robust perennial with pinkish-purple

Dahlia imperialis, the last flowers in April in Menton

Dahlia merkii at Hadspen, Somerset

Dahlia excelsa in a cottage garden near Potosi, NE Mexico

Dahlia coccinea in woods on Volcan Colima, SW Mexico in November

flowers, native of S Mexico and Guatemala, growing in rich damp oak and pine woods at around 1800m, flowering in October–December. Stems to 2m. Leaves usually pinnatisect. Flowers on arching stalks, yellow towards the middle, around 10cm across. Easily grown, given ample water in summer. Min. –5°C provided the roots do not freeze.

Mutisia spinosa Ruiz & Pav., syn. *M. retusa* Remy var. *glaberrima* Phil.(*Compositae*) An evergreen climber with simple often untoothed leaves and pale pink or white flowers, native of Chile and Argentina, around 40°S, in the Andean foothills at 1200–1500m, scrambling over scrub, flowering in summer. Stems to 6m. Leaves to 12cm long, lobed at the base and clasping the stem, retuse at apex, ending in a tendril. Flower heads with around 8 rays, oblanceolate, 3.5cm long. For a sheltered position with soil moist in summer. Min. –5°C.

Mutisia decurrens Cav. A suckering climber with narrow glaucous leaves and vermilion, orange or deep yellow flowers, native of Chile and Argentina, climbing among shrubs on open hillsides in hot dry sandy or loamy soil or in woodland margins at 800–1500m, flowering in spring–summer. Stems to 3m; leaves glaucous, tapering to a long slender tip with a tendril. Flower heads 12.5cm across with around 15 rays. Easily grown in dry sandy soil with the suckering rhizomes carefully protected. Min. –5°C.

Mutisia spinosa in Ventnor Botanic Garden, Isle of Wight

Mutisia decurrens (yellow form) from M. Pellizzaro, Vallauris, S France

Bracteantha bracteata (Vent.) Anderberg & Haegi, syn. *Helichrysum bracteatum* (Vent.) Andrews (*Compositae*) Strawflower, Golden Everlasting, Yellow Paper Daisy   An erect annual or perennial herb or sub-shrub with bright yellow (or more rarely) white flowers, native of Australia in all states, growing in open woodland and forest, also found naturalised in Spain, flowering all year in gardens. Stems 20–150cm, simple sometimes branched at base, minutely hairy. Leaves 1.5–10cm long, alternate, spear-shaped, smooth or slightly hairy or woolly. Flowers up to 8cm across; bracts lemon to deep gold (rarely white); disc florets yellow. Min. –5°C. Annual cultivars of this species are the ones most frequently grown for cutting and drying because such a variety of colours and heights is available. To dry, cut before buds are fully open, strip leaves off the stems, tie into small bunches and hang upside down to dry away from direct heat.

'Dargon Hill Monarch'   Has bright yellow petals and a darker yellow centre. A shrubby cultivar selected from plants from the McPherson ranges of SE Queensland.

Helichrysum adenophorum F. Muell. var. **waddelliae** J. H. Willis (*Compositae*) A creeping perennial with pink and white flowers, native of Australia south from the Hunter Valley to SE Victoria and SE New South Wales, growing in subalpine rocky areas and on open sites in woodland and sclerophyll forest, flowering from spring–autumn. Stems 20–50cm. Leaves to 2.5–5cm, spear-shaped, green, white-hairy beneath. Flowers 3–4.5cm across, solitary, white (often tinged pink in bud) with yellow centres. Min. –5°C. This species is good in pots and rockeries although it is often short-lived.

Helichrysum apiculatum (Labill.) D. Don., syn. *Chrysocephalum apiculatum* (Labill.) Steetz. (*Compositae*) Common Everlasting Flower, Yellow Buttons   An erect perennial with numerous bright yellow daisy flowers, native of Australia, found widespread on open or disturbed sites in a variety of soils, flowering throughout the year but especially in spring. Stems to 60cm, erect, often suckering. Leaves to 4cm, alternate, thickly spear-shaped, green, woolly below. Flowers to

1.5cm, numerous, growing in loose clusters; ray and disc florets golden yellow. Min. –7°C. A variable species closely related to *H. semipapposum*. Further study is needed to clarify the variants. Several named varieties are grown in Australia.

Helichrysum bellidioides (Forst fil.) Willd. (*Compositae*) Everlasting Daisy   A prostrate perennial herb or shrub with numerous white flowers, native of New Zealand, found in lowland rocky terrain, grasslands and open scrub, flowering from October–February. Stems rooting, branching, somewhat hairy, to 20cm. Leaves to 6mm, alternate, roundish, green and softly woolly below. Flowers to 3cm, solitary, white ray florets with pale yellow disc florets. Min. –17°C. This plant is especially suitable for a sunny position in a rock garden in well-drained soil and needs protection from too much rain in the winter.

Helichrysum petiolare Hilliard & B. L. Burtt. (*Compositae*) Liquorice Plant   A climbing or spreading shrub with numerous sweetly scented, creamy white flowers, native of South Africa from the SE Cape to the Transkei, growing on forest edges and in clearings, often covering large areas, also found naturalised in Portugal, flowering from November–January. Stems slender, branched, to 1m. Leaves to 3.5cm, numerous, broadly round to oval shaped, heart-shaped at the base, silvery green and thinly woolly. Flowers tiny, forming loose corymbs, opaque white. Min. –1° C. This plant is frequently grown as an annual for ground-cover or edging and prized for its attractive silver foliage.

Helichrysum semipapposum (Labill.) DC., syn. *Chrysocephalum semipapposum* (Labill.) Steetz. (*Compositae*) Clustered Everlasting, Yellow Buttons   An aromatic perennial herb or sub-shrub with numerous yellow daisy flowers, native of all Australia, found widespread in woodland, hilly grasslands or rocky rises flowering throughout the year but especially from spring–early summer. Stems to 1m, simple or branched, hairy. Leaves to 2–5cm, alternate, crowded, spear-shaped, green, woolly-white below. Flower clusters from 3–9cm across, with 50–100 flower heads up to 7mm across with

numerous golden yellow ray and disc florets. Min. –7°C. A variable species closely related to *Chrysocephalum apiculatum* but has larger flower heads and fewer in a cluster. Further study is needed to clarify the variants.

Helichrysum vestitum (L.) Schrank (*Compositae*)   A woolly sub-shrub with large white flowers, native of South Africa from Paarl and the Cape Peninsula to Knysna, growing on flats and middle slopes, flowering in November–January. Shrub to 1m. Leaves narrow, crowded along the stem. Flower heads about 5cm across, with a dark purple centre. This is one of the commonest and most striking of the 75 or so species in the Cape.

Ozothamnus diosmifolius (Vent.) DC., syn. *Helichrysum diosmifolium* (Vent.) Sweet (*Compositae*)   An erect shrub with masses of small white daisy flowers, native of Australia north from the Eden District, C Queensland and New South Wales, found widespread in heath and on ridges and on margins of rainforest, flowering in early winter–spring. Stems 2–5m, with short woolly hair on branches. Leaves 10–15mm long, thin, green above, woolly-white below. Flower heads 4mm across, tiny, numerous, in dense clusters, opaque white. Min. –5°C.

Ozothamnus hookeri Sonder, syn. *Helichrysum hookeri* (Sonder) Druce (*Compositae*) Kerosene Bush   An aromatic sticky shrub with greenish-white flowers, native of Australia from Scabby Range to Victoria and Tasmania, found in boggy sites and subalpine heaths and occasionally in low alpine habitats, flowering from summer–autumn. Stems 0.5–1m, branches hairy white. Leaves 1–3mm long, scale like, green and sticky above, woolly-white below. Flowers 2mm across, tiny, numerous, in dense clusters, opaque white. Min. –10°C for the alpine forms.

Phoenocoma prolifera (L.) D. Don (*Compositae*)   A densely branched shrub with large everlasting flowers of red to silvery-pink bracts, native of South Africa in the W and SW Cape, growing in heathy scrub on rocky hills and mountains near the coast, flowering in September–April. Stems to 60cm, densely branched, spreading. Leaves 2mm, very small heath-like, glandular. The flower heads are about 4cm across; the ray florets cerise or white or cerise below and white or pinky-white above. A lovely shrub for well-drained, acid sandy soil; drought-resistant in summer. Min. –3°C.

Helichrysum vestitum growing on Cape Point, South Africa

Bracteantha bracteata, the white form

Helichrysum apiculatum   *Helichrysum petiolare* naturalised in Tresco   *Helichrysum bellidioides*

Helichrysum semipapposum in Canberra   *Ozothamnus diosmifolius*

Bracteantha bracteata 'Dargon Hill Monarch'   *Helichrysum adenophorum* var. *waddelliue*   *Ozothamnus hookeri*

Phoenocoma prolifera at Cape Point Reserve, South Africa   *Phoenocoma prolifera*

COMPOSITAE

Eupatorium sordidum in Menton Botanic Garden, France

Eupatorium ligustrinum in Trebah, Cornwall

Ageratum corymbosum

Eupatorium sordidum

Ageratum corymbosum Zucc. ex Pers.
(*Compositae*)   A shrub with blue, lavender or
white flowers, native of C America, flowering
throughout the summer. Stems to 2m. Leaves
to 10cm, ovate to spear-shaped, subentire or
toothed, dull green above, pale green and
hoary below. Flower heads numerous forming
dense round clusters, blue, lavender, white.
Min. –6°C. The pretty brush-like bushy
blooms flower over a long period, sometimes
continuing from summer until the first frost.

Berkheya armata (Vahl) Druce
(*Compositae*)   A perennial herb with bright
yellow daisy flowers, native of the Cape
Province in South Africa, growing on sandy
plains and low hills flowering from
September–December (summer). Stems to
40cm, erect, simple or moderately branched.
Leaves to 18cm, alternate, oval to spear-
shaped; margin toothed and spiny. Flower
heads 6–10cm; ray florets and disc florets
bright yellow. Min. –8°C. This plant will grow
in almost any fertile soil if well drained and in
a sunny position.

Cassinia aculeata (Labill.) R. Br.
(*Compositae*) Dolly Bush   A shrub with white
flowers, native of New South Wales,
Victoria, Tasmania and S Australia, growing in
openings in forests in partial shade, usually in
damp areas, flowering in the summer. Stems
to 4m, much-branched, woolly. Leaves to
3cm, alternate, linear, rough above, woolly
below. Flower heads small, numerous in a
terminal cluster, white. Min. –5°C. This
species is tender and may not tolerate such a

low temperature as that given, probably
preferring to be grown in a cool greenhouse in
such conditions. Prune quite hard in spring to
retain a compact shape.

Cotula lineariloba (DC.) Hilliard.
(*Compositae*)   A rhizomatous tufted perennial
herb with bright yellow to red flowers without
petals (rays), native of South Africa from the
W Cape to Natal, growing on mountain
slopes, flowering in summer (November–
January). Stems to 20cm, erect, simple, leafy.
Leaves to 3cm, oblong, upper leaves smaller,
pinnate and bract-like. Flower heads 1–2.5cm,
round, ray florets bright yellow to red. Min.
–6°C. This plant makes an attactive low
ground-cover for lawns, paving and rockeries.

Cotula turbinata L., syn. *Cenia turbinata*
(*Compositae*)   An ascending to erect annual
herb with yellow flowers, found in New
Zealand, Australia and South Africa, growing
in waste places, roadsides and disturbed areas
near towns as well as pastures, riverbeds,
coastal areas and forests, flowering from
January–December. Stems 10–20cm, slender,
much-branched from the base, very hairy.
Leaves 10–35mm, deeply pinnatisect, feathery
Flower heads 3–6mm, yellow. Min. –3°C.

Dendranthema indicum (L.) Desmoul.,
syn. *Chrysanthemum indicum* L. (*Compositae*)
A strongly scented stoloniferous perennial
with yellow flowers, native of S Japan and E
China, growing in scrub and grassy places,
flowering in the autumn. Stems to 60cm,
leafy, decumbent and softly hairy. Leaves to

Dendranthema indicum growing wild in Hong Kong

Cotula turbinata

Cotula lineariloba

5cm, egg-shaped, oblong, toothed and lobed. Flowers 2.5cm, in corymbs, ray florets to 13mm, yellow. Min. –10°C. This, with the white or pink flowered *D. morifolium*, is one of the wild ancestors of the garden Chrysanthemum, which was developed in China around 600BC and later brought to perfection in Japan. These Japanese varieties were first sent to England around 1861.

Eupatorium ligustrinum DC., syn. *Ageratina ligustrina* (DC.) R. King & H. Robinson (*Compositae*)   A large shrub with creamy-white or rose-tinged flowers, native of Mexico to Costa Rica, flowering in autumn. Stems to over 5m, erect, densely branched. Leaves 5–10cm, elliptic; margin sparsely toothed, lighter green below. Flower heads to 20cm wide, in large clusters; 4–8 ray florets, creamy white or rose-tinged, fragrant. Min. –1°C.

Eupatorium sordidum Lee., syns. *Eupatorium macrophyllum* Hort. *Bartlettina sordida* (Less.) R. King & H. Robinson. *(Compositae)*   An erect shrub with fragrant pink to violet flowers, native of Mexico, growing in forests, scrub or waste places, flowering in winter. Stems to 3m, densely covered in red woolly hairs. Leaves to 10cm, broadly egg-shaped, coarsely toothed. Flower heads to 12mm, in large, terminal clusters, sweet-smelling, pink to violet. Min. –5°C. A very variable plant differing greatly in size of leaves, hairiness and colour and size of flower heads. The form shown here is a particularly good large one, commonly grown along the Riviera.

Podolepsis gracilis (Lehm.) Graham, syn. *Podolepsis rosea* Steetz. *(Compositae/Asteraceae)* An annual herb with pink flowers, native of W Australia, flowering in the summer. Stems to 50cm. Leaves to 8cm, attached to the stem, spear-shaped, green above woolly white below. Flower heads to 2cm, single or many, ray florets to 1.5cm, pink, disc florets pink. Min. –6°C. This plant can be dried for everlastings.

Sonchus ortunoi Svent. *(Compositae)* A robust shrub with yellow daisy flowers, native of the Canary Islands on Gomera in the central and SW regions and the N coast to 200–1000m, flowering in spring. Stems to 1m. Leaves to 30cm pinnatisect, bright green, semi-smooth. Flower heads 4–5cm, in small clusters, yellow. Min. –5°C.

Berkheya armata flowering after a bush fire

Podolepsis gracilis in Canberra, Australia

Sonchus ortunoi in the Huntington Gardens San Marino, California

Cassinia aculeata in Melbourne, Australia

Calochortus barbatus at Harry Hay's

Calochortus weedii at Sellindge, Kent

Calochortus barbatus (H. B. & K.) Painter (*Liliaceae*) A small bulb with grass-like leaves and hanging yellow hairy flowers, native of Mexico, growing in grassland and open oak and pine woods, below 2500m, flowering in July–September. Leaves 5–10mm wide, with bulbils in the axils. Stems 10-30cm, branched. Flowers with 3 narrow and 3 broader, pointed segments, 2–3cm across, with purple hairs. For rich soil, moist in summer, dry in winter. Do not attempt to start into growth before June. Min. –3°C.

Calochortus catalinae Wats. A small bulb with grass-like leaves and upright white flowers, native of S California along the coast from San Luis Obispo to San Diego Co., growing on grassy clay hills near the coast below 600m, flowering in March–May. Leaves 3–6mm wide. Stems 20-60cm, branched. Flowers with 3 large segments, white tinged with purple, 3–5cm long, with a small dark oblong gland, surrounded with hairs near the base. For rich soil, moist in winter, dry in summer. Min. 0°C.

Calochortus purpureus Baker A small Fritillary-like bulb with grassy leaves and hanging, purple and green flowers, native of Mexico, growing on rocky banks in oak and pine woods below 2500m, flowering in July–September. Leaves 5–10mm wide, with bulbils in the axils. Stems 10–30cm, little branched. Flowers 2.5–3.5cm across, with 3 narrow and 3 broader segments fringed with yellow hairs. For leafy soil, moist in summer, dry in winter. Do not attempt to start into growth before June. Min. –3°C. We found this growing with *Achimenes mexicana* (*see page 183*).

Calochortus madrensis S. Wats. A small bulb with grass-like leaves and upright yellow flowers, native of W Mexico, growing in dry pine woods at around 2500m, flowering in September–October. Leaves 5–10mm wide. Stems 10–20cm, branched. Flowers 2.5cm across, with 6 almost equal segments with brownish hairs near the base. For leafy soil, moist in summer, dry in winter. Do not start into growth before June. Min. –3°C.

Calochortus weedii Wood A small bulb with grass-like leaves and upright yellow hairy flowers, native of S California, from the Santa Ana Mountains to San Diego Co., growing on dry rocky hills near the coast, below 1500m, flowering in May–July. Leaves 10–15mm wide. Stems 30–60cm, branched. Flowers with 3 very narrow and 3 broad segments, yellow with a brown edges and spots, rarely all red-brown or purplish, 2.5–3cm long, with a small round gland near the base. For rich soil, moist in winter, dry in summer. Min. –3°C.

Lapageria rosea Ruiz & Pavon (*Liliaceae-Philesiaceae*) Copihue An evergreen twiner with large waxy bells of red, pink or white, native of Chile and Argentina, south to 41°S, growing in moist forests, flowering mainly from late summer–spring. Stems twining to 3m or more. Leaves 3–10cm long, very stiff and leathery. Flowers mainly in the leaf axils of old stems, around 7.5cm long, sometimes pink spotted with white as in **'Nash Court'** (*shown here*), or even striped. Fruit an elongated fleshy berry. For moist leafy soil and shelter; an ideal plant for a cold conservatory, needing little care except protection of the young shoots from slugs and snails. Slow to establish, but very long-lived. Min. –5°C.

Calochortus catalinae near Los Angeles

Calochortus purpureus in September

Lapageria rosea white form

Calochortus catalinae on grassy hills near Long Beach, California in March

Calochortus madrensis wild in pine woods at Punta de Buenos Aires above Copala in late October

Lilium brownii Miellez var. ***viridulum***
Baker, syn. var. *colchesteri* (Van Houtte) Elwes
(*Liliaceae*)   A tall slender lily with few large
white flowers, greenish outside, native of
S China from Hong Kong (var. *australe*
(Stapf) Stearn), westwards to N Burma,
growing in rock crevices among coarse grass
and scrub below 1500m, flowering in
July–September. Bulbs usually rather small.
Stems to 1.25m, green. Leaves 1–2.5cm wide,
without bulbils in the axils. Flowers 1–4, rarely
flushed purple outside, yellowish inside on
opening, fading to white, 12–18cm long. For a
very well-drained position, moist in summer,
dry in winter. Growth does not start till May
Min. –3°C.

Lilium formosanum Wallace   A tall lily
with masses of narrow leaves and an umbel of
scented narrow-tubed white flowers, native of
Taiwan, growing in open grassy places, in
sandy or volcanic soil, particularly among
Miscanthus, at up to 3000m, flowering much
of the year. Bulbs small with many narrow
scales. Stems to 2m. leaves 5–10mm wide.
Flowers 1–10, 12–15cm long, usually purplish
outside. Easy to grow from seed, flowering in a
year and growing continually in warm
climates. This lovely lily grows well in the
tropics and is naturalised in parts of Africa. It
grows well with the bulbs crammed into a pot,
with crocks below the bulbs and good loose
compost above. Min. –3°C. Var. *pricei* Stocker
is a dwarf high altitude form with stems as
short as 10cm. Min. –10°C.

Lilium longiflorum Thunb. Easter Lily
A rather stout lily with an umbel of long white
trumpet flowers, native of S Japan, in
Yakusima and the Liukiu Islands including
Okinawa and in Taiwan, growing in pockets in
coral rock, flowering in May–June. Stems to
1m, green or purplish. Leaves 5–15mm wide.
Flowers 1–6, 13–20cm long, sometimes
flushed with brown outside. For well-drained
limestone soil. Min. 0°C. This lily is widely
grown for the cut flower trade and in the past
Bermuda was the main source for the North
American market, the mild climate and coral
soil suiting the plant perfectly.

Lilium longiflorum in Bermuda in April

Lilium formosanum naturalised in Limbe, Malawi

Lapageria rosea 'Nash Court' in an unheated
vinery at Sellindge, Kent

Lilium brownii var. *viridulum* at Harry Hay's

Sandersonia aurantiaca at Harry Hay's

Gloriosa superba, Virescens group, wild in Malawi, near Monkey Bay in January

Gloriosa superba L. (*Liliaceae-Colchicaceae*)
A summer-growing perennial climber with a
V-shaped or simple tuberous root, leaves
modified to tendrils and flowers with reflexed
petals, native of tropical Africa from Ethiopia
south to Natal and Madagascar and of Asia
from Sri Lanka to NW India, Thailand and
Malaysia, growing in grassland, scrub and
forest margins, flowering in summer–autumn.
Stems to 5m (on Mount Elgon), though
usually less than 2m. Flowers with tepals
4–10cm long, red, yellow, red and yellow, or
very rarely white. Stamens arching outwards;
style bent to one side. A superb plant, very
variable in the wild in size and colour. Several
variants have been named as species, a
selection of which is shown here. Needs good
rich soil and ample heat, water and feeding
while growing; dry in winter. Start in heat.
Min. 5°C while dormant.
'Rothschildiana' A fine cultivar with
striped crisped flowers, red with a yellow base
and margin, fading to all red.
Lutea group Flowers all pale yellow; a
frequent colour form found from Malawi to
Tanzania. Tepals sometimes crisped,
sometimes smooth in this colour form, fading
to pinkish-orange.
Virescens group A common form in
Malawi and elsewhere in Africa, petals yellow
with a red centre, strongly incurved, wavy but
not crisped, fading brownish-red.

Littonia modesta Hook. (*Liliaceae-
Colchicaceae*) A summer-growing perennial
with a tuberous root, leaves modified to
tendrils and pale orange nodding flowers,
native of tropical Africa from Botswana, the
Transvaal and Orange Free State south to
Natal, growing in scrub and forest margins,
often among bracken, flowering in
January–February. Stems to 1.8m. Leaves
lanceolate, to 12cm long. Flowers with tepals
around 4cm long. An attractive plant needing
the same treatment as *Gloriosa*.

Gloriosa superba Lutea group, wild in Malawi

Wurmbea latifolia on Garcia Pass, S Cape in
October

Onixotis triquetra growing in shallow water in a marsh near Citrusdal, in October

Littonia modesta on Ngeli Mountain, Natal

Onixotis triquetra

Onixotis triquetra (L. fil.) Mabberley, syn. *Dipidax triquetra* (L. fil.) Bak. (*Liliaceae-Colchicaceae*)   An aquatic winter-growing perennial with rush-like leaves and spikes of pink or white flowers, native of South Africa in Namaqualand, the W and SW Cape east to Port Elizabeth, growing in seasonal marshes and pools, flowering in August–November. Root a corm. Stems to 45cm, the flower spike subtended by a leaf; leaves triangular in section; flowers to 2.5cm across. An attractive plant for a pool edge. Min. 0°C.

Sandersonia aurantiaca Hook. (*Liliaceae-Colchicaceae*)   A summer-growing perennial with small 2-lobed tuberous roots, leaves not modified to tendrils and pale orange, inflated nodding flowers, like Chinese lanterns, native of South Africa in Natal, reaching 1950m in the Drakensberg, growing on steep slopes in scrub along streams and on forest margins, flowering in December–January. Stems to 2m. Leaves lanceolate, to 12cm long. Flowers around 4cm long with tepals united and crimped at the base into spur-like points. An attractive plant needing the same treatment as *Gloriosa*. Min. –3°C when dormant.

Wurmbea latifolia (Bak.) B. Nordenstam (*Liliaceae-Colchicaceae*)   A dwarf winter-growing perennial with a corm, flat leaves and a spike of starry white flowers with dark spots and stamens, native of South Africa growing in damp sandy places in the Langkloof, flowering in October. Stem 5–10cm. Stem leaves 3, overlapping. Flowers around 25, 1.5cm across. The larger *Wurmbea spicata* (Burm. fil.) Durand & Schinz, a winter-growing species from the Cape, has stems to 20cm, crowded with flowers which are scented in the evening. Min. –3°C, perhaps.

Gloriosa superba 'Rothschildiana' with leaves of *Vitis vinifera* 'Purpurea'

Bulbine latifolia in Madeira

Bulbine caulescens in the Huntington Gardens

Bulbine praemorsa in the Little Karroo

Kniphofia typhoides in Devon

Thysanotus dichotomus in the Moore River National Park near Perth, WA

Kniphofia rooperi flowering in January at Les Cèdres, Côte d'Azur

Arthropodium cirrhatum (Forst. fil.) R. Br. (*Liliaceae-Asphodelaceae*) A large perennial with evergreen leaves and branched panicles of nodding white flowers, native of New Zealand in North Island and N South Island growing in forest and shady places, flowering in November–January. Leaves rather fleshy, narrowly lanceolate to 30–60cm long. Stems to 75cm. Flowers 2–4cm across with curved and bearded tails on the anthers. For rich leafy soil. Min. –3°C. *A. candidum* Raoul is deciduous and smaller with linear leaves 10–30cm long and less than 1cm wide and flowers around 1cm across.

Bulbine latifolia (*Liliaceae-Asphodelaceae*) A perennial with a basal rosette of succulent leaves and spikes of small yellow flowers, native of S Africa in Natal, growing in rocky places, flowering most of the year. Leaves soft and fleshy to 10cm long. Stems to 45cm. Flowers around 1cm across with bearded stamens. For well-drained soil. Min. –3°C. *Bulbine natalensis* Baker is very similar, but has longer narrower inflorescences.

Bulbine caulescens (L.) Willd., syn. *B. frutescens* (L.) Willd. A perennial or sub-shrub with rosettes of soft narrow leaves and spikes of small yellow or brownish flowers, native of South Africa throughout the Cape and in the Little Karroo to the E Cape and Natal, growing in rocky and grassy places, flowering in August–December. Leaves soft and fleshy around 16cm long. Stems to 40cm. Flowers around 1cm across, sometimes white with bearded stamens. For well-drained soil. Min. –3°C overnight. A variable plant, sometimes forming shrubby patches.

Bulbine praemorsa (Jacq.) Roem. & Schult. A perennial with rosettes of soft narrow leaves and spikes of small yellow flowers, native of South Africa throughout the W Cape and in the Little Karroo, growing in rocky and grassy places, flowering in August–December. Leaves soft and fleshy around 20cm long. Stems 40–60cm. Flowers around 1cm across, sometimes white, with bearded stamens. For well-drained soil. Min. –3°C overnight.

Chlorophytum species in Malawi A tall slender perennial with broad upright leaves and a branched inflorescence of small white flowers, native of Malawi, growing in grassy places with bracken on Mlanje Mountain, at around 2000m, flowering in December–January. Leaves around 1m, 5–8cm wide. Stems to 1.8m. Flowers around 1.5cm across. For moist peaty soil with shade in hot climates. Min. 0°C.

Kniphofia northiae Baker (*Liliaceae-Asphodelaceae*) A huge perennial with rosettes of broad long-pointed leaves and thick spikes of orange or yellowish flowers, native of the NE Cape, E Lesotho and Natal, growing among rocks and on peaty hills, at 1500–3000m, flowering in October. Leaves to 1.5m long and 15cm wide. Inflorescence around 50cm, in most areas with pinkish buds opening whitish, as shown here, but rarely orange-red, opening yellow. For rich peaty soil. Min. –10°C. Though very hardy this is one of the most exotic-looking species for a tropical effect.

Kniphofia rooperi (Moore) Lem. A clump-forming perennial with narrow spreading leaves and short dense spikes of

Kniphofia northiae at Bustervoedpad, NE Cape in October

Chlorophytum species on Mlanje Mountain, Malawi in January

Kniphofia thomsonii in Tanzania, with Embagai Crater Lake behind

Arthropodium cirrhatum in Wellington in January

orange or yellow or green flowers, native of the SE Cape and S Natal, growing in marshy places near the coast, at 1500-3000m, flowering mainly in June–September (winter–early spring). Leaves to 1.1m long, 3.5cm wide. Inflorescence around 150cm, the flowers crowded onto the top 8–11cm, with red, orange or green buds opening orange or yellow. For rich peaty soil. Min. –5°C. This species is valuable for flowering in mid-winter in mild climates.

Kniphofia thomsonii Baker A tall slender perennial with long curving flowers, native of E Africa from Ethiopia to Kenya, Tanzania, and Zaire, growing usually in marshy places at 1000–3900m, flowering much of the year.

Leaves flat or keeled. Stems to 1m. Flowers crowded or spaced out, red to yellow. An elegant plant for a mild area. Min. –5°C provided the root does not freeze. Var. *snowdenii* (C. H. Wright) Marais, only from Kenya and Uganda, has a lax inflorescence and hairs inside the floral tube.

Kniphofia typhoides Codd A tall, very slender perennial with small chocolate-brown scented flowers, native of South Africa from Natal and Orange Free State to Transvaal, growing in marshy places in black clay soil at 1000–1500m, flowering in February–March. Leaves greyish, mainly in 2 ranks, 35–65cm long. Stems to 1m. Flowers crowded into the top 15–30cm, 4.5–6.5mm long with exserted

stamens and style. Min. –5°C, perhaps. Two other species, *K. umbrina* Codd and *K. brachystachya* (A. Zahlbr.) Codd, have similar brownish flowers.

Thysanotus dichotomus (Labill.) R. Br. (*Liliaceae-Asphodelaceae*) A tufted perennial with bluish-mauve flowers, the inner three petals fringed with long hairs, native of Western Australia, growing in sandy heathy places, flowering in spring–summer. Leaves linear-lanceolate, 8–14cm. Stems to 60cm, branched, with umbels of flowers; petals to 18mm long. Stamens 6. For sandy soil, not too wet. Min. 0°C. In the commoner *T. patersoni* from E Australia, the stems twine or hang down if unsupported.

235

Aloe ferox near Oudtshoorn with the Great Swartberg in the background in October

Aloe arborescens, close-up of inflorescence

Aloe ferox on the Côte d'Azur, flowering in January

Aloe arborescens at le Clos du Peyronnet, Menton in January

Aloe tenuior in the Huntington Gardens, San Merino in March

Aloe striata at la Mortola, NW Italy

Aloe africana Mill.(*Liliaceae-Aloeaceae*) A stout shrubby succulent with an unbranched stem and branching inflorescence of yellow or orange flowers, native of South Africa in E Cape Province from Humansdorp to Port Elizabeth, growing in rocky places, flowering in July–September (early spring). Stems 2–4m. Leaves to 65cm long, 12cm wide. Inflorescence with 2–4 branches, to 80cm. Flowers to 5.5cm. For a dry sunny position. Min. –2°C.

Aloe arborescens Mill. A tree-like succulent with a much-branched stem and simple inflorescence of scarlet or yellow flowers, native of South Africa in the Cape, from Caledon to Uitenhage and north to Zimbabwe and Malawi, growing in bush and open forest, flowering in May–June (winter). Stems 2–3m. Leaves to 60cm long, greyish. Inflorescence to 80cm. Flowers to 4cm, with green tips, on thin pedicels. For a warm, sunny position. Min. –2°C.

Aloe cooperi Baker subsp. ***pulchra*** A stemless succulent perennial with long narrow channelled leaves and a simple

Aloe africana in the Huntington Gardens, San Merino in March

Aloe plicatilis in the Botanic Gardens, Funchal, Madeira

inflorescence of pinkish-red flowers, native of South Africa in Swaziland, growing in grassland, flowering in November–December (summer). Stems absent. Leaves to 80cm long, green, spotted. Inflorescence to 1m, unbranched. Flowers pinkish with green tips, hanging on thin pedicels. For a warm sunny position. Min. 0°C. Subspecies *pulchra* appears to be smaller then subspecies *cooperi*.

Aloe ferox Mill.   A stout shrubby succulent with an unbranched stem and branched inflorescence of bright scarlet flowers, native of South Africa in E Cape Province from the Little Karoo and Swellendam to Mossel Bay and east to the E Cape, Lesotho and Orange Free State, growing in scrub and rocky places, flowering in May–November (early spring). Stems 2–3m. Leaves to 1m long, 15cm wide. Inflorescence with 2–4 branches, to 80cm. Flowers to 3.5cm, rarely orange. For a dry sunny position. Min. −2°C.

Aloe plicatilis (L.) Mill.   A tree-like succulent with a much-branched stem, stiff flattish non-spiny leaves in 2 ranks and a simple inflorescence of large red flowers, native of South Africa in the Cape from Tulbagh to Stellenbosch, growing on rocky mountain slopes, flowering in August–October (spring). Stems 3–5m. Leaves to 30cm long, greyish. Inflorescence to 50cm. Flowers to 5cm. For a warm sunny position. Min. −3°C perhaps less overnight.

Aloe striatula Haw.   A shrubby succulent with a much-branched stem and simple

inflorescence of scarlet to yellow flowers, native of South Africa in the E Cape and Lesotho, growing in bush and rocky places, flowering in October–December (summer). Stems 1–2m. Leaves to 25cm long, glossy with small teeth. Inflorescence to 40cm, dense. Flowers to 4.5cm, pointing down. For a warm sunny position. Min. −5°C. *Aloe ciliaris* Haw. differs in its more slender stems and flowers with green tips. It is commonly cultivated in S France and California.

Aloe striata Haw.   A large succulent with a stemless rosette of thick leaves and a much-branched inflorescence of bright pink flowers, native of South Africa in the Cape from Worcester east to the Little Karoo, Port Elizabeth and the E Cape, growing in dry bush and rocky places, flowering in August–September (spring). Stems decumbent. Leaves to 50cm long, greyish, without teeth. Inflorescence to 1m, much-branched at the top. Flowers to 2.5cm, hanging down. For a warm sunny position. Min. −5°C. *Aloe saponaria* Haw. differs in its smaller spiny-edged brown-banded leaves.

Aloe tenuior Haw.   A shrubby succulent with an elongated scrambling stem and simple inflorescence of yellow flowers, native of South Africa in the E Cape, growing in bush, flowering in October–December (summer). Stems to 3m, visible between the leaves. Leaves to 15cm long, greyish with small teeth. Inflorescence to 30cm, dense. Flowers to 1.5cm, pointing down, sometimes red. For a warm sunny position. Min. −5°C.

Aloe cooperi subsp. *pulchra* at Harry Hay's

Aloe striatula in the Abbey Gardens, Tresco

Agave americana 'Mediopicta Alba'

Agave attenuata, detail of flowers

Cordyline terminalis in S California

Agave filifera in the Abbey Gardens, Tresco, Isles of Scilly

Agave attenuata growing on a precipice in the mountains above Copala, SW Mexico

Furcraea bedingshausii flowering in the open in Barnstaple, North Devon

Agave americana L. **'Mediopicta Alba'** (*Agavaceae*) Century Plant   The species forms a huge succulent rosette of glaucous spiny leaves with a branching inflorescence of yellow flowers, native of Mexico, but commonly planted in Mediterranean countries and spreading underground by suckers. Rosette to 3m across. Leaves 15–30cm wide, with spines on the margin and a terminal spine 3–5mm long. Inflorescence 5–8m, with yellow flowers. **'Mediopicta Alba'** (*shown here*) has a broad white stripe along the centre of the leaf; the commoner 'Variegata' has leaves edged white. For well-drained soil. Min. –3°C if dry.

Agave attenuata Salm-Dyck   A succulent with a rosette of glaucous leaves and a long curving inflorescence of pale greenish flowers, native of Mexico in the Sierra Madre Occidentale, growing along the tops of cliffs in cloud forest of pine and oak, flowering in November–January (winter). Rosettes often on a short prostrate trunk. Leaves without spines and with a soft point, 50–70cm long, 12–16cm wide. Inflorescence to 3.5m with plantlets after flowering, hanging out over the cliff. Easily grown with water in summer. Min. –3°C.

Agave filifera Salm-Dyck   A succulent with a rosette of glaucous leaves and an upright inflorescence of reddish-brown flowers, native presumably of Mexico but not known wild, flowering in summer. Rosettes trunkless, around 65cm across. Leaves 2–4cm wide, without spines, dark green with white lines on the surface, the margins splitting into 5–6 long threads. Inflorescence to 2.5m; flowers 3–3.5cm long. Easily grown with water in summer. Min. –3°C.

Beschorneria yuccoides Hook. (*Agavaceae*) A succulent with a rosette of soft glaucous leaves and an arching inflorescence with pinkish-red bracts and green flowers, native of Mexico, flowering in summer. Rosettes trunkless. Leaves 30–60cm long, around 5cm wide, without spines, rough beneath. Inflorescence to 1.2m, the branches drooping; flowers 5–7.5cm long. Easily grown with water in summer; also tolerant of drought. Min. –3°C.

Cordyline australis (Forst. fil.) Endl. (*Agavaceae*) Cabbage Tree   A little branched tree with large tufts of leaves on the ends of the branches and large pyramidal panicles of small scented flowers, native of New Zealand on North and South Islands, growing on the margins of forest and in open places near swamps, flowering in October–December (summer). Trunk to 12m. Leaves 30–100cm long, 3–6cm across. Panicles 60–150cm long. One of the hardiest of the palm-like trees, widely planted by the sea in SW England and California. Cut back when young to encourage branching. Min. –10°C for short periods. Other cultivars (*not shown*) include 'Torbay Red' with red leaves, and 'Albertii' with leaves striped with cream and pink, red in the centre.

Cordyline indivisa (Forst. fil.) Steud. A little branched tree with broad leaves and compact panicles of small white flowers, native of New Zealand on North and South Islands, growing in openings in wet forest, flowering in December–January. Trunk to 8m. Leaves 1–2m long, 10–15cm across. Panicles 60–160cm, pendulous when large. A grander but tenderer plant than *C. australis*, also good by the sea. Min. –3°C.

Cordyline stricta (Sims) Endl.   A slender clump-forming shrub with narrow lax leaves, and open panicles of small purple flowers, native of Australia in Queensland and New

Beschorneria yuccoides at M. Pellizzaro's, Vallauris, S France

Cordyline australis at Tapeley Park, near Bideford, Devon

South Wales, growing in openings in rainforest and along streams, flowering in December–February. Stems 2–5m. Leaves 20–60cm long, 1–2.5cm across. Panicles 30–70cm, arching, producing purple or blackish berries. A graceful plant, often grown in conservatories, needing water all year. Min. –3°C.

Cordyline terminalis (L.) Kunth. A tall clump-forming shrub with few broad, often red leaves and open panicles of white or purplish flowers, native of Australia in Queensland and New South Wales, north to tropical SE Asia and Hawaii, growing in openings in rainforest and along streams, flowering in July–September in Australia. Stems 2–7m. Leaves 30–50cm long, 3–8cm across, lanceolate. Panicles 30–60cm, arching, producing bright red berries around 1cm across. A common plant in tropical gardens, with many cultivars, eventually forming large spreading clumps. Min. –3°C.

Doryanthes excelsa Corr. (*Agavaceae*)
A huge clump-forming perennial with upright leaves and tall stems with a head of red flowers, native of Australia in New South Wales, growing in sandstone areas in open forest or heathland around Sydney, flowering in August–February. Scape 2–5m. Leaves to 1.5m long, 10cm across, linear-lanceolate. Flower heads 30cm across, the flowers around 10cm long, with 6 nearly equal lobes. An easy plant to grow, but takes 5–10 years to reach flowering size. Min. –3°C. *D. palmeri* W. Hill ex Benth. has the inflorescence arching, with an elongated flower head to 1m long.

Furcraea bedinghausii Koch (*Agavaceae*)
A soft yucca-like plant producing a giant inflorescence of hanging green branches, native of Mexico, flowering in summer. Plant with short trunk. Leaves 60–120cm long, 5–10cm wide, with small teeth, rough on the keel beneath. Inflorescence to 6m, the branches to 2m; the flowers pale green, eventually replaced by bulbils. For any good soil in a warm position. Min. –5°C for short periods.

Cordyline indivisa in Cornwall

Cordyline australis flowers

Doryanthes excelsa in the Huntington Gardens, San Merino, California

Cordyline stricta in the Temperate House, Kew

Spiloxene aquatica at Harry Hay's

Spiloxene capensis

Bessera elegans (red form) at Harry Hay's

Bessera elegans (pink form) at Harry Hay's

Tulbaghia cominsii at Harry Hay's

Milla biflora

Milla biflora wild in wet fields in C Mexico, north of Guadalajara in October

Agapanthus praecox Willd. subsp. **orientalis** (Leighton) Leighton (*Liliaceae-Alliaceae*) An evergreen clump-forming perennial with dense umbels of blue flowers, native of South Africa in the S and E Cape to Transkei and W Natal at Port Shepstone, growing in rocky places and cliffs by the sea, flowering in December–February. Leaves 2.5–5.5cm wide. Scape 50–100cm. Flowers 4–5cm long. This species is commonly grown in warm gardens and in tubs, put outdoors in summer. For good soil, with water in summer, dry in winter. Min. −3°C. This is naturalised on the sand dunes on Tresco, Isles of Scilly. *Agapanthus africanus* (L.) Hoffmans. from rocky mountains from the Peninsula to Swellendam, has leaves less than 35cm long, 9–12mm wide and very thick fleshy flowers. It needs water in winter, dry conditions in summer.

Bessera elegans Schultes (*Liliaceae-Alliaceae*) A corm with nodding bell-shaped pinkish-purple, orange or scarlet flowers with protruding stamens, native of SW and SC Mexico, flowering in late summer. Leaves 60–80cm linear. Scape to 90cm, with 2–30 flowers. Perianth lobes 3–4cm, paler inside. Stamens united below into a tube. For good soil with water from midsummer to autumn. Min. 0°C.

Leucocoryne ixioides (Hook.) Lindl. (*Liliaceae-Alliaceae*) A slender bulb with lovely pale blue and white or white flowers, native of C Chile, growing in dry sandy places, flowering in spring. Leaves narrowly linear. Scape to 45cm, with 6–9 flowers, each 2.4–3cm across. For good sandy soil, with water in winter, dry in summer. Min −3°C.

Milla biflora Cav. (*Liliaceae-Alliaceae*) A small bulb with stiff slender stems and starry white flowers, native of Arizona, S New Mexico, Mexico and Guatemala, growing in damp grassy places or open oak and pine woods, up to 2000m, flowering in August–November. Leaves 2–7, narrowly linear. Scape with an umbel of 1–6 scented flowers, each 3–7cm across, with a long tube 10–20cm long. For good soil with ample water in midsummer, dry in winter and spring. Min. −3°C.

Spiloxene aquatica (L. fil.) Fourc., syn. *Hypoxis aquatica* (L. fil.) Druce (*Hypoxidceae*) A small perennial with a corm, narrow leaves and white starry flowers, native of South Africa throughout the Cape from Clanwilliam to Port Elizabeth, growing in pools and marshes, flowering in June–October. Stem 10–30cm. Flowers 2cm across, in an umbel of 1–7. For peaty soil with water in winter, dry in summer. Min. 0°C.

Spiloxene capensis (L.) Garside, syn. *Hypoxis capensis* (L. fil.) Druce A small perennial with a corm, narrow leaves and yellow, pink or white starry flowers, often with an irridescent purple centre, native of South Africa through the W Cape from Clanwilliam to the Peninsula and east to Humansdorp, growing in rocky and stony places, along seepage lines and in wet fields, flowering in August–October. Stem 10–30cm. Flowers 1.5–10cm across, solitary. For sandy soil with water in winter, dry in summer. Min. 0°C.

Tulbaghia cominsii Vosa (*Liliaceae-Alliaceae*) A dwarf clump-forming perennial

Agapanthus praecox subsp. *orientalis* in the Abbey Gardens, Tresco, Isles of Scilly

Tulbaghia violacea in Devon

Tulbaghia natalensis at Marwood Hill, Devon

with small bulbs and very thin leaves smelling of onion, and scented white flowers, native of South Africa in the E Cape near King William's Town, growing in rocky areas, flowering in August–October. Leaves glaucous, to 20cm long, 1mm wide. Umbel with 7–9 white flowers, each 14–18mm across, the corona of 3 simple white lobes. Very free-flowering and pretty in a pot for its sweet scent. Good well-drained soil. Min. −3°C.

Tulbaghia natalensis Baker A clump-forming perennial with small bulbs and grassy leaves smelling of onion, native of South Africa in the Natal Drakensberg, growing in damp places and rocky areas with seepage, at 800–1800m, flowering in August–October.

Leaves glaucous, to 20cm long, 4mm wide. Umbel with 3–12 white flowers, each 16–20mm across, the corona greenish-orange with blunt teeth. For any good soil. Min. −5°C.

Tulbaghia violacea Harvey A clump-forming perennial with narrow bulbs and grassy leaves smelling of onion, native of South Africa in the E Cape from Knysna eastwards to East London, growing in rocky places, flowering in December–April. Leaves glaucous, 28–35cm long, 6–8mm wide. Umbel with 12–14 soft purple flowers, each 2–2.2cm across, the corona of 3 fleshy scales. For any good soil. Min. −10°C if the rootstock is protected.

Leucocoryne ixioides in the Alpine House, Kew

Hippeastrum × johnsonii in a village garden near Dali, Yunnan

Hippeastrum reticulatum in Devon

Hippeastrum argentinum (Pax.) Hunz (*Amaryllidaceae*) An ovoid bulb with broad leaves and horizontal long-tubed scented flowers with wavy segments, native of South America in Argentina and Bolivia, flowering mainly in summer. Leaves to 4cm wide. Scape to 50cm. Flowers 2–3, to 15cm long; the tube 5.5cm, the lobes oblanceolate. Stigma capitate, slightly 3-lobed. For sandy leafy soil, dry in winter, moist in summer. Min. 0°C. Very similar to *H. solandriflorum* (Lindl.) Herbert, which has 2–6 narrower flowers 18–25cm long, sometimes striped or tinged with red. It comes from South America, south to Peru.

Hippeastrum calyptratum (Ker Gawl.) Herbert A rather rounded bulb with broad leaves and pale greenish flowers, native of Brazil, flowering in winter–spring. Leaves to 4cm wide. Scape to 40cm. Flowers 2–3, 10–12cm long; the tube 2–2.5cm, with scales closing its throat. Outer lobes incurved, inner outcurved. Stigma 3-fid at apex. For sandy leafy soil, dry in winter, moist in summer. Min. 0°C.

Hippeastrum 'Lemon 'n' Lime' In this recent garden hybrid the flowers are an unusual shade of greenish-yellow, fading to pink. The flowers are slightly smaller than the huge modern hybrids sold at Christmas time. These were first raised and improved by John Seden, the famous hybridist at Veitch's in Chelsea from 1867 onwards, using the Bolivian *H. leopoldii* Dombrain. As well as

concentrating on large flowers with clear colours, they raised a yellowish-green hybrid called 'Veldt', which must have been similar to the modern 'Lemon 'n' Lime'.

Hippeastrum 'Pamela' A fine hybrid with perfectly formed flowers of intense red, easily grown and free-flowering, in early spring in England, even without extra heat. This has been a popular show variety in America in the miniature hybrid class. Water in summer, keep dry in winter. Min. –3°C.

Hippeastrum psittacinum (Ker Gawl.) Herbert A rather large bulb with broad leaves and greenish zygomorphic flowers, the upper petals heavily marked and veined with chocolate-red, native of S Brazil, flowering in spring. Leaves to 4cm wide. Scape to 50cm. Flowers 2–4, 10–12cm long; the tube short, with scales closing its throat. Lowest lobes with the margins inrolled. Stigma 3-fid at apex. For sandy leafy soil, dry in winter, moist in summer. I have not found this easy to flower regularly, but have heard that the bulbs should be crowded in the pot. Min. 0°C. Sometimes sold under the name 'Papillo'.

Hippeastrum puniceum (Lam.) Urban, syn. *Amaryllis belladonna* sensu Traub A rather rounded bulb with broad leaves and horizontal orange-red flowers on tall stems, native of N South America and the Caribbean, flowering in winter–spring. Leaves 2.5–4.5cm wide. Scape to 60cm. Flowers 2–4, 10–13cm long; the tube 2.5cm. Stigma

capitate. For sandy soil, dry in winter, moist in summer. Min. 5°C.

Hippeastrum reticulatum (L'Hérit.) Herbert A rather rounded bulb with broad leaves and nodding pale crimson flowers with faint tessellations, native of S Brazil, flowering in autumn–winter. Leaves to 5cm wide with a diffuse central stripe. Scape to 30cm. Flowers 2–5, 10–12.5cm long; the tube 1.3–2.5cm. Stigma capitate, slightly 3-lobed. For sandy leafy soil, dry in winter, moist in summer. Min. 0°C.

Var. **striatifolium** is larger with a more distinct stripe on the leaves and larger very pale flowers with much clearer crimson veining.

Hippeastrum × johnsonii This is an old hybrid between *H. vittatum* (L'Hérit.) Herbert and *H. reginae* (L.) Herb., first made in the 1790s, but named after a Mr Johnson, a shoemaker or possibly a watchmaker in Lancashire who made the cross in 1811. The flowers are red, variably striped with green. This is still widely cultivated in warm areas such as SW China, where it is common in pots in village gardens.

× Hippeastrelia hort., syn. × *Sprekeliastrum*, × *Hippeaspreckelia* A hybrid between *Spreckelia* and *Hippeastrum* making a dwarf plant with small flowers of intense scarlet in summer. Easily grown in well-drained soil, kept dry in winter, watered in summer. Min. 0°C. A clone 'Mystique' is in cultivation.

Hippeastrum argentinum at Harry Hay's, Surrey

Hippeastrum calyptratum at Harry Hay's, Surrey

Hippeastrum psittacinum in Sellindge, Kent

Hippeastrum puniceum on the E coast of the Yucatan, Mexico in March

× *Hippeastrelia* in Devon

Hippeastrum reticulatum var. *striatifolium* in the open in Hong Kong in October

Hippeastrum 'Lemon 'n' Lime' in Devon

Hippeastrum 'Pamela' in Devon

253

Eichhornia crassipes in Malawi with grazing hippo and *Pistia*

Cyperus papyrus at La Mortola

Ottelia alismoides in Malawi

Hydrocleis nymphoides

Dichorisandra thyrsiflora at Edinburgh
Botanic Gardens

Cyperus papyrus L. (*Cyperaceae*) Papyrus
A large but graceful perennial aquatic, native
of tropical and S Africa, north to Egypt and
also naturalised in Sicily. Stems dark green, 3-
angled, leafless, to 3m or more high. Rhizomes
short and stout. Inflorescence an umbrella-
like umbel with numerous pendent, threadlike
green branches. Good as a marginal plant for
conservatory pools, as a pot plant in a shallow
tray of water, or outside in subtropical
gardens. Min. 8°C for short periods.

Dichorisandra thyrsiflora Mikan.
(*Commelinaceae*) A perennial, native of
Brazil, flowering in gardens in autumn. Stems
erect, to 2m. Leaves elliptic-lanceolate, to
30cm long, spirally arranged in a rosette, shiny
green on upper surface, purplish below.
Inflorescence a dense terminal raceme, to
around 20cm; flowers numerous, short-
stalked, sepals and petals 3 each, both around
1cm across, violet-blue (too pink in our
photo). For a warm humid place out of direct
sun. Min. 12°C.

Eichhornia crassipes (Mart.) Solms-Laub.
(*Pontederiaceae*) Water Hyacinth An invasive
perennial aquatic with floating rosettes of
leaves and spikes of pale blue flowers, native of
tropical South America and naturalised
throughout the subtropics and tropics. Stems
thick; roots long, hairy. Inflorescence to 15cm;
flowers several, to 3cm across, usually blue
with yellow blotch in centre, but sometimes
pale pink. For a sunny but cool pool; can be
removed and potted up in moist compost

during long spells of cold weather. Min. 0°C.
Edible to cattle, especially when half-dried.

Elegia capensis (Burm.fil.) Schelpe
(*Restionaceae*) A tussock-forming perennial,
native of South Africa throughout the Cape
from Clanwilliam to Port Elizabeth where it
grows by streams and in wet places. Stems
green, up to 2.5m, with numerous needle-like
branches at the nodes, and pinkish-brown
bracts which drop off. Inflorescence a dense
cluster of numerous minute brown flowers.
Min. 0°C.

Hydrocleis nymphoides (Willd.) Buchenau
(*Limnocharitaceae*) An attractive perennial
aquatic with glossy green leaves and long-lived
simple yellow flowers, native of tropical South
America, flowering in summer in gardens.
Leaves broadly-ovate, usually floating, to 8cm
across. Flowers held above surface of the
water, solitary, to 7cm across; petals 3, yellow,
rounded. For shallow water in a warm
greenhouse or outside in the subtropics or
tropics. Min. 10°C.

Ottelia alismoides (L.) Pers.
(*Hydrocharitaceae*) An annual or perennial
aquatic with white, pink or pale blue flowers,
native of N Africa, NE India to W China, SE
Asia and Australia and naturalised in Europe.
Leaves submerged, variable in shape, to
around 40cm long and 20cm across; midrib
prominent, veins making distinctive pattern.
Spathes on long stalks with several 'wings';
sepals 3, green, up to 15mm long; petals 3, to

30mm, often yellow at base. For warm water; good as an oxygenator. Min. 0°C.

Sagittaria montevidensis Cham. & Schlecht. (*Alismataceae*)   A perennial marginal aquatic plant, native of Uruguay, growing in shallow water, flowering in late summer. Leaves ovate to lanceolate on slender stalks. Inflorescence with long branches at the lowest node, but little-branched above. Flowers short-stalked to about 2.5cm; petals 3, larger than the sepals. A larger-flowered relative of the well-known water plantain, *A. plantago-aquatica*. For a sunny wet site. Min. –3°C

Tradescantia fluminensis Vell. (*Commelinaceae*)   A trailing plant, native of S Brazil to N Argentina, flowering throughout the year. Leaves green, sometimes flushed purple beneath, up to 12cm long, variable in shape but more or less ovate; there are variegated forms in cultivation. Flowers white, to around 1.8cm in diameter. Good for a hanging basket or as a ground-cover plant, as it roots at the nodes. Best in a warm, slightly humid place. Min. 5°C.

Tradescantia pallida (Rose) D. Hunt, syn. *Setcreasa purpurea* Boom   A low-growing clump-forming plant, thought to be native of Mexico where we saw it growing, apparently wild, on limestone pavement. Stem to 40cm, usually purple, but varies according to growing conditions. Leaves to around 15cm long and 4cm across, oblong-elliptic-lanceolate, purple or greyish-green. Flowers solitary, pale pink, to 3cm diameter. Min. 0°C.

Tradescantia sillamontana Matuda, syns. *Cyanotis veldthoutiana, T. pexata, T. velutina, T. villosa, T.* 'White Gossamer', *T.* 'White Velvet'   A trailing plant with velvety leaves, native of NE Mexico, flowering in summer in cultivation. Stems ascending and spreading, to 30cm, purplish, branched at the base. Leaves ovate, to around 6cm long and 3cm across, green flushed purple underneath; both leaves and stem covered with long white hairs, densely below. Flowers terminal and often solitary, 3-petalled, to around 2cm across; petals longer than sepals, bright pink. Easy to grow; good for a hanging basket. Min. 0°C.

Tradescantia spathacea Sweet, syn. *Rhoeo discolor, R. spathacea* (L'Hérit.) Hance   An erect semi-succulent plant with a rosette of fleshy sword-like leaves, native of Belize, Guatemala and Mexico and naturalised in the West Indies, flowering throughout the year. Stem up to 20cm. Leaves to 30cm long, dark green, tinged and margined with reddish-purple on upper surface, purple below. Bracts purple, boat-shaped, partly enclosing tiny white flowers, to about 1.5cm across, which are produced throughout the year. Easy to grow and good as ground-cover in the subtropics or indoors in a pot. Min. 5°C.

Tripogandra multiflora (Swartz) Rafinesque (*Commelinaceae*)   A creeping perennial rooting at the nodes, native of Costa Rica, Jamaica, Trinidad, W tropical South America, flowering throughout the year. Stems slender, to 80cm. Leaves ovate, up to 9cm long and around 3cm across. Inflorescence a cyme, with numerous flowers; flowers to 8mm across, petals and sepals, same length, white or sometimes pink. For a warm humid place out of direct sun. Min. 12°C.

Sagittaria montevidensis at Clos du Peyronnet

Elegia capensis at Kirstenbosch

Tripogandra multiflora

Tradescantia fluminensis with *Pelargonium* leaves

Tradescantia sillamontana

Tradescantia spathacea

Tradescantia pallida in Central Mexico

Tillandsia andrieuxii on a tree in Mexico

Tillandsia aeranthos at Holly Gate, Sussex

Tillandsia is the largest with over 400 species and most widely distributed genus of Bromeliads. The plants are epiphytic herbs and normally have rosettes of leaves. A few (usually the larger green-leaved varieties) can be grown as pot plants in a special free-draining compost, but the majority are true epiphytes and need to be grown fixed to bark or branches. A number of the smaller grey-leaved species, sometimes known as 'atmospherics', are marketed as 'air plants' and are sold attached to pieces of cork bark, on which they can be grown for several years if regularly sprayed with uncontaminated water. Most *Tillandsias* prefer a warm, rather humid atmosphere and plenty of light, but some will survive arid conditions and extraordinary extremes of temperature.

Tillandsia aeranthos (Loisel.) L. B. Smith *(Bromeliaceae)* A variable species with rosettes of narrow leaves, pink bracts and violet flowers, native of Argentina, Brazil, Paraguay and Uruguay, growing as an epiphyte. Leaves linear, to about 15cm long and about 1.5cm wide at base, green. Inflorescence a loose spike, either upward- or downward-facing, to about 25cm, bright pinkish-red, multiflowered. Flowers arranged spirally, rich violet-blue, to about 2.5cm long. One of the easier *Tillandsias* to grow in a pot indoors or outside in warmer climates such as the Mediterranean or W California. Min. −5°C, perhaps.

Tillandsia andrieuxii (Mez.)L. B. Smith A small clump-forming epiphyte with a loose rosette of leaves and pendulous red inflorescence, native of Mexico and Costa Rica where it grows on oaks and conifers at up to 3000m. Leaves narrow, silvery-grey, scaly, to about 12cm long and 1cm wide at base. Inflorescence pendulous, to about 15cm, bracts red, to about 3cm long. Flowers violet-blue fused into a tube, to about 5cm long. A beautiful but rather demanding plant for growing epiphytically; needs plenty of light. Min. −3°C.

Tillandsia cyanea K. Koch A small perennial with rosettes of narrow dark green leaves, a bright pink inflorescence and dark violet flowers, native of Ecuador and Peru, growing as an epiphyte. Leaves linear, to about 30cm long and 1.5cm wide at base, striped maroon at the base on the upper surface and suffused with brown at the base of the lower surface. Inflorescence to about 15cm long, 6cm across, elliptic, flat, bright pink, with up to 20 flowers. Flowers short-lived, sessile, rich violet-blue, three-petalled, to about 3cm long. A showy plant for growing in a pot indoors in Europe or outside in warmer climates, such as W California. Min. 0°C perhaps less. *T. lindeni (not illustrated)*, also from Ecuador and Peru is similar, but has a longer, narrower inflorescence on a stalk and dark violet flowers, but with a white throat.

Tillandsia prodigiosa (Lem.) Baker A very variable plant with long showy hanging inflorescences, growing mainly on oak trees in the Mexican cloud forest at around 1500–2300m. Leaves to about 50cm long and 6cm wide at base, forming a large funnel-shaped rosette. Inflorescence to 1m or sometimes 2m long, growing upright at first, but later hanging, as shown here. Flower bracts red, pink or greenish-yellow; flowers usually blue or green to about 5cm long.

Small adventitious offshoots sometimes appear at the base of the rosette and these can be detached and grown independently. A showy plant for growing in damp slightly shady conditions, definitely not for the novice. Min. 10°C, perhaps less.

Tillandsia recurvata (L.) L. Ball-moss A clump-forming epiphyte with narrow silvery leaves, native of much of Central America, from the southern USA down to Argentina and Chile, where it is found growing on mesquite bushes, cacti, trees, cliffs and houses. Leaves narrow, silvery-grey in clumps of variable size up to about 20cm high. Flowers 1–5, small, pale blue, each about 1cm long. Like *T. usneoides (see below)* it requires plenty of light, but will survive extremes of temperature and drought, and can easily be grown for several years on a piece of bark indoors (if regularly sprayed with pure water) or outside, providing there is not too great a rainfall. Min. −3°C.

Tillandsia species in Mexico A large rosette with an upright stem covered with pink bracts, native of Mazatlan Province in NW Mexico, growing on oaks at around 2000m, flowering in late October. Rosette stemless, spike to 30cm, bracts pinkish-red, petals yellow with long spreading stamens. For a cool humid atmosphere. Min. 0° C.

Tillandsia usneoides (L.) L. Lousiana Moss, Spanish Moss, Old Man's Beard An extraordinary plant with long grey stems which hang in festoons from trees, rocks, houses and so on in many parts of America, where it is sometimes regarded as a pest; native of SE USA to C Argentina and Chile Normally rootless, except in young seedlings where a small short-lived root provides an initial means of attachment. Stems up to 5m long, thread-like, no more than 1mm in diameter. Leaves grey, scaly, 2–5cm long in two rows. Flowers single, fragrant, stalkless; sepals narrow, to about 6mm, petals to about 10mm, varying from pale yellowish-green to whitish-blue. In the wild the plant is distributed by the wind, which tears off small pieces. A curiosity for growing epiphytically indoors in Europe or outside in warmer climates. Min. 0°C, possibly less.

Tillandsia cyanea grown as a houseplant

Tillandsia recurvata in Mexico

Epiphytic bromeliads with *Tillandsia* species above Copala, Mexico

Tillandsia usneoides (Spanish Moss) in Mexico

T. prodigiosa growing in oak and pine forest near Morelia, C Mexico

Tillandsia recurvata in the Sierra Madre Orientale near Los Linios, Mexico

Puya chilensis in full flower

Puya venusta in the Huntington Gardens

Puya alpestris

Puya laxa in the Huntington Gardens

Puya berteroniana in full flower

There are over a hundred species of *Puya*, which are terrestrial Bromeliads with flowering stems ranging in height from 50cm up to 10m in *Puya raimondii* (*not illustrated*). They are all native of the Andes, where they grow at a higher altitude than any other Bromeliad, with a resulting tolerance of drought and often surprisingly low temperatures. Only a few of them are generally available commercially, partly because the time between raising from seed and flowering can be several years, but they are worth seeking out for their exotic and unusual forms and colours.

Puya alpestris (Poepp. and Endl.) Gay (*Bromeliaceae*)   A terrestrial perennial with rosettes of spiny grey leaves and large spikes of dark bluish flowers, native of S and C Chile, where it grows on arid hillsides, usually near the coast, flowering in October–December (spring). Flowering stems to 1.5m. Leaves narrow, recurved, arching, around 60cm long, about 2cm across at the base; the upper side glabrous, the undersides densely coated with white scales. Flowers with narrow green sepals, shiny dark bluish-green petals to about 4cm long and bright orange anthers. An attractive plant for a container or sunny dry well-drained site, outside in mild areas only; less hardy than some others, it will nevertheless survive a degree or two of frost. Min. –2°C, for short periods only.

Puya berteroniana Mez.   A terrestrial clump-forming perennial with greyish-green spiny leaves and dense spikes of very dark bluish-green flowers, native of C Chile where it grows on arid hillsides, usually near the coast, flowering in October–December (spring). Flowering stems to 4m. Leaves recurved, around 1m long, 6cm across at the base, with sharp spiny margins; the undersides are densely coated with white scales. Flowers with narrow green sepals, very dark, almost black, bluish-green petals and bright orange anthers. A striking plant for a sheltered well-drained site in a mild area; will survive a few degrees of frost. Min. –5°C for short periods.

Puya chilensis Molina   A terrestrial perennial with a rosette of numerous narrow spiny leaves and dense spikes of yellowish flowers, native of C Chile where it grows on arid hillsides, often spreading across large areas, flowering in October–December (spring). Flowering stems to 5m. Leaves pale green, straight, around 1m long and 6cm

across at the base, with sharp margins and large viciously hooked spines (formerly used by the Indians as fish hooks). Flowers to about 7cm long with green sepals, yellowish-green petals and bright yellow anthers. A self-sterile species, this is pollinated in the wild by the Tordo, a small black bird which perches on the tips of the branches; in cultivation cross-pollination with *P. alpestris* can be effective. A large striking plant for a sheltered well-drained site in a mild area; will survive a few degrees of frost. Min. –5°C for short periods.

Puya laxa L. B. Sm.   A terrestrial perennial, different from the other Puyas, with grey spiny leaves and a loose inflorescence of dark purple flowers, native of Argentina and Bolivia where it grows in dry places, flowering in October–December (spring). Flowering stems slender, to 1m. Leaves grey, white underneath, around 60cm long, grass-like at apex with small hooked spines on the margins. Bracts white, woolly. Flowers to about 4cm long, spirally arranged up stem, with scaly greenish sepals and small dark violet petals, striped with green on the outside. A peculiar-looking plant, for a container where it will tolerate long periods of drought, or for a sheltered well-drained site outside in a very mild area; hardiness uncertain, probably 0°C for short periods.

Puya spathacea Mez.   A terrestrial perennial with a rosette of grey spiny leaves and spikes of dark blue flowers, native of N Argentina where it grows in dry stony places, flowering in October–December (spring). Flowering stems red, to 1m. Leaves narrow, recurved, around 1m long and 5cm across at the base, with sharp spiny margins; the undersides are densely covered with fine white hairs. Bracts red, flowers with pinkish-red sepals and dark bluish-purple petals. A plant for a sheltered well-drained site in a mild area; will survive a few degrees of frost. Min. –2°C for short periods only.

Puya venusta Philippi.   A terrestrial perennial with a rosette of narrow grey leaves and spikes of deep purple flowers, native of Chile where it grows in arid places, flowering in October–December (spring). Flowering stems bare at base, upper part alternately branched, to about 80cm. Leaves grey on both sides, around 30cm long and 3cm across at the base, with sharp spiny margins. Flowers with pink sepals and deep purple petals. For a sheltered well-drained site in a mild area. Min. 0°C for short periods.

Puya chilensis at Tresco, Isles of Scilly being visited by a Starling

Puya berteroniana in the Berkeley Botanic Garden, California

Puya spathacea at the Huntington Botanic Gardens, California

Babiana stricta at Berkeley Botanic Garden, California

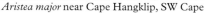

Aristea major near Cape Hangklip, SW Cape

Homeria comptoni in California

Anomatheca grandiflora Baker, syn. *Lapeyrousia grandiflora* (Baker) Baker (*Iridaceae*)   A short plant with a corm and bright red flowers with a long style and stamens, native of SE Africa from Natal to Malawi, growing in grassy places, rocky hillsides and by streams, flowering in January–September. Stems 10–60cm. Flowers 5–7, with the tube 3cm, lobes 2–2.5cm, the lower marked with dark brown. For good soil, with water in summer, dry in winter. Min. –3°C when dry. *Anomatheca laxa* (Thunb.) Goldblatt, syn. *Lapeyrousia cruenta* (Lindl.) Baker, has small red, blue or white flowers with long upright tube and spots on the lower lobes.

Aristea major Andrews, syn. *A. thyrsiflora* (Del.) R. Br. (*Iridaceae*)   A tall perennial with long flat leaves and a branched spike-like raceme of blue flowers, native of South Africa from the Piketberg to the Peninsula and east to Caledon, growing in moist places on steep lower mountain slopes, flowering in October–December. Leaves to 1.5m long, 3cm wide. Stems as long as the leaves, subterete; bracts brown and papery, with white margins. Flowers 1.2–1.6cm long. A fine plant for a mild climate, in sandy peaty soil. Min. –3°C.

Babiana stricta (Ait.) Ker Gawl. (*Iridaceae*) Stompstertbobbejaantjie   A short plant with hairy pleated leaves and actinomorphic usually blue flowers, native of South Africa in the Cape from Piketberg to the Peninsula and Ceres to Caledon, growing on mountain slopes, flowering in August–October. Leaves

to 12cm. Stems 10–20cm. Flowers with the tube 1–1.8cm, lobes 1.5–2.5cm, often purple, sometimes with a dark red centre, rarely all cream or yellow. For good soil with water in winter and spring, dry in summer. Min. –3°C. Many other species have markings on the lower 3 perianth lobes.

Dierama luteoalbidum Verdoorn (*Iridaceae*)   A graceful perennial with a small corm and hanging bell-shaped white or pale buff flowers, native of South Africa in the Natal Midlands around Nottingham Road, at 1100–1700m, growing in grassland on clay soils, flowering in October–December. Corm solitary, not forming large clumps. Leaves to 60cm long, 4mm wide. Inflorescence 65–110cm, with few branches. Bracts silvery with brown veins. Flowers 3–5cm long. For good well-drained soil with water in summer. Min. –3°C.

Dierama floriferum Hilliard   Grows in the same places as *D. luteo-albidum*, but extends to Transvaal and the NE Cape. It has shorter stems, forms clumps and has many smaller bluish flowers, 1.5–2cm long.

Freesia corymbosa (Burm. fil.) R. Br. (*Iridaceae*)   A tufted plant with scented yellow flowers on an angled spike, native of South Africa in the Cape from Uniondale east to East London, growing in dry rocky places, flowering in August–November. Leaves 5–40cm. Stems to 20–50cm. Flowers 2.4–3.8cm long, usually yellow, rarely creamy white or pink. For good soil with water in

winter and spring, dry in summer. This is an ancestor of the florists' freesia. Min. –3°C.

Homeria comptonii L. Bolus (*Iridaceae*) A tall plant with a lax flat leaf, branched stem and tulip-shaped yellow flowers, native of South Africa in the S Cape from Villiersdorp to Caledon and Stanford, growing on clay slopes, flowering in August–September. Leaves to 60cm. Stems to 30cm. Flowers 6–7cm across, usually yellow with a green splash, but sometimes with pink or orange segments and a yellow centre. For good soil with water in winter and spring, dry in summer. Min. –3°C. *H. ochroleuca* Salisb., with stems to 75cm, is commonly grown.

Ixia viridiflora Lam. (*Iridaceae*)   A tall slender plant with a corm and pale bluish green flowers with dark centres, native of South Africa in the S Cape from Clanwilliam to Tulbagh, growing on rocky bush-covered lower slopes, flowering in September–November. Stems 40–50cm. Flowers 12–18, 3–5cm across. For good soil with water in winter and spring, dry in summer. Min. –3°C. Other ixias, mainly hybrids, with pink, red or white flowers, are commonly cultivated.

Sparaxis tricolor (Schneev.) Ker Gawl. (*Iridaceae*)   A small plant with a corm and orange or reddish flowers, with a black and yellow centre, native of South Africa in the W Cape near Nieuwoudtville, growing in dry clay flats and slopes, flowering in August–October. Stems 20–35cm. Flowers 2–5, the tube 6–8mm, the lobes 1.8–2.2cm. For sandy

soil with water in winter and spring, dry in
summer. Min. -3°C.

Sparaxis grandiflora (Del.) Ker Gawl.
from the W Cape, has paler flowers, purplish
outside. Sometimes naturalised in
Mediterranean areas, for example, near Nice
and on Madeira.

Tritonia crocata (L.) Ker Gawl., syn.
T. hyalina (L. fil.) Baker(*Iridaceae*)   A small
plant with a corm and orange or reddish
flowers, native of South Africa in the S Cape
from Heidelberg to Humansdorp, growing in
dry clay flats and slopes, flowering in
September–November. Stems 25–50cm.
Flowers 6–10, the tube 8–1.5mm, the lobes
2–2.8cm, with a transparent area near the
base. For good soil with water in winter and
spring, dry in summer. Min. –3°C.

Tritonia crocata near Mossel Bay

Ixia viridiflora at Harry Hay's, Surrey

Freesia corymbosa at Oliphant's Kop, E Cape

Anomatheca grandiflora

Sparaxis tricolor at Quince

Dierama floriferum

Dierama luteoalbidum at Nottingham Road

Dierama luteoalbidum from Karkloof

Sparaxis grandiflora in Madeira

BOBARTIA

Bobartia indica on a recently burnt area near Hout Bay on the Cape Peninsula in October

Iris wattii in the Temperate House at Kew

Neomarica northiana

Dietes bicolor in Sydney Harbour Botanic Garden

Moraea aristata

Bobartia indica L. (*Iridaceae*) A stiff rush-like perennial with a head of yellow flowers, native of South Africa in the SW Cape from the Peninsula to Caledon and Worcester, growing on sandy flats and slopes, flowering in October–March, especially following a fire. Leaves long and trailing, terete. Stems to 80cm, arching. Flower heads of 6–40 cymes, each flower around 5cm across, lasting 1 day. For sandy soil with water mainly in winter. Min. 0°C.

Cypella aquatilis Rav. (*Iridaceae*) A small *Tigridia*-like bulb with yellow flowers with recurved outer segments and smaller spotted inner segments, native of Brazil in Rio Grande do Sul and Parana, growing in streams, flowering in summer. Leaves pleated. Stem to 50cm; flowers with the outer segments 3–4cm long, the inner forming a cup, with recurved tips, spotted with purple. For sandy peaty soil, wet in summer, dry in winter. Min. 5°C.

Cypella osteniana Beauv. A small *Tigridia*-like bulb with yellow flowers with recurved outer segments and smaller, incurved inner segments, native of Uruguay and possibly NW Argentina, growing in moist fields, flowering in late summer. Leaves pleated. Stem to 15–20cm; flowers with the outer segments 1.7cm long, deflexed, the inner strongly folded foreward, then back. Stamens brown with pale pointed tips. For sandy peaty soil with water in summer. Min. −5°C. Some Cypellas have blue flowers.

Dietes bicolor (Steud.) Klatt (*Iridaceae*) An iris-like perennial with upright green leaves and pale yellow flowers, native of South Africa in the E Cape from Bathurst to East London, growing in forest, flowering in December–March. Leaves to 70cm. Stems to 100cm. Flowers with 3 large outer segments 3–4cm long, with a brown blotch. Drought-resistant and tolerant of poor soil; needs water mainly in summer. Min. 5°C.

Ferraria crispa Burm., syn. *F. undulata* L. (*Iridaceae*) A soft fleshy plant with wavy-edged brown-spotted flowers, native of South Africa in the SW Cape from Lambert's Bay to the Peninsula and into the Little Karoo, growing on sandy flats and slopes, mainly along the coast, flowering in July–October. Stems to 80cm, leafy, much-branched and flattened. Flower heads of short cymes, each flower around 4cm across, pale yellow, sometimes very heavily spotted. For sandy soil with water mainly in winter. Min. 0°C.

Iris wattii Baker (*Iridaceae*) A tall perennial with large fans of shiny green leaves and branching stems of pale bluish or white flowers, native of the W Himalayas from Manipur east to Yunnan, growing in woods and by rivers at up to 2000m, flowering in April–May. Stems below the leaves cane-like, 1–2m. Leaves to 90cm long. Inflorescence much-branched; flowers around 6cm across, spotted with orange and purplish-blue, the falls hanging down vertically. Needs shelter from wind and frost, with water and feeding in summer. Min. 0°C.

Melaspherula ramosa (L.) N. E. Br. (*Iridaceae*) A delicate much-branched perennial with small yellowish wispy flowers, native of S Namibia and South Africa in the Cape from Nieuwoudtville to Bredasdorp, growing in moist places, flowering in

Melaspherula ramosa at Quince House

Cypella aquatilis at Clos du Peyronnet, Menton

Cypella osteniana at Harry Hay's, Surrey

Nivenia binata on the Swartberg Pass in October

Ferraria crispa at Cape Point

Rigidella orthantha at Harry Hay's, Surrey

July–September. Stems to 50cm, leafy, much-branched. Flowers around 1.5cm across, pale yellow or white. For sandy soil with water in winter and spring. Min. 0°C. Easily grown and self-seeds in frost-free gardens.

Moraea aristata (Del.) Asch. & Graeb. (*Iridaceae*)   A slender perennial with single white flowers, the outer 3 segments with a large electric blue spot, native of South Africa in the SW Cape near Cape Town, growing on clay flats and slopes, flowering in September, but now virtually extinct in the wild. Leaves flat, long and trailing. Stems 25–35cm. Outer segments 3–3.5cm across; inner 15–20mm long, reduced to 2 lobes and a long point, purple spotted. For sandy soil with water in winter and spring. Established in cultivation. Min. 0°C.

Neomarica northiana (Schneev.) Sprague (*Iridaceae*)   An iris-like perennial with upright dark green leaves and white to yellow flowers, banded with brown, the inner segments blue, native of Brazil to Peru and Nicaragua, flowering in spring–summer. Leaves to 60cm, 5cm wide. Stems to 90cm. Flowers with 3 large outer segments 3–5cm long, inner shorter, with blue veins. For good soil and sun or partial shade with water in

summer. Min. 5°C. *Neomarica caerulea* (Ker-Gawl) Sprague has larger flowers with blue outer segments.

Nivenia binata Klatt (*Iridaceae*)   A shrubby clump-forming perennial with stiff 2-ranked leaves and branching inflorescence of starry blue flowers, native of South Africa in the Cape in the Swartberg Mountains, growing on rocky slopes at up to 1700m, flowering in September–November. Leaves 6–10cm long. Stems 15–90cm. Inflorescence of 20–60 flowers in pairs. Tube 9–15mm; lobes 7.5–10mm long, 5mm wide. For well-drained soil with water through the year, but drier in summer. Min. –3°C. This interesting genus has heterostylous flowers.

Rigidella orthantha Lem. (*Iridaceae*) An upright perennial with a small corm, pleated leaves and flowers with 3 reflexed segments, native of S Mexico in Chiapas and Oaxaca, growing in open areas in the forest at over 2500m, flowering in May–August. Leaves to 35cm; stems to 60cm. Flowers with outer segments 3–6cm, with the lower part forming a cup, the upper part reflexed; inner segments 2.5–3cm long. Style and stamens erect. For peaty soil with water only in summer. Min. 0°C when dormant.

Gladiolus gregarius on Mlanje Mountain

Gladiolus dalenii subsp. *dalenii* in Malawi

Gladiolus candidus in a dambo near Moshi on the road to Arusha, Tanzania

270

Gladiolus gregarius

Gladiolus tristis

Gladiolus dalenii subsp. *dalenii*

Gladiolus cardinalis from Gary Dunlop, Ballyrogan, Co. Down, N. Ireland

Gladiolus alatus L. var. **meliusculus** Lewis syn. *Gladiolus alatus* var. *alatus* A striking dwarf with orange flowers, the upper 3 lobes broad, the lower 3 narrow, bright yellow tipped with red. In var. *meliusculus* (*shown here*) the flowers are pinker and the lower lobes have a small lime-green area edged with dark red, the 2 laterals being spoon-shaped. Both are native of South Africa in the Cape from Nieuwoudtville to Worcester and from the Peninsula to Bredasdorp, growing on sandy slopes among rocks, flowering in August–October (spring). Stems 15–25cm. Leaves 4–5, with hairy ribs, shorter than the spike. Flowers scented, usually 1–6, 4–6cm across, the style and stamens curved downwards. For sandy soil, moist in winter and spring, dry in summer. Min. –3°C.

Gladiolus bullatus Thunb. ex Lewis A small delicate *Gladiolus* with blue bell-shaped flowers, native of South Africa in the Cape from Caledon to Bredasdorp, growing on sandy slopes among rocks, flowering in August–October (spring). Stems 35–70cm. Leaves 3–4, sheathing the stem, free only at the top, shorter than the spike. Flowers usually 1–2, around 5cm long, with blue spots and white patches on the lower lobes. For sandy soil, moist in winter and spring, dry in summer. Min. –3°C.

Gladiolus candidus (Rendle) Goldblatt, syn. *Acidanthera ukambanensis* Baker A graceful *Gladiolus* with scented pure white flowers with a straight tube, native of Oman in the Dhofar Highlands, S Ethiopia, Somalia, Kenya and Tanzania, growing in wet grassland, open woods and rocky outcrops in the mountains, flowering in the wet season, (March–May in Kenya). Stems 20–40cm. Leaves 2–3, 10–20cm. Flowers 2–4; tube 80–100cm; lobes 2.5–3cm, rarely with purple streaks on the lower lobes. A lovely plant for a warm climate with ample water in summer; close to the familiar *Gladiolus murielae* (syn. *G. callianthus* Marais) which has a longer arching tube and blotched segments. Min. 0°C when dormant.

Gladiolus cardinalis Curtis A spectacular *Gladiolus* with large scarlet flowers, native of South Africa in the Cape from Paarl and Wellington to Worcester, growing by waterfalls and on wet cliffs, at up to 1400m, flowering in December–January (midsummer). Stems in clumps, 60–115cm, usually arching. Leaves bluish-green, 5–9, the lower 40–90cm long, 1.5–2.8cm wide. Flowers usually 5–12, sometimes crimson, with a large white or cream spot on the lower three lobes. Lobes spreading, the upper slightly hooded. For good soil, moist in summer. Min. –3°C when dormant. This species survives well in the open in W England and Ireland.

Gladiolus dalenii van Geel subsp. **dalenii**, syns. *G. natalensis* Reinwardt ex Hook., *G. psittacinus* Hook., *G. primulinus* Baker A tall *Gladiolus* with brownish-orange or yellow downward-pointing hooded flowers, native of Natal north to Saudi Arabia and Madagascar, west to Senegal, growing in grassy places and open woods at up to 2000m, flowering in the rainy season. Stems 70–120cm. Leaves 4–6, 10–20mm wide, well-developed at flowering. Flowers 3–7, tube curved, 3.5–4.5cm; lobes 4–5cm long, the upper curved over the style and stamens. For well-drained soil with water in summer. Min. 0°C when dormant. This is one of the parents of the large-flowered garden Gladioli.

Gladiolus decoratus Baker A small *Gladiolus* with bright orange-red flowers, a large pale yellow blotch on the three lower petals, native of Mozambique, Malawi and Tanzania, growing in rocky places in open woodland at up to 2000m, flowering in December–February (wet season). Stems 45–80cm. Leaves 4–5, to 60cm long, 8–18 mm wide. Flowers 5–9, tube short, 2.5–3.5mm; lobes lanceolate, unequal 4.5–5.5cm long, the upper arched over the style. For well-drained soil with water in summer. Min. 0°C when dormant.

Gladiolus gregarius Welwitsch ex Baker A tall slender *Gladiolus* with several stems in a group and small spotted flowers, native of Senegal east to Tanzania, Malawi and Mozambique, growing in grassy and rocky places and open woods at up to 2000m, flowering in the rainy season, usually January–March. Stems 30–80cm. Leaves 4–7, 19–16mm wide. Flowers 8–20, light to dark purple, with a pale throat, the lower tepals each with a dark purple diamond-shaped spot. Tube 12mm; lobes 2.2–2.6cm long, the upper curved over the style and stamens. For well-drained soil with water in summer. Min. 0°C when dormant.

Gladiolus liliaceus Houtt. Large Brown Afrikaaner A *Gladiolus* with a few large brown flowers, fragrant at night, native of South Africa in the Cape from Clanwilliam to Port Elizabeth, growing in sandy or clay soils on flats and mountain slopes at up to 1800m, flowering in August–December. Stems 30–80cm. Leaves 3, to 3mm wide, longer than the stem. Flowers 1–3, 7.5–11cm long, yellowish, flecked with brown, changing in the dark to dark mauve or blue. Tube 3.8–6cm; lobes 3.5–5.5cm long, wavy, recurved. For good sandy soil with water in winter and spring, dry in summer. Min. –3°C .

Gladiolus maculatus Sweet Small Brown Afrikaaner An autumn-flowering *Gladiolus* with few scented large brownish flowers, native of South Africa in the Cape from Ceres to the Peninsula and east to Port Elizabeth, growing in grassy places at up to 1000m, flowering mainly in March–July. Stems 30–80cm. Leaf solitary, to 40cm long, 5mm wide, appearing after the flowers. Flowers 1–3, 5–10cm long, yellowish, heavily streaked and spotted with brown; lobes wavy, reflexed, the upper not, or only slightly, hooded. For well-drained soil with water in winter, dry in summer. Min. 0°C .

Gladiolus tristis L. Marsh Afrikaaner A slender *Gladiolus* with few large creamy yellow flowers, fragrant at night, native of the Cape Province from Clanwilliam to Humansdorp, growing in marshy places, up to 1800m, flowering mainly in September–December. Stems 40–150cm. Leaves 2–4, 1.5–5mm wide, cruciform in section, separate from the stems. Flowers 1–20, tube curved above the middle, 4–6cm; lobes ovate-elliptic to lanceolate, 2–3.3cm long, slightly spreading. For sandy peaty soil, moist in winter, dry in summer. Min. 0°C

Gladiolus liliaceus in South Africa in October

Gladiolus decoratus in Malawi

Gladiolus bullatus near Betty's Bay, in October

Gladiolus maculatus in South Africa in October

Gladiolus alatus var. *meliusculus* on the Swartberg Pass, near Oudtshoorn

Watsonia pillansii in the Abbey Gardens, Tresco, Isles of Scilly in July

Watsonia pillansii detail from near Humansdorp

Watsonia borbonica subsp. *ardernei*

Watsonia spectabilis on a rocky hill near Ceres in October

Watsonia borbonica subsp. *borbonica* on the Cape Peninsula in October

Watsonia borbonica subsp. *ardernei* on du Toit's Kloof in October

Watsonia aletroides (Burman. fil.) Ker Gawl. (*Iridaceae*)   A large perennial with shiny green leaves and a spike of tubular nodding orange flowers, native of South Africa in the S Cape from Caledon to Mossel Bay and in the Langkloof E to Humansdorp, growing in heavy clay, often wet in spring with seepage, flowering in August–October. Leaves 4–5, 5–10mm wide. Stems to 1.2m. Spike with up to 20 flowers; outer bracts, just overlapping the one above, 11–24mm, green below, dry and brownish above; inner bract similar; perianth tube 4–5.5cm long, down-curved, tubular, the segments obovate, 1cm long. For rich soil, growing mainly in winter, hot and dry in summer. Min. –3°C.

Watsonia borbonica (Pourr.) Goldblatt subsp. **ardernei** (Sander) Goldblatt, syn. *W. ardernei* Sander   A large tufted perennial with evergreen leaves and branched spikes of pink flowers, native of South Africa in the SE Cape from Paarl to the Breede River valley, growing on rocky hillsides, flowering in October–January. Leaves 5–6, 2–4cm wide. Stems usually unbranched to 1.2m. Main spike with around 20 flowers; outer bracts not or just overlapping the one above, 10–18mm, green below, dry and brownish above, soon becoming all brown; inner bract to 3mm shorter; perianth tube 2.6–3.5cm long, curved, the lower half narrow, the upper flared, the segments obovate to oblanceolate, 3–3.6cm long; stamens curving upwards. For good well-drained soil, growing mainly in spring. The white form is commonly grown but rare in the wild. Min. –3°C.
Watsonia borbonica subsp. **borbonica** is found further south and on the Peninsula. It has a shorter upper perianth tube, 8–15mm long, the stamens curving downwards.

Watsonia coccinea Herbert ex Baker   A small perennial with pale green leaves and a spike of a few red, orange or pink flowers, native of South Africa in the S Cape from Malmsbury to Bredasdorp and common on the Peninsula, growing in moist sandy areas or mountain plateaux, wet in spring, flowering in August–November, in the two years following a burn. Leaves 4–6, 2–5mm wide. Stems usually unbranched, 15–30cm. Spike with 3–6 flowers; outer bracts 2–2.5cm, pale green below, dry and brownish in upper 1–2mm; inner bract similar, greenish; perianth tube 3.8–4.8cm long, curved, upper part not flared, the segments obovate, 1.6–2.3cm long; anthers violet, held below the upper segment. For sandy peaty soil, growing mainly in winter, drier in summer. Min. –3°C.

Watsonia fourcadei Mathews & L. Bolus
A large tufted perennial with evergreen leaves
and a spike of pink, orange, orange-red or
rarely purplish flowers, native of South Africa
in the S Cape from Wuppertal and Citrusdal
to Villiersdorp and in the Langeberg and
Outeniqua mountains, E to Humansdorp,
growing in rough grassland on moist
mountain slopes, flowering in October–
January. Leaves 5–8, lanceolate, 2–4cm wide.
Stems usually branched, to 1.8m. Spike with
25–40 flowers; outer bracts just overlapping
the one above, 10–18mm, reddish, dry and
brown above, soon becoming all brown;
perianth tube 4.5–5.6cm long, curved, the
lower half narrow, the upper slightly wider, the
segments lanceolate, 2.4–3.3cm long. For
good well-drained soil, growing mainly in
summer. If the plant stops flowering, try
putting hot ashes on it at the end of the dry
season or in early spring. Min. –3°C.

Watsonia marginata (L. fil.) Ker Gawl.
A large tufted perennial with broad evergreen
leaves and branched spikes of actinomorphic
pink flowers, native of South Africa in the W
Cape from Nieuwoudtville to Caledon and
the Peninsula, growing on sandstone soils in
places wet in spring, flowering in mid-
September–December. Leaves 3–4, glaucous,
3–5cm wide, with thickened margins. Stems
usually branched to 2m. Main spike with
10–20 flowers; outer bracts overlapping the
one above, 10–18mm, dry, brown and torn by
flowering; inner bract 1–2mm longer; perianth
tube 13–16mm long, the lower half narrow, the
upper short, flared, the segments obovate,
2–2.2cm long, all equal, blotched at the base;
stamens grouped around the style. Winter-
growing, needing good soil, moist in winter,
dry in summer. Min. 0°C.

Watsonia pillansii L. Bolus, syn. *W. beatricis*
Mathews & L. Bolus, *W. socium* Mathews &
L. Bolus   A large tufted perennial with
evergreen leaves and a spike of orange flowers,
native of South Africa from the S Cape above
Swellendam to the Natal Drakensberg,
growing in grassland and among rocks at up
to 2400m, flowering in October–March.
Leaves 4–6, 12–18mm wide. Stems usually
unbranched to 1.2m. Spike with 25–35
flowers; outer bracts just overlapping the one
above, 23–33mm, green with a dry, brown
margin 3–5mm wide, covering the inner bract;
perianth tube 4–5cm long, curved, the lower
half narrow, the upper wider, the segments
lanceolate, 2–2.6cm long. For good well-
drained soil, growing mainly in summer; a
commonly grown species, requiring moisture
in spring and summer. Min. around –5°C
depending on place of origin.

Watsonia spectabilis Schinz   A small
perennial with a spike of a few bright red to
pale orange flowers, native of South Africa in
the SW Cape from Nieuwoudtville to
Bredasdorp, but no longer found on the
Peninsula, growing on rocky slopes and by
streams, in places wet in spring, flowering in
August–October. Leaves 3–5, 2–8mm wide.
Stems usually unbranched, 20–50cm. Spike
with 2–5, rarely to 10 flowers; outer bracts
2–4cm, green or flushed red; inner bract
similar; perianth tube 3.8–4.7cm long, curved,
lower part narrow, enclosed in the bracts,
upper part not flared, the segments lanceolate,
3.5cm long; anthers violet, held below the
upper segment. For sandy soil, growing
mainly in winter, drier in summer. Min. –3°C.

Watsonia aletroides, close-up of flowers

Watsonia aletroides in the Langkloof in October

Watsonia fourcadei, pink-flowered form

W. fourcadei on Prince Alfred's Pass, Knysna

Watsonia marginata between Wolseley and Ceres

Watsonia coccinea (pink-flowered form) in
Cape Point Reserve in October

Watsonia coccinea (orange-flowered form) at
Betty's Bay in October

Zantedeschia pentlandii at Harry Hay's

Zantedeschia rehmanii at Harry Hay's

Zantedeschia albomaculata, *Helichrysum petiolaris* and ferns by a spring on the Outeniqua Pass, Langklorf, South Africa

Dracunculus vulgaris Schott. (*Araceae*) An attractive and unusual white form of the ordinary Mediterranean *Dracunculus* (*see Bulbs, page 193*) which appears to be confined to Crete; introduced into cultivation by John Fielding. For a dry place in well-drained soil. Min. −3°C for short periods only.

Pistia stratiotes L. (*Araceae*) Water Lettuce A floating aquatic plant, native throughout the tropics and subtropics where it sometimes becomes an invasive pest. Rhizome floating with numerous roots. Leaves green, pubescent, to 15cm long, in a rosette. Inflorescence shorter than leaves; spathe to 4cm long, greenish. Spadix partly fused to spathe, with a flask-shaped female flower below and a few male flowers above. Min. 0°C.

Tacca leontopetaloides (L.) O.Kuntze (*Taccaceae*)   A tuberous perennial, native of SE Asia and Africa where it is found in monsoon forests. Also naturalised and cultivated in India and Sri Lanka for its edible starchy tubers and rhizomes, which are valued for their starch when cooked. Stem erect, to 1m. Large leaves trifid, up to 1m across. Flowers funnel-shaped, purple, in a dense umbel, surrounded by numerous thread-like bracteoles. A curiosity for a warm humid place in rich soil. Min. 13°C.

Xanthosoma violaceum Schott. (*Araceae*) One of nearly 50 species, this perennial herb is native of the West Indies, widely naturalised and sometimes cultivated throughout South America. Leaves green, with purple midrib and veins, to 70cm long and 40cm wide, roughly arrow-shaped on a long thick purple stalk to 2m high. Spathe pale green on outside, creamy-yellow within, to 15cm long; spadix to 18cm long, white and purple. Tubers starchy, pink inside, both leaves and tubers being edible when young and properly cooked. For a damp warm place. Min. 0°C.

Zantedeschia aethiopica (L.) Sprengel (*Araceae*)   A tuberous, usually perennial evergreen, native of the SW and S Cape area of South Africa where it grows in damp places, flowering from June–February; also widely naturalised and cultivated throughout the subtropics. Stems to 1m high. Leaves dark glossy green, to 45cm long and 20cm wide, hastate. Spathe to 25cm, white, tinged green at base; spadix to 8cm, yellow. For a moist place in full sun, outside or in the cool greenhouse. Min. −8°C for short periods, but the roots must not be allowed to freeze.

Zantedeschia aethiopica 'Green Goddess' Grows to 90cm. Leaves large, dull green. Spathe large, green with white centre. Min. −8°C for short periods.

Zantedeschia albomaculata (Hook.) Baill. A perennial herb, native of South Africa and tropical E Africa where it grows in damp places among rocks up to 2400m. To 120cm high. Leaves to 40cm long and 22cm wide, glossy green, splashed with white, more or less hastate, with waved margins. Spathe up to 10cm, often shorter, on long stem, white or cream, shaded with green at the base on the outside; spadix yellow. Min. −3°C for short periods only.

Zantedeschia pentlandii (Wats.) Wittm. A striking species from the Transvaal where it

Xanthosoma violaceaum with *Pistia stratiotes* in the foreground

Zantedeschia aethiopica at Betty's Bay, S Cape

Zantedeschia (Calla Lily) cultivars at Auckland Botanic Garden, showing coloured spathes

Dracunculus vulgaris, a white Cretan form

grows on rocky hillsides. Plant up to 60cm. Leaves to 35cm long and around 15cm across, hastate, green, sometimes splashed with white. Spathe to 12cm, deep yellow with purple blotch on inside base. Min −3°C for short periods only.

Zantedeschia rehmanii Engl.
A deciduous species, native of South Africa and Swaziland where it grows in shady damp places, on woodland margins or sometimes among rocks. Stems to 80cm. Leaves narrow, dark green, up to 40cm long and around 5cm wide. Spathe pale or dark pink, sometimes white or maroon, to 12cm long and around 2cm across. Min. −3°C for short periods only.

Zantedeschia aethiopica 'Green Goddess'

Tacca leontopetaloides in Malawi

Chrysalidocarpus lutescens in the courtyard of an old house in Guadalajara, Mexico

Neodypsis decaryi

Livistona chinensis in Bermuda

Trachycarpus fortunei at Trebah, Cornwall

Trachycarpus martianus at Dali, China

Bismarckia nobilis

Phoenix canariensis in the gardens of the Generalife, Granada, Spain

Chamaerops humilis at the Villa Thuret, S France

Bismarckia nobilis Hildebrandt & H. Wendl. (*Palmae*)   A majestic fan palm, native of Madagascar. Trunks up to 60m high with foliage in a terminal crown. Leaves palmate, greyish-green, to 3m across. Fruit fleshy, brown, to 3cm long, in large clusters on female trees. Min. 15°C.

Chamaerops humilis L. (*Palmae*) Mediterranean Fan Palm   A small palm, native of the W Mediterranean region where it grows in rocky or sandy places up to 1000m or higher; large wild plants are rare but it is commonly grown in gardens. In poor soil it will stay quite small, but in good conditions it can eventually reach 5m. Trunks sometimes clump-forming, often curving. Leaf blades deeply divided, to around 70cm, glossy green or blue-green. Inflorescence short and stiff, the male flowers bright yellow, female greenish-yellow. Fruit round, yellow or orange. Drought-resistant, so it is good outside in dry areas or in containers; will also make a thick hedge. Min. –10°C for short periods only.

Chrysalidocarpus lutescens Bory. (*Palmae*)   A graceful clump-forming pinnate palm, native of Madagascar, the Comores Islands and Pemba Islands where it grows in damp places. Its stems are slender and clustered, eventually reaching up to 6m or more tall and around 15cm in diameter. Leaves pinnate, to 2m, yellow-green, upright and arched at tips. Fruit to 2cm, ellipsoid, yellow to purple. Good in a pot in light shade in a sheltered frost-free place. Min 0°C for short periods only.

Livistona chinensis (Jacq.) R. Br. ex Mart. (*Palmae*) Chinese Fan Palm   Similar in appearance to *Washingtonia*, native of China, Taiwan and Japan. Trunk grey, ringed and patterned with old leaf base scars, swollen at base; slow-growing, will eventually reach about 5m or more tall. Leaves green on a long stalk, to around 2m long and across, entire for first third, remainder segmented, drooping at edges. Inflorescence shorter than leaves. Fruit bluish-green to grey, more or less ovoid, to 2.5cm. Needs good soil and plenty of water. Min –5°C down to freezing for short periods.

Neodypsis decaryi Jumelle (*Palmae*) Triangle Palm   A pinnate palm, native of Madagascar where it grows in dry barren areas. Slow-growing, eventually up to about 6m. Trunk is unusual, being triangular in cross-section, due to the leaf bases growing in 3 rows around the outside. Leaves to 5m, greyish green, upright but arching at the tips. Min. 15°C.

Phoenix canariensis Chabaud (*Palmae*) Canary Island Date Palm   A majestic tree, native of the Canary Islands where it is common at lower altitudes and is also frequently cultivated. Tree slow-growing at first but eventually up to 20m, with a roughly surfaced unbranched trunk. Pinnate leaves to 6m long, green, arched, in a large terminal rosette with numerous narrow leaflets arising from the central midrib. Old leaf bases and leaves persistent. Flowers small, yellow, in pendent spray. Fruit a pale orange fleshy berry, to about 2cm long.

The different types of date palms hybridise very freely, *caveat emptor*! Good as a pot plant when young before the trunk has formed, thereafter suitable only for very large conservatories or outside in a hot dry climate; this particular plant is especially useful near the sea as it is salt-tolerant. Min. –5°C for short periods only.

Trachycarpus fortunei (Hook.) H. A. Wendl. (*Palmae*) Chusan or Hemp Palm   A very hardy fan palm, native of China and Japan and possibly also Burma where it grows in oak forest at up to 2400m. Trunk solitary, growing to 8m or more in favourable conditions, slender at base, thicker at top, with a ruff of decaying leaf sheaths; dark in colour due to the characteristic layer of black fibre. Leaves in a terminal crown, fan-shaped, divided to about halfway, to about 80cm long and 1m across on 45cm long stalks. Flowers yellow. Can be grown outside in some mild temperate climates or indoors in a cool greenhouse; needs plenty of water. Min. –8°C for short periods, to –15°C when mature.

Trachycarpus martianus (Wall.) H. A. Wendl.   Similar to *T. fortunei* but with a thinner trunk and black fibres at the top only, native of the Himalayas from Nepal to Burma. Slower-growing than *T. fortunei*, this eventually overtakes the latter, growing up to 15m. Leaves bluish-green, to 1.5m, divided halfway. Male inflorescence to 1m, flowers cream; female flowers yellowish-green in longer inflorescence. Fruit orange. Less hardy than *T. fortunei* when young. Min. –5°C.

277

Musa × paradisiaca in Malawi

Heliconia champneiana

Heliconia champneiana Griggs. (*Heliconiaceae*) A banana-like evergreen perennial, native of Guatemala. To 5m with leaves to 2m. Inflorescence erect to around 50cm, oblong, bright orange with red markings; bracts to 14cm, alternate with numerous greenish flowers to each bract. Good for a warm greenhouse or a moist partly shaded place outside in subtropical or tropical areas. Min. 15°C.

Heliconia rostrata Ruiz & Pav. Hanging Lobster Claw A banana-like evergreen perennial, native of South America from Peru to Argentina. Stems to 2m. Leaves banana-like, green, leathery, to 80cm or more. Inflorescence to 60cm, pendent; bracts alternate, red, tipped with yellow, edged with green; flowers yellowish-green. Good for a warm greenhouse or a moist partly shaded place outside in subtropical or tropical areas. Min. 15°C.

Musa 'Dwarf Cavendish' (*Musaceae*) A small variety, probably a form of *M. acuminata*, grown commercially in the Canaries and Israel, suitable also for the conservatory or outside in subtropical areas. If fruit is required, the temperature should

Heliconia rostrata in the Fairchild Botanic Garden

Musa velutina at Kew

Strelitzia reginae

Strelitzia nicolai cultivated in Natal

Musella lasiocarpa in a village in Yunnan

be kept at around 20°C. Min. 10°C for ornamental use.

Musa × paradisiaca L. A cross between *M. acuminata* and *M. balbisiana*, this is the most commonly grown edible banana, making a giant perennial herb to 8m high. Leaves spirally arranged, to 2.5m long, and 70cm wide, green. Inflorescence pendulous, to around 15m; bracts purplish-brown, flowers yellow. Fruit yellow, to about 20cm long. There are numerous cultivars which are grown commercially throughout the tropics, especially in E Africa. Suitable only for the largest greenhouse, in bright, humid conditions. Min. 15°C.

Musa uranoscopus Lour. A small species, native of Indochina, it grows to 1m with oval to elliptic leaves, glossy light green on upper surface and conspicuously veined, with a greenish-pink midrib. Inflorescence erect, to 75cm, with shiny red bracts to 15cm long. Fruit pink, cylindrical, to around 5cm long. Very attractive when in fruit; to obtain these, maintain a temperature of at least 20°C.

Musa velutina Wendl. & Drude. A small species, native of NE India where it grows to 1.5m or more. Stem and petioles pinkish. Leaves to 1m long and around 30cm wide,

pinnately veined, mid-green above, lighter below, with conspicuous pink midrib on underside. Inflorescence erect, with red bracts and yellow flowers. Fruit pinkish-red, to around 9cm long. Min. 18°C.

Musella lasiocarpa (Franchet) C.Y. Wu ex H.W. Li A relation of the banana, native of the Jinshajiang valley from Yongshan to Lijiang in NW Yunnan. Stem short, erect, with terminal head of flowers, with large colourful fleshy bracts. Min. −5°C.

Pandanus utilis Bory (*Pandanaceae*) Screw Pine A branching tree, native of Madagascar. To 20m eventually, with distinctive stilt roots. Leaves strap-like, to about 60cm long and 10cm wide, stiff, glaucous, with reddish spines. Fruit to about 15cm across, solitary, drooping on a long peduncle with about 100 drupes. Good for the warm greenhouse when young, although it needs large amounts of water during the summer. Min 0°C for short periods.

Strelitzia juncea Link, syn. *S. × kewensis* var. *juncea* (*Strelitziaceae*) A rush-like plant, native of Uitenhage in the South African Cape, where it grows to 1.5m, with very narrow leaves and bright orange and blue flowers. Min 10°C.

Strelitzia nicolai Reg. & Körn. A large tree, native of South Africa from East London to Natal, where it grows on river banks or in clearings in the coastal bush. Stems woody, forming large clumps up to 10m high. Leaves large, to 2m long and 80cm across, oblong or ovate-oblong, on a stalk up to 2m long. Inflorescence short-stalked, with 3–5 dark purple-red glaucous spathes; flowers white, to 20cm, with light blue tongue. For a subtropical garden or can be grown in a very large conservatory, if given a really good deep rich soil and plenty of sun. Min. 10°C

Strelitzia reginae Banks ex Dryand. Bird-of-Paradise, Crane Flower A shrubby clump-forming perennial, native of South Africa in the E Cape coastal bush; also cultivated commercially for cutting in warm countries. Plant to 2m high, 1m across. Leaves up to 70cm long, glaucescent, oblong-lanceolate. Inflorescence on long stem, spathes greenish purple and orange, glaucous, to about 12cm long. Flowers to about 10cm, with orange calyx and arrow-shaped blue corolla, produced in succession on each spathe during the spring, autumn and sometimes winter. For a sunny place in good rich soil; it will do well in pots if well fed and watered regularly. Min. −2°C but for short periods only.

Strelitzia juncea in the Kirstenbosch Botanic Gardens, Cape Town

Musa uranoscopus

Pandanus utilis in Bermuda

Musa 'Dwarf Cavendish'

Hedychium flavescens by a forest stream in Kerala

Hedychium gardnerianum in the greenhouse at Sellindge, Kent

Hedychium coronarium in Malawi

Hedychium chrysoleucum

Hedychium greenii in Malawi

Hedychiums (*Zingiberaceae*) are perennials with fleshy aromatic rhizomes, tall stems with leaves in 2 opposite ranks and a short or long inflorescence at the top. The flowers are usually scented, individually short-lived, but produced in large numbers. All thrive in good leafy soil with heat, feeding and ample moisture in summer, dry and frost-free in winter. They are ideal for large tubs in the conservatory or for putting outdoors in shade in areas with hot summers.

Hedychium chrysoleucum Hook.   Stem with with large heads producing a mass of scented yellowish flowers with an orange-pink stamen, native of NE India to SW China?, growing in damp places and by streams in the forest, flowering in summer–autumn. Stems to 3m; bracts overlapping, forming a cone-like head. Flowers with a long tube to 8cm and a pale orange stamen about as long as the lip; lip shallowly 2-lobed, 3.5cm wide. Min. 0°C. This fine species was seen growing in a village garden near Dali, SW Yunnan.

Hedychium coccineum Smith   Stem with long heads of scented brick-red, orange or salmon-pink flowers, native of India in the C and NE Himalayas, Nepal, Bhutan and Burma, growing in broad-leaved forest and secondary scrub, at 250–2280m, flowering in July–September. Stems to 1.5m; inflorescence 15–25cm. Flowers with a short tube and a straight orange stamen much longer than the lip; lip deeply 2-lobed, 1.5–2cm wide.

Min. 0°C. Some clones of this species, such as 'Tara' from Nepal, are hardy in S and W England.

Hedychium coronarium Koenig   Stem with short heads producing a succession of wonderfully scented white flowers, native of India to Indonesia, growing in damp places and by streams in the forest, flowering in spring–summer. Stems to 2m; bracts overlapping, forming a short cone-like head. Flowers with the stamen not exserted, the lip 2-lobed, 5cm wide, with a yellow or greenish blotch. Very tender, sensitive to the slightest frost. Min. 5°C.

Hedychium flavescens Roscoe   Stem with short heads producing a succession of scented yellowish flowers, native of India from the Himalayas to Kerala, growing in damp places and by streams in the forest, flowering in spring and summer. Stems to 3m; bracts overlapping, forming a cone-like head. Flowers with a long tube and a pale orange stamen longer than the lip, the lip 2-lobed, 3cm wide, with a yellowish blotch. Min. 0°C.

Hedychium gardnerianum Ker Gawl. Stem with long heads of well-scented lemon-yellow flowers, native of India in the Himalayas, growing in broad-leaved forest at 910–2130m, flowering in July–September. Stems to 2m; inflorescence 25–40cm. Flowers with a long tube and a red stamen much longer than the lip, the lip entire or 2-lobed,

Hedychium speciosum in the Royal Botanic Garden, Edinburgh

Hedychium chrysoleucum in a village garden near Dali, SW Yunnan

Hedychium thyrsiforme in the Royal Botanic Garden, Edinburgh

2cm wide. Min. −3°C or less if the root is protected from freezing. A very fine and easily-grown plant.

Hedychium greenii W. W. Smith   Stem with short heads producing a succession of bright red flowers, native of Bhutan, Sikkim and Assam, growing in damp places on low hills, flowering in July. Stems to 2m; leaves purple beneath. Bracts overlapping, forming a short ellipsoid head. Flowers upright, with a short tube, the stamen as long as lip; the lip 2–lobed, 4–5cm wide, with an orange blotch. Min. 5°C.

Hedychium speciosum Wallich   Stem with long heads of scented white spidery flowers with straight orange-red stamens, native of India in the NE Himalayas, growing in forest, flowering in August–November. Stems to 2.5m; inflorescence to 30cm. Flowers with a tube 4–5cm, staminodes linear and a straight orange-red stamen 6–7cm long, longer than the lip; lip entire, to 1.5cm wide. Min. 0°C.

Hedychium thyrsiforme Smith   Stem with long heads of scented white spidery flowers, native of Bhutan and India in the NE Himalayas, growing in forest, sometimes as an epiphyte, at 300–2000m, flowering in August–November. Stems to 1.5m; inflorescence 6–10cm. Flowers with a short tube and a curved white stamen 6–7cm long, much longer than the rest of the flower, the lip deeply 2-lobed, 2cm wide. Min. 0°C.

Hedychium coccineum in the Royal Botanic Garden, Edinburgh

Canna indica near Karkloof, South Africa

Canna hybrid at Stone Drum on the Yangtse

Canna 'Striped Beauty' in Malawi

Globba winitii

Canna iridiflora in South Devon

Alpinia zerumbet in Bermuda

Alpinia zerumbet (Pers.) B. L.Burtt & Rosemary M. Smith (*Zingiberaceae*) Shell Ginger   A tall rhizomatous perennial, native of E Asia. Stems arching in clumps to 4m. Leaves mid-green, lanceolate, to 60cm long and around 10cm across. Inflorescence pendent to 30cm; flowers numerous, fragrant, bracteoles pink, corolla white, tipped dark pink, lip yellow, striped with reddish-brown. For a cool conservatory. Min. 5°C, perhaps

Canna edulis Ker Gawl. (*Cannaceae*) A tall leafy perennial with broad purplish leaves, native of S America and the West Indies. Stem stout, tinged purple, to 3m. Leaves oblong, to 60cm, glaucous, tinged purple when young. Flowers small, in racemes, yellowish orange to red. This plant is commonly cultivated in China for its edible rhizomes and differs from *C. indica* in its taller stems and broader purplish leaves. Min. 5°C.

Canna indica L. Indian Shot   A perennial with green leaves and small bright red flowers, native of Central and South America, but naturalised and cultivated throughout the tropics. Stem to 1m, sometimes more. Leaves green, narrowly ovate with uneven pointed tip, up to 50cm long and around 15cm across. Flowers solitary or in pairs, in a raceme, usually bright reddish-orange, the lip yellow or orange often splashed with red. Seeds black, like large shot. For rich soil; needs plenty of water. Min. 5°C or less for short periods only if the rhizome is well protected.

Canna iridiflora Ruiz & Pav.   A large, leafy rhizomatous perennial, native of Peru. To 3m tall. Leaves green, ovate with uneven pointed apex, to 1m or more long and around 40cm across, downy on the underside when young. Flowers to 10cm, nodding, deep rose pink, in terminal panicle raised well above the leaves. For a warm greenhouse in temperate climates. Min. 5°C or less for short periods only if the rhizome is well protected.

Canna × generalis   An old variety of this showy hybrid, possibly 'Speciosa', with glaucous leaves and bright red flowers. Min. 5°C or less for short periods only if the rhizome is well protected.

Canna × generalis 'Striped Beauty' Another form of *Canna × generalis*. Leaves yellow-green striped with cream and gold. Flowers scarlet. Min. 5°C or less for short periods only if the rhizome is well protected.

Costus malortieanus H.Wendl. (*Zingiberaceae*)   A rhizomatous perennial, native of Central America, flowering throughout the year. Stems to 1m high. Leaves broadly elliptic, fleshy, bright green with dark lengthwise stripes, to 25cm long and around 18cm across. Inflorescence a dense terminal spike; flowers yellow, lip yellow with reddish-brown markings. For warm humid shady conditions in rich soil; better in a greenhouse border than a container. Min. 18°C.

Costus pictus D. Don.   A rhizomatous perennial, native of C America from Mexico to Costa Rica. Stem erect, to 45cm. Leaves to 20cm, oblanceolate, dark glossy green. Inflorescence a spike; flowers yellow-orange, lip 3-lobed, sometimes marked with purple. For warm humid shady conditions in rich soil; needs unrestricted root run. Min. 18°C.

CANNACEAE

Canna edulis cultivated for food, between Dali and Kunming, Yunnan, China

Kaempferia pulchra at Kew

Costus malortieanus in the stove house at the Royal Botanic Garden, Edinburgh

Siphonochilus kirkii in Malawi

Costus speciosus in Kerala, India

Costus pictus at Kew

Costus speciosus (Koenig) J. F. Smith
A rhizomatous perennial, native of India and
SE Asia to New Guinea, also cultivated
throughout the tropics, flowering all year.
Plant to 2m. Leaves up to 25cm long and 5cm
across, short-stalked, elliptic, downy beneath.
Inflorescence a terminal spike; bracts green
flushed red, flowers 1 per bract, white with
yellow centre. For warm humid shady
conditions in rich soil; needs unrestricted root
run. Min. 18°C.

Globba winitii Wright. (*Zingiberaceae*)
A slender perennial, native of Thailand where
it grows in forest. Plant to 1m. Leaves
lanceolate, green above, whitish and downy
beneath, to 20cm long, on stalks to 10cm.
Inflorescence pendent, to 15cm; bracts bright
magenta-pink, to 3cm, 5–7 yellow flowers to
each bract; each flower has a short slender
tube, petal-like staminodes and a stamen with

a long curved filament, in which is the hair-
like style. For a warm humid place; needs
plenty of water in growing season. Min. 15°C.

Kaempferia pulchra Ridley (*Zingiberaceae*)
A stemless perennial, native of E Bengal,
Burma, parts of Malaysia and Thailand where
it flowers during the rainy season, dying down
completely in dry weather. Leaves to 15cm,
elliptic, dark green, sometimes streaked with
paler green. Inflorescence nestles among the
leaves; flowers lilac. Min. 15°C.

Siphonochilus kirkii, (Hook. f.) B. L. Burtt,
syn. *Kaempferia rosea Baker* (*Zingiberaceae*)
A perennial with scented flowers, found in
tropical S and E Africa growing in light
woodland, flowering in December–January.
Flowering stems 15-30cm. Leafy stems to
60cm, appearing with or after the flowers.
Keep dry in winter. Min.5°C.

MARANTACEAE

Ctenanthe lubbersiana

Calathea bachemiana

Calathea libbyana 'Windows'

Calathea argyraea

Calathea magnifica

Ctenanthe opennheimiana

Calathea ornata 'Roseo-lineata'

Ctenanthe burle-marxii

Calathea dressleri var. dressleri

Specimens from the Royal Batanic Gardens, Kew, 23 July, ¼ life-size

Alocasia × amazonica hort. *A. lowii* var. *grandis × A. sanderiana* André (*Araceae*) There are about 70 species of *Alocasia* native of tropical S Asia, many of which are suitable for the warm greenhouse or as houseplants when small. The plant illustrated here is of garden origin and has a bushy habit. Leaves dark green with white veins and white scalloped margins. A plant for a warm humid greenhouse, shaded from direct sun. Min. 15°C.

Caladium **'Florida Cardinal'** and **'Rosebud'** (*Araceae*) Caladiums are tuberous herbaceous perennials, native of the tropical rainforests of South America, particularly Brazil where they grow in forest clearings in moist, slightly shady places. There are 7 species and numerous hybrids, with an enormous variety of brightly coloured leaf markings; shown here are two of the most spectacular varieties. For a warm humid place or as a bedding plant. Min. 12°C.

Calathea argyraea Körn. (*Marantaceae*) Wild origin uncertain, but probably native of Brazil. Leaves to about 10cm long and 5cm wide, roughly ovoid, with wavy margins and a pointed apex, silvery greyish-green, with dark green midrib and numerous narrow dark green vein markings. Flowers yellow. Needs warmth, humidity and shade. Min. 15°C.

Calathea bachemiana Morren, syn. *Maranta kegeliana* hort. A stemless herb, native of Brazil, that grows to around 45cm. Leaves narrow, greyish-green, to 30cm long and 12cm wide, with broad dark green bands on either side of the midrib. Flowers white, to around 5cm, on stalk to 8cm. Needs warmth, humidity and shade. Min. 15°C.

Calathea dressleri H. Kennedy var. *dressleri* A species of unknown origin, with round leaves. Needs warmth, humidity and shade. Min. 15°C.

Calathea libbyana Kenn. **'Windows'** This is a form of the species from Ecuador. Plant forms a large clump to at least 1m. Leaves to about 40cm, broadly ovate, dark bluish-green with wavy margins and broad light green markings either side of the midrib. Flowers white and purple. Needs warmth, humidity and shade. Min. 15°C.

Calathea magnifica Morton. & Skutch., syn. *C. utea* (Aubl.) Mey. A large striking plant, possibly to 4m tall, native of tropical America, especially Panama. Leaves mid-green with distinctive 'peacock-feather' markings. Flowers yellow. Needs warmth, humidity and shade. Min. 15°C.

Calathea ornata (Lind.) Körn **'Roseo-lineata'** A form of *C. ornata* that eventually grows to 1m or more tall. Leaves to 20cm long or more, marked with pairs of narrow pink lines when young. Needs warmth, humidity and shade. Min. 15°C.

Ctenanthe burle-marxii H.Kenn. (*Marantaceae*) Native of Brazil, plant to 40cm or more. Stem purplish. Leaves oblong, pale green with dark green markings on veins either side of midrib. Inflorescence to 6cm; flowers white. Needs warmth, humidity and shade. Min. 15°C.

Epipremnum aureum, showing juvenile and mature leaves

Alocasia, Dichorisandra (*see page 256*) and *Fittonia* (in front)

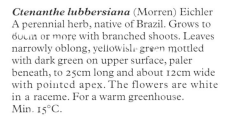

Thalia dealbata in the Huntington Gardens, California

Caladium 'Florida Cardinal'

Caladium 'Rosebud'

Maranta leuconeura var. *kerchoviana*

Monstera deliciosa

Ctenanthe lubbersiana (Morren) Eichler
A perennial herb, native of Brazil. Grows to
60cm or more with branched shoots. Leaves
narrowly oblong, yellowish-green mottled
with dark green on upper surface, paler
beneath, to 25cm long and about 12cm wide
with pointed apex. The flowers are white
in a raceme. For a warm greenhouse.
Min. 15°C.

Ctenanthe oppenheimiana (Morren)
Schumann   A perennial herb, native of
E Brazil, where it grows in damp wooded
places. Grows to 1m. Leaves to 40cm, ovate-
lanceolate with pointed apex, greyish-green
with dark green midrib and veins. Flowers
white. Needs warmth, humidity and shade.
Min. 15°C.

Epipremnum aureum (Lind. & André)
Bunting, syn. *Scindapsus aureus* (Lind. &
André) Engl. (*Araceae*)   A fleshy vine, native
of the Solomon Islands and South Pacific.
Plant eventually to 15m, but a small bush
when young. Juvenile leaves to 30cm, ovate,
bright glossy green splashed with yellow;
mature leaves to 80cm, similar in appearance
to *Monstera*, but variegated. Spathe and spadix
to 15cm. For a warm greenhouse or as a
houseplant in temperate zones; outside in the
tropics. Min. 15°C.

Fittonia verschaffeltii (Coem.) Nichols.
'Argyroneura' (*Acanthaceae*)   A creeping
spreading perennial herb, native of Peru.
Leaves oval, to around 10cm long, bright
green netted with white veins. Flowers white.
Good as a ground-cover plant for greenhouse
borders. Needs warm semi-shaded humid
conditions. Min. 15°C.

Maranta leuconeura E. Morr. var.
kerchoviana (*Marantaceae*) Morren Prayer
Plant   A low-growing herb, this is a garden
variety of the species which is native of Brazil
where it grows in forest clearings. Leaves oval,
to 15cm long, greyish green, with a row of
dark brown blotches each side of the midrib;
leaves fold up in the evening. Inflorescence
solitary; flowers small, white, on slender stem.
Good as a ground-cover plant in tropical or
subtropical gardens or as a houseplant in
temperate climates. Min. 10°C.

Monstera deliciosa Liebm.(sometimes
known as *Philodendron pertusum* in its juvenile
form) (*Araceae*) Swiss Cheese Plant   A
woody climber with long aerial roots, native of
Guatemala, Panama and South Mexico where
it grows up trees; also cultivated commercially
for its fruit in Florida. Leaves large, leathery,
glossy green, to 1m, entire when young but
later pinnately cut and perforated with holes
which increase in number as plant ages.
Spathe white, to 30cm; spadix to 25cm,
cream. Fruit (ceriman) edible. For a warm
greenhouse or as a houseplant in temperate
zones; outside in the tropics. Min. 15°C.

Thalia dealbata L. (*Marantaceae*)
A moisture-loving perennial, native of S
Carolina to Florida and Missouri to Mexico
growing in swampy woodlands and marshes.
Leaf stems up to 2m long. Leaves ovate-
lanceolate, greyish-green on upper side,
whitish below, to around 50cm long and 25cm
wide. Flowers numerous, small, to around
8cm, purple, in panicles on long stalks which
rise above the leaves. For pool margins in the
warm greenhouse or outside in subtropical
areas. Min. −5°C for short periods only.

DENDROBIUM

Bletilla ochracea on the road to Baoxing

Bletilla striata on Mount Omei

Dendrobium aphyllum

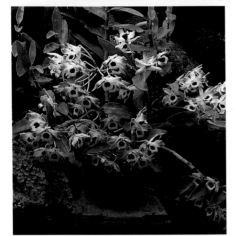

Dendrobium nobile at Sellindge

Dendrobium nobile

Dendrobium nobile 'Yukimusume'

Dendrobium speciosum

Bletilla ochracea Schltr. (*Orchidaceae*)
A terrestrial orchid, native of China from
Hubei to SW Sichuan where it grows on rocky
grassy slopes, flowering in May–June. Stem
erect, to 50cm. Leaves arching, narrow,
oblong-lanceolate, pleated, to 30cm long, 5cm
across. Inflorescence slender, erect; flowers to
5cm across, pale yellow. For a pot in light
shade or a sheltered border outside.
Min. –5°C or less for short periods.

Bletilla striata (Thunb.) Rchb. fil., syn.
Bletia hyacinthina (J. E. Smith) R. Br
A terrestrial orchid, native of China, Japan
and E Tibet where it grows on rocks, grassy
slopes and scrub, flowering in May–June.
Stem erect, to 70cm. Leaves narrow, oblong-
lanceolate, pleated, to 45cm long, 5cm across.
Inflorescence slender, erect; flowers purplish-
pink, to around 5cm across. For a pot in light
shade or a sheltered border outside.
Min. –5°C or less for short periods.

Coelogyne cristata Lindl. (*Orchidaceae*)
An epiphytic orchid with scented white
flowers, native of the foothills of the
Himalayas from N India to Sikkim, growing
on trees and rocks at 1000–2000m, flowering
in March–April. Pseudobulbs bright green.
Leaves narrow, dark green, to about 30cm
long. Inflorescence pendent, to 30cm long,
with up to 10 flowers, each to 8cm across,
white; lip with fimbriate keels, streaked bright
yellow. Good for a hanging basket. Min. 0°C
for short periods only. **'Lemoniana'** is an old

selection of *C.cristata*, with a paler lemon-
yellow blotch on the mid-lobe.

Coelogyne ochracea Lindl.   An epiphytic
orchid with small white flowers, native of the
foothills of the Himalayas from N India to
Bhutan and Burma, growing on trees and
rocks at 1300–2500m, flowering in April–May.
Pseudobulbs yellow green. Leaves upright,
narrow, dark green, to about 30cm long.
Inflorescence upright, to 20cm long, with 6–8
flowers to 4cm across, white, the lip with
yellow, red-margined blotches and two ridges.
Min. –3°C for short periods only.

Dendrobium aphyllum (Roxb.) C. E.
Fischer, syn. *D. pierardii* (Roxb.) C. E. Fischer
(*Orchidaceae*)   An epiphyte with pendulous
cane-like pseudobulbs and small pale pink
and cream flowers on leafless stems which can
be so thick on trees that they look like *Wisteria*.
Native of NE India and Bhutan, E to China
and south to S India and Malaya, growing
on large trees and cliffs at up to 300m, flowering
in March–May. Stems to 90cm long, 10mm
thick. Leaves 5–12cm long, deciduous.
Inflorescence of 1–3 flowers at each
node.Flowers 5cm across, fragrant. Requires
heat and humidity with ample water while
growing, cooler and drier in winter.
Min. 10°C.

Dendrobium chrysanthum Wall. ex. Lindl.
An epiphytic orchid with pendulous cane-like
pseudobulbs and small golden yellow flowers,
native of Nepal to N Burma and Thailand,
growing on trees and rocks at 1300–1800m,
flowering in May–October. Stems 1–2m.
Leaves acuminate, 10–20cm long. Flowers
1–3, produced opposite the leaves, to 4cm
across, scented; lip with 2 round brownish
patches. Easily grown, kept dry and cool in
winter, warm and humid in summer.
Min. 5°C.

Dendrobium chrysotoxum Lindl.
An epiphyte with a clump of fleshy
pseudobulbs, 2–4 leaved at the top and

Coelogyne cristata 'Lemoniana'

Dendrobium chrysotoxum

Coelogyne ochracea

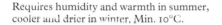

Dendrobium densiflorum at
Quince House, Devon

Dendrobium chrysanthum

hanging inflorescences of golden yellow flowers, native of NE India, Burma, Thailand, Yunnan and Laos, growing on trees and rocks, flowering in April–May. Stems 12–30cm. Leaves very stiff, 10–15cm long. Inflorescence 15–20cm long. Flowers 4–5cm across, scented; lip densely hairy with a fringed margin. Easily grown, kept dry and cool in winter, warm and humid in summer. Min. 5°C.

Dendrobium densiflorum Wall. ex. Lindl. An epiphyte with a clump of fleshy pseudobulbs, 3–5 leaved at the top and hanging inflorescences of yellow and white or all yellow flowers, native of the Himalyan foothills from C Nepal to Bhutan and Burma, growing on trees and rocks at 600–1600m, flowering in April–May. Stems 30–50cm. Leaves to 16cm long. Inflorescence to 25cm; flowers 4–5cm across, pale yellow or, in var. *alboluteum* hort., white and cream sepals and petals and a yellow lip. Easily grown, kept dry and cool in winter, warm and humid in summer. Min. 5°C.

Dendrobium farmeri Paxton An epiphyte with 4-angled pseudobulbs, 2–4 leaves at the top and hanging inflorescences of white or pale lilac flowers with a yellow lip. Native of the E Himalayas to Thailand and Malaysia, growing (in Malaysia) on large trees overhanging rivers in the forest, flowering in February–April. Stems 15–30cm. Leaves rather thin, ovate-lanceolate, to 8–18cm long. Inflorescence 20–30cm; flowers to 5cm across with pink stalks; lip white with a yellow base. Easily grown, kept dry and cool in winter, warm and humid in summer. Min. 10°C.

Dendrobium heterocarpum Lindl. An epiphytic orchid with upright or pendulous cane-like pseudobulbs and pale creamy yellow flowers with a brown to crimson blotch on the lip, native of India, Sri Lanka, Burma to Philippines, growing on trees, flowering in December–January. Stems to 150cm. Leaves 10–18cm long. Flowers 2–3 at each node on leafless stems, 5–8cm across.

Requires humidity and warmth in summer, cooler and drier in winter. Min. 10°C.

Dendrobium nobile Lindl. An epiphytic orchid with upright cane-like pseudobulbs and lovely white and mauve flowers at each node, native of NE India to S China and S to Laos and Thailand, growing in full sun at up to 1800m, flowering in February–April. Stems 30–50cm. Leaves 7–11cm long. Flowers 2–4 at each node, 6–8cm across, waxy, scented; petals and sepals white at the base, shading to rose or purple above. Easily grown, kept dry and cool in winter, warm and humid in summer. Min. 5°C. There are some very good new hybrids raised in Japan, with large flowers of various colours; shown here is **'Yukimusume'**.

Dendrobium speciosum Smith Rock Orchid An epiphyte with 2–5 leaves at the top and arching inflorescences of small spidery white to yellow flowers, native of Queensland, New South Wales and Victoria, growing on rocks or trees in rainforest, cliffs or gorges, from the coast into the mountains, flowering in July–October. Plants forming large clumps to 3m across. Stems 10–100cm. Leaves 4–25cm long, ovate to obovate, thick and leathery. Inflorescence 10–60cm; flowers 2.5–5cm across, strongly scented; lip with purple or red spots and streaks. Very hardy and easy to grow; requires full light with ample water and fertiliser in summer. Min. 0°C.

Dendrobium farmeri from Burnham Nurseries

Dendrobium heterocarpum

Cymbidium lowianum in a temple in Lijiang

Cymbidium hookerianum at Kew

Cymbidium old hybrid

Cymbidium 'Calle del Mar'

Cymbidium 'Kiwi Sunrise'

Cymbidium new hybrid

Cymbidium hookerianum Rchb. fil., syn. *C. grandiflorum* Griff. (*Orchidaceae*)   A large epiphyte with long grassy leaves and large scented green flowers, with a white lip with small red spots, native of the Himalayas from E Nepal to SE Tibet, growing on trees at 1600–2500m, flowering in April–May. Pseudobulbs 7cm long. Leaves to 60cm long, 2.5cm wide. Inflorescence arching and pendent, to 60–150cm, with 7–20 flowers, each 7.5–10cm across. For a large pot, moist in summer, dry and cooler in winter. Min. –3°C.

Cymbidium lowianum Rchb. fil.   A large epiphyte with long grassy leaves and large scented green flowers, native of Burma and NE India, growing on trees at up to 1500m, flowering in April–May. Pseudobulbs 10–15cm long. Leaves to 75cm long, 1.8cm wide. Inflorescence pendent, to 150cm, with up to 25 flowers, each 7.5–10cm across; sepals and petals yellowish-green, lip creamy white, with red W-shaped blotch near the apex. For a large pot, moist in summer, dry and cooler in winter. Min. –3°C.

Cymbidium tracyanum Rolfe   A large epiphyte with long grassy leaves and large scented green, brown-striped flowers, native of Burma, Thailand and Vietnam, growing on trees, flowering in April–May. Differs from *C. lowianum* in its flowers, which are 10–12.5cm across, scented, with sepals and petals curving downwards, greenish-yellow striped brown or reddish, and lip creamy with hairs and red and brown streaks. For a large pot, moist in summer, dry and cooler in winter. Min. –3°C.

Cymbidium hybrids   Modern *Cymbidium* breeding began around 1911, when H. C. Alexander, orchid grower at Westonbirt House, Gloucestershire, crossed Veitch's hybrid *Cymbidium eburneo-lowianum* with *C. insigne* to produce the hybrid *C. × alexanderi* 'Westonbirt'. Since then many hundreds of hybrids have been named, some very large, others with small flowers, and in every colour

Epidendrum ibaguense in Madeira

Laelia anceps 'Guerrero'

Laelia anceps or possibly *L. autumnalis* on Volcan Collima, SW Mexico in November

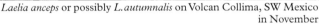

Odontoglossum pulchellum at Quince House, Devon

Phalaenopsis stuartiana

Cymbidium tracyanum

except crimson and blue. All are easily grown in an airy greenhouse and will tolerate a degree or two of frost. They should be kept on the dry side in winter and watered and fed well while growing in summer. They benefit by being stood outdoors in late summer and flower best after being subjected to warm days and cool nights. Shown here are four hybrids, including two miniatures:

'**Kiwi Sunrise**' with pink spotted flowers.
'**Calle del Mar**' with green flowers and a red spotted lip.
An old tall free-flowering and easy variety which we have grown since 1950.
An unnamed large-flowered modern hybrid with ice-green flowers whose parentage is *C. alexanderi album* × Sussex Dawn 'Cold Springs'.

Epidendrum ibaguense H. B. & K., syn. *E. radicans* Pavon ex. Lindl. (*Orchidaceae*) A scrambling or climbing orchid with long stems, short two-ranked leaves and heads of small, usually red, flowers, native of tropical America, usually growing in soil or on rocks, flowering most of the year. Stems to 1m or more. Leaves to 10cm long, 3.5 cm wide. Flowers variable, from magenta to orange or white, 1.6–3.2cm across with a 3-lobed fimbriated lip. Easily grown in full sun and tolerant of dry conditions; commonly cultivated in the tropics. Min. −3°C.

Laelia anceps Lindl. (*Orchidaceae*) An epiphytic orchid with long narrow pseudobulbs, tough leathery leaves and flowers pale and dark purple, native of

Mexico, growing on tree trunks and branches and sometimes on rocks, often in full sunlight, flowering in winter. Leaves 15–22cm, one or two at apex of each pseudobulb. Inflorescence 60–75cm, a 5 flowered; flowers to 10cm across. Easily grown, requiring full sun with water in summer, dry in winter and spring. Min. 0°C.

Odontoglossum pulchellum Lindl. (*Orchidaceae*) An epiphytic orchid, often making large clumps, with small scented white flowers and a yellow red-spotted lip, native of Mexico, Guatamala and El Salvador, growing in montane forests up to 2600m, flowering in early spring. Pseudobulbs to 10cm long, 2-leaved at apex. Leaves erect, 10–35cm long. Inflorescence erect, 12–50cm long, 3–10 flowered. Flowers held with lip uppermost, 2–4cm across. Easily grown in a cool greenhouse, kept rather dry in winter. Min. 0°C.

Phalaenopsis stuartiana Rchb.fil. An evergreen epiphytic orchid with broad fleshy mottled leaves and white flowers spotted with purple on the lower petals and lip, native of the Philippines, flowering in winter. Plant with very short stem and without pseudobulbs. Leaves thick and fleshy, to 35cm long and 8cm wide. Inflorescence arching or pendulous, to 60cm; flowers slightly scented, to 6cm across. This species and the commoner white-flowered *P. amabilis* require heat and humidity throughout the year; good for a luxurious bathroom. Winter night temperature should be above 15°C.

Pinus pinea and *Cupressus sempervirens*

Widdringtonia whytei on Mount Mulanje, Malawi

Pinus canariensis, showing cones

Cupressus macrocarpa at Point Lobos, near Monterey, California

A grove of *Pinus canariensis* on Tenerife

Amentotaxus argotaenia (Hance) Pilger (*Cephalotaxaceae*)   A rare evergreen shrub or small tree, native of S China from Sichuan to Hong Kong and Guangdong. Leaves green, glossy above, whitish underneath, needle-like, to 7cm long, 5mm wide. Male cones to 7cm long, 4cm wide; usually solitary, but sometimes in groups of 2–3. A shrub for cultivation outside only in areas with high summer temperatures (such as Florida), to enable the wood to ripen; although frost-tolerant for short periods, it requires glasshouse treatment in cool temperate regions. Min. –3°C.

Araucaria heterophylla (Salisb.) Franco. (*Araucariaceae*) Norfolk Island Pine
An evergreen tree, eventually up to 60m, native of SW Pacific and S America. Leaves narrow, soft, pale green, to 1cm long, becoming smaller and scale-like with age. Female cones subglobose, to about 10cm long and round. Planted as a windbreak in subtropical areas and in temperate climates often used as a decorative plant in large covered areas; suitable for conservatory use for only a few years as it grows quickly. Min –2°C for short periods only.

Cupressus macrocarpa Gord. (*Cupressaceae*) Monterey Cypress
A pyramidal tree which becomes flat-topped with age, native of California where it grows on coastal cliffs near Monterey. To about 20m in the wild, where it is subjected to gales, but up to 35m in cultivation in favourable conditions. Bark pale brown when young, turning greyer or pinkish-brown later. Leaves minute, about 3mm long with sharp points, becoming scale-like when the tree matures, lemon-scented when crushed. Cones oblong, to about 4cm long, 3cm wide, on short stalks. One of the hardiest cypresses, does well in warm maritime areas where it can be clipped back to form a hedge; rather tender when young. Min –10°C for short periods only.

Phyllocladus trichomanoides D. Don (*Podocarpaceae*)   A graceful evergreen tree, native of both islands of New Zealand where it grows from sea level to 800m. To 20m or so in the wild, with whorled branchlets. Leaves (known as phylloclades) dark green, shallowly lobed at top, in opposite rows on short branchlets to 12cm long, giving the general effect of a maidenhair fern frond. Min. –5°C.

Pinus ayacahuite Ehrenb. ex Schldl. (*Pinaceae*) Mexican White Pine   A large conical-shaped tree, native of Guatemala and S and C Mexico where it is found in sheltered valleys and on mountain slopes, at 2400–3300m. To 50m or more in the wild, usually less in cultivation. Trunk grey and smooth when young, fissured and purplish-brown when older. Leaves needle-like, silvery-blue-green, in groups of 5, to 15cm long, falling after 3–4 years. Cones short-stalked, 15–30cm long, cylindrical, usually in groups of 2 or 3. Good for moist areas. Min. –15°C.

Pinus canariensis C. Smith Canary Island Pine   A fine large pine, native of the Canary Islands where it grows on the islands of Gran Canaria, Hierro, La Palma and Tenerife, in bare rocky places at about 1200–2000m. Tree conical in shape, up to 30m. Bark thick, reddish-brown. Leaves needle-like, usually to 20cm, sometimes up to 30cm long, in groups of three. Cone to about 20cm long. Does well in warm temperate climates, especially along the Mediterranean coast. This is one of the few pines that has the ability to sprout from the trunk after damage either by fire or frost. Min. –3°C for short periods only.

Pinus culminicola Andresen & Beaman. A shrub to 5m, native of NE Mexico, on El Potosi, where it grows in cloud forest at above 3000m. Crown compact, widely branching. Bark greenish-grey. Leaves needle-like, in fives, glossy green on upper surface, whitish below. Min. –3°C when young and with its juvenile foliage, but will tolerate lower temperatures when mature.

Pinus pinea L. Stone Pine   A tree with a wide dome-shaped head, native of S Europe from Spain and Portugal east to Greece and cultivated in Britain for at least 4 centuries. Variable in height, up to around 35m. Bark greyish-orange, deeply fissured when mature. Leaves dark green, in pairs (occasionally threes) to 12cm long. Cone greyish-brown, ovoid, to 12cm long. Hardier than generally thought, but tender when young. Min. –10°C.

Widdringtonia whytei Rendle (*Cupressaceae*) Mulanje Cedar   A large tree, native of Malawi, Mozambique, Transvaal and Zimbabwe, where it grows in cool wet mountains at around 2500m. Young trees narrowly columnar, becoming more pyramidal up to 15m, after that spreading until they become flat-topped, reaching nearly 50m; a shrubby form with adult foliage is also found. Juvenile leaves glaucous, linear, to about 1cm long, are produced until the tree is about 2m high; adult foliage has congested scale-like leaves on much-branched twigs. Min. 0°C.

Araucaria heterophylla in California

Amentotaxus argotaenia in China

Pinus ayacahuite near Tequila, Mexico

Phyllocladus trichomanoides on Madeira

Pinus culminicola, a dwarf shrubby pine in cloud forest of El Potosi, Mexico

293

CYCADS

Encephalartos altensteinii with Erythaea behind

Encephalartos gratus in the Fairchild Garden

Cyathea dregei in the Natal Drakensberg, near
Cathedral Peak

294

Equisetum giganteum at Kew

Ephedra campylopoda in fruit at La Mortola

Dicksonia squarrosa in Cascades Park,
Yaitakari, Auckland

Cycas revoluta Thunb. (*Cycadaceae*) Sago
Palm   A squat palm-like tree, native of Japan.
Extremely slow-growing cylindrical stem
eventually to 3m or higher, dark brown,
usually single, but sometimes branched.
Leaflets leathery in pinnate fronds, stiff dark
green, glossy, to around 1m long, in a terminal
crown. Increases by offsets. Female plants
bear orange fruits (*see picture*). The hardiest
and most commonly grown cycad, it will do
well as a pot plant in a frost-free greenhouse
or outside in a lightly shaded spot in
Mediterranean climates. Min −5°C for short
periods only, if the crown is protected.

Dioon purpusii Rose (*Zamiaceae*)
A palm-like cycad from S Mexico with a short
trunk and numerous stiff pinnate leaves in a
terminal crown. Male cones cylindrical to
20cm; female cones ovate, woolly to 45cm
long. For a warm humid greenhouse in rich
well-drained soil. Min. 15°C.

Encephalartos altensteinii Lehm.
(*Zamiaceae*) Prickly Cycad   A rare and
endangered plant in the wild, native of the
E Cape in South Africa. Trunk up to 5m.
Leaves to 2.5m long, glossy green, pinnate;
pinnae to 15cm long and 2.5cm wide. Cones
in groups of 2–5; male cylindrical, to 40cm
long; female oval, to 45cm. A plant for a shady
humid place in the warm greenhouse or
outside in the tropics. Min. 12°C.

Encephalartos gratus Prain.   Rare in the
wild, native of tropical Africa. Trunk to 1m or
more. Leaves green, to 1.5m with pinnae to
25cm long in pairs. Male cones cylindrical, to
30cm long; female cones to 60cm long. A
plant for a shady humid place in the warm
greenhouse or outside in the tropics.
Min. 12°C.

Ephedra campylopoda C. A. Meyer
(*Ephedraceae*)   A scrambling shrub, native of
the Mediterranean region, including Turkey,
the Balkans, Cyprus and W Syria, where it
grows in scrub. Branches arching, lax,
pendent. Leaves greyish. Fruit an orange
berry, to 8mm in diameter. Min. −5°C.

Tree Ferns on Mount Mulanje in Malawi
Tree ferns occur in suitable habitats in Asia,
Europe, Africa, Australia and South America
and are most abundant in warm temperate
forest. In southern Africa they are represented
by about 5 species of the family *Cyatheaceae*.
Cyathea dregei is the most widespread and
conspicuous, growing in open places such as
stream-banks and grassland in the cooler
parts. The other species are confined to shady
ravines in temperate forests at up to 2000m
and in areas of very high rainfall. These
woodland species are the least amenable to
cultivation but *C. dregei* is well suited to
conservatory cultivation, being tolerant of low
temperatures and, to some extent, of dry
conditions.

Cyathea dregei Kunze (*Cyathiaceae*)
A large tree fern, native of much of tropical
and South Africa from Cape Province
northwards, usually growing in open places in
mountain grassland and by streams, to 2300m
in the Drakensberg. Plant forming a small tree
up to 5m tall with a very stout trunk to 45cm
thick, the leaves in a whorl at the top. Leaves
to 2m long or more, the stalk with dense long
brown scales at the base. Fertile leaves with
spore clusters in very small cup-like structures

Dioon purpusii in Mexico

Cycas revoluta showing the orange fruits

Tree ferns on Mount Mulanje in Malawi

on the undersides. Grows best in slightly shaded conditions in light soil but needs moist atmosphere and plenty of water during dry weather. Very slow-growing. Min. 0°C.

Dicksonia squarrosa (Forst. f.) Sw. (*Dicksoniaceae*)   Native of North and South Islands of New Zealand, growing in open forest and by streams at up to 800m. Plant tree-like, to 6m tall, sometimes spreading by runners. Trunk about 10cm thick, formed of a slender rhizome surrounded with dense fibrous roots. Leaves up to 2m long and 60cm wide, bearing spore-clusters in cup-like sori beneath the margins. The young unfurling leaves (croziers) are very striking. Grows well but slowly in moist well-drained compost in light shade and moist atmosphere. In dry weather the trunk should be sprayed regularly. Min. 5°C.

Equisetum giganteum L.   A huge horsetail, native of the West Indies, Central and South America, generally in mountainous areas and growing in clay on spring-lines, stream banks and other moist places. Plant with a deep-running rhizome, forming colonies of erect stems to 3m tall. The evergreen stems are jointed like all horsetails, up to 2cm thick. From the upper joints arise whorls of slender branches of similar structure. Spores borne in cone-like bodies at the ends of branches or sometimes at the tip of the main stem. Once established it grows well in moist soil and light shade. Min. 10°C.

Cycas revoluta at the Elbow Beach Hotel, Bermuda, showing young leaves

Drynaria rigidula 'Vidgenii'

Pteris argyraea

Blechnum occidentale

Osmunda banksiifolia

Anemia dregeana

Dicranopteris linearis

Specimens from the Royal Botanic Gardens, Kew, 10 September, ¼ life-size

Lygodium japonicum at Kew

Blechnum attenuatum var. *giganteum* in the Knysna forest, SE Cape

Blechnum gibbum at Kew

Anemia dregeana Kunze (*Schizaeaceae*)
Native of South Africa from the Transvaal to the E Cape, where it grows along shady stream banks and river valleys in deciduous or evergreen forests, at up to 1500m. Plant with a short erect rhizome and a tuft of simply pinnate fronds to 25cm long. The fertile fronds bear spores on two modified pinnae arising from the base of the leafy part of the frond. Best grown in pots in a well-drained, acid or neutral soil. Min. 5°C.

Blechnum gibbum Labill. (*Blechnaceae*)
Native of Fiji, New Caledonia and the New Hebrides, where it grows in open forest and by streams. Plant clump-forming, slowly developing a black fibrous trunk up to 1m tall. The arching light green sterile leaves form a rosette at the apex and are up to 1m long.

A wonderful gathering of tree ferns and other pteridophytes in the last remnants of the rainforest near Auckland, New Zealand

Mature plants have erect fertile leaves with narrower segments. Grows well in containers or in moist shady ground. Min. 5°C.

Blechnum attenuatum (Sw.) Mett. var. **giganteum** (Kaulf.) Bonap.   Native of southern Africa from Malawi and Zambia to South Africa in Cape Province, growing on mountain stream banks in the open and in evergreen forests in wet places, especially by waterfalls. Plant clump-forming or slowly creeping, with a thick short rhizome. Leaves arching, to 1.8m long, the segments tapering to a fine point. The young leaves are sometimes bright pink. Fertile leaves more erect with very narrow segments. Grows best in shade with plenty of moisture. Min. 5°C.

Blechnum occidentale L.   Native of South and Central America and the West Indies, generally growing on shaded but well-drained slopes. A short rhizome bears a tuft of arching, once-pinnate fronds up to 60cm long. The young fronds are rosy-pink or coppery, becoming light green when mature. Spores are borne in a continuous line either side of the midrib. Easily grown in any moist well-drained and slightly shaded place. Min. 5°C.

Dicranopteris linearis (Burm. f.) Underw., syn. *Gleichenia dichotoma* Hook. (*Gleicheniaceae*)   Widely distributed in the tropics and subtropics of E Asia, where it forms very extensive thickets in shrubby places and rapidly colonises roadsides and other cleared ground. The long-creeping rhizome bears fronds at wide intervals, each with a slender wiry rachis bearing paired leaflets which are divided pectinately (comb-like) into many narrow segments. The spores are borne in round heaps either side of the midrib under the frond. Difficult to cultivate as the plants are very susceptible to dry conditions. They are best established from young pot-grown seedlings planted out in an open but retentive peaty compost. Min. 5°C.

Drynaria rigidula (Sw.) Beddome   Native of much of SE Asia and NE Australia, usually growing as an epiphyte on trees in tropical to warm temperate forest clearings. The fern forms a 'basket' of lobed leaves round the short rhizome, soon becoming brown and papery but persisting many years; the much larger drooping foliage leaves grow to 1.5m or more and are divided into narrow stalked pinnae. These leaves are deciduous and bear the spore heaps in a single row either side of the midrib of each pinna. Slow-growing but easily cultivated in a coarse well-drained compost or mounted on a moss pole. Min. 10°C and fairly drought-resistant when established. **'Vidgenii'** is a cultivar in which the pinnae are attractively lobed.

Lygodium japonicum (Thunb.) Sw. (*Schizaeaceae*)   Native of India, China, Japan, Malaysia, New Guinea and Australia, growing into shrubs and small trees in woodland margins, in lowlands and low mountains. Plant with a slender creeping underground rhizome. Leaves to 6m long with long twining leaf rachises, bipinnate, the fertile pinnae with smaller segments than the sterile ones. Spore-clusters in two rows on the margins of the smallest segments. Grows well in a well-drained leafy compost in partial shade. Leaves die back in cool conditions. Needs some support or can be grown in a basket as a trailer. Min. 5°C.

Osmunda banksiifolia (Presl) Kuhn (*Osmundaceae*)   Native of the warmer parts of China and Japan, where it grows in shady wet places such as the flood plains of small rivers and streams at low altitudes. Plants with a stout erect rhizome, and tufted fronds which can be as much as 1.5m long, but are more usually up to 90cm, divided into several pairs of slender, deeply toothed leaflets, often with contracted fertile leaflets in the middle of the frond. Requires a moist or intermittently wet position in light shade. Min. 5°C.

Pteris argyraea Moore (*Pteridaceae*)   Native probably of S or SE Asia but long cultivated elsewhere, this is a robust clump-forming species with long-stalked fronds to 1.5m. Fronds broadly ovate and bipinnate, a rich dark green with a broad silvery stripe down the centre of each main division. Spores borne under the in-rolled frond margins. This striking fern needs a shaded position in a leafy light but moist soil and dislikes wide temperature variations. Min. 10°C.

Pteris cretica 'Albolineata'

Pteris cretica 'Parkeri'

Pteris cretica 'Wimsettii'

Pteris ensiformis 'Victoriae'

Pteris cretica 'Rivertoniana'

Pteris cretica 'Albolineata Cristata'

Specimens from the Royal Botanic Gardens, Kew, 10 September, ¼ life-size

Pyrrosia lingua with cushions of the moss *Leucobrymum glaucum* on Victoria Peak, Hong Kong

Cyrtomium fortunei J. Smith var. **clivicola** (Makino) Tagawa (*Dryopteridaceae*) Native of C and S Japan where it grows in woodland in the low mountains. Rhizome short, with a tuft of fronds to 80cm long and widest at the base. Fronds simply pinnate with up to 15 pairs of ovate leaflets to 15cm long, their margins scarcely toothed. Easily grown in any well-drained leafy compost. Min. 0°C. The frond illustrated is close to typical *C. fortunei*, with numerous narrower leaflets.

Pteris cretica L. Native of S Europe and much of Africa and Asia, from the Mediterranean to China and Japan, growing in temperate to subtropical forests and more open places. Plant with a short rhizome bearing a tuft of erect pinnate fronds, the narrow segments bearing abundant spores under the in-rolled margins. Easily cultivated in pots or planted out in any well-drained compost. They form copious roots and may need repotting twice a year. Min. 0°C. The following are cultivars of *P. cretica*:
'Albolineata' A variant known from the wild (although possibly as an escape from cultivation) and very commonly cultivated. It differs from the wild type in having a white or pale green stripe down the centre of each segment.
'Parkeri' A vigorous selection with larger and broader leaflets, giving it a distinctly bold appearance.
'Wimsettii' A plumose form in which the leaflets are deeply toothed and lobed. Very popular and widely available.
'Albolineata Cristata' A crested form derived from 'Albolineata'. The leaflets have a white central stripe and each divides into a broad fan-shaped crest at the tip.
'Rivertoniana' A strong-growing variant in which the leaflets are deeply and irregularly lobed along the margins.

Pteris ensiformis Burm. fil. **'Victoriae'**
This species is native of E Asia, Polynesia and Australia, growing in forest clearings and disturbed ground in tropical and subtropical areas. It is a compact tufted fern with erect long-stalked, dark green fronds to 60cm long. In the variety 'Victoriae', which comes true when raised from spores, each segment has a silvery-white band either side of the midrib. It is a popular and easily grown variety for

growing in pots in a peaty open compost. Min. 5°C.

Pteris fauriei Hieron. (*Pteridaceae*) Native of China and Japan, growing in forests, often near streams. Plant clump-forming with arching, broadly triangular or ovate evergreen leaves up to 50cm long, divided into even-sized segments. Sori under the in-rolled leaf margins. Needs shade and a well-drained humus-rich soil. Min. 0°C or slightly lower.

Pyrrosia heteractis (Mett.) Ching (*Polypodiaceae*) Native of Sikkim and Bhutan in the Himalayan foothills, growing on banks, rocks and tree trunks in moist forests. Rhizome slender and far-creeping, densely scaly. Fronds to 15cm long, oblong with long-tapering points, borne on stalks to 18cm long. The lower surface is covered with whitish or pale brown scales, among which are rounded spore heaps. Easy to grow, either in a shallow pot or pan with very coarse peaty compost, in a hanging basket or on the trunk of a tree fern. Min. 10°C.

Pyrrosia lingua (Thunb.) Farwell (*Polypodiaceae*) Native to E Asia from Thailand and Laos to China and Japan, growing on rocks and stony places in forests in the low mountains. Plant creeping from a slender rhizome, eventually forming extensive colonies. Leaves up to 25cm long, evergreen, very thick and somewhat scurfy, especially when young. Fertile leaves bear spore clusters in a regular dense pattern beneath. Grows well in well-drained leafy soil and stands bright light if kept humid. Very tolerant of dry conditions when well established. Min. −5°C.

Pyrrosia polydactyla (Hance) Ching Native of Taiwan where it grows on trees and mossy rocks in shady places in a tropical climate. Rhizome short-creeping, with shiny deep green fronds to 20cm long and wide,

Woodwardia radicans in laurel forest on Madeira

Woodwardia unigemmata on Omei Shan

Pteris fauriei at Kew

divided almost to the base into up to 8 narrow, finger-like pointed lobes covered with pale green, later brownish scales beneath. This distinctive species should be quite easy to grow, either in a shallow pot or pan with very coarse peaty compost, in a hanging basket or on the trunk of a tree fern. Min. 10°C.

Quercifilix zeylanica (Houtt.) Copel. (*Dryopteridaceae*) Native of subtropical parts of SE Asia, growing in rocky places in well-drained soil in light shade. Rhizome short, the hairy fronds resembling oak leaves, to 15cm long. Each is oblong, with shallow rounded lobes and often a pair of free leaflets at the base. The spore-bearing fronds are similar but much contracted. Needs a lightly shaded airy place in well-drained loamy compost in a pot or in the ground. Min. 10°C.

Woodwardia radicans (L.) J. E. Sm. (*Blechnaceae*) Native of SW Europe and the Atlantic Islands, growing in woodland margins, often by streams. Plant clump-forming with several arching broadly ovate evergreen leaves up to 2m long. Sori chain-like, in two rows either side of the midrib. Each leaf has a large bud near the tip which develops into a plantlet that roots if the leaf reaches the ground. Best in a shady place in moist humus-rich acid or neutral soil. Min. −5°C when established.

Woodwardia unigemmata (Makino) Nakai Native of much of Asia from India to China and Japan, this fern is usually found in moist habitats like stream banks in woodlands or shady cliffs. Clump-forming plant to 90cm tall. Leaves rather thick-textured, often with a single plantlet developing just below the apex. Fertile leaves have spore clusters in chains either side of the midrib beneath. Needs a moist acid or neutral soil with plenty of humus and will stand some sun. Min. −5°C, perhaps, when established.

Cyrtomium fortunei

Polypodium species

Pyrrosia heteractis

Pyrrosia polydactyla

Quercifilix zeylanica

Specimens from the Royal Botanic Gardens, Kew, 10 September, ⅓ life-size

Araiostegia faberiana (C. Chr.) Ching (*Davalliaceae*)   Native of the Himalayas and W China growing in mountain woodland up to 3500m. The stout creeping rhizome produces fronds up to 60cm long including the stalk. The fronds are broadly triangular and rather finely divided with deeply lobed segments bearing inconspicuous spore heaps near the veins beneath. Should be quite easily cultivated in a basket or shallow pan using a well-drained leafy compost. Min. 5°C.

Araiostegia pseudocystopteris (Kunze) Copel.   Native of N India and W China where it grows on trees and rocks, less often in the ground, at up to 2800m. Slender creeping rhizomes bear arching or drooping fronds to 60cm long. The fronds are very finely divided into narrow pointed segments. Probably quite easily cultivated in a basket or shallow pan using a well-drained leafy compost. Min. 5°C.

Davallia canariensis (L.) Sm. (*Davalliaceae*)   Native of Portugal, Spain, Madeira and the Canary Islands, growing on rocks and walls and sometimes epiphytic on trees. The rather thick rhizome is covered with conspicuous chestnut-brown scales. The fronds are triangular, very finely divided and lacy, the small spore heaps under the fronds show as a small bump in the upper surface. Slow-growing but easy in a basket or shallow pan with a well-drained coarsely leafy compost. The plant goes briefly dormant in summer before the new leaves emerge in autumn. Min. 0°C.

Davallia fejeensis Hooker   Native of Polynesia where it grows as an epiphyte on trees and rocks. Plant with a creeping rhizome, the evergreen leaves arising singly on long stalks. Leaves triangular-ovate, up to 90cm long, elegantly divided into very fine segments. Needs shade and even moisture and is best grown over a rock or branch or in a shallow container or basket. Min. 5°C.

Davallia fejeensis Hook. **'Plumosa'**
Native of Fiji where it grows on rocks and tree trunks in forests. The thick creeping rhizome often arches away from the soil and bears very finely divided triangular fronds to 90cm long. In the variety 'Plumosa' these are particularly lacy and droop elegantly. Easily grown in any leafy soil. Min. 5°C. The wild form of the species is illustrated opposite.

Davallia solida (Forst.) Sw.   Native of SE Asia, Polynesia and N Australia, growing on trees and rocks especially near the sea. The stout creeping rhizome produces long-stalked triangular fronds to 50cm long. They are finely divided and a deep glossy green but sometimes tinged purple when young. Easily grown in a basket, planted with the rhizome creeping over the surface of a coarse leafy compost or allowed to run among rocks in a shady greenhouse border. Min. 0°C.

Humata griffithiana (Hook.) C. Chr. (*Davalliaceae*)   Native of India, China and Taiwan, growing on trees and rocks in the hills at up to 1800m. The stout creeping rhizome is covered with long silvery scales. Fronds triangular, finely divided, to 30cm long, on a wiry stalk to 15cm long. Resembles *Davallia mariesii* in the structure of the spore but differs in the structure of the sporangia. Easily cultivated in baskets, shallow pots or among rocks in a greenhouse border. Min. 5°C.

Leucostegia immersa (Wall.) Presl var. ***amplissima*** Copel. (*Davalliaceae*)   Native of tropical and subtropical parts of the Philippines and Borneo where it grows in open places either on tree trunks and rocks or in the soil. The thin creeping rhizome produces very finely divided, broadly triangular fronds to 60cm long, on stalks to 40cm. Needs an open and well-drained compost, even moisture and some shade; a good plant for a basket but does not like low temperatures. Min. 10°C.

Peltapteris peltata (Sw.) Morton (*Lomariopsidaceae*)   Native to the West Indies and tropical America from Mexico southwards, growing epiphytically on mossy tree trunks and rocks, especially near streams. A plant with a very slender creeping scaly rhizome, forming colonies. Sterile leaves curiously dissected to form a fan-shaped lacy frond to 5cm wide, on a stalk to 12cm long. Fertile leaves taller, with an undivided blade to 2cm wide, the lower side covered with sporangia. Best grown in live sphagnum moss as shown in the photograph, with some shade and constant humidity. Min. 15°C perhaps.

Sphenomeris chusana Copel. (*Dennstaedtiaceae*)   Native of much of E Asia, Madagascar and Polynesia, growing on lightly shaded banks in forest clearings and stream sides. Plant clump-forming or slowly creeping, to 60cm. Leaves arching on long slender stalks, light green, very lacy in appearance. Fertile leaves bear small spore clusters under the tips of the finest segments. Grows best in well-drained mixture of sand and coarse humus in light shade. Min. 0°C.

Davallia canariensis on a volcanic cliff

Peltapteris peltata on top of a tree-fern stump

Leucostegia immersa var. *amplissima* at Kew

Sphenomeris chusana on Mount Omei, SW Sichuan

Davallia fejeensis in the Princess of Wales House at Kew

Davallia fejeensis 'Plumosa'

Leucostegia immersa var. *amplissima*

Davallia solida

Davallia canariensis

Araiostegia faberiana

Araiostegia pseudocystopteris

Humata griffithiana

Specimens from the Royal Botanic Gardens, Kew, 10 September, ⅓ life-size

Diplazium donianum

Asplenium oceanicum

Asplenium aethiopicum

Asplenium nidus
'Plicatum'

Asplenium viviparum

Bolbitis subcordata

Specimens from the Royal Botanic Gardens, Kew, 10 September, ⅓ life-size

Asplenium aethiopicum (Burm.) Becherer (*Aspleniaceae*)   Native of subtropical and tropical parts of southern Africa, Mauritius and Madagascar, growing in a range of habitats including deciduous woodland, cliff faces and mist forest. Rhizome short with tufted leathery fronds to 60cm long. Fronds bipinnate, with wedge-shaped segments bearing linear spore heaps beneath. Best grown in a rather small pot in a coarse leafy or peaty compost. Light shade and an airy situation are required. Min. 5°C, depending on provenance.

Asplenium aenonicum Olin, syn.
A. bipinnatifidum Bak.   Native of Polynesia, growing on rocks in evergreen forests. The short rhizome bears a tuft of fronds to 20cm long, each with about 12 pairs of pinnae, themselves more or less deeply divided into narrow segments. Needs well-drained leafy compost which is neutral to alkaline and kept moist in summer, drier in winter. Light shade. Min. 10°C.

Asplenium nidus L. **'Plicatum'**   Native throughout the Old World tropics, generally as an epiphyte on trees in deep forest. Rhizome very short, bearing a tuft of stalkless or short-stalked fronds forming a 'nest'. Fronds entire, to 1.5m under optimum conditions. In the cultivar 'Plicatum' they are narrower than normal and regularly pleated or goffered. Easily grown in an open humus-rich compost in pots or on an indoor rockery. Needs warm humid shady conditions. Min. 10°C.

Asplenium viviparum L.   Native of Mauritius and Madagascar, growing in relatively dry shady places. Rhizome short and stout, bearing clusters of arching fronds to 40cm long. Fronds tripinnate with very narrow final segments, each with a single spore heap beneath. Fronds bearing numerous small plantlets scattered over the upper surface, giving a ready source of new plants. The commonly cultivated Australasian *Asplenium bulbiferum* Forst. has the same characteristic but the fronds are less finely divided. Min. 5°C.

Bolbitis subcordata (Copel.) Ching (*Lomariopsidaceae*)   Native of China, Indochina, Taiwan and S Japan, growing in forest in low mountains, generally on rocks and sometimes in deeply shaded ravines. Rhizome short, bearing two sorts of fronds up to 90cm long. Sterile fronds ovate, pinnate, the segments strongly lobed or toothed. Fertile fronds with fewer, much narrower segments. Needs a humus-rich acid soil, plenty of moisture and moderate shade. Min. 10°C.

Diplazium donianum (Mett.) Tard. Blot. (*Woodsiaceae*)   Native of subtropical E Asia from the Himalayan foothills to China and the southernmost islands of Japan, growing in considerable shade in dense mountain forests. The short thick rhizome produces large, simply pinnate fronds up to 1m long, each with up to 7 lanceolate leaflets 15–20cm long. The spores are borne in narrow lines along the minor lateral veins. Should be easily cultivated in a well-drained leafy compost in a large pot or a border. Needs moist shady conditions. Min. 5°C.

Platycerium willinckii

Platycerium superbum

Platycerium bifurcatum (Cav.) Christens. Native of Indonesia, New Guinea and Australia where it grows epiphytically on trunks and branches of trees. Plant clump-forming with two sorts of leaves. The erect 'nest' leaves clasp the branch and are wavy-edged at the top. The scurfy-hairy arching fertile leaves are up to 90cm long, up to 4 times forked into pairs of oblong lobes in the upper half and taper to a slender base. The spores are borne in patches under the tips of the lobes. This fern is usually grown on a branch or a suspended slab of cork or in a well-drained coarse peaty compost and needs good light. Min. 5°C but better grown at 10°C winter minimum.

Platycerium superbum de Jonkheere & Hennipman   Native of Australia growing as an epiphyte on trees in Queensland and northern New South Wales. Plant forming a clump with large erect 'nest' leaves which are deeply lobed along the top margin. The arching or drooping scurfy, grey-green fertile leaves are up to 2m long, forking several times and bearing a single large spore patch in the angle of the first fork. Best grown on a large moss pole, tree trunk or well-fixed cork slab in a warm greenhouse with good light. Should be watered quite freely while in growth, but kept rather dry in winter. Min. 10°C.

Platycerium willinckii T. Moore (*Polypodiaceae*)   Native to Indonesia and New Guinea, growing as an epiphyte on trunks and branches of trees. Plant clump-forming with two sorts of leaves. The erect 'nest' leaves clasp the branch and are deeply lobed at the top. The drooping fertile leaves are up to 1m long, repeatedly divided into pairs of oblong lobes in the upper half and taper to a slender base. The spores are borne in patches under the tips of the lobes. This fern is usually grown on a branch or a suspended slab of cork or in a well-drained coarse peaty compost and needs good light. Min. 10°C but better grown at 15°C or higher.

Platycerium bifurcatum

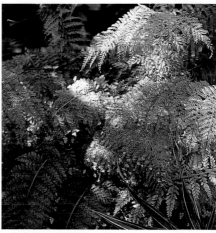

Asplenium bulbiferum showing young plants on the leaves

303

ADIANTUM

Adiantum macrophyllum

Adiantum trapeziforme

Adiantum diaphanum

Adiantum formosum

Adiantum peruvianum

Adiantum henslovianum

Adiantum reniforme var. chinense

Adiantum reniforme var. asarifolium

Specimens from the Royal Botanic Gardens, Kew, 10 September, ¼ life-size

Adiantun reniforme on Madeira

Adiantum diaphanum Bl. (*Adiantaceae*)
Native of E Asia, Australia, New Zealand and
Pacific islands, forming extensive colonies on
wet boulders, clay banks and cliff faces in wet
and shady places. The arching translucent
green fronds are up to 30cm long, pinnate or
bipinnate with small oblong leaflets. Easily
grown in a well-drained acid compost needing
shade and moisture. Min. −5°C, depending on
provenance.

Adiantum formosum R. Br. Native of E
Australia, New Zealand and Pacific Islands,
forming extensive colonies in wet alluvial
forests and rich woods. Tall evergreen fronds
up to 150cm long, 4-pinnate, glabrous, with
rhomboidal leaflets. Easily grown in a well-
drained acid compost, needing shade and
moisture. Min. −3°C depending on
provenance.

Adiantum henslovianum Hook. Native of
tropical forests of South America and the

Galapagos Islands. Rhizome short, bearing
thin-textured, triangular-ovate fronds to 60cm
long. These are divided into fan-shaped
leaflets, finely hairy on the underside. Easily
cultivated where fairly high temperatures can
be maintained. Best in pots in a coarse leafy
neutral soil in light shade and kept rather dry
in winter. Min. 15°C.

Adiantum macrophyllum Sw. Native of
the West Indies, Mexico, Central and South
America, generally growing in clay soils in
moist shaded ravines and banks at low
altitudes in tropical regions. Rhizome shortly
creeping, covered with glossy brown scales.
Fronds up to 30cm tall on a glossy black stalk
15–30cm long, simply pinnate with up to 8
pairs of narrowly triangular leaflets. Young
fronds are coppery-pink. The spores are borne
under the margins of the leaflets. Best in a
slightly alkaline well-drained compost in a
small pot, in shaded humid conditions. Min.
10°C. The frond illustrated is from a plant
collected in Trinidad.

Adiantum peruvianum Klotsch Native of
tropical and subtropical South America where
it grows in moist forest conditions. Rhizome
short, producing triangular-ovate fronds to
1m long, divided into dark green diamond-
shaped leaflets up to 7cm long. The young
fronds are often a silvery-pink colour,
especially when grown in good light. Needs a
buoyant humid atmosphere with some air
movement and should have a neutral leafy
compost, kept nearly dry while dormant in
winter. Min. 10°C.

Adiantum raddianum Presl. Native of
tropical and subtropical America from Mexico
and the West Indies south to Argentina,
growing on rocks, cliffs and stream banks
within forests. Rhizome short-creeping with
narrowly triangular fronds borne on shiny
black stalks to 10cm long. Fronds up to 40cm
long, tripinnate, with many small leaflets
wedge-shaped at the base and more or less
lobed on the upper margin. Easily cultivated
in pots in a frost-free, lightly shaded
conservatory or greenhouse, using a well-
drained neutral or slightly limy compost.
Min. 5°C or lower. This species has given rise
to many cultivars varying in size and habit:
'Deflexum' A plant with fronds to 45cm
long, the segments small and distinctively
folded down, especially towards the apex of
the frond, not very clearly shown in the
photograph.
'Fasciculatum' A compact plant to 20cm
tall with relatively large slightly overlapping
leaflets, which are more deeply lobed than
normal. The general appearance is rather
congested.
'Goldelse' Broadly triangular fronds to
30cm long on red-brown stalks to 20cm. The
segments are regularly lobed and the plant has
a luxuriant appearance. New growth may be
pink or pale yellow.
'Kensington Gem' A robust variety with
luxuriant fronds up to 70cm long when well
grown. The rather large segments are deeply
and regularly divided, and are a pleasant pale
green. It is sterile and is propagated by
division.
'Lawsonianum' A robust cultivar with an
attractive lacy appearance. Fronds to 70cm
long, arching, with small wedge-shaped
leaflets which are deeply and regularly lobed.
'Legrand Morgan' A compact cultivar
with congested fronds to 40cm long, divided

into many tiny rounded leaflets, the whole effect being of a mass of lacy greenery. The plant illustrated was grown under another name but appears to be close to this cultivar.

'Pacific Maid' A distinctive cultivar up to 40cm tall, with congested upright fronds bearing many overlapping broad finely toothed leaflets.

'Pacottii' A dwarf variety of congested growth with broad dense fronds to 30cm long, borne on rather long black stalks. The leaflets are broad, strongly lobed and finely toothed.

'Pelican' Fronds to 40cm long, broadly triangular with a wiry black stalk. Segments broad, wedge-shaped, deeply and regularly lobed.

'Waltonii' This cultivar differs from others in its more regularly arranged frond and in the rounded bases to the deeply lobed leaflets. The narrow fronds are up to 40cm long. Some authorities place this plant under *Adiantum excisum*, another South American species.

Adiantum reniforme L. Native of the Canary Islands, Madeira, Kenya and W China (var. **_chinense_** Y. X. Lin), a curiously broken distribution pattern. It grows in open situations on rock faces and among boulders, often in apparently dry places. Plant loosely tufted with a short scaly rhizome. Leaves rounded or kidney-shaped, 3–5cm wide, on wiry stalks up to 15cm long. The spores are borne under reflexed flaps on the margin. Good for pot cultivation in a well-drained leafy, slightly alkaline compost. Very tolerant of dry airy conditions, less so of warm humid ones. Min. −5°C depending on provenance. Plants from the Mascarene Islands are larger, with more scaly stalks and overlapping lobes at the base of the blade. They are:

A. reniforme var. _asarifolium_ (Willd.) C. Chr., sometimes considered a distinct species.

Adiantum trapeziforme L. Native of Jamaica, Cuba and tropical Central America, growing on wooded hillsides. Rhizome short and thick. Fronds arching, to 1m or more, on a shiny black stalk to 50cm long, much divided into diamond or trapezium-shaped leaflets 3–5cm long. An imposing fern for a large pot, but best grown in a border in a conservatory in a well-drained humus-rich neutral compost in good light. Min. 10°C.

'Lawsonianum' 'Fasciculatum' 'Pacific Maid' *Adiantum raddianum* 'Waltonii' 'Kensington Gem' 'Legrand Morgan' 'Goldelse' 'Deflexum' 'Pelican' 'Pacottii'

Varieties of *Adiantum raddianum* from the Royal Botanic Gardens, Kew, 10 September, ¼ life-size

Adiantum raddianum close to 'Lawsonianum' at Kew

SELAGINELLA

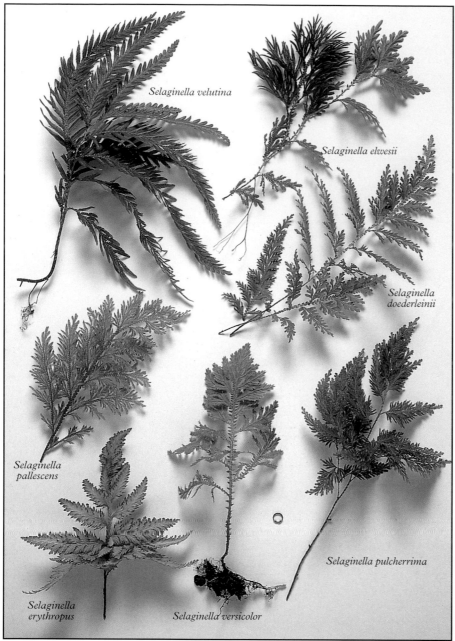

Selaginella velutina

Selaginella elwesii

Selaginella doederleinii

Selaginella pallescens

Selaginella pulcherrima

Selaginella erythropus

Selaginella versicolor

Specimens from the Royal Botanic Gardens, Kew, 10 September, ¼ life-size

Selaginella erythropus at Kew

Pilea involucrata (Sims) Urban **'Norfolk'**, syn. *P. spruceana* hort. A spreading dwarf with distinct, silver-veined leaves, native of Central and South America. Several varieties with different leaf patterns are grown; all prefer deep shade and humidity. Min. 5°C. *Pilea* 'Moon Valley' is shown in vol. 1, p.213.

Selaginella Beauv. (*Selaginellaceae*)
The club-mosses or spike-mosses. This is a genus of over 700 species, predominantly tropical and subtropical in distribution but with a few species in the temperate and Arctic regions. Most have small scale-like leaves arranged in frond-like sprays on creeping, scandent or erect stems. The spores are of two kinds and are commonly borne in spike-like strobili. Many are very easy to grow.

Selaginella doederleinii Hieron. Native of subtropical parts of W China, S Japan, Taiwan and Indochina, this grows in shady moist woodlands at low altitudes. It has a slender, much-branched main stem with flattened sprays of fern-like foliage to 30cm long or more. The leaves are bright light green. This species grows well in a conservatory where it should have a well-drained but leafy moist compost and fairly good diffuse light. It is satisfactory both in baskets and in the ground. Min. 5°C.

Selaginella elwesii Dark green with upright fronds, the shoots becoming crowded in the fertile state (*shown here*).

Selaginella erythropus (Martius) Spring Native of tropical America, south to Chile, growing in shady moist woodland conditions. It has a short main stem with regularly branched, flattened triangular sprays of fern-like foliage to 30cm long. The stems are often crimson and the leaves may be pale green or reddish. This is a beautiful species for a warm conservatory, where it should have a well-drained but leafy moist compost and fairly good diffuse light. Min. 10°C.

Selaginella kraussiana (Kunze) A. Braun Native of E and S Africa and the Azores (but commonly naturalised elsewhere), growing on shady roadside banks and forest glades. Plants with trailing stems to 30cm long, rooting from the stem. The stems are much branched, forming flattened sprays clothed in tiny scale-like leaves. Spores are borne in slender, erect strobili about 5mm long, just below the tips of the shoots. Easily grown in a moist shady place in almost any soil; in sun the foliage is paler and may scorch. It sometimes becomes quite invasive but makes an effective ground-cover under larger ferns or other plants. Min. 0°C or lower.

Selaginella kraussiana (Kunze) A. Braun **'Aurea'** A selection in which the foliage is light yellow-green, especially when grown in good light.

Selaginella martensii Spring **'Variegata'** Native of Mexico and Central America, *S. martensii* grows in lime-free soils in moist shady places. It forms a plant with clumps of erect short stems densely clothed with glossy green scale-like leaves to 8mm long. This variegated form has irregular patches of white leaves scattered over the plant. Easily grown in a warm moist shady place, either in pots or for ground-cover. Min. 0°C.

Selaginella versicolor with *Pilea involucrata* 'Norfolk'

Specimens from the Royal Botanic Gardens, Kew, 10 September, ¼ life-size

Selaginella pallescens (C. Presl) Spring
Native of Central America, Cuba, Jamaica and
Mexico, growing in shady banks where there
is little competition from other plants. Plant
forming a flat rosette of much-branched
fronds to 15cm long, which curl inwards when
the plant is dry. The small scale-like leaves are
yellow-green above and silvery-green on the
underside. The spores are borne on spikes to
1cm long. Easily grown in a pot in a well-
drained leafy soil in shade. Min. 10°C.

Selaginella pulcherrima Liebm. &
Fournier   Native of Mexico, this has a short
main stem from which arise elegant frondose
branches to 20cm long, with yellow stems.
Each branch has rounded lateral sprays of
bright green scale-like leaves which contrast
with the main stems. Easily grown in pots in a
warm conservatory, given a moist, well-
drained compost. Min. 10°C.

Selaginella serpens (Desv.) Spring   Native
of the West Indies where it grows in lime-free
soils on shady banks and rock ledges at up to
700m. Plant with branched creeping stems to
20cm long, forming dense bright green mats.
The wiry stems are clothed in very small
scale-like leaves and the spores are borne in
short erect strobili to 1cm long. In the wild the
foliage becomes silvery in the evening (for
physiological reasons), but this is seldom seen
in cultivated plants. Easily grown in warm
moist and partially shaded conditions, where
it makes useful ground-cover. Also effective in
a hanging basket. Min. 5°C.

Selaginella uncinata (Desf. ex Poir.) Spring
Native of S China, growing on shady banks in
the forest. Plant with trailing stems to 60cm,
rooting from the stem. Branches short,
alternate; leaves often with a remarkable blue
sheen. The spores are borne in short erect
angular strobili, 6–12mm long. For warmth
and humidity in summer, cooler and drier in
winter. Min. 5°C.

Selaginella velutina   Native of New
Guinea, with large triangular frond-like
shoots. Requires warm humid conditions.

Selaginella versicolor   Native of tropical
W Africa from Senegal south to Angola,
growing in shady moist conditions. It has a
short main stem with erect stems and broad
compound overlapping pinnae, dark to light
green and yellowish in colour. Min. 10°C.

Selaginella uncinata and other species on Victoria Peak, Hong Kong in October

Bibliography

General

The New Royal Horticultural Society Dictionary of Gardening Macmillan 1992. A new version of the old *Dictionary*.

The Royal Horticultural Society Dictionary of Gardening Oxford University Press 1976–77. Old but still valuable.

The European Garden Flora I–V to be completed, Cambridge University Press 1986–. Scientific account of cultivated plants.

Exotica International by A. B. Graf, 12th ed. 1985. 2 vols; 16300 B & W photos of exotic plants; short text.

Sunset Western Garden Book Lane Publishing Co., Menlo Park, California, 6th ed. 1988. An excellent source book for gardening in California.

Andersen Horticultural Library's Source List of Plants and Seeds University of Minnesota 1996. A source list for North America.

The RHS Plant Finder 1996–7 etc. A good source of modern plant names, as well as a source list of nurseries for Great Britain.

Wild Flowers of the World by Barbara Everard & Brian Morley, Ebury Press & Michael Joseph 1970. A geographical sample of interesting plants with excellent and fascinating text.

Flowering Tropical Climbers by Geoffrey Herklots, Dawson 1976. A clear and detailed account of many genera of climbers with excellent line drawings.

Cultivated Plants of the World: Trees, Shrubs and Climbers by Don Ellison, Flora Publications International, Brisbane 1995. 4500 small coloured photographs, mainly for Australia; little text.

Butterflies

The Butterfly Gardener by Miriam Rothschild and Clive Farrell, Michael Joseph 1983. Describes in detail, how to set up a butterfly house as well as how to encourage wild butterflies into the garden.

Keeping and Breeding Butterflies and other Exotica by John L. Stone, Blandford Press 1992.

Floras and Books on Different Regions of the World

AFRICA:

Plants of the Cape Flora. A Descriptive Catalogue by Pauline Bond & Peter Goldblatt, Journ. of South African Botany suppl. vol. 13 (1984).

The Botany of the Southern Natal Drakensberg by O. M. Hilliard & B. L. Burtt, National Botanic Garden 1987.

Wild Flowers of East Africa by Sir Michael Blundell, KBE, Collins 1987.

Wild Flowers of Malawi by Audrey Moriarty, Purnell 1975.

Spring and Winter Flowering Bulbs of the Cape by Barbara Jeppe, Oxford University Press, Cape Town, 1989.

AUSTRALIA:

Encyclopaedia of Australian Plants by W. Rodger Elliott & David L. Jones, vols. 1–5 1980–1990.

Australian Native Plants by John W. Wrigley & Murray Fagg, Collins 1986.

Flora of New South Wales ed. Gwen J. Harden, New South Wales University Press, 4 vols., 1990–93

CANARY ISLANDS:

Wild Flowers of the Canary Islands by David & Zoë Bramwell, Stanley Thornes 1974.

EUROPE:

Flora Europaea by V. H. Heywood *et al.* Cambridge University Press 1964–80.

INDIA, CHINA AND THE HIMALAYAS:

Flowers of the Himalaya by Oleg Polunin & Adam Stainton, Oxford 1984; and Supplement, Dehli 1990.

Flora of Bhutan by A. J. C. Grierson & D. G. Long, Royal Botanic Garden, Edinburgh 1983–94.

Plantae Wilsonianae by J. S. Sargent, 1913: reprinted by Dioscorides Press 1988.

Travels in China by Roy Lancaster, Antique Collectors Club 1989.

NEW ZEALAND:

New Zealand Flowers and Plants in Colour by J. T. Salmon, Reed 1973.

Native New Zealand Flowering Plants by J. T. Salmon, Reed 1991.

NORTH AMERICA:

A California Flora and Supplement by Philip A. Munz, University of California Press 1973.

Arizona Flora by Thomas H. Kearney, Robert H. Peebles and collaborators, University of California Press 1951.

MEXICO

Catalogues of Yucca Do Nursery at Peckerwood Gardens, Waller, San Antonio, Texas 77484.

SOUTH AMERICA:

Plant Hunters in the Andes by J. Harper Goodspeed, Robert Hale undated (around 1941).

References for Particular Genera

Acanthaceae, with annotated list of the species known to have been in cultivation by Col. R. H. Beddome, FLS, Journ. Roy. Hort. Soc. 34:54–96 (1908).

Adenium see Plazier in Meded. Landb Hoogesch, Wageningen 80–12:13 (1980).

Agapetes see *The Plantsman* vol. 8, pt.2 (1986).

Bottlebrushes, Paperbarks and Tea Trees by John W. Wrigley & Murray Fag, Angus & Robertson 1993.

The Bromeliad Lexicon by Werner Rauh, edited by Peter Temple, 2nd ed., Blandford 1990.

Brugmansia: see *Notes on the Species of Tree Daturas* by M. L. Bristol, Bot. Mus. Leafl. Harvard Univ. 21:229–248 (1967); and the Supplement to the old *RHS Dictionary*, p. 260, 1969.

Cosmos: see Sherff in Publ. Field Mus. Nat. Hist. Chic. Bot. Ser. VIII, 401–447 (1932).

Cuphea see Engler, *Das Pflanzenreich*, IV, 216: 80–179 (1903).

Dunalia: *Iochroma australis – A New British Alien* by Julian M. H. Shaw, in *BSBI News*, 68, Jan. 1995: 41–42 (1995).

Ericas in Southern Africa by H. A. Baker & E. G. H. Oliver, Purnell, Cape Town 1960.

Eurycles and *Vagaria (Amaryllidaceae)* by G. A. C. Herklots, *The Plantsman*, vol. 3, pt. 4 March 1982, p. 220.

Fuchsia: Wagtails Book of Fuchsias, vol. V by E. Saunders, 1987.

A Revision of the Genus Fuchsia (Onagraceae) by Philip A. Munz, Proc. California Acad. Sci., vol. XXV, No. 1 1943 (reprinted by Johnson Reprint Corporation 1970).

Gladiolus in Tropical Africa by Peter Goldblatt, Timber Press 1996.

A Revision of the South African Species of Gladiolus by C. J. Lewis & A. A. Obermeyer, *Journal of South African Botany* suppl. vol. 10, 1972.

Haemanthus: A Revision of the South African Species of Haemanthus L. (Amaryllidaceae) by D. Snijman; *Journal of South African Botany* suppl. vol. 12, 1984.

Impatiens of Africa by C. Grey-Wilson, A. A. Balkema 1980.

Kniphofia: The South African Species of Kniphofia by L. E. Codd Bothalia vol. 9, parts 3 & 4 (1968).

Nivenia: The Woody Iridaceae, Nivenia, Klattia & Witsenia by Peter Goldblat, Timber Press, Missouri Botanical Garden and National Botanical Institute, South Africa 1993.

Nerine see *The Garden*, Journ. Roy. Hort. Soc. vol. 121, pt. 10, p. 646–9

Passion Flowers by John Vanderplank, Cassell 1991.

Pelargoniums by Derek Clifford, Blandford Press 1970.

Pelargoniums of Southern Africa by J. J. A. Van der Walt & P. J. Vorster vols. 1–3, National Botanic Gardens, Kirstenbosch 1979–88.

Proteas of Southern Africa by J. P. Rourke, Purnell 1980.

Watsonia: The Genus Watsonia by Peter Goldblatt, National Botanic Gardens (South Africa) 1989.

INDEX

INDEX

INDEX

INDEX